The Rise and Fall of Japan's LDP

The Rise and Fall of Japan's LDP

Political Party Organizations as Historical Institutions

Ellis S. Krauss and Robert J. Pekkanen

Cornell University Press
Ithaca and London

Cornell University Press gratefully acknowledges receipt of a grant
from the School of International Relations and Pacific Studies
at the University of California, San Diego, which assisted in the
publication of this book.

First published 2011 by Cornell University Press
First printing, Cornell Paperbacks, 2011

Printed in the United States of America

Library of Congress Cataloging-in-Publication Data

Krauss, Ellis S.
    The rise and fall of Japan's LDP : political party organizations as
historical institutions / Ellis S. Krauss and Robert J. Pekkanen.
        p. cm.
    Includes bibliographical references and index.
    ISBN 978-0-8014-4932-1 (cloth : alk. paper)
    ISBN 978-0-8014-7682-2 (pbk. : alk. paper)
    1. Jiyu Minshuto—History.   2. Japan—Politics and government—
1945– I. Pekkanen, Robert.   II. Title.
    JQ1698.J5K73   2011
    324.252'04—dc22   2010035753

Cornell University Press strives to use environmentally responsible suppliers and materials to the fullest extent possible in the
publishing of its books. Such materials include vegetable-based,
low-VOC inks and acid-free papers that are recycled, totally
chlorine-free, or partly composed of nonwood fibers. For further
information, visit our website at www.cornellpress.cornell.edu.

Cloth printing   10 9 8 7 6 5 4 3 2 1
Paperback printing   10 9 8 7 6 5 4 3 2

For Martha and for Sophia

Contents

Figures and Tables

Tables

Acknowledgments

We began the intellectual journey that resulted in this book with a simple sense of curiosity about what was happening at the intersection of theory and empirical reality in Japan. We owe a debt of gratitude to all of those who aided us along the way to our answers. Because it has been a long journey, with many twists and fascinating diversions along the way, we ask forgiveness for our overlooking anyone inadvertently omitted here.

This book, like many others, greatly benefited from the intellectual engagement of friends and colleagues. Kuniaki Nemoto was the best research assistant any scholar could ever hope for. He contributed to the manuscript in innumerable ways, always going well above and beyond the call of duty. Steve Reed and Yves Tiberghien also provided extensive and insightful comments on the entire manuscript, and Steve sent a number of valuable readings to the authors. Naoto Nonaka and Michio Muramatsu (a wonderful friend to and collaborator with Krauss for many years) organized a workshop at Gakushuin University to discuss an earlier draft of this book, and they and Sadafumi Kawato provided invaluable suggestions and comments. Ben Nyblade and Yves Tiberghien of the University of British Columbia organized a workshop in Vancouver where they and their graduate students, Go Murakami, Nick Fraser, and Konrad Kalicki, gave us very useful critiques and advice. The manuscript also benefited from a workshop at the Jackson School of the University of Washington organized by Scott Radnitz, at which he, Gadi Barzilai, Dan Chirot, Sabine Lang, Joel Migdal, and Saadia Pekkanen furnished important comments—with Barzilai, Lang, Radnitz, Migdal, and S. Pekkanen even writing up feedback memos to share with both authors. In spring 2007, first Krauss, then in spring 2009, Pekkanen gave presentations at Harvard University based on the ideas in this book sponsored by the Reischauer Institute and the U.S.-Japan Relations Program, and the comments and feedback there, especially from Ted Bestor, Susan Pharr (who in a sense started this all off for Robert years ago with his first class on Japanese politics), and Shin Fujihira, were very useful. Pekkanen gave a presentation at the University of Tsukuba and received valuable comments from Yutaka Tsujinaka (as always a good colleague and good friend), Shuichiro Ito, Hiroki Mori, Shinsuke Hamamoto, Jaeyoung Choe, and Takafumi Ohtomo.

In addition to these face-to-face meetings, we also benefited from interacting with friends, colleagues, and students. Erik Bleich read and provided written comments on the entire manuscript and, in particular, stimulated our thinking about qualitative methods. Daniel Markham Smith also provided us with excellent comments on each chapter, sharpening our logic with his incisive feedback. Martha Walsh did yeoman's service with her excellent copyediting on the manuscript that we submitted to Cornell University Press. Peng-Er Lam, T. J. Pempel, Michael Strausz, and Bob Uriu sent us written comments that aided us considerably in framing our arguments. Ethan Scheiner and Steven Reed provided data we used (as acknowledged in the text), and we thank them and Masahiko Tatebayashi, who shared an early data set that grew to become our Japanese Legislative Organization database (J-LOD). The Jiji Press either provided or sold us the data on cabinet and LDP party support rates used in the chapters on party leadership. Students in Pekkanen's SISEA 536 Political Parties in Japan and East Asia course at the University of Washington read and provided good feedback on an early version of the manuscript. We thank them all, especially Thomas Abrahamson, Chris Acheson, Garrett Bredell, Heewon Kang, Deirdre Martin, Alex Simmons, and Cassidy Werner.

We acknowledge the help of many students and research assistants, including Kuniaki Nemoto, Dan Smith, Hasegawa Tomoko, Imaoka Rieki, Kohmoto Aki, Saori Mitsuya, Yuriko Ohira, and Andre Toyama at the University of California at San Diego; also Brittain Barber, Garrett Bredell, Gregory Buehler, Rebekah Harmon, Deirdre Martin, Brian Mayer, and Hironori Sasada at the University of Washington. Itaru Yanagi of the University of Tsukuba provided stellar research assistance over two summers.

We also thank our many interview sources, although they must remain anonymous. Of course, we can name Katsuei Hirasawa and Yoshinori Ohno, and we thank them for allowing us to speak and travel with them on so many occasions, even during the frantic election campaigns. As scholars, we are extremely grateful for their overwhelming generosity in supporting our research. We also benefited from the kind introductions or advice about interviews from William T. Breer, Amy Catalinac, Yoso Furumoto, Ryozo Hayashi, the Keizai Koho Center staff, Yoji Kitamura, Kazutaka Maeda, Takakazu Matsuda, Naoyoshi Otani, Len Schoppa, Hideya Taida, Yutaka Tsujinaka, Tsuneo Watanabe, and, especially, Gerry Curtis.

Krauss thanks Gakushuin University and its Faculty of Law for providing the research funding that greatly aided him in the writing of this book, and especially Michio Muramatsu and Naoto Nonaka of that faculty. He also thanks the University of California Pacific Rim Program and the Japan Foundation for travel and maintenance support that allowed him to conduct interviews in Japan. Lisa Woinarski was of invaluable help in her efficient management of funding accounts and reimbursements. Pekkanen acknowledges the support of and thanks the Abe Fellowship of the Center for Global Partnership, the East Asia Center of the University of Washington, and the Japan Studies Program at the University of Washington. Mieko Kimura and the staff at Ninomiya House and Takezono House in Tsukuba provided excellent help to Pekkanen for periods of field work. Pekkanen also thanks the staff at the Jackson School of International Studies at the University of Washington. Annette Bernier (now in another job), Ellen Eskenazi, Lydia Gold (moved to the history department, sadly), Eva Greuhlich, Mark ("can't write a book without a computer") Haslam, Emily Ngo, "big cheese" Dvorah Oppenheimer, Toni Read, Diane Scillo, Sandra Scott, Martha Walsh, and Beverly Winner-Coates helped him with many reimbursement requests and other support without which this research would simply not have been possible. Anyone who has ever worked at a university knows what he means.

This book would never have reached its publication fruition in whatever good shape it is in, without the help of several people. Lynne Bush expertly aided us with the figures. Karen M. Laun and Julie Nemer did a great job shepherding our original draft through copyediting. The inimitable Roger Haydon gave us excellent advice throughout for which we are grateful.

In addition, Pekkanen thanks his "Japanese family" (Hirokuni, Ikuko, Hirotaka, and Takahisa Tanaka; and Tomomi and Masaki Okazaki), and his American family, John, Lynn, Sarah, Benjamin, and daughter Sophia Pekkanen, once again. Finally, we give our gratitude and love to our spouses, Martha A. Leche and Saadia Pekkanen, who put up with us and provided us with support and encouragement during the process of researching and writing this book.

Abbreviations

CEFP	Council on Economic and Fiscal Policy
CGP	Clean Government Party (Kōmeitō)
DPJ	Democratic Party of Japan
DSP	Democratic Socialist Party
FILP	Fiscal Investment and Loan Program
HHI	Herfindahl-Hirschman Index
JCP	Japanese Communist Party
J-LOD	Japanese Legislative Organization database
JMA	Japan Medical Association
JSP	Japan Socialist Party
KSD	SME Managers' Welfare Corporation
LDIs	Liberal Democrat independents
LDP	Liberal Democratic Party
MMD	multi-member district
MMM	mixed-member majoritarian [system]
MMP	mixed-member proportional [system]
NET	Network Movement political party
NFP	New Frontier Party
NLC	New Liberal Club
NRP	New Renaissance Party
PARC	Policy Affairs Research Council (Seimu Chōsakai; also called Policy Research Committee)
POEL	Public Office Election Law
PR	proportional representation
SAP	Social Democratic Party [Sweden]

SMD	single-member district
SMEs	small and medium-size enterprises
SNTV MMD	single nontransferable vote multimember district system
SNTV	single nontransferable vote

Chapter 1

The Liberal Democratic Party in Time

The Liberal Democratic Party's organizational structure, whose basic units are individual *kōenkai, zoku,* and factions, is decentralized and flexible, and it is not the orderly centralization which can be seen in the so-called organized parties of Western Europe.
Seizaburō Satō and Tetsuhisa Matsuzaki (1986, 3)

Indeed, the institutions that define the political party are unique, and as it happens they are unique in ways that make an institutional account especially useful.
John H. Aldrich (1995, 19)

If the LDP does adopt new electoral rules, readers will have a chance to test the claims so many observers have made about Japanese politics: to examine the resulting changes in the LDP's internal organization, in its electoral strategy, in its relations with bureaucrats and judges, and in its basic policies. It is an opportunity not to be missed.
Mark J. Ramseyer and Frances McCall Rosenbluth (1993, 201)

How do we best explain how political parties develop and organize themselves? In other words, why do political parties develop the way they do? Why do their organizational structures persist or change over time? These are the central questions this book seeks to answer for one of the most successful political parties in the democratic world, the Liberal Democratic Party (LDP) of Japan. Formed in 1955 from the merger of two smaller conservative parties, until 2009 it had continuously held the reins of government, either singly or as the dominant party in a coalition, with the exception of ten months in 1993–1994. Then, in 2009, it overwhelmingly lost an election and fell from power. Considering that the organization and development of political parties should be at the heart of any study of democratic institutions and politics, systematic empirical studies focusing on these issues outside the United States have been surprisingly lacking, especially in parliamentary democracies. This book focuses on the development of the distinguishing institutions of the LDP, and asks why and how they came into being and were maintained, and with what consequences.

Writing on party development in the United States, John Aldrich argues that "political outcomes—here political parties—result from actors seeking to realize their goals, choosing from within and possibly shaping a given set of institutional arrangements, and so choosing within a given historical context" (1995, 6). This has not been the way the LDP has been considered; rather, the most favored recent approach involves looking for an explanation in the kinds of electoral systems existing before and after electoral reform in 1994. As a result, several adherents of the electoral explanation predicted that the organizational form of the LDP in pursuing its goals would be fundamentally altered by electoral reform. Yet for a decade and a half after that reform, the LDP continued to win key elections—scoring its greatest success at the polls in 2005—and hold power before finally succumbing. Electoral system explanations by themselves are ill-equipped to explain this particular pattern of the surprising success of a party and then its equally surprising abrupt failure.

In this book, we offer an alternative explanation as to why and how the LDP developed the way it did and as to why its pre- and postelectoral reform organization formed and persisted, and with what consequences. We show that the LDP was, in Aldrich's language, a result of key actors seeking to realize their goals by shaping a given set of institutional arrangements within a given historical context. As a result, we also demonstrate why the predictions of those who believed the electoral system alone would transform the form and processes of the LDP were wrong—the unique institutional forms developed under the old electoral system continued even after Japan experienced electoral reform in 1994, although in slightly altered form. We find that, although electoral systems did play a role, they did so only in conjunction with other important factors. The conflict and rivalry within the LDP, both among its leaders and between these leaders and the LDP backbencher representatives, were probably just as (or more) important in shaping the development of the party.

This book, then, is about how the LDP became the party that it was at the time of the 1994 electoral reform, how it became the party that it was after that reform, and why. We treat the main units of the LDP organization as institutions; political parties should be treated as institutions because they are durable patterned organizations composed of established rules and relationships (Aldrich 1995). Therefore, we tell this story through an analysis of the most important LDP institutional components for carrying out the actions for which political parties are formed—vote-seeking, office-seeking, and policy-seeking (Strøm 1990, 569–98; Müller and Strøm 1999)—and for managing the collective action, social choice, and ambition problems of political parties (Aldrich 1995). These three party institutions—the party in the electorate, party in the legislature, and party as organization—also parallel both V. O. Key's (1964) three faces of political parties: the party on the ground, party in office, and party as central office (see also Katz and Mair 1994, 4). It also parallels the mix of legislators' goals posited by Barbara Sinclair (1995, 17): reelection, good public policy, and influence.

First, we examine *kōenkai*, the candidate-support organizations in the electoral districts; these are technically not part of the party but are the main way in which LDP candidates usually mobilize votes. Second, we look at LDP factions, the key, deeply structured groups of the major party leaders and their loyal followers that determined for many years not just who became a party leader and the prime minister but also the posts that every representative was given in the party, the parliament (the National Diet), and the government, including the cabinet. Third, we analyze the development of the Policy Affairs Research Council (Seimu Chōsakai; PARC), the highly organizationally developed, extra-legislative party institution that formulated the party legislative policies that were usually, more or less, adopted into law by the Diet. Finally, no book on a political party would be complete without also a look at the party leadership, especially the party president, who, because of the LDP majority in the Diet, in practice became the prime minister. (The only exceptions were when the LDP was out of power in 1993–1994 and when, for two years subsequently, the LDP returned to power and kept most cabinet seats but not that of prime minister, which went to Tomiichi Murayama, a Socialist.) Examining party leadership in the LDP is especially appropriate because its influence and power, or lack thereof, were inextricably involved in the development of our other three party institutions and because it has, arguably, changed the most of all the party institutions over the past quarter century. The examination of the development of these four party institutions before and after electoral reform forms the core of the book.

Studying these institutions provides us with the rare opportunity to conduct a great natural experiment to observe how a major political party adjusts (or does not adjust) to an important change in the electoral system. Although in the pages that follow we come to different and alternative answers to why these LDP institutions developed, and therefore why they did not disappear or change as much as predicted, we do agree completely with the challenge that Ramseyer and Rosenbluth (1993, 201) laid out (see the beginning of the chapter) just as the new electoral system was being adopted. Conducting a study of the LDP prior to and subsequent to the electoral reform of 1994, focusing primarily on its internal organization and electoral strategies and on how these changed or did not change as a result of this great institutional change, is indeed "an opportunity not to be missed."

Most especially, we seek to answer several interrelated questions: How and why did the LDP develop before the reform under the single nontransferable vote (SNTV)? How did it adapt after the reform to the new mixed-member majoritarian (MMM) system? Did the prior organizational development of the party affect how and to what extent it adapted to the new electoral environment? What other changes contributed to revisions to the party organization and behavior? Why did its major institutional structures not disappear, as some predicted? And, finally, why was the LDP able to stay in power for so long despite the predictions of its demise with reform, and then suddenly, at the height of its postreform strength, did it lose power?

Why Study the Liberal Democratic Party?

There are several reasons for studying the development and organization of the LDP in depth. First, we cannot understand the politics and policy-making of postwar Japan, the world's second largest economy and one of the largest liberal democracies, without understanding the LDP. The LDP has been at the core of Japanese politics, pre- and postreform, ever since its formation.

Second, the LDP was probably the most successful political party in the democratic world simply in terms of its number of years in power. Other political parties have had long periods in power, such as those in Italy, Sweden, and Israel (Pempel 1990), but none but the LDP was still in power by 2009 or had had as long a period as a governing party. It ruled from 1955 continuously until 2009, fifty-four years, with only a ten-month break when it lost power to a coalition of opposition parties, some of which were composed of former LDP Diet members who had split from the party.

Only one other political party in any democracy even approaches this record—the Social Democratic Party (SAP) of Sweden. It has been in power a total of approximately sixty-five years, since 1932. The SAP, however, was out of power for approximately six years between 1976 and 1982, between 1991 and 1993, and then again in 1996. Its longest consecutive time in power was the forty-four years, from 1932 to 1976. This was almost matched by the LDP time in power from its formation until 1993, but the LDP term took place entirely in the postwar period. Further, during its time in power the SAP was rarely a majority government; instead, it almost always shared power in a coalition government. In contrast, the LDP shared power only by occasionally providing one or two cabinet portfolios during its many years governing.

Several explanations for the success of the LDP have been advanced, ranging from the Cold War and postwar polarized political culture, through the weakness and division of its opposition parties, to the SNTV electoral system. Yet even after all these variables had changed—the Cold War had ended, the 1994 electoral reform had occurred, and a more unified main opposition party had developed after the electoral reform—the LDP managed to cling to power. And rarely have the explanations put forward accounted for the organizational strengths of the party instead of just the environmental conditions or the weaknesses its rivals. Surely, the LDP party organization, how it carries out the main purposes of a political party, and how it adjusted to changes in its environment, had something to do with its remarkable record. It is important for comparative political scientists to understand how one successful political party in a parliamentary democracy was organized and why, and thus how the LDP *qua* party accomplished its governing dominance.

This question becomes even more noteworthy given the surprising LDP defeat in the 2009 election. After having won one of its greatest electoral victories ever in 2005, the LDP was roundly defeated by and ceded power to the Democratic Party of Japan (DPJ) in the August 30, 2009, general election. Did the same institutions that helped the LDP succeed under both the old and the new electoral systems now also contribute to its sudden downfall?

The LDP organizational structure is particularly interesting because in Westminster-style parties, backbenchers delegate the decisions about mobilizing votes, allocating offices, and making policy to their party leaders (while holding them accountable for the outcomes) (Strøm, Müller, and Bergman 2006 [2003]), and thus top-down cabinet government becomes the norm. In some parties, however, this delegation is more limited and backbenchers or competing leaders retain the responsibility for these party functions.

In contrast, the LDP has been a prime and extreme example of a decentralized[1] "un-Westminster" party (George Mulgan 2003) with an elaborate and large decentralized structure, perhaps the largest in the industrialized democratic world and existing below the top party leadership, to perform these functions (Nonaka 2008, 113–17). This is the case despite its having formal institutions—parliamentary and cabinet forms of government—similar to those in the much more centralized democracies. Part of these Japanese institutional parliamentary structure, however, is different from Westminster systems in that there is a contradiction between cabinet government and "parliamentary supremacy" in the Japanese system that gives parliament more influence on policy than in the Westminster-style systems in the United Kingdom or New Zealand (Kawato 2006, 2005).

These partial institutional differences in the parliamentary system, nonetheless, cannot fully explain why the Japanese system of policymaking and the LDP as a governing party became so extremely decentralized, to the point of being the polar opposite of a centralized Westminster parliamentary party. Many analysts assume that such decentralized party functions are the result of LDP leaders' "allowing" backbenchers to have these functions

---

1. Although we use the term *decentralized* to characterize the LDP and emphasize the conflicts and relationships between leaders and backbenchers, it should be noted that the LDP leadership was in fact oligarchical with perhaps up to twenty leaders being influential in party decisions, with mid-level politicians in PARC also having influence. We characterize it as decentralized primarily to contrast it with the cabinet-government, top-down leadership style in Westminster systems.

as a rational response to the SNTV electoral system that was in effect from 1947 to 1993. This explanation is inadequate, however, because it does not explain exactly how these functions became decentralized and never demonstrate that the decentralization was a response to the electoral system and not, instead, to other variables.

These were the initial concerns that motivated this book. As we attempted to find the solutions to these puzzles, we made two important discoveries, one theoretical and one empirical. Theoretically, we noticed that analysts had made several wrong, or partially wrong, or unfulfilled, predictions about what would happen to the LDP organization after the 1994 electoral reform and wondered why. Analysts predicted that many of the LDP institutional components—kōenkai, factions, and PARC—would disappear because their origins lay in a rational and intentional response by the party to its SNTV electoral environment. For example, Haruhiro Fukui and Shigeko Fukai argue that the kōenkai "are likely to undergo a significant change, since they are devices geared primarily to electoral competition among candidates of the same party. Under the new system in which only one seat is available in each district and no party is likely to run more than one candidate in a district, the rationale for the electoral line as we know it will be lost" (1996, 284). They go on to say, "With only one official candidate in a district, a party's local branch will be in a position to devote all its resources to that candidate's campaign, thus potentially making the *koenkai* unnecessary and even irrelevant" (1996, 284–85). They offer the caveat that this outcome depends on the party's devoting sufficient resources to the local branch, but in fact the electoral reform allows contributions directly to the local branch and not only to the national party organization.

Predictions of institutional disappearance also included the entrenched personal leadership factions of the party. Ramseyer and Rosenbluth (1993, 59) explicitly argue that factions existed in the LDP due to the need for vote division in the SNTV electoral system: "the electoral system alone is sufficient to explain the survival of LDP factions."[2] Masaru Kohno (1992, 385, 391), only a bit less certain of the determining qualities of the electoral system, argues that "factions persist because they meet the electoral incentives of rational LDP candidates," even if there were also "secondary incentives" in the form of their function in aiding promotion to party and government positions.

And when it came to PARC, "If it is true that the raison d'etre of the PARC committee structure is to aid in district-level vote division, then we should expect to see nothing short of its demise" (Cowhey and McCubbins 1995, 257–58). "PARC committees would grow relatively inactive, as

---

2. By contrast, however, Thayer (1969, 21) argues that the electoral system was only one contributing cause of the growth of LDP factionalism, and that the most important was the means of selecting the party president, a view much closer to our findings in this book.

members lost their need to scramble for budgetary and regulatory favors for their constituents," and in general, the LDP "would grow to resemble more closely British parties. Personnel, electoral strategy, and policy decisions would be centralized" (Ramseyer and Rosenbluth 1993, 197).

The electoral reform was enacted over fifteen years ago, but the LDP did not change nearly as much as these analysts predicted. It did become a bit more centralized, but it did so mostly because of the enhanced influence of the party leadership and not because the factions, PARC, or kōenkai disappeared thanks to the new electoral system. Why? This outcome alone should stimulate us to look more closely at the approach that led to these partially erroneous predictions. Scientific analysis advances as much, and perhaps more, by explaining the reasons for failed predictions and hypotheses as it does by confirming accurate ones.

These predictions were based on an intellectual approach that looked at the success of the party and its structure under the old electoral system and then assumed that, because the party and its representatives had benefited from this organization in this electoral system, that must be the reason the party had intentionally adopted those forms in the first place. We came to realize that this "actor-centered functionalism" might not be the most valid explanation and that an approach that looked more closely at the evolution of the party and its institutions over time might yield a better explanation and an answer to why those predictions were wrong. Perhaps institutions can persist for reasons other than the fact that they seem to conform (or not) to the analyst's deduced incentives of the existing electoral system. Perhaps other variables intervene between an electoral system and the party structures that develop under that system. For example, after the electoral reform in New Zealand, David Denemark (2003) found that the incentive to conform to the new electoral system to avoid defeat was a necessary but not sufficient condition for parties to change their campaigning strategies. Other variables were important as well. Indeed, we find that other variables were important in Japan as well.

Empirically, as we delved into the most important organizational dimensions of the LDP before and after the electoral reform, we discovered that the actual historical development of these forms sometimes bore little relationship to what some analysts had posited about them. Indeed, the more we investigated, the more we found that the way the party and its fundamental organizations developed to carry out its fundamental goals was often not simply or directly the result of the electoral system per se. The LDP may be a somewhat unusual party, but the incentives of the party and its representatives are similar to those in other countries, and although these incentives certainly include electoral ones, politicians everywhere respond to other incentives as well, including incentives to attain higher office and to achieve policy aims. The real causation was much more complex and often involved intraparty conflict over career ambition or policy, both among leaders and between the leaders and the rank-and-file representatives (Longley and

Hazan 2000), and other, more complicated processes in which the electoral system was only a part of the equation.[3]

The importance of the LDP as a successful parliamentary political party in a major stable democracy and the opportunity to study the effects of the electoral change on the LDP argue for a systematic study of the party. Surprisingly, although there were several significant books on the LDP prior to electoral reform (Thayer 1969; Fukui 1970; Ramseyer and Rosenbluth 1993; Satō and Matsuzaki 1986; Inoguchi and Iwai 1987), there have been only a few after the reform (e.g., Nonaka 2008) and none in English.

Alternative Explanations

The first major answer to the important questions of how and why political parties (in this case, the LDP) develop, is a cultural explanation. Although there are valid uses of cultural explanations in social science, the one most popularly used for Japan tends to be a cultural determinist approach that attributes political behavior, belief, and organization to some vague but permanent structural characteristics inherent in Japanese society and the Japanese people. Perhaps the most famous of these approaches sees a fundamental and unchanging organizational pattern that both characterizes and determines Japanese individuals' behavior and its institutional consequences (Nakane 1970).

This cultural approach was particularly popular in the study of Japanese politics up until the 1980s. By the 1990s, it had been widely discredited for being tautological at best and just plain historically wrong or unfalsifiable at worst. At the extreme, such explanations said little more than "Japanese behave the way they do because they are Japanese" or "the LDP has factions because it is Japanese"—hardly useful social scientific explanations.

By the 1990s, these models of Japanese politics had been supplanted by electoral explanations, in particular, a form of rational choice, that to this day are the dominant approach to studying Japanese politics (as well as politics in other countries). Rational choice, however, is only one particular variant, although the most prominent, of the new institutionalisms (Hall and Taylor 1996; Weingast 2002; Pierson and Skocpol 2002; Mahoney and Rueschemeyer 2002; Pierson 2000; Steinmo, Thelen, and Longstreth 1992; Schickler 2001). The electoral connection (Mayhew 1974) has been deemed especially important because of the way elections structure incentives for politicians and political parties and frame choices for voters. Among the most accepted propositions along these lines is that the type of electoral

3. Kreuzer (2009), for example, combines "Election Marketplaces" with historical legacies, institutional contexts, and "elite coordination strategies," and their interaction to show how the German political party system became institutionalized through path-dependent processes after World War II.

system—especially whether a polity has a single-member or a proportional representation (PR) district system—affects the number of viable political parties that can compete and whether the resulting government is most likely to be formed by a single party or a coalition.[4] Electoral system incentives also have been linked to the organization of legislatures and the party organizations within them, as well as to the strength or cohesion of political parties in general (Kingdon 1981; Fiorina 1974; Cox and McCubbins 1993; Cason 2002; Morgenstern 1996; Mair, Müller, and Plasser 2004).

Political scientists in recent years, however, have gone much further in their attributions of the influence the electoral system on parties, especially as applied to Japan. *Japan's Political Marketplace* (Ramseyer and Rosenbluth 1993), easily the most influential book on Japanese politics in the past quarter century, and several articles have enhanced our knowledge greatly about the LDP under the SNTV system and how party strategies have adapted to the new electoral system.

The electoral system approach has several major conceptual and methodological advantages. It is parsimonious, it is deductively logical, and often it can be tested by empirical data. It may even accurately predict the general direction that political processes eventually take. Nevertheless, it also can result in far from satisfying intellectual explanations for reality. First, these analyses can sometimes sacrifice too much in the name of parsimony, becoming a form of electoral determinism rather than a probabilistic and multivariate form of analysis. Second, in contrast to historical institutionalism, this approach may not examine the origins of institutions but focus, instead, only on the contemporary incentives they have created, thus ignoring the potential influence of the developmental process of the institutions on those very incentives. Ignoring time and process can mislead analysis; eschewing process tracing raises severe methodological issues in assessing causality (discussed in chapter 10).Third, even though electoral system variables may indeed influence the direction in which political systems eventually go and their ultimate destination, they do not tell us anything useful about the process by which they get there or how long it takes. As Steven Reed and Michael Thies have stated, "As important as where the system is headed is when and how it will get there" (2001b, 381).The more historically oriented account presented here takes into account other political variables and more comprehensively explains not only how the reform of the electoral system in Japan is finally, more than fifteen years after the actual electoral reform, showing signs of moving politics toward the kind of political processes that electoral analysts predicted but also the processes

4. This literature is too voluminous to cite. The godfather of all the studies on this relationship between electoral systems and party systems is Maurice Duverger (1954). A bibliography is available from the Section on Representation and Electoral Systems of the American Political Science Association. A good edited volume evaluating Duverger's law as well as the effects of different kinds of electoral systems is Grofman and Lijphart (1986).

by which it has reached this point and why it took so long for the electoral system to produce these changes.

Fourth, electoral system analyses sometimes commit the error of retrospective determinism—the analyst, knowing the outcome, projects back in time that this outcome was bound to occur because no other outcome was possible. This, of course, may not be the case; it is likely that the outcome is only one of several possible outcomes or rational ways of responding to the incentives and situations that created the institution.

Finally and most important, when electoral system analyses do consider how and why institutions originated, the studies may fall into the trap of actor-centered functionalism, assuming that an institution exists because it must serve the interests of those who created and benefited from it. This implies an inevitable intention and also the omniscience of the creators, who could anticipate any unintended consequences (Pierson 2004, 105–6). Indeed, because these theorists often ignore the historical process of development, they project current institutional arrangements backward in time to their creation and assume that the contemporary benefits were the rationale for their creation, again falling into the trap of retrospective determinism. In short, such analyses have analytical shortcomings, "particularly with regard to their inability to capture the complexity, multidimensionality, and interactive nature of the objectives parties and their leaders pursue, the strategies they adopt, and their actual behavior in the real world of politics" (Gunther and Montero 2002, 12).

We firmly believe that electoral systems can be important and potentially powerful variables that shape incentives and influence outcomes, as our chapters on postelectoral reform indicate. But we do not simply assume them to be the dominant causal variables promoting the development of the LDP or the changes that occurred in Japanese politics before and after electoral reform. Although electoral systems may be necessary explanations, they are not sufficient. In this book, we take into account other variables, the possibility of unintended consequences, and that the actors who created and developed the LDP might have done so while pursuing benefits and interests only indirectly related to electoral victory per se, such as attaining leadership positions and power, advancing their careers, achieving policy goals, and settling or managing intraparty conflicts. Our premise is that electoral incentives work in combination with these other goals, not independently of them, because in the real world politicians pursue multiple interrelated goals simultaneously. Electoral systems provide the rules under which political actors play the game of politics, but they do not alone or invariably determine the specific outcomes of the game, why and how the actors play that game, or how well they play it.

A sports analogy perhaps can more clearly and concretely illustrate our problems with an electoral determinist approach. In sports, as in politics, there are different rules of the game. They determine in a general way how the game is played, what the field or court looks like and where its boundaries are, and how may players can be on that field at a time. Similarly, electoral systems and the rules governing how elections are held and how a candidate wins or loses powerfully shape how many players are usually in the party system (the game). And, as in sports, the particular rules of the game can certainly help shape the incentives for the players' behavior and probably the range of strategies used to win the game, for example, whether to try harder to mobilize "personal votes" for a candidate[5] or votes for the party.

Do we expect, however, the rules of a particular sport to decide, for example, which team will have an autocratic coach and which a more player-friendly one? Or necessarily determine which strategies or formations a team will use? Of course not. How particular teams organize, develop, and play the game *within* those common rules can vary, and thus clearly other factors must shape these dimensions of the game, not the rules alone.

The organization of a particular team might be strongly affected by factors that have nothing to do with the rules about the play on the field. In some leagues, owners may agree on salary caps and on the pooling and distribution of advertising income to equalize the chances of more teams' acquiring star players. Thus, in politics, political funding regulations can make a difference in how parties organize and play the same electoral game. Or institutions external to the sport may impose new rules regarding recruitment or payment to players that can profoundly affect which team is likely to win more games. The ending of the reserve clause by a mediator and the development of free agency in U.S. baseball after the agreement for binding arbitration; the "Bosman ruling" in European soccer; and the Spanish decision to provide tax breaks for foreign workers in 2005, making it more appealing for foreign players to play for Real Madrid, are prime examples. Similarly, in politics, term limits at the local level, a legislature passing a law instituting primary elections, or a court decision imposing (or removing) restrictions on political advertising can affect how a party develops and its strategies. In other words, other factors and other norms, rules and practices related to, but not part of, the basic electoral system rules themselves (called here *complementary institutions*), can greatly affect how political parties operate.

What would happen if one team introduced an innovation to the game that was perfectly legal under the rules but that gave it a major advantage over the other teams, resulting in its winning more and more games and dominating the league? Surely, other teams would eventually follow suit and adopt the same innovation rather than be permanently consigned to the bottom of the standings. This is what happened after the Scots (yes, the Scots) revolutionized English soccer in the 1800s by passing the ball for the

---

5. As discussed in chapter 2, the *personal vote* is a vote for a candidate based on his or her personal characteristics, as distinguished from a vote based on platforms (Cain, Ferejohn, and Fiorina 1987).

first time (Turnbull 2007). Over time, sometimes sooner and sometimes later, other teams emulate such innovations in order to compete (Finkelstein and Urch 2001). The initial competitive advantage of the first innovator eventually decreased with time as its rivals adopted the same practice.

But what would happen if some rivals were locked out from emulating this advantage and, as a result, suffered an ever-increasing disadvantage? For example, say there is a new sports league in which all the teams are all evenly matched. Then one team by chance wins the inaugural championship. As a result, its revenue increases because more fans come to see the winning team and it sells more jerseys. With these proceeds, the winning team signs contracts with better players (who might even play for less money for the chance to be on a championship team). The winning team is more likely to win the championship in the second year and, should it repeat, even more likely to win in the third year. The process is path dependent. And what really keeps the winning team at the top of the race after that is that the other teams cannot keep up. With less revenue from weaker ticket and jersey sales, they cannot afford and cannot attract as many good players (they experience negative externalities), and they are locked into a cycle in which they win fewer games and make less and less money. Perhaps the winning team even contracts a lucrative deal to broadcast its games, contributing further to the process. Even from a position of absolute initial equality, after a few years, clear winners and losers can become entrenched through these time-dependent processes. Soon, the winners may establish dynasties and take up residence at the top of the league for years to come.

Although the example is perhaps easier to understand when we start with a blank slate, a similar transformation can take place in an established league. For example, new rich owners could buy a team—Real Madrid in Spanish football, the Yomiuri Giants in Japanese baseball, or the New York Yankees in U.S. baseball—which then goes on to win and to reap the gains described. Of course, most sports leagues have elaborate rules and mechanisms in place to prevent precisely this kind of thing from happening and to maintain a competitive balance, but readers should easily be able to think of a few real-world teams that fit this scenario nonetheless.

Similarly, in politics, if factions within a political party are able to recruit members and give them exclusive advantages that nonmembers cannot get, those who do not join any faction will suffer major and continuing costs and disadvantages over time, changing the incentives for the politicians in that political party and its internal relations for good. Such situations in sports or politics are called path dependent because each step down the path makes a further step on the same path more likely.

Now let us suppose that major league baseball or European soccer imposed a strict salary cap on the amount of money any team could spend on any future newly acquired players' salaries (but not on the salaries for those it already had). And let us suppose that this new rule was imposed *before* those rich businessmen bought the Yankees or Real Madrid and turned it into the dominant team. Given this, it is unlikely that those rich businessmen would have bought the team or, if they had, would be able to turn it into a champion under these conditions. Yet, if the salary cap had been imposed *after* the rich businessmen had bought the team, the outcome—that the team would become a frequent champion—would not have changed much. So, a change in the sequence of events has changed the results.

Political parties too may be affected by decisions made at a certain time, which then limit one line of development but provide greater incentives to continue with another in the future, and the order in which the decisions are made matters. This is called sequencing. For example, a political party is formed and establishes strong local branches, which are successful in helping it win elections. Years later, its leaders decide they would like to centralize the party now that the television media has started to make the image of the party leader more important, and they try to abolish those local branches as archaic and less useful relics of the past. But all the local branch leaders in the party successfully resist, and the party continues with its prior organizational style. Now let us reverse this and say that the television coverage and centralizing leaders come earlier, around when the party is first formed. It is more than likely that this party will wind up becoming more centralized because there are no established local branch leaders to strenuously resist. Which comes first—the established party branches or the centralizing leaders—matters, and changing the sequence of events changes the outcome.

Therefore, the extent to which we should emphasize the rules of the game as determining outcomes depends on the question being asked. To know the broad outlines of how the (political) game is played or generally how many competitive parties there might be or the range of vote-gaining strategies that might have a better chance of succeeding than others, studying only the electoral system incentives is a good and powerful means of doing so. Let there be no equivocation: we absolutely believe electoral systems are important in structuring outcomes, including party organization to some extent, and can shape the way parties operate. Indeed, we ourselves often have used electoral system incentives to study how the LDP adapted its strategies to the new electoral system after 1994 (e.g., Pekkanen, Nyblade, and Krauss 2006, 2007).

But using the electoral system alone to explain LDP party organization (and to explain political party organization in general) has been oversold. Here we are asking a very different question than whether political parties adapt their strategies to new electoral systems; now our question is the equivalent of asking why sports team organizations develop the way they do. Electoral ground rules cannot tell us everything about the exact way a particular political party developed, only the context in which it did and to which it had to eventually adapt. Which of several possible ways it might have adapted within that electoral context, how long it took it to do so, and whether that adaptation was enough to win elections, however, depend on the way several factors have combined over time. If we want to know why a particular political party gradually organized itself to play the political game the way it did and was successful (or not) at it, we must look beyond just the rules of the game to other variables. These variables are internal to the party and external to it, they are beyond the electoral rules themselves, and, most important, they are found in the historical development of that party. This is the approach we take here to study the LDP before and after the 1994 electoral reform.

The Liberal Democratic Party before Electoral Reform: The '55 System

The LDP was formed from the merger of two smaller conservative parties in 1955. Its major policy orientation was anticommunist during the Cold War and supportive of capitalism. Other than these two basic principles, however, its conservative orientation would seem a bit alien to Americans, although more familiar to Europeans. Generally, the LDP stood for a strong but small national government with centralized relationships with local governments and provided large-scale government aid to farmers, small and medium-size enterprises, and the economically less affluent (Pempel 1982). These policies produced the most equitable distribution of income and wealth in the industrialized world outside of Sweden, with its usually long-term socialist governments (McKean 1989). Some of the other conservative principles of the LDP were honored as much in breach as in practice, as when its usual fiscal conservatism went by the board during a period of challenge in the 1970s from opposition parties and its spending to shore up its base and popularity produced massive debt (Calder 1991).

One of the greatest strengths of the party has been its flexibility. Rather than being narrowly and ideologically fixated on particular conservative principles, it has been able to tack with the prevailing strong winds and alter, even if belatedly, its previous policies when they proved to be unpopular later on. Thus when opposition parties began to make huge gains at the local level on the issue of the environment, the LDP shifted its singular emphasis on rapid economic growth in the 1960s, which had produced horrendous negative externalities in the form of environmental degradation, to controlling pollution instead. After winning a large victory in the 1980 election, the LDP shifted from its huge debt-producing spending back to its original fiscal conservatism. After decades of not challenging the doctrine of its own former prime minister, Shigeru Yoshida, that Japan should trade bases for U.S. protection and rearm only lightly, in the 2000s the LDP developed a much stronger military (the Self-Defense Forces); now it has the second most powerful navy in the Pacific after the United States and is a growing space power (Pekkanen and Kallendar-Umezu 2010). This flexibility and ability to change in response to changed external and internal circumstances and public opinion have been called "creative conservatism," to distinguish it from the more ideological variety often practiced elsewhere (Pempel 1982).

Perhaps the party was so flexible and pragmatic because the LDP was also a diverse political party. Its representatives ranged from those who in the United States would be considered centrist Democrats to ultra-right-wing Republicans, moderate liberals to extreme conservatives. In part because of the Cold War and in part because of the prereform SNTV electoral system, all the LDP opposition parties were to its left, ranging from the moderate Clean Government Party (CGP) and Democratic Socialist Party (DSP) to the much more leftist Japan Socialist Party (JSP) and Japanese Communist Party (JCP). And the LDP represented all social interests from rural farmers through small shopkeepers to urban big business owners. The main opposition party, the JSP, had its primary strength in the labor unions and to some extent urban white-collar workers.

This very diversity of the LDP as a coalition of interests and pragmatic nonleftist viewpoints was paired with its highly decentralized political party structure, possibly a boon to such a diverse party, enabling it to stay together. As noted, although Japan on paper looks as if it should not be different from a Westminster system such as the United Kingdom or New Zealand, it was actually almost on the opposite of a relatively top-down strong prime minister and cabinet parliamentary system.

The most important functions of the party had devolved down its organizational structure. Vote mobilization was mostly left to individual representatives and their kōenkai supporter organizations in the district. Appointments to party posts and parliamentary committees were the results of negotiations and bargains among the leadership factions, not at the command of the prime minister. Even cabinet positions, although the prime minister made the final decisions, were the result of factions' nominations to him and generally subject at the height of the prereform system to proportional representation (or balance) among the factions, greatly constraining the prime minister's appointment choices. Policymaking did not come from the cabinet and then go to the party for approval; rather, legislative proposals determining the policy started in the bureaucracy and the PARC party bureaus before they went up to the top party executives and the cabinet for final approval. In few actions of the party did the party leader exercise as much influence or power as leaders in other democratic nations (Hayao 1993).

Many of the academic studies and journalistic accounts of Japanese politics and the LDP prior to the 1994 electoral reform refer to *the '55 system,* and this has become a common term in the parlance of Japanese politics.

Nevertheless, there are many definitions of this term, and its application has sometimes been vague.

1. The dominance of the LDP as the governing party from the time of its formation until the electoral reform.
2. The prereform period, in which the ruling party was characterized by decentralized vote-, office-, and policy-seeking structures and processes and weak prime ministerial leadership.
3. The prereform party system, in which the LDP was the dominant governing party and the JSP, the main opposition party, had too few seats and support to ever take power.
4. The prereform system, in which the LDP was the dominant party but there was a strong national bureaucracy heavily involved in policymaking (and which some saw as even more influential in that process than the LDP).

In discussing prereform Japanese politics, observers have used variations of these definitions with different emphases or even various combinations of these definitions (and others) for the '55 system. In this book, we use the term frequently, primarily to refer to the first and second definitions: the nature and organization of the LDP, the dominant ruling party from 1955 to 1993. But we are not interested in imposing our definition on the field or getting involved in sterile definitional debates. Probably each of the four definitions has varied somewhat during the almost forty years of this period, and examining all the elements of LDP rule during this period, including its relations with the opposition and bureaucracy, would require many volumes; indeed, it is a subject that has already provided many volumes. In this book, we use *the '55 system* simply as a term of convenience, shorthand if you will, to mean the period from 1955 to 1993 when the LDP developed its organizational components of kōenkai, factions, and PARC in the SNTV electoral system environment to rule continuously and attain that governing dominance. Our focus is on the organizational development of the LDP rather than on a comprehensive examination of all its important relationships.

From 1947 until 1994, Japan had a medium district–size, multimember, SNTV electoral system.[6] Between three and five (and later, in a few districts, between two and six) candidates competed in the same district even though the voter cast only one ballot (thus the *single* in SNTV), and there was no run-off ballot. Votes cast for one candidate of a party could not be transferred to another candidate of that party (thus the *nontransferable* in SNTV). Simply, the highest vote-getters won election to the Diet, the number of winners determined by the district allocation of three, four, or five seats.

---

6. A multimember SNTV system had also been used during a period before World War II.

After these electoral rules had been operating for almost half a century, however, they came to be perceived as undergirding the entire pattern of politics and policymaking that had come to be dubbed *the '55 system*. Political scientists (Curtis 1971; Thayer 1969, 36–39; see also Fukui 1970, 100–101; Rochon 1981) saw the electoral system as helping to produce the personal vote, kōenkai, and factional roles in nominations and funding. Others also described the increasing specialization of LDP Diet members and the growth and influence of *zoku giin* ("policy tribe representatives," politicians who were veteran representatives with expertise and influence in a policy sector), produced by long-term LDP rule and the PARC system of policymaking within the LDP (e.g., Inoguchi and Iwai 1987; Muramatsu and Krauss 1987, 540–42; Satō and Matsuzaki 1986, 78–104). The most influential of the more recent analyses of the consequences of the previous Japanese system, especially of how electoral rules stimulating intraparty rivalry led to policy specialization, is found in Ramseyer and Rosenbluth (1993, 17–37, 99–141; see also McCubbins and Rosenbluth 1995). Let us look at the major institutions of the LDP under the '55 system that came to be attributed to the SNTV electoral system.

Kōenkai

At the heart of the LDP vote-gathering dominance under this system were the kōenkai, through which its individual Diet candidates constructed or incorporated a network of groups in which their constituents participated. The candidate also provided kōenkai members with recreational and constituency service opportunities. Participation in this network induced loyalty to the candidate—kōenkai were *not* party organizations or branches but personal support groups for a particular candidate—and members repaid the services and attention provided by the candidate by voting for him and by mobilizing friends, neighbors, and relatives to do the same. At the same time, local politicians, all with kōenkai of their own at local levels, would fold their groups and members into the network of the Diet candidate in return for his or her support when local elections came around as well as good access to the candidate if and when he or she won national office (Curtis 1971).

In many ways, kōenkai were like personal political machines for each candidate whose purpose was to help build the LDP candidate's personal vote and loyal network of supporters within the district because he or she was competing against other LDP candidates there. Kōenkai served another important function under this electoral system—to get around the draconian campaign laws that restricted candidates from doing almost any of the activities that citizens of other countries take for granted, such as door-to-door campaigning, campaigning and campaign speeches outside the short period after an election is officially promulgated but before it is held, and campaign advertising (including purchasing television time—only a political party can buy time—and hanging posters). In other words, kōenkai, as officially only private social groups independent of parties or politics, allowed the politician to reach constituents and induce a loyal, personal vote without violating the very restrictive campaign laws. Although all political party candidates had kōenkai, even the Japanese Communist Party (JCP) candidates, all the other parties relied more or as much on their own party mass organization (Clean Government Party and the communists) or labor union activists (JSP and DSP) as on these networks. But for LDP candidates kōenkai *were* the main grassroots vote-mobilizing organization.

Factions

Intraparty rivalry was encouraged because candidates from the same party, especially in the LDP, competed against one another more than against the candidates of other parties. Even before winning office, most candidates—including independents, who were mostly LDP local politicians who had failed to get the party nomination but ran anyway—were already committed to joining a leadership faction in the party if they won. Almost all incumbents were members of such factions, making the faction the second major party institution under SNTV. The reasons were simple—factions provided aid in getting candidates the party nomination in that district and financing to help candidates win their seats, and party leadership factions managed the allocation of all positions in the party, parliament, and government. There were at various times in LDP prereform history between five and ten major leadership factions in the LDP. Each was led by one of the most senior party veterans, highly organized (with staffed offices and weekly members' meetings), and structured by seniority (by the number of times elected, not by age per se).

   Although informal and often highly criticized by the press and by some prime ministers as well, factions were an indispensable aid to the careers of LDP Diet members. They existed as a mutual exchange relationship between the veteran party leader, who had strong ambitions to become party president and thus prime minister, and the Diet members in his or her faction. As previously noted, the faction leader helped get the nomination for an aspiring local politician or bureaucrat who wanted to run for the first time for a Diet seat in a district—decided by an electoral strategy committee of the party on which all the major factions had representatives. The faction leader provided extra funding to support the politicians' kōenkai and campaigns, and also represented the winning Diet members in the annual interfactional bargaining over the distribution of party, parliamentary, and government positions. A Diet member advanced to eligibility for all positions through his or her seniority in the faction—not in the party itself—and there were norms governing which types of positions were allocated to which level of seniority. Without factional backing, a candidate might as well not aspire to any important post at the national level.

The Policy Affairs Research Council

PARC (now also sometimes called the Policy Research Committee) was the chief policymaking body within the party and because by party rule all proposals for legislative bills had to go through the party first before going up to the cabinet and then to the Diet for passage, it was essentially the chief political organ making government policy. The PARC divisions paralleled the structure of both the parliamentary functional committees and the government bureaucracy (thus, divisions in education, health and welfare, agriculture, construction, etc.). Most executives of PARC divisions were also on the parliamentary committees with the same specialty, providing direct a linkage and conduit between party policy decisions and the parliamentary process. Effectively, once PARC approved the bills that came up through its divisions and relevant committees, if the top party elders and then the cabinet signed off on the proposal, it was likely to become law with only minor revisions because of the LDP majorities in the Diet (highly controversial bills fiercely resisted by the opposition parties were the only exceptions).

It has been widely accepted that by joining specific policy divisions of the LDP PARC LDP representatives acquired influence over policymaking to secure pork for constituents and claim credit for doing so, as well as expertise and contacts with interest groups and officials in a particular policy area useful to the Diet member's constituents. Some analysts also believe that LDP Diet members from the same constituency differentiated themselves from their intraparty rivals by specializing in different policy sectors of PARC, thus dividing the vote at election time.

Frequent membership on the same PARC policy-sector divisions and committees helped to train LDP experts in particular policy areas. Indeed, after many years in the key positions on PARC, on House committees, and in subcabinet and cabinet positions in a particular sector, politicians became known as zoku giin, representatives who had expertise as well as contacts in the key bureaucracy and interest groups in that policy sector and were the veteran influential representatives who knew how to articulate interests and aggregate them into policy in that legislative area.

The Party President (Prime Minister)

The electoral system was also said to undermine the unity of the LDP and to produce national leaders who were weak and not necessarily qualified. The reader might have noticed that the highest party leader is so far almost nowhere to be found in this analysis of LDP organization. Indeed, all three of the LDP institutions—kōenkai, party factions, and PARC—essentially undermined the ability of the party president and prime minister to lead effectively. The party leader, in fact, owed his achievement of that post completely to the creation of winning interfactional coalitions at the party convention. The three most important party executives posts below him (collectively known as the "Big 3" of the party)—the party secretary-general (*kanjichō*) and the chairs of the Executive Council (Sōmukai) and PARC—were traditionally given to the leaders of other factions. Although the party leader had the final choice over the specific individuals appointed to his cabinet, he had to choose from a pool of candidates advanced by the factions according to seniority and give cabinet portfolios to members of all the factions. Because the personal vote was so important in elections, especially with the salience of kōenkai, his image and popularity played little role in mobilizing votes. With PARC vetting all legislative proposals *before* they even came to the cabinet, he had a much lesser role in policymaking than most prime ministers elsewhere. In short, the prime minister had a minimal role in party vote-seeking, office-seeking, and policy-seeking functions.

Without a major role in procuring votes at election time; beholden to faction leaders for his achieving power, the factions that controlled or influenced appointments to almost all party, parliamentary, and government posts; and presiding over a decentralized policymaking process, the LDP prime minister's power and influence in policymaking was undermined (Hayao 1993, 96–121, 141–56; George Mulgan 2002, 2003), and some of the main intraparty policy conflicts, when they occurred, were between the prime minister and the factions and PARC. The main qualifications for being a national leader seemed to be merely the talents to make backroom bargains, raise money, and longevity, not abilities in electoral, party, or policy leadership.

How the Components Fit Together

There were important relationships, note, among all these major LDP institutions for vote-seeking, office-seeking, and policy-seeking. The factions helped candidates attain nomination and helped fund the candidates' kōenkai. The kōenkai were crucial to the politicians' ability to win elections and join a faction. Becoming a member of a faction put a candidates on the career-advancement escalator to higher party, legislative, and government posts; long-time service in the faction could lead to important PARC positions, enabling a candidate to claim credit for bringing benefits to his or her own district and kōenkai members, reinforcing the personal vote in the next election. The three party institutions were also integrally and often inversely related to how much influence the prime minister had within the party and government.

This, then, is the description of the LDP under the '55 system as an organization and of the important political components in Japan that has come down to us through the most important analyses done before reform (Inoguchi and Iwai 1987; Ramseyer and Rosenbluth 1993). Certainly, this was the characterization of the structure and process of the LDP by the mid-late 1980s when these studies were done. As noted, however, the problem is that observers could assume that the party organization and processes they saw in the late 1980s and early 1990s, when the system had developed to its height, also characterized the LDP from the beginning of its formation in 1955; they this led to sound functional and logical—but not empirically verified—reasons why the SNTV system must have caused these organizational structures.

In this book, we put forward a different explanation. The development of the LDP occurred over time and only became the archetype of that party in the 1980s, rather later than analysts have assumed. Further, without understanding the true causes and development of kōenkai, party factions, PARC, and party leadership, we cannot sufficiently explain how and why electoral reform had the consequences it did (and did not).[7]

The 1994 Electoral Reform

Political scientists were not the only ones who attributed the LDP organization and the '55 system to the influence of SNTV. Critics and reformers did so too and also thought the electoral system underlay much of what was wrong with Japanese democracy.

Among these faults (or evils) was the one-party dominance of the LDP, which had ruled Japan uninterruptedly, although occasionally with a smaller party in coalition, since its formation in 1955. Because only the largest parties, almost exclusively the LDP, had enough support in any districts to elect more than one candidate, the system was thought inherently to make it easier for only the LDP to obtain a majority of seats in the Diet. Further aiding LDP dominance was that the other parties, like the LDP, could elect a candidate of their own with only 15–20 percent of the vote in districts in which they had sufficient support. Thus, they had no incentive to combine to elect candidates, splitting the opposition into at least four major parties and thus also making LDP hegemony possible. Finally, adding unfair insult to the injury of perennial LDP control of government was the fact that the districts over time had become severely malapportioned, allowing rural voters to, on average, elect a representative with one-third or fewer votes than urban voters. Because the LDP had greater support in the countryside than in the cities, this disparity in vote representation added enough seats to the LDP column to give it a majority or near majority even though it had not obtained a majority of the popular vote since 1967.

Another problem was the lack of interparty competition based on policy differences because the personal vote delivered by kōenkai meant that

7. Although we hope it is clear from our analysis, we want to state explicitly here that we value the scholars and scholarship in the rational choice tradition, including those cited in this chapter. We have personally learned a great deal from them about the subjects of this book. Indeed, our own expectations were that predictions about LDP party organization would be fulfilled, and probably the major motivation for this book is to find out why they were not.

votes were induced not by policy but by personal loyalty. This led to the surfeit of particularistic benefits—from bridges and dams to roads and agricultural subsidies—to the district.

Thus by the early 1990s, after a long and almost constant stream of scandals were revealed, political scientists, as well as the press and much of the public, attributed to the multimember SNTV system in whole or part most of the characteristics we have come to associate with the LDP and its rule. Even some representatives of the LDP, the chief beneficiary of the system, were calling for change and reform. Dissatisfaction with the electoral system reached a peak in 1993 when LDP Prime Minister Kiichi Miyazawa failed to gain sufficient support of the party to pass an electoral reform bill, despite his very public promise previously made on television to do so (Altman 1996, 172–73). Several members of the LDP, with a mixture of both self-interested electoral and sincere reform goals (Reed and Scheiner 2003), bolted the party over the issue, and they and others who had left the party previously formed smaller conservative parties pushing for political reform.

One of these young former LDP politicians, Morihiro Hosokawa, and a veteran former LDP politician, Ichirō Ozawa, then managed to do in summer 1993 what many had considered previously to be impossible—unite all the opposition parties except the communists to form a coalition to take power away from the LDP. The new coalition ranged from conservative former LDP members to their arch-ideological rivals, the socialists, and every stripe in between; consequently, the coalition agreed on only one issue, the one that had brought it to power—electoral reform. Over the course of much of the next year, Hosokawa attempted to get an electoral reform bill through the Diet, one that would combine first-past-the post, single-member district (SMD) seats with proportional representation (PR).

Faced with some recalcitrant members within his own coalition, however, Hosokawa ultimately had to engage in tough negotiations with the LDP to get the bill through the House of Councilors. Many of the smaller parties in the coalition favored national PR seats because these would allow them to gain seats commensurate with their strength, which lay primarily in urban areas. The LDP favored having as many SMD seats as possible; being by far the largest party, it would gain the most seats. In PR, the LDP pushed regional PR because it thought this would allow for more seats determined by the rural vote where the LDP was dominant than would national PR. The final reform law that emerged was a definite compromise on the part of the smaller parties of Hosokawa's coalition and was more favorable to the LDP than the original bill. Ironically, it was also in essence the same bill that an advisory council had proposed three years earlier but that had not been passed by the Diet, to a large extent because of the antipathy of many of the Diet members of the former opposition parties that were now in power and pushing reform (Curtis 1999, 137–70; Reed and Thies 2001a, 152–72)!

The new electoral system adopted was a mixed-member district (MMD) system combining 300 SMD seats with 200 PR seats elected from eleven regional districts (this was later reduced to 180 PR seats). Japan was not unique in moving toward this MMD hybrid system around this time. Indeed, so many nations recently have moved toward this form to gain the benefits of both an equitable distribution of seats to votes and the individual representation of geographical units that such MMD electoral systems may well "prove to be *the* electoral reform of the twenty-first century, as PR was in the twentieth century" (Shugart and Wattenberg 2001b, 1). Italy, New Zealand, and Venezuela reformed their electoral systems to variations of this hybrid system about the same time as Japan (Shugart and Wattenberg 2001a; 2001b, 1–2). Later, Taiwan and Korea did the same, also abolishing their former SNTV systems.

These new MMD systems, however, differ greatly in their operation. There are two common forms of such systems. One is a compensatory version, similar to that in Germany, in which the results of the SMD races are compensated for to produce overall seat results that emulate proportionality of seats to votes. This was the form to which New Zealand and Venezuela moved. The other type is the parallel form, in which the SMD and PR portions are largely separate and the overall results are not necessarily proportional. Japan and Italy adopted this type (Shugart and Wattenberg 2001a, 178). In the Japanese system, the voter receives two ballots, one for his or her local SMD and one for the regional PR constituencies. The balloting is therefore separate for the two types of districts representing the voter, and the PR seats are not used to adjust the overall distribution of seats for the party (as in compensatory MMD systems).

The Japanese version of the parallel form also has a distinctive dimension—there is a simple "best loser" provision that links the SMD and PR portions indirectly. Candidates in the SMD districts are also allowed to be listed on the party PR list. Furthermore, candidates on the PR list can be ranked more than once on that list. For example, all the LDP SMD candidates running in districts in the Shikoku region can each be ranked number one on the party regional PR list for Shikoku. The party can run a candidate in each of the thirteen SMDs in the Shikoku region and then list seven of these also as number one for the seven seats in the Shikoku regional PR election, possibly the seven weakest of the candidates in SMDs. It might then list five others who were not running in SMD elections at lower ranks. If a candidate ranked for both types of seats wins in his or her SMD, his or her name is removed from the PR list.

Then, let us assume that in an election the party wins four seats in the regional PR election. If three of the seven candidates ranked in PR win their SMD seats and drop off the PR list, then of course there is no problem—the four remaining losing candidates take the four seats that the party won in the PR election.

But what if the party wins only two seats in SMD, leaving five losing SMD candidates who are identically ranked number one on the party regional PR list to compete for the four PR seats that the party has won? Who fills the seats is determined by taking the proportion of the votes that each losing SMD candidate has won compared to those of the winning SMD candidate (who belongs to another party). The higher the proportion, the more likely the losing SMD candidate will be considered for one of the four PR seats. Thus, if candidate A wins 21,000 votes in his SMD district to his winning rival's 25,000 votes (a proportion of 84 percent), he will be more eligible for a PR seat than candidate B, who wins 20,000 votes to his winning competitor's 29,000 (a proportion of 69 percent). In our example, the losing LDP SMD candidates who have the four best proportions of votes compared to the winners in their districts will take the four party PR seats, and the remaining candidate, with the worst proportion, will be out of luck in both his SMD and PR candidacies (Jain 1995; Christensen 1996; Reed and Thies 2001b, 383).

Clearly, the incumbents in 1994 who voted this system into place were concerned about their own futures in politics under the new system and favored a way to build into the reform a potential insurance policy in case they did not continue to succeed with the redrawn boundaries and constituents of the new SMDs. In the view of the public and the media after the first election, however, this ability to "rise from the dead"—to win a PR seat even after constituents in the SMD rejected the candidate in favor of someone else—made the legislator a "zombie" Diet Member! And this somewhat pejorative label is still in use today, although decreasingly so. This process has been reviled in the press, which treat it as a repudiation of the people's will and destructive to democracy.[8] This antipathy should not disguise the reality that dual candidates are quite common in mixed systems. The reform in Italy also has an unusual feature called *scorporo* that compensates smaller parties in the PR portion of the Chamber of Deputies, and the Italian Senate also features a "best loser" provision.[9]

The impetus for reform in 1994 extended also to attempting to fight the endemic corruption that seemed to plague the old SNTV system. In a separate law, the Diet passed a campaign finance bill that features some public financing of campaigns and severe restrictions on or outlawing of donations to individual politicians or factions. The purpose was to channel money through political parties to a greater extent than in the past. Although each individual candidate can have one personal fund-raising organization, the distribution of public monies and other contributions has to go through the political parties, either the national organization or the local branches.

---

8. Press complaints began almost from the moment the first zombie representative was elected, but diminished somewhat after 2000 revisions in the electoral law disqualified candidates who failed to collect at least one-tenth of the effective vote in a SMD election (nine candidates were elected in 1996 with fewer than one-sixth of the votes in the SMD in which they ran).

9. We thank Matt Shugart for emphasizing the importance of this provision and giving it the "best loser" provisional appellation. See also McKean and Scheiner (2000, 447–77). On the system in Italy, see Katz (2001, 96–122).

Responsibility for illegal campaign activities by supporters or aides is now legally pinned on the Diet member him- or herself, and penalties for violations are much more severe, including the courts having the ability to void an election and to ban candidates in some cases for violations by supporters, relatives, or aides (Christensen 1996, 56–57; Curtis 1999, 165).

The malapportionment between urban and rural districts was addressed, but only partially. Prior to the reform, the average ratio of voters needed to elect a representative in urban districts compared to rural ones was nearly 3:1; after the new SMD electoral district boundaries had been redrawn, this was reduced to about 2:1. Although this ratio increased again over the next decade, the Diet responded by redrawing some districts and got the ratio back down to almost 2:1 (*Japan Times* 2002; Horiuchi and Saito 2003).

One important part of the old system that was not reformed was the draconian restrictions on campaign activities. The prohibited activities under SNTV remained (Christensen 1998).

In early 2009, fifteen years after the reform and four general elections later, although its hold on power was under a much greater challenge because of the rise of a major centrist alternative party, the DPJ, after the reform (something that had been accurately predicted by many after the change of systems), the LDP was still in power, with its greatest number of seats in the House of Representatives than at any other time since the 1960s.

As important, the LDP remained in power with all its major institutional components—kōenkai, factions, and PARC—intact, contrary to the predictions of many analysts that they would disappear without the SNTV electoral environment from which they ostensibly arose. If these LDP institutional components were just the consequence of the functions they performed under the SNTV electoral system, why did they not disappear? Did they change after the reform, and if so, how and why? And if they did not disappear because they developed for reasons other than just to perform electoral functions, how, why, and when did these components develop into their full structures and functions prior to the reform? Can answering the last question inform us why the LDP did not change as much as was predicted for fifteen years and also, then, why the LDP suddenly and massively lost the August 2009 election? Answering these questions should enable us to differentiate among the actual effects of the electoral system, effects caused by the electoral system in combination with other factors, and effects that electoral system did not shape at all.

How to Study the Liberal Democratic Party:
A Historical Institutional Approach

We look at the LDP as an institution that had evolved through time. An alternative new institutionalism approach to rational choice—the historical institutional approach (Steinmo, Thelen, and Longstreth 1992; Mahoney and Rueschemeyer 2002; Skocpol 2006)—allows us to explain how the constraints and opportunities that characterize the institution evolved over time and also why they operate the way they do. We assume that different, multiple paths of development and outcomes were all possible at the point of origin, rather than merely one, and we treat electoral rules not only as constraints that force parties to develop in a certain direction but also as opportunities for parties to creatively organize to achieve their multiple goals within those rules. Often what the rules do *not* say provides space for political entrepreneurs and decision makers to innovate and make decisions that provide alternative ways of organizing within the same electoral rules.

This approach has a number of strengths for the analyst. It avoids the problems that have beset other approaches—retrospective determinism and actor-centered functionalism, for example—by looking at the actual process of institutional development and the motives, intent, and interests of the actors involved at the time they occurred. It further allows us to focus our attention on effects and consequences that can be revealed only by historical analysis, rather than at one cross section in time, as well as on the effects of prior arrangements on the next stage of institutional development.

The approach also has some potential pitfalls, however. Often such analyses argue that what came before determined what came after, that the outcome was path dependent and therefore that history matters. But as Paul Pierson argues, "To assert that 'history matters' is insufficient; social scientists want to know why, where, how, and for what" (Pierson 2004, 6). A further, related problem is that historical analyses use discrete and unique concepts and variables for each case, preventing a real comparative analysis that can be replicated elsewhere.

We attempt to avoid these pitfalls by using Pierson's (2004) concepts, which combine both the advantages of using parsimonious but dynamic concepts drawn from economics of rational choice analysis and the attention to history, path dependence, and developmental analysis of historical institutionalism. We especially use three of his general analytical concepts to explain why some institutional practices were adopted, persisted, and became institutionalized.

The first concept, *institutional complementarity,* comes from Pierson's seminal work but also resonates with a stream of studies on organizations. Institutional complementarity exists when other institutions, with their consequent network of interdependent relationships, have mutually reinforcing effects (including intensifying positive feedback and making costs of change higher) on the institution being studied (Pierson 2004, 149–50, 162). The concept of institutional complementarity is similar to organizational populations, ecology, or niches, which has been used in organizational sociology since at least the 1960s (for reviews, see Aldrich and Pfeffer 1976; Amburgey and Rao 1996), although only occasionally in political science (see Gray and Lowery 1996), to explain the success, duration, and development of organizations. In other words, relationships with other institutions and organizations can increase the likelihood of one institution of a particular type originating, persisting, and thriving. Recall our sports analogies about player selection and the court and legislative decisions affecting how teams may develop differently even when playing under the same rules on the field. This concept represents the organizational environment into which each of the LDP institutional components fits at a particular time and that relates to its primary goals.

The second concept we use is *sequencing*. Some decisions, once made, and some paths, once set on, may generate positive returns that make it difficult later to reverse course. Because of this, the sequence in which events occur or decisions are made also becomes important because the first stage or step or decision or set of actions may in fact determine the options and viability of decisions or actions at later stages. In short, which action comes first or when the action occurs in a developing sequence matters (Pierson 2004, 66–67, 54–78). Our sports analogy of a salary cap being instituted before or after a group of rich owners acquires a team is one example. In the chapters that follow, we will show that the practices and organizational forms that the LDP adopted at one stage affected the next stage of its organizational development.

The third concept is *path dependence* or increasing returns (also known as positive feedback). This concept is based on the notion that some decisions generate positive feedback for those who take a particular path, making it increasingly difficult to change it later. "In the presence of positive feedback, the probability of further steps along the same path increases with each move down that path. This is because the *relative* benefits of the current activity compared with once-possible options increases over time. To put it a different way, the costs of switching to some previously plausible alternative rise" (Pierson 2004, 21, italics in the original; see also Pierson 2000, 251–67; 2004, 17–53). In other words, rather than just using the term *path dependence* to mean that what came before influenced what comes after (again, a not very useful truism), Pierson defines the term to give us a specific analytical tool to understand why some decisions and activities undertaken earlier were continued and became solidified as institutional practices in later stages of development.

In contrast, Scott Page (2006) has argued that path dependence is based on negative externalities rather than increasing returns. Negative externalities are the costs imposed on others who are left out when actors adopt some forms or behavior. For example, the increasing number of people who adopted the QWERTY keyboard (whose longevity has no rational defense) gained relative benefits from being able to use the keyboards that many others were also using (relative increasing returns); but, perhaps more important, they also avoided the large costs of having to learn to type on many different keyboards (negative externalities) (Page 2006, 110). Thus, although both reasons for path dependence may have been operative in this case, it was probably the negative externalities that were more important.[10] In a sports example, a baseball team's gaining advantages from a metropolitan area's giving it tax and stadium breaks, which also imposed continuing and increasing costs on teams that could not gain those concessions, is an example of negative externalities.[11] This concept thus represents the process by which organizational forms become established and self-sustaining over time through the imposition of costs on others.

These three concepts—complementary institutions, sequencing, and path dependence through negative externalities—allow us to examine how, individually and together, key events at an earlier stage, the process of establishment over time, and the organizational interdependence of the LDP institutional components help explain their origin and development. These are particularly powerful concepts for understanding why other perfectly rational and plausible alternative paths were not followed instead. These concepts help us explain, much more concretely than a simple stimulus-response model, how and why the LDP developed the way it did, both under SNTV before the electoral reform and under a totally different electoral system after the electoral reform. We also examine how these concepts explain the different stages of the LDP development.

10. Note that path-dependent processes do not necessarily result in one standardized model, as any American who has been frustrated when trying to type by rote or find the ampersand on a French or Belgian AZERTY keyboard or on an Italian QZERTY keyboard can attest (as, of course, also can those nationals trying to type on an American keyboard). The path dependence of the QWERTY keyboard was clearly adapted to the differences in the use of different letters and punctuation in different languages. There can be variation even within the dominant outcome of negative externalities.

11. In contrast, the advantages of adopting the pass after Scottish teams did in nineteenth-century soccer and of hiring African American baseball players after the Brooklyn Dodgers did in U.S. baseball illustrate competitive advantage.

Chapter 2

The Kōenkai

Origins and Development of a Vote-Mobilization Machine

Japanese parties are like ghosts. They have heads but no feet.
A former minister of education

In this chapter, we take a much closer look at kōenkai. Kōenkai are an excellent example of an institution that we would expect to be powerfully affected by a change in the electoral system. As we show here, the electoral reform of 1994 did affect kōenkai, but not nearly as much as predicted. In fact, kōenkai have altered less than either the LDP factions or PARC, the other two party institutions we examine in detail in this book. Why have kōenkai not succumbed to the potent electoral forces at work? More generally, what lessons can we draw from this about institutional change? To answer these questions, we first need to devote ourselves to an examination of the kōenkai. This chapter begins with a definition of *kōenkai* and an exploration of their most salient characteristics. At the outset, it is important to clearly relate the kōenkai to the concept of the personal vote in electoral studies. The remainder of the chapter explores the twin questions of the origin and development of the kōenkai under the '55 system.

What Are Kōenkai?

A prominent feature in Japanese electoral and party politics, kōenkai play a number of roles. Kōenkai transmit local demands to party politicians. Membership in the kōenkai socializes political society, familiarizing citizens with the political process and establishing a mode of political interaction.

The epigraph quotation appears in a few places, attributed sometimes to a "former Minister of Education" (see Foster 1982, 856). Thayer attributes it to a LDP party worker in Hiroshima who says, "The Liberal Democratic Party is like a ghost. It has no feet" (1969, 85).

Kōenkai also provide the opportunity for constituency service (which augments the personal vote) (Abe, Shindō, and Kawato 1994, 177). Their key function from the perspective of the candidate, however, is vote mobilization; kōenkai are organizational devices by which politicians get out the vote.

Kōenkai are permanent formal-membership organizations, or overlapping sets or networks of organizations, devoted to supporting an individual politician and are heavily involved in electoral mobilization. Their permanence distinguishes them from large-scale campaign organizations such as those developed in U.S. presidential elections. Kōenkai do kick into high gear for elections, but they certainly do not dissolve after the campaign. Far from it, they continue to work actively and incessantly. Kōenkai also differ from large-scale mass-membership political party branches because the basis of kōenkai membership is the support of an individual politician, not a party. Let there be no confusion—kōenkai are distinctly *not* party organizations. Although there are, of course, similarities to the support bases devised by legislators in other countries, there are also differences. Unlike most U.S. congressional support groups, for example, kōenkai are mass-membership groups. Voters join a kōenkai, typically receiving a formal membership card or other status marker. Although most Japanese politicians retain a conception of overlapping circles of support similar to the differing constituencies described in Fenno (1978), these are institutionalized into different formal membership groups. Indeed, although references to a Japanese politician's kōenkai sometimes make it appear monolithic, in practice there is usually not a single kōenkai but a sometimes overlapping network of dozens of groups of supporters. Each of these groups is dedicated to the politician as an individual. Although different personal characteristics of the politician might serve as the glue for the different groups, they are all groups dedicated to supporting that individual. In effect, they are all organizations designed to cultivate a personal vote.

The Personal Vote and Particularism

Because kōenkai are multifaceted organizations that involve a variety of politicians and supporters, they bind voters to politicians in various ways. Analytically, we can distinguish among concepts such as the personal vote and particularism or a particularistic or pork-barrel vote. A single kōenkai might induce one constituent to vote for the politician for personal reasons while tempting another with more tangible particularistic benefits and still a third for other reasons. It is worthwhile to outline briefly here how kōenkai as organizations relate to concepts from the political science literature such as the personal vote and particularism.

Brude Cain, John Ferejohn, and Morris Fiorina define the *personal vote* as "that portion of a candidate's electoral support which originates in his or her personal qualities, qualifications, activities, and record" (1987, 9). Technically, the personal vote and kōenkai are not identical; the politician may receive many personal votes from people who do not belong to the kōenkai, and some in the kōenkai might be attracted to the politician for policy reasons. Still, kōenkai are indeed ideal vehicles to develop a personal vote because they are dedicated to a person, not an ideology, a policy, or a party. As Steven Reed and Michael Theis note, "Japan has often been cited as holding down the extreme end of candidate-based personalistic politics" (2001b, 390). John Carey and Matthew Shugart (1995) rank electoral systems based on how they provide incentives to cultivate personal reputations. In their analysis, the single nontransferable vote multi-member district system (SNTV MMD) creates the greatest incentives for politicians to cultivate a personal vote: "of all the systems in which parties control nominations, this is clearly the most personalistic" (Carey and Shugart 1995, 429). Kōenkai fit this perfectly in that they mobilize voters by what Gerald Curtis calls "social obligation voting" (1971, 35). Kōenkai mobilize the personal vote primarily through the personal touch.

Voters rarely join kōenkai because of their affinity with a political party. Typically, there is some personal connection to the politician, although sometimes party support or a connection through a group to which the voter belongs plays a role (Moriwaki 1984, 546). And there is no doubt that the personal vote has loomed large for Japanese voters. Scholars have long emphasized that Japanese make voting decisions based on personal characteristics (Ward 1951). Surveys reveal that the emphasis on the candidate, rather than the party, in choosing how to vote was strong until the late 1960s, and even after that, a very substantial portion of the electorate chose to vote based on the candidate instead of the party.

Particularism is another way the LDP was said to divide the vote within districts. The idea is that the LDP funneled government resources to Diet members for them to build a personal vote and to differentiate themselves through their distribution of different flavors of pork (Cox and Niou 1994). Fukui and Fukai (1996) and Ethan Scheiner (2006) have argued for the particularistic connection between local politics and national politicians, and Shigeo Hirano (2006) and Masahiko Tatebayashi (2004) have demonstrated the geographical concentration of votes within a district, indicating some local or personal attraction. Certainly kōenkai and particularism as a means to divide the vote can overlap in practice, as when favored interest groups are members of the kōenkai of one Diet member in a district but of not others. Nevertheless, the two are not the same. A kōenkai can cultivate the personal vote without dispensing pork, for example through constituency service or by subsidizing social activities; and particularism in many other states flourishes without kōenkai. In practice, too, scholars such as Junnosuke Masumi (1995) differentiate kōenkai as electoral machines from kōenkai as pork-barrel machines. Accordingly, our discussion of particularism is somewhat limited.

Who Belongs to Kōenkai?

Kōenkai are ideal vehicles to develop a personal vote because the organizing principle of the kōenkai is the support of an individual person. This clearly distinguishes them from party organizations, and it is worth emphasizing again that kōenkai are *not* party organizations. Let us look at examples from the old and new electoral systems.

Under the old SNTV system, an LDP supporter in a particular district might belong to the kōenkai of politician A, politician B, or politician C, or none of them. Although LDP supporters were more likely to join LDP politicians' kōenkai than were other voters (and more likely to join LDP kōenkai than the kōenkai of politicians of other parties), party support and kōenkai membership were clearly separate.

Under the new system, this separation remains. In a given electoral district, the same voter might now consider herself a DPJ supporter (and vote DPJ with her PR ballot) but belong to the kōenkai of an LDP politician. So, although not totally independent, membership in kōenkai and the support of a party are clearly separate. Just as separate are membership in a kōenkai and membership in a particular political party.

Diet members are, naturally, keenly interested in the sources of their support. They understand that the kōenkai organizational form allows non-LDP supporters to line up behind them. "About 30 percent of my kōenkai members support another party, but they like me personally" (Interview HH, August 6, 2004).[1] "In the urban areas of my district, about half of my supporters are LDP supporters. In the rural areas, the LDP is stronger, and about 70 percent of my supporters also support the LDP" (Interview A, June 27, 2002). One former LDP prime minister, Toshiki Kaifu, showed us an article from a regional newspaper during the 2000 election that indicated that he had retained close to 70 percent of the vote of LDP supporters in his district even though he was in the Conservative Party. Admittedly, Kaifu had once been a prominent LDP politician, but the article also indicated that he had received over 80 percent of the vote of CGP (Kōmeitō) supporters and even 10 percent of the vote of Communist Party supporters (*Chūnichi Shimbun*, June 20, 2000). An LDP member who later became one of the notorious *zōhan* postal "rebels" in 2005 commented, "My kōenkai has 10,000 members. The LDP organization has 5,000 members.... In my kōenkai there are of course those who don't like the LDP but like [me] personally" (Interview C, December 7, 2001).

In our own analysis of Meisuikyō data[2] from 1972 to 2003, we see interesting patterns in the kinds of people who join kōenkai. Men have been

---

1. Please see the coded interview lists at the end of the book.

2. We use two databases throughout the book: the Meisuikyō data and the Japanese Legislative Organization database (J-LOD). The Meisuikyō is widely available and well known to scholars researching Japanese elections. Our prereform J-LOD is based on an earlier and less complete dataset developed by Masahiko Tatabayashi, the receipt of which we gratefully

consistently more likely to join kōenkai than women, although the gap has shrunk. In 1972, women joined at only 61 percent the rate of men. In 1983, this rate rose to 75 percent and in 2003 was 80 percent (having slipped from its high in 1993 of 96 percent). Kōenkai members are also relatively old. The peak of kōenkai membership occurs in people in their fifties, and those in their twenties are the least likely to belong to kōenkai. In general, kōenkai membership tracks life-cycle expectations of political involvement, rising from a low in people's twenties, through their thirties and forties, and peaking in their fifties before falling in their sixties to about the same level as their forties.[3] Kōenkai members are more politically active than nonmembers, at least in terms of their reported voting turnout. From 1972 through 2003, kōenkai members were about 10 percent more likely to vote than nonmembers. Breaking down kōenkai membership by party is a bit more complicated (see figure 2.1 later in the chapter). For our purposes now, we can sum up by saying that CGP supporters are the most likely to belong to a kōenkai, followed by the JCP supporters until 1980, when the LDP became the party whose supporters were second most likely to belong to a kōenkai. JCP supporters in 1996–2003 ran neck and neck with DPJ supporters in kōenkai membership rates. We also find that kōenkai members are much more stable supporters of a particular political party. In 2003, kōenkai members were slightly more than half again as likely to have supported the same party for more than ten years than non-kōenkai members. This number is slightly higher even than the proportion from 1972 (137 percent), but the trend is strong through the entire period of the Meisuikyō surveys (see figure 2.1).

How Do Kōenkai Mobilize?

Kakuei Tanaka's devotion to his kōenkai, the Etsuzankai, was legendary. He poured enormous effort into building it up over many years. Launched in the 1950s with only 80 members, by the early 1970s the Etsuzankai had nearly 98,000 members—nearly 20 percent of the Niigata voters (Schlesinger 1999, 105; Fukuoka 1983b, 34–38). Visits to hot springs are a typical feature of many a smoothly run kōenkai, but Tanaka's kōenkai excursions border on the mythic in scale. Tanaka once took 11,000 people to the Nukumi hot springs in Yamagata Prefecture at a cost of $1.4 million (Richardson 1998, 28).

Although Tanaka no doubt set the bar in terms of scale, most LDP Diet members are no slouches when it comes to keeping their kōenkai busy and

acknowledge. We developed the current J-LOD to incorporate district characteristics such as urbanization, electoral characteristics such as the votes won by all candidates and parties, and individual legislator characteristics ranging from occupational and educational background to party, government, and Diet committee and leadership positions held.

3. Earlier analysts found that self-employed merchants and manufacturers (small businesspeople, in other words) were disproportionately likely to join kōenkai, at least through the 1980s (Watanuki 1991).

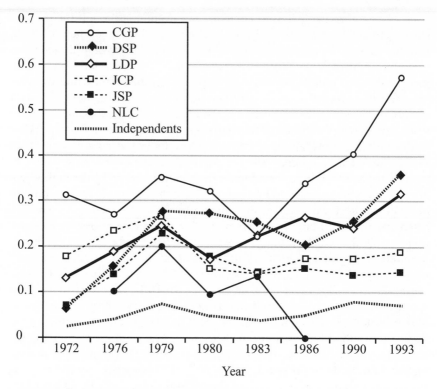

Figure 2.1 Kōenkai membership by party, 1971–1993
Source: Calculated from Meisuikyō data.
Note: CGP, Clean Government Party; DSP, Democratic Socialist Party; JCP, Japanese Communist Party; JSP, Japan Socialist Party; LDP, Liberal Democratic Party; NLC, New Liberal Club.

happy. Activities vary widely depending on the type of subgroup; even a representative list would include a dizzying range. Remarkably, many meetings of kōenkai have little to do with politics. In many cases, to be sure, there is some political discussion. One Diet member described a typical meeting: "I try to put a name on the [kōenkai] meeting, Diet Report Meeting under the sponsorship of [Diet member's name] Kōenkai and the local LDP District Branch. I do a short report on the Diet to the people. And after that we have a little bit of snacks and sake" (Interview B, October 5, 2007). Such political and current-events discussions abound, but these are probably overwhelmed numerically by sports contests of all types—baseball games, sumo contests, golf tournaments, marathons, fishing competitions, volleyball matches, and even Japanese chess make an appearance. Diet members use these nonpolitical activities as a means to connect to the voters:

> For example, I organize a volleyball tournament. I don't put my name on it anywhere, but I do organize this volleyball tournament and also a baseball

tournament. In the volleyball tournament, about a hundred teams from my district participate, which means about a thousand people turn up at the gymnasium for the tournament. I give a little speech but don't touch on politics really. Then, I pose for a photo with each team. This is surprisingly effective. Everyone feels close after this. About 50 teams participate in the baseball tournament, with 10 people per team. That tournament attracts mainly younger people so these aren't really "firm" votes, but it does help to appeal to the floating voter. Still, I do this kind of activity. It's pointless to try to appeal to younger voters through talking about policy. (Interview A, June 27, 2002)

Education is another theme of kōenkai activities. Classes are held for cooking, the tea ceremony, and how to wear a kimono and lectures are given on farming issues. Chorus groups form in the kōenkai and compete for members' interest with folk song and folk dance groups. Visits from celebrities spice up the kōenkai calendar, as does the occasional group outing to hot springs or sightseeing trip, as well as field trips to the National Diet, karaoke parties, bus excursions, and of course the annual New Year's celebration (Yamada 1993, 10–20; Ishikawa and Hirose 1989, 14–28, 138–40; Kitaoka 1985, 50–63; Ramseyer and Rosenbluth 1993, 24).

But when elections roll around, things are quite different. The tempo of meetings picks up, and the topics become more avowedly political. Kōenkai members are implored to mobilize their friends and acquaintances to vote for the Diet member. Speeches from the Diet member or key members of the kōenkai reinforce the urgency of getting out the vote.

Voters typically join kōenkai not because of an attraction to a political party but because of some connection to the politician (Moriwaki 1984, 546). Once a voter joins the kōenkai, of course, the battle for her vote is far from won, but the Diet member can rest assured that the likelihood that the voter will turn out and vote the right way is much higher. Naturally, Diet members are constantly seeking new kōenkai members. They use two means for this. First, they pick up voters one by one (*ipponzuri*). The personal touch is what cements kōenkai members to their Diet member. "A good kōenkai has to create connections to people horizontally, vertically, and sideways" (Interview HH, August 6, 2004). A Diet member's appearing at critical life junctures signals a commitment to the voter and is far more likely to be remembered than a visit at other times. Weddings and funerals are rich venues for the Diet member to fortify ties or forge new links. One Diet member disclosed to us that he attends around three hundred weddings a year and:

I personally attend about 6 or 7 funerals a week. [Another Diet member] told me that he attends 2,000 a year! The real issue is how to obtain information about these funerals. This is very important. Sometimes people will tell me about this, but since these things can be very sudden, there are times when they don't tell us. So, my organization has connections to funeral homes, and they provide us with the information. (Interview N, June 29, 2004)

For similar reasons, the summer *obon* festival, New Year's parties, and graduation ceremonies rank high for Diet members. "Tomorrow evening, starting at something like 5:30 or 5:00 I think, I shall go to seven *bon* festival events. Six, I think, six" (Interview KK, August 26, 2004). "I attend funerals every other day....At New Year's time, I attend about a hundred New Year's parties in the month of January.... I just go from one to another the whole month" (Interview CC2, August 26, 2004). "I attend ceremonies of some sort or another for the firefighters all the time. At the New Year, there's one every single day. It's cold outside in January in the early morning, but I wear a *happi* coat and appear at the ceremonies" (Interview CC2, August 26, 2004).

In addition to pressing the flesh, Diet members also strive to provide constituency service whenever possible. The logic is the same as in making a personal connection and, indeed, the same that drives members of the U.S. Congress in their constituency service. Kissing babies, attending weddings, and performing constituency service all help cultivate the personal vote. Diet members are called on to help kōenkai members get their children into the best schools and to secure jobs. They also "assist supporters in securing loans and business connections, mediate in disputes, and help people get out of minor trouble with the law" (Iwai 1990, 138–43, cited in Ramseyer and Rosenbluth 1993, 24; Kitaoka 1985, 56–62; Inou 1984, 22–215; Curtis 1971, 153–78).

Another means that Diet members use to boost kōenkai membership is making connections with groups. The LDP has always been comfortable working with organized groups. Some kōenkai are even organized around interest groups, such as the postmasters, construction industry, and agriculture (Ishikawa and Hirose 1989, 144). Diet members sometimes tap interest groups to supply members for their general or specialized kōenkai. Commonly, the LDP Diet member will make a request of a group to round up a certain number of new kōenkai members. One of the authors once saw the haggling that can accompany this. A Diet member met with a group that had not traditionally supported him. During the meeting, the group pressed forward with a legislative demand. To satisfy them, the Diet member agreed to make an attempt to do this but made it clear that a positive result could not be guaranteed. The promise of an effort was enough for the group, however. In exchange, the Diet member handed over a block of nine hundred blank membership applications with the agreement that they would be filled out by the group for its members. When these membership roundups are implemented, it is unlikely the group will seek volunteers to join the kōenkai or will publicize the opportunity; rather, it probably just pulls names off of its rolls and pays the kōenkai dues directly for them.[4]

4. This occurred during our field work in 2003. The accounts and descriptions in this section are meant to apply generally to kōenkai throughout the postwar period. One of the remarkable things about kōenkai is that the types of activity, reasons voters have for

Kōenkai members can also be recruited from the ranks of other politicians' kōenkai. To do this, one politician, say the national Diet member, asks local politicians to get their kōenkai members to join the national Diet member's kōenkai. This is often effective, but certainly members who join the kōenkai in these ways can have quite a different relationship to the Diet member than those who join because of intimate personal connections.

Overlapping Organizational Structures

Several organizational features distinguish most kōenkai. First, kōenkai are typically not single organizations; instead, the kōenkai for a lone Diet member comprises dozens of groups, some of which overlap in membership. Second, there are three major different types of organizing principles for the groups: personal connection to the Diet member, geography, and function (which commonly includes gender, age, occupation or former occupation, and some interest or hobby). Diet members are typically strategic in how they use these three principles to form kōenkai. For example:

> Counting the smaller groups, I have about 300 kōenkai organizations. For example, I maintain about 100 geographically based groups. Some of these are in rural areas and can be quite small, perhaps only a hundred households in them. So, I have some small kōenkai with only a hundred households as members. But, these also have presidents, secretary-generals, directors, too. I form kōenkai wherever I can form kōenkai. In the urban areas, the geographic ties are weaker. So, I form "group-based kōenkai" instead, for example, women's groups and youth groups. My organizing principles are geographic areas and also groups. Sometimes I incorporate a pre-existing group of like-minded people organized around something into my kōenkai, too. (Interview A, June 27, 2002)

Third, most Diet members begin their kōenkai in one area—typically their hometown—with a group of intimates and then expand in concentric circles, organizing geographically until they have blanketed the district. For rural Diet members, this results in at least one organization in every village, town, and city in the district; for urban Diet members, the geographical organizations are based on some subunit, such as school districts or neighborhoods.

So, kōenkai are typically not single organizations but webs of groups. Jean-Marie Bouissou describes it well: "the *kōenkai* is not a neatly arranged, hierarchically ordered, and coordinated structure but rather a heterogeneous patchwork of small groups born from parochial identification with a local community, material interest, personal histories, common likes"

---

joining, and even organizational strategies display surprising consistency from the 1950s to the early 2000s.

(1999, 107). Still, geography plays a central role, with most groups confined to one city or town.

Moreover, the initial period of kōenkai building reveals a personal core. The first step for most politicians building their kōenkai is to start close to home. Diet members commonly form an early group around a nucleus of high school friends (a separate group is formed for college friends, and another for middle school friends, elementary school friends, etc.). An LDP politician told us, "I created my first kōenkai with former high school classmates" (Interview A, June 27, 2002). Another fit the same pattern: "Therefore what I did for the first time is to organize a kōenkai which is composed of the people who graduated from my high school. They are very enthusiastic in their support for me. That's why I had confidence in winning the election. That's the first thing I did" (Interview Z, December 17, 2003). A third politician said, "I ran in my first campaign as an independent. My first kōenkai was formed by classmates from my high school, my old teachers, some of their other students, middle school and elementary school classmates of mine" (Interview HH, August 6, 2004). DPJ politicians use the same tactics. "In my district, there is no real DPJ party organization. DPJ supporters are basically the unaffiliated voters. I only had 50 days, so I formed a kōenkai of my old classmates, from elementary, middle, and high school" (Interview PP, October 4, 2007). Another DPJ politician remarked, "I first stood for election at 28 in the area I was born and raised. My first kōenkai was naturally formed by former classmates, seniors and juniors to me, and their mothers and fathers" (Interview Q, June 27, 2002). In Ibaraki, one LDP representative organized kōenkai groups initially around local ties, kinship ties, classmates, and people in the same industry as his family (water transportation), whereas another first organized a group for relatives, then moved to organizing a group for his elementary and middle school classmates, and next created a local network centered where he lived (Yamada 1993, 8, 15).

Wherever the core group, a typical pattern is for politicians to extend their kōenkai outward from their hometown in concentric circles (Kitaoka 1985, 141; Ishikawa and Hirose 1989, 144). Tanaka, ever prodigious, maintained over three hundred groups, divided into several branches and covering all the cities, towns, and villages in the district. Even he, however, started in his home county of Kariwa before blanketing the area. His district Etsuzankai formed liaison councils at the city or county level, and these in turn combined to form the Niigata Prefecture Etsuzankai. The Etsuzankai boasted nearly 100,000 members and its monthly *Gekkan Etsuzan* had a circulation of more than 50,000 (Fukuoka 1983b, 34–38).

Aurelia George Mulgan chronicles the kōenkai building by Toshikatsu Matsuoka, a well-known LDP politician who rose to the cabinet before taking his own life in 2007 amid a financial scandal. Matsuoka hailed from Aso, in Kumamoto Prefecture. His primary electoral mobilization machine was the Matsutomokai (Friends of "Matsu" Association), based primarily on his hometown and Aso County but also on his network of old school ties in Kumamoto City. This organization fell under the jusdiction of the Kumamoto Prefecture Election Administration Commission and raised $1.3 million for his first electoral bid in (George Mulgan 2006, 14–27).

Other kōenkai organizations take a predominant activity as their focus, for example, centering around a particular hobby or the discussion of current events. In addition to the hometown and old school ties that fueled Matsuoka in Kumamoto Prefecture, he also constructed organizations connecting to special interests in agriculture and forestry: the Matsuoka Toshikatsu New Century Politics and Economic Discussion Association (Matsuoka Toshikatsu Shinseiki Seikei Konwakai), the 21st Century Discussion Association (21 Seiki Konwakai), the Green Friends Association (Ryokuyūkai), and the Matsuoka Toshikatsu Policy Research Association (Matsuoka Toshikatsu Seisaku Kenkyūkai). This last alone raised over a quarter million dollars for his first election bid (George Mulgan 2006, 14–27, 53–54). Tanaka's kōenkai reportedly included several hundred industry-based groups (Fukuoka 1983b, 34).

Although these subgroups have separate organizational lives, they are really part of a single organism. In the minds of both supporters and Diet members, they are dedicated to a common purpose. In many cases, an umbrella organization also subsumes all or many of these subgroups. For example, in the 1960s Yoshizō Hashimoto in Ibaraki organized his kōenkai in the typical fashion, with a general kōenkai that had branches in every city, town, and village in the district working in parallel with two other groups (see figure 2.2): one group for the postmasters and another group pressing for rural telephone service. The latter was a merely a front for a traditional kōenkai; some voters did not want to join Hashimoto's kōenkai, but felt comfortable joining a group he led that was dedicated to an issue they cared about.

We commonly observe in strong kōenkai this pattern of opening a branch in every incorporated locality. In 1967, Richardson quoted a "conservative politician" as reporting on his kōenkai in this way: "People would not support me unless there was some kind of a connection between me and them....I have a kōenkai, a regional organization, which has twenty three branches. There are branch chiefs in each place, several directors and a central head. The branch chiefs and the group heads meet each month, even if there is no election that year" (1967, 866). Masumi Ishikawa and Machisada Hirose (1989, 134) provide an example of an anonymous Diet member from Oita 1st District in Kyushu with offices in each of the forty-one localities in his district. In Ibaraki, Fukushiro Nukaga adopted a similar strategy of establishing a branch of his kōenkai in each of the thirty-nine cities, towns, and villages of Ibaraki Prefecture. In larger population centers, Nukaga organized more intensively. In Mito City, the largest city in Ibaraki, Nukaga used school districts to establish areas for branches, putting up a branch of his kōenkai in almost every one of the twenty-eight

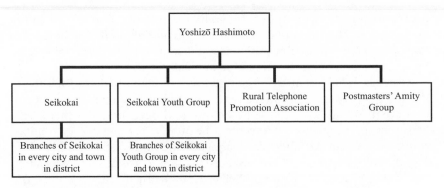

Figure 2.2 Early kōenkai of Yoshizō Hashimoto (Old Ibaraki 3rd District), 1960s
Source: Adapted from Yamada (1993, 11).

school districts in the city (Yamada 1993, 19). Another urban Diet member told us that he had geographically based groups centered around neighborhoods (Interview N, October 5, 2007), and many rural Diet members informed us that they had a kōenkai in each of the cities, towns, and villages in their districts (e.g., Interview K, July 1, 2002; Interview CC2, October 4, 2007).

These organizational webs become more complex over time. Politicians entrench themselves in the district, building new ties to different groups of the population. This targeting helps them maximize the loyalty they earn from kōenkai membership. As politicians become entrenched in the district, more specialized organizations are also a natural development from an organizational perspective. Masahiro Yamada's analysis of Yoshizō Hashimoto's kōenkai shows this development over time (see figure 2.3). For example, he added a second youth group, which might seem strange, but the simple reason for this is that members of the original Seikokai Youth Group had aged. To keep the organizational integrity and friendship bonds tight, the original youth organization continued with its membership unchanged, even though, even by the most generous standards, its members could not be consider youths any longer. Instead, new members who happened to be young were directed into the new Seikokai Young People's Group. The Yoshikai and the Yuumikai brought together the more youthful supporters of another local politician who died, these organizations then switching support Hashimoto. And the Yūeikai formed around Sumitomo subcontractors concentrated in the Kashima area (Yamada 1993, 13).

Developing a kōenkai takes a lot of time. It also requires a lot of money. All of the service involved gets expensive, after all. Indeed, one of the central pillars of the popular argument for electoral reform was that Japanese politics was too expensive because the SNTV system made politics too personal. In turn, this bred corruption because politicians were forced

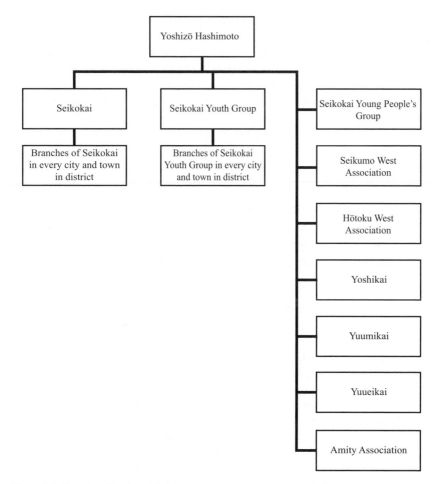

Figure 2.3 Kōenkai of Yoshizō Hashimoto (Old Ibaraki 3rd District), 1980s
Source: Adapted from Yamada (1995, 13).

to scramble, sometimes unethically, for the funds needed to lure voters. The expense of running a kōenkai is also an entry point for factions into the process. The factions provided financial support for their members to launch kōenkai (Asahi Shimbun Seijibu 1968). In this way, kōenkai and factions were complementary institutions, fitting together as neatly as a hand in a glove.

Some estimates put the costs of running a kōenkai in the 1980s at over $1 million per year, with one-third of the amount used for overhead, including personnel costs (Ishikawa and Hirose 1989, 141). Shinichi Kitaoka (1985, 54) provides an example of an anonymous politician who spent $700,000[5]

---

5. All of Kitaoka's figures in 1975 currency.

to start his kōenkai. His own estimates of the yearly expense of running a kōenkai in 1975 ran from a minimum of $500,000 in one case to a typical $700,000 to $1 million in more expensive cases (Kitaoka 1985, 141). Writing a few years later, Ishikawa and Hirose (1989, 141) set a similar average yearly expense of $700,000–1 million for kōenkai maintenance.

Many of the activities that sustain the kōenkai are underwritten by the Diet member herself, at a yearly cost of hundreds of thousands of dollars at least. Japanese custom dictates that guests bring large gifts of cash when they attend weddings or funerals. Diet members attending weddings are not exempt from this expectation, and because Diet members are prodigious in their attendance of weddings and funerals, they face a significant financial outlay simply from this, which in the 1980s ran to hundreds of thousands of dollars (Kitaoka 1985, 141).[6] Constituency service is done for free, of course, but it costs money to have staff or the Diet member spend time finding a job or securing admission to a school for the supporter or her children. Fukushiro Nukaga of Ibaraki maintained three offices at a cost of around $50,000 per month. Fortunately for him, he also was able to raise money; he disclosed revenue of $700,000 in 1992. These costs ratchet up as the Diet member adds staff as he or she gains seniority. Staff for newly minted Diet members number in the single digits (although one Hokkaido first-termer set a record by employing over thirty staff members), but senior LDP members might have over forty staff members on their payroll (Yamada 1993, 18; Yamada 1996, 1997; Ramseyer and Rosenbluth 1993, 24; Iwai 1990, 127; Kitaoka 1985, 141; Ishikawa and Hirose 1989, 141). Recently, kōenkai activities have become more likely to be revenue generating or, at least, revenue neutral. Diet members are now more likely to collect a fee for the food served, as per campaign regulations (Interview F, June 22, 2004; Interview B, October 5, 2007). Still, dues remain modest for individual members. One Diet member told us he had dropped his dues from $30 to $10 to increase kōenkai membership after his third year in office, out of recognition that individual-membership kōenkai still are not good vehicles for raising funds (Interview HH, October 6, 2004).

The Broader Role of Kōenkai in Japanese Politics

Simply to maintain a kōenkai requires a huge amount of money. On the other hand, a well-run and well-financed kōenkai offers considerable advantages to the incumbent. Because building a kōenkai takes time and money, this creates barriers to entry for challengers. The demands of the kōenkai contribute to two significant and oft-noted trends in Japanese politics: the

6. Wedding gifts are typically $300–$500, whereas funerals require a more modest $50. The Public Office Election Law (POEL) prevents the staff of Diet members from making these donations; if the Diet member wants to bestow this gift, he or she must attend in person.

rise of hereditary politicians (*nisei giin*) and the diminished number of re-tired bureaucrats turned politicians.

The rise of hereditary politicians has attracted considerable attention of late (Ishibashi and Reed 2000; Usui and Colignon 2004; Taniguchi 2008). According to Naoko Taniguchi (2008), in 1958 fewer than one out of seven LDP Diet Members were hereditary politicians. In 2003, this had risen to two out of five (Taniguchi 2008, 67). These politicians had a much greater chance of electoral success—81.3 percent in 2003—than other newcom-ers (70). Nevertheless, Gerald Curtis (1988, 97) called attention to this phenomenon in the 1980s, calling it one of the most notable changes in LDP Diet membership in the postwar period. Of course, hereditary politi-cians are not unique to Japan; after all, the 2000 U.S. presidential election featured the son of a president running neck and neck with the son of a senator. But Japan has developed this trend, comparatively, to an extreme (Ishibashi and Reed 1992). Moreover, Michihiro Ishibashi and Steven Reed argue that "[k]oenkai have evolved into selectorates, organizations that select candidates for elective office," and that the easiest new candi-dates to rally everyone in the organization around are those closely tied to the previous incumbent (1992, 369). Chikako Usui and Richard Colignon see the cause for this clearly: "[t]he rise of hereditary politicians reflects the strength of *kōenkai* in specific local constituencies" (2004, 410).

In the second trend, retired bureaucrats turned politicians were once a staple of the LDP, but in recent years their number has dwindled. In some ways, this is concomitant with the rise of hereditary politicians (see figure 2.4); however, the decline is marked. Usui and Colignon (2004) per-suasively demonstrate this decline through an analysis of the prime min-istership, cabinet membership, and membership in the lower house as a whole. The percentage of ex-bureaucrat cabinet ministers declined from 25 percent in 1953 to only 11.1 percent in 2004 (Usui and Colignon 2004, 406). In figure 2.4, we show the number of LDP ministers who were either hereditary politicians or former bureaucrats. Beginning in the 1980s, the number of ministers who were hereditary politicians clearly began to sur-pass the number who were former bureaucrats. Bureaucrats, who retire at the pinnacle of their careers, are without exception too old to build senior-ity in a party where hereditary politicians sometimes first win seats in their twenties.

Why Are There Kōenkai?

Now that we have carefully reviewed exactly what kōenkai are and have es-tablished that they are an important feature in Japanese politics, we turn to the main thrust of this chapter—an explanation of the origin and transfor-mation of kōenkai that will provide evidence for our larger argument about institutional origin and transformation (see chap. 1).

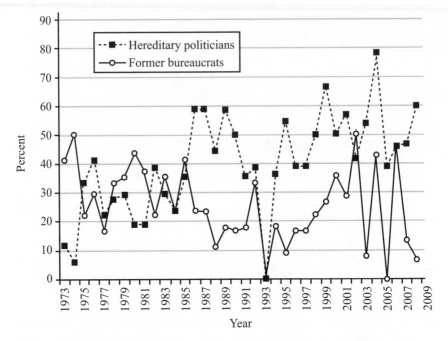

Figure 2.4 Percentage of LDP ministers who are former bureaucrats and hereditary politicians, 1973–2009
Source: Analysis of data from J-LOD.

There are two main sets of arguments for the origin of kōenkai in the academic literature, both having considerable merit: the urban village explanation and the electoral explanation. Both also have the virtue of explaining why kōenkai arose in Japan but not in other countries. Nevertheless, neither suffices as a full explanation for the origin of kōenkai.

Urban Village Explanation of Kōenkai

The first view is that kōenkai are primarily social mobilization networks that developed because of the nature of Japanese social networks or because of their transformation during economic growth, urbanization, and political changes in the postwar period. We call this the urban village explanation of kōenkai. Not intrinsic to the argument but implicit in some of this literature is a view that kōenkai are effective because Japanese democracy is stunted or because Japanese voters are unduly swayed by social networks instead of just making up their own minds.

Masao Soma (1963) was one of the first to analyze kōenkai in postwar Japanese politics. He argued that the old community-based relationships, which traditionally provided communal services such as water and farm tool management, had been weakened by ongoing agricultural modernization and urbanization. As the local traditional societies were structurally transformed, new types of social and personal networks emerged, and kōenkai were examples of such networks (Soma 1963).

Kitaoka (1985) adds that the rapid economic development that Japan enjoyed after 1955 transformed the societal structure in rural Japan. Although local bosses, such as officials in the local government or local assembly members, played a major role in organizing local networks, such networks were unstable because the society was changing at such a rapid clip (Kitaoka 1985, 50–51). In response, Diet members created kōenkai as their own personal networks (52). Kōenkai began as small groups of comrades (*dōshi*) immediately after World War II, but they grew rapidly. They expanded first in small and medium-size cities, but then spread to both larger cities and rural areas (53).

Advocates of cultural causes of kōenkai typically see them as reflecting and in part being caused by the nature of Japanese society, constituting "a peculiarly Japanese 'society of connections' that utilizes blood and regional ties based on the family and including in-laws, neighborhood groups, trade unions and so on as mediums to create a supportive social network centered on the Diet Member" (Fukuoka 1983b, 38). Others have argued that the use of social organizations and networks for political purposes constitutes the cultural roots of electoral or campaign practices (Richardson 1974).

Neighborhood associations have also been seen as another of these village-surrogate organizations. The argument is similar to the urban village explanation of kōenkai, although neighborhood associations and urbanization have probably come under closer scrutiny by sociologists than kōenkai and urbanization have by political scientists. Still, sociologists have argued that the vitality of neighborhood associations in postwar urban Japan reflects phenomena similar to those sketched out by Soma (Kikuchi 1990, 221; for a discussion, see also Pekkanen 2006, 116–17). Ralph Falconieri terms neighborhood associations "a product of Japanese village orientations carried over into the urban setting" (1990, 34). Henry Smith argues that the neighborhood associations reflected genuine community desire for a community organization to face urbanization, "essentially a means of sustaining local community solidarity in the face of rapid population turnover" (1978, 66). Ronald Dore sees neighborhood associations as a surrogate or "some substitute for the security and sense of belonging which a rural community provides" (1958, 258, 264).

Arguments that the source of kōenkai or neighborhood associations lies in the dramatic social and economic changes of postwar Japan—urbanization and industrialization being foremost among them—undoubtedly touch on important factors. Recent scholarship by sociologists, historians, and political scientists on neighborhood associations, however, has found the urban village arguments wanting because they ignore certain factors, such as the role of the state (Akimoto 1990;

Hastings 1985; Pekkanen 2000, 2003, 2004, 2006; Tsujinaka, Pekkanen and Yamamoto 2009). Similarly, we cannot fully accept the urban village explanation for kōenkai. After all, many societies experienced rapid economic modernization in the postwar period without developing kōenkai.

Electoral Explanations of Kōenkai

A second view of the origin of the kōenkai originates from a completely different perspective. Whereas the urban village explanation looks to large-scale changes, the electoral explanation sees the origin of kōenkai in the Japanese electoral system. As discussed in chapter 1, the peculiar SNTV MMD creates a host of problems for a political party intent on gaining a majority in the legislature. Foremost among these are that the party must gain multiple seats in a single district and, to do so, must solve a coordination problem to spread votes evenly among its candidates. If one candidate gains a disproportionate share of the votes in a district at the expense of other party candidates, this uneven distribution will probably result in the party's failing to maximize its seat total. In the electoral explanation, kōenkai are seen as a means to coordinate vote distribution, and they are thus a logical solution to the problems posed by the electoral system.

In the words of Mark Ramseyer and Frances Rosenbluth, "Building personal loyalty is the key to the LDP electoral strategy. The personal bonds that develop between support group members and their Dietmember aid the LDP in apportioning the vote efficiently among competing LDP candidates" (1993, 26; see also Rochon 1981). Haruhiro Fukui and Shigeko N. Fukai appear to endorse this logic when they summarize, "Under the multiseat district system, which was in place from 1925 to 1994, a local branch of a major party that ran more than one candidate in the same election district could not campaign for one at another's expense and, therefore, the kōenkai replaced a party organization as a candidate's primary campaign organization" (1996, 284).

Hitoshi Abe, Muneyuki Shindō, and Sadafumi Kawato (1994) offer a rich explanation that relies largely, but not entirely, on the electoral system. According to these authors, the poverty of local finances in the 1950s created acute problems for local politicians. These local politicians were forced to offer national politicians an exchange that cemented the primacy of kōenkai. The local politicians traded access to their base (jiban) of supporters to the national politicians in exchange for government largess (Abe, Shindō, and Kawato 1994, 174; see also Scheiner 2006).

There is much to be said for the electoral explanation; the reasoning behind it is sound, and a close connection is to be expected between the electoral system and kōenkai, which are, after all, vote-mobilization organizations. Nevertheless, this explanation suffers from what Paul Pierson calls the defect of "actor-centered functionalism—that is the claim that a particular institution exists because it is expected to serve the interests of those who created it" (2004, 104–22; see also chap. 1). In other words, the clean logical links between the coordination problem created by the electoral system and the persuasive conclusion that kōenkai mitigate this problem are not in themselves evidence of causality. Instead, they are the basis for a plausible hypothesis. To determine causality, we must look more closely at the historical record. Abe, Shindō, and Kawato (1994) are on the right track when they combine such an analysis with their keen understanding of the incentives created by the electoral system.

Historical Institutionalist Explanations

Given our emphasis on assessing the historical record before making causal claims, we need to examine the evidence first and then return to clarify the claims of our argument. In fact, we plunge into the historical examination in the next section. But first, to orient the reader to the type of analysis we conduct, we briefly frame our argument here.

A combination of institutional and contingent factors led to the establishment, development, and supremacy of the kōenkai (vs., say, party branches) for the LDP. Our notion of causality foregrounds time as a variable. Therefore, our argument about the origin and development of kōenkai emphasizes sequence—critically, the merger of the LDP comes after the early development of kōenkai, conjoint or complementary institutions such as factions and electoral campaign laws, and positive returns that successfully reinforced the development of kōenkai over time. We avoid the problems of actor-centered functionalism by causal process tracing.

Before tracing the trajectory of kōenkai in postwar Japan, let us consider the complementary institutions of kōenkai: factions and restrictive campaigning laws. Factions work well with kōenkai because the separate electoral bases that are the kōenkai permit factions more independence from one another. Without kōenkai, too, faction leaders would find it harder to sponsor new faction members, and nomination constitutes a key role for factions. Moreover, the development of factions spurred the development of kōenkai, especially in the late 1950s and early 1960s.

Scholars have widely recognized that the tight campaigning restrictions in Japan contributed to the significance of kōenkai. It is important to emphasize, however, that although they work together to shape the electoral environment, campaign regulations are distinct from the electoral system. In Japan, campaign regulations have severely restricted the avenues available to politicians as they seek to deliver their message to voters. These regulations restrict activities, prohibiting, for example, canvassing door to door; signature campaigns; and dispensing cash, food, or drink to voters. Moreover, written campaign materials are prohibited unless expressly allowed by law, so campaigns may create only officially approved campaign posters and these posters may be placed only in publicly provided and designated locations, campaigns may produce only two types of brochures and distribute a limited total number, and direct mailings are limited to only an approved postcard mailed (at government expense) to a limited number of voters. Media advertisements are limited to government-approved settings in which all candidates follow identical regulations concerning content and format, among other restrictions on use of the media (indeed, Diet members are even forced to close their websites during the election campaign!). Campaign offices and cars and the amount of expenditures made on campaign workers are also closely restricted and regulated by the government. Sidewalk speeches may only be made between 8 a.m. and 8 p.m. (Christensen 1994; Usaki 1990; Public Officials Election Act 1950).

Politicians commonly seek to evade these restrictions to some degree by engaging in "organization activities" with their kōenkai rather than in "campaign activities" (Christensen 1994, 991). With so many points of contact with voters closed down, kōenkai are especially important to Diet members. In other words, the campaign restrictions shape the electoral environment in a way that heightens the value of kōenkai; as such, the restrictive campaign regulations become a complementary institution for kōenkai. Of course, for politicians who already have strong kōenkai, the restrictive campaign regulations serve as entry barriers for opponents, and this accounts for their being maintained so ardently (McElwain 2008) despite the improbability that loosening them would imperil Japanese democracy (the original rationale behind the restrictions). This is the same kind of mutual reinforcement found between factions and kōenkai.

Origin of the Kōenkai

Why and how did politicians come to develop kōenkai? Looking at how and when kōenkai came about and rose to prominence provides crucial evidence for our understanding of institutions, and in this section we provide this historical analysis. In probing the origin of kōenkai, we find that kōenkai existed after the readoption of SNTV electoral rules in 1947 but that they did not grow and develop until after the 1955 merger of the LDP. Another crucial finding is that the LDP attempted to eliminate kōenkai and replace them with party branches in 1963. Despite the fact that the electoral merits of kōenkai for the LDP have been persuasively laid out by scholars, it appears that party leaders, at least, were not convinced.

Early Kōenkai

Although it is difficult to be conclusive, it appears that the SNTV electoral system was used in Japan for many years before kōenkai became widespread. The earliest record of a kōenkai that we found is that of Yukio Ozaki. In 1910, Ozaki's kōenkai took the name Gakudokai (*Gakudo* was a nickname for Ozaki), but the group had existed as a strong personal network for some time before this renaming. Kōenkai members supported Ozaki, who engaged in political struggles with oligarchs, bureaucrats, the political parties, and the military.

Japan originally adopted the SNTV MMD system in 1900. The Meiji oligarchy believed that intraparty competition would prevent a dominant party from appearing. The system remained in place until 1993, except for two brief periods in 1919–1925 and 1946. In 1925, the Elections Act changed the electoral system from one comprising 295 single-member, 63 two-member, and 11 three-member districts to one comprising 53 three-member, 38 four-member, and 31 five-member districts (Hirano 2006, 21).

In 1945, the Japanese government adopted a complicated large-district system that allotted voters one, two, or three votes depending on the number of representatives to be elected from their district. The election on April 10, 1946, was held under this prefecture-size district system (although seven prefectures—Hokkaido, Tokyo, Niigata, Aichi, Osaka, Hyogo, and Fukuoka—had two districts) of 455 seats. Voters in single- to five-member districts wrote down one name, voters in six- to ten-member districts wrote down two names, and voters in eleven- to fourteen-member districts wrote down three names. The average number of representatives for a district was nine. This complicated system was quickly scrapped, and a new electoral law passed on March 31, 1947. So, the next election (the twenty-third general election) in 1947 was held under the SNTV MMD system, which remained in place until 1993 (Wada 1996, 54).

It is important to examine the years between the 1947 readoption of SNTV and the LDP merger in 1955. Interestingly, kōenkai were scarce for years after the initial readoption of SNTV in 1947, and they were far from dominant as electoral mobilization devices. This is somewhat surprising, given that Japanese democracy itself was arguably untried, party labels were still somewhat fluid, and voters were reported to vote substantially based on personal characteristics (*Asahi Shimbun*, September 19, 1952, 1). Kakuei Tanaka, famous as the founder of the Etsuzankai, the foremost Japanese kōenkai, did not bother to establish a kōenkai during his first campaign in 1946; instead, he relied on local notables to get out the vote for him (Igarashi 1989, 87–88).

Even though major party candidates faced competition from within their own party, kōenkai were not widespread in the first several elections in the postwar period. This is strange in that the three major parties in the 1947 and 1949 elections certainly faced a problem in evenly distributing their votes (see tables 2.1 and 2.2).

Only after the reversion of sovereignty in 1952 did kōenkai really begin to emerge (*Asahi Shimbun*, September 18, 1952, 1; *Asahi Shimbun*, September 23, 1952, 3; *Asahi Shimbun*, January 6, 1967, 14). By then, the SNTV system was firmly in place, but kōenkai also grew, in part, due to their usefulness in skirting campaign restrictions. Candidates were permitted to have only one election campaign office, but they could have an unlimited

TABLE 2.1

Number of districts where parties ran multiple candidates, 1947–1955

Year	Total Number of Districts	Liberals	Democrats	Socialists	Left Socialists	Right Socialists
1947	117	98	99	90		
1949	117	111	69	54		
1952	117	113	70		5	21
1953	117	103	54		11	21
1955	118	88	100		13	22

Source: Calculated using data generously provided by Steven Reed.

TABLE 2.2

Percentage of districts where a party ran multiple candidates, 1947–1955

Year	Liberals	Democrats	Socialists	Left Socialists	Right Socialists	JCP
1947	85.2	88.4	76.9			2.6
1949	94.9	61.6	46.6			0.9
1952	96.6	63.1		5.6	23.6	0.9
1953	88.0	50.5		11.1	22.3	0.0
1955	75.2	84.7		12.0	22.0	0.0

Source: Calculated using data generously provided by Steven Reed.
Note: JCP, Japanese Communist Party.

number of "kōenkai offices" (*Asahi Shimbun,* September 23, 1952, 3). And candidates used kōenkai meetings, in which supporters only "voluntarily" got together for a drink with candidates, to evade restrictions (*Mainichi Shimbun,* September 22, 1952, 3).

Shigeru Hori had built a kōenkai of 5,000 members in Saga Prefecture by 1952, and Tanaka first established his more celebrated kōenkai the following year.[7] Moreover, kōenkai had already taken their distinctive form. They were easily distinguished from the labor union bloc support because kōenkai, as today, comprised members with different occupations, backgrounds, and hobbies (*Asahi Shimbun,* September 18, 1952, 1). In the period 1952–1955, kōenkai still remained relatively scarce or weak. Even in fiercely competitive districts such as Oita 2 and Yamaguchi 2, not all the conservative candidates had even built kōenkai (*Asahi Shimbun,* September 18, 1952, 1). Despite, or perhaps in part because of, this scarcity and the severity of election campaign restrictions, elections were widely reported to be marred by outright vote buying (*Asahi Shimbun,* January 5, 1955, 1). Local notables worked as election brokers, buying and selling blocks of votes both in remote villages and in large cities (*Mainichi Shimbun,* March 22, 1953, 6;

---

7. See *Asahi Shimbun* (September 18, 1952, 1); Igarashi (1989, 91). For journalistic descriptions of Etsuzankai, see Asahi Shinbun Niigata Shikyoku (1982); Kobayashi (1983); Niigata Nippō Sha (2004).

Asahi Shimbun, January 7, 1955, 1; *Asahi Shimbun,* January 6, 1955, 1). In this period, too, the party label was weak, which no doubt worried candidates and influenced campaign strategies. An *Asahi Shimbun* survey found that voters cared most about the personalities of the candidates. The number of voters who said they would vote based on the candidates' personal characteristics (43 percent) was almost double the number who said they would make their decision based on political party (25 percent) (*Asahi Shimbun,* September 19, 1952, 1). The personal vote dominated the election and electoral mobilization was obviously a problem to the point that vote buying was widely reported, yet kōenkai were far from the universal solution. At the time, the relatively weak party labels of new parties probably made kōenkai more attractive to candidates. On the other hand, given such weak party labels and such a fluid political landscape, we can view the primary aim of kōenkai as getting out the vote rather than dividing the vote.

On November 15, 1955, the Liberal Party and the Democratic Party merged to form the Liberal Democratic Party (LDP). Neither had secured a majority in the election in February of that year, although they were the largest two parties in the Diet. The democrats held 185 seats (39.6 percent) and the liberals 112 (24.0 percent), each far outpacing the left socialists, with 89 seats (19.1 percent), and right socialists, with 67 seats (14.3 percent). The communists, with 2 seats (0.4 percent), were hardly in the legislative picture. Even after the merger of the two socialist parties, the democrats were the largest party in the Diet.

Kōenkai were active to a degree in the 1955 elections. They had already formed their character as general vote-collecting organizations relying on constituency service and subsidized social activities, which persisted for decades. In the month before the elections, election staff members reported that in the upcoming elections they felt that even more important than campaign finances would be whether candidates had established a firm organizational base. This organization should have held all-you-can-eat meetings, sent letters, provided job introductions, and hosted drinking outings. A crucial part of this organizational base was the women's association, which was easily developed into another part of the kōenkai (*Asahi Shimbun,* January 5, 1955, 1).

The role of local notables loomed large in the minds of politicians and reporters alike. If these local notables recommended a candidate, it was felt that the community as a whole would vote for the candidate (*Asahi Shimbun,* January 6, 1955, 1). In rural areas, these local bosses were the moneylenders who controlled access to capital, the right to allocate seed rice, and the coordination of the use of common lands. Naturally, incorporating these local notables into an election campaign was seen as critical. In some ways, it was not important whether these local notables actually had the electoral leverage ascribed to them. What matters is that politicians apparently believed these local notables held the key to electoral success, and the kōenkai structure was a natural one in which to incorporate these local leaders.

Local notables were important in urban areas as well. Figures such as the town meeting chairs and crime-prevention committee members were tapped for leadership positions within the kōenkai. Comparing rural and urban areas, however, the *Asahi Shimbun* concluded that bosses were more important in rural areas. Junnosuke Masumi also finds in later (1958 and 1960) surveys that kōenkai activities were not as active in urban areas as in semiurban areas (1964, 58–59; 1965)), and Kitaoka reports that kōenkai became popular first in small and medium-size cities and then expanded into large cities and rural areas (Kitaoka 1985, 58–59).

In the countryside, local notables held some coercive power, and the level of voter sophistication was much lower. But, even in the cities, electoral competition pushed candidates to develop kōenkai (*Asahi Shimbun,* January 7, 1955, 1). Because many city dwellers were fairly recent immigrants from the countryside or still maintained close links to a rural area, a large number of candidates created kōenkai to strengthen the regional relationship with their districts. Much more than the party label, incorporating the voters into this organizational base held the key to electoral victory (*Asahi Shimbun,* February 29, 1955, 1).

The Liberal Democratic Party Merger and Kōenkai

The electoral system and the needs of a dominant party seem clearly related to the development of the kōenkai. Nevertheless, it is important also to remember that the electoral system had been around since 1947 but kōenkai really began to boom only a few years after the 1955 LDP merger. A glance at tables 2.1 and 2.2 shows that, in multiple elections spanning nearly a decade before the merger, the liberals, democrats, and even socialists ran multiple candidates in many districts. In other words, even before the LDP merger, multiple candidates from the same party constituted the reality in almost all districts, yet kōenkai did not really come to dominate electoral mobilization until *after* the 1955 LDP merger. Of course, the electoral system certainly played a part in the development of kōenkai; but by the time the LDP contested the 1958 election, major parties had fought five national elections (1947, 1949, 1952, 1953, and 1955) under SNTV, in which a majority of districts had multiple competitors from at least two parties. It is the *sequence* of the limited initial development of kōenkai followed by the merger of the LDP that matters. Had the LDP formed as a unified conservative party in, say, 1947, it could have pursued an alternative vote mobilization strategy, one that did not involve kōenkai. As things played out, however, the LDP formed after some politicians had already developed kōenkai, although these kōenkai were not widespread or deeply rooted enough to constitute a general solution to the problem of vote division. As research in chaos theory has shown, these small initial perturbations can have exaggerated effects on equilibrium states or later outcomes.

It is also important to realize that we cannot assume that the merger of the two conservative parties was the inevitable result of the electoral system (which was, thus, indirectly a cause of whatever stemmed from the merger); as Masaru Kohno has argued, the "conventional perspectives that view the creation of the LDP as largely as a product of change in Japan's underlying socio-ideological foundations" go too far (1997, 90).

It is possible that things could have played out differently had the Democratic Party succeeded in forming a minority government; the socialists had been unable to agree on a merger before the 1955 election; or Ichiro Hatoyama, the Democratic Party head, been able to prevent a merger. In other words, let us assume for a moment that the development of kōenkai was a result of the LDP merger and that the kōenkai would not have developed under SNTV absent the merger. Then, if the merger is properly seen as not being the inevitable consequence of the electoral system but a contingent event, the causal relationship between SNTV and kōenkai is undermined.

The 1958 election was the first election following the LDP merger. In this election and its immediate aftermath, kōenkai activities increased substantially. Tanaka's Etsuzankai, for example, became much more sophisticated organizationally. In 1959 the group created a liaison council, and in 1960 a headquarters completed its pyramidal structure. Around this time, too, the kōenkai introduced a "competition rule," spurring local branches to compete to achieve higher vote shares in every election (Igarashi 1989, 86–93). Rapid economic development after 1955 also transformed the societal structure, particularly in Japanese rural areas. The local notables, so frequently remarked on, began to fade from prominence only an election or two before this. Kitaoka (1985, 50–53) writes that networks based on local notables became unstable during this rapid transformation and that as a consequence Diet members began to build up their kōenkai to mobilize votes (see also Masumi 1965, 58). But kōenkai were still not completely dominant, despite the fact that the candidates had three years after the merger to plan their election campaigns. This slow rise to dominance of the kōenkai is consistent with both the kōenkai's existing before the merger and this preexistence of kōenkai's crucially affecting later developments; it is not necessary to argue that kōenkai magically manifested in 1955 after the merger. The slow development over time favors our historical institutionalist argument, which recognizes the positive returns that set path dependence over an explanation based on strategic calculations rooted in electoral calculus.

The New Liberal Democratic Party Fails to Replace Kōenkai

When the LDP was launched, one of its major goals was to develop local branches. In a December 1955 meeting, the LDP decided to set up local branches (*Asahi Shimbun,* December 4, 1955, 1); however, it substantially failed in this goal. This is directly relevant to our analysis of the origin and development of kōenkai as election mobilization organizations. From its inception, the LDP, far from seeing the kōenkai as ideal vehicles to divide the vote, aimed to subsume them into a robust network of party branches.

On November 15, 1955, the LDP announced its "Organization Activity Outline" ("Soshiki Katsudō Yōkō"). This document urged the rapid development of local party organizations to compete effectively with the Socialist Party (see Takahara 1959). The LDP effort to build up local organization was not limited to this pronouncement alone. In addition, the fledgling party invested resources in building its local organizational strength. Starting in 1956, several workshops were held to train local leaders. The following year, the party established a Central Institute of Politics to advance the training of local party operatives. It is important to recognize that the party proclamation in 1955 was not lip service and that these were not token efforts. By 1964, in fact, the LDP had trained over 22,000 local leaders through these efforts (Masumi 1964, 1965). But the effort to build a strong local party organization was doomed to failure because the national Diet members resisted the growth of their own party organization (Masumi 1995 [1985]).

Before the merger, the Liberal Party and the Democratic Party had clashed fiercely in campaigning for the conservative vote. There was no electoral coordination between the conservatives of rival parties, and each fought the election independently (*Mainichi Shimbun*, April 10, 1953, 2). So, these rival organizations could not be merged easily. The liberals and the democrats had run head to head in 117 out of 118 districts in 1955. Former liberals and democrats squabbled about who would hold power in the local party branches (*Asahi Shimbun* [evening ed.], January 8, 1956, 1). The task of coordinating the LDP candidates was made even more difficult because in some districts the kōenkai had already formed sticky web-like personal networks (*Mainichi Shimbun*, November 20, 1955, 1; *Mainichi Shimbun*, November 21, 1955, 3). In other words, the existence of kōenkai themselves thwarted party efforts to build a network of party branches. And it was the conflictual merger that really spurred the growth of kōenkai, not the electoral system that had been in place for nearly a decade.

Hurdles to the creation of local branches also sprang up in districts where the local assembly seats were not evenly distributed among Liberal Party and Democratic Party local legislators (*Mainichi Shimbun*, November 20, 1955, 1). In districts such as Kumamoto and Nagasaki, ex-Democratic Party and ex-Liberal Party leaders haggled over who would become the head of the local branch (*Mainichi Shimbun*, November 21, 1955, 3). In Gifu, Kagawa, Aichi, and other districts, local assembly members even resisted the LDP merger. In the run up the 1958 election, tensions ran high as Diet members strove to integrate their kōenkai into local networks by tying up with local assembly members' kōenkai; conflicts between kōenkai struggling for local links were visible in Shimane, Okayama, and other districts (*Mainichi Shimbun*, April 24, 1958, 9). A prefectural office opened in Hyogo in 1956, but national and local legislators ignored it so completely that no party branch office opened until 1967 (Foster 1982, 847). The intensity of these problems should not be dismissed. Indeed, some national Diet members were forced to contemplate changing districts because of the difficulties in coordinating local offices (*Mainichi Shimbun,* November 21, 1955, 3). Junnosuke Masumi called the increased integration of the national Diet members' and local assembly members' kōenkai the "conglomeratization" (*keiretsuka*) of kōenkai (Masumi 1964, 1965).

It is impossible to know what would have happened had the LDP formed as a majority party in 1947 and fought from its inception as a unified party, but it is plausible that the development of kōenkai and party branches would have taken a very different path. Sequence matters. The sequence of fighting the first few elections followed by the merger of the LDP laid down different tracks into the future than if the LDP had formed earlier. As it was, by the early 1960s, the time of the next LDP attempt to centralize, kōenkai had extended their roots even deeper into local soil. In the run up to the 1960 election, the *Asahi Shimbun* featured a story on a Tokyo-area Diet member who appeared relaxed amid the usual flurry of candidates frantically campaigning. His strong kōenkai gave him peace of mind, and the *Asahi* opined that it was even more advantageous to have a strong ongoing kōenkai than to have a large war chest for the campaign (*Asahi Shimbun,* November 9, 1960, 11). Kōenkai activities remained the same as earlier times: drinking parties, excursions, and dinner parties, all overlapping when possible with any other kind of group meeting, such as volunteer firefighters and drought prevention meetings (*Asahi Shimbun,* November 23, 1960, 2). The newspaper also reported that LDP candidates generally boasted kōenkai membership figures of around 10,000–20,000 (*Asahi Shimbun,* November 9, 1960, 11; *Asahi Shimbun,* November 23, 1960, 2).

Some kōenkai existed immediately after the introduction of the SNTV system,[8] but it was the LDP merger in 1955 that stimulated the growth of kōenkai. To connect these dots, however, is not to proclaim kōenkai the inevitable or even logical solution to a vote-division problem. After all, the major parties had faced considerable vote-division problems in the first four elections, before the merger (see tables 2.1 and 2.2). Moreover, even then, kōenkai did not immediately blossom, as we might expect if the parties suddenly had to divide the vote even more, but grew slowly over a period of years. Kōenkai membership for LDP candidates grew gradually from the 1960s to the 1990s (see figure 2.5). This pattern of growth is very much consistent with a positive returns explanation.

---

8. It is impossible to be certain how many existed or what the membership levels were like. The first reliable data we have are from 1967, which indicate fewer than 6 percent of all Japanese voters were kōenkai members, although the rate for LDP members was higher at 8 percent (Masumi 1995 [1985], 485). We can reasonably guess that fewer than 5 percent of Japanese voters were in kōenkai in the 1950s, perhaps many fewer.

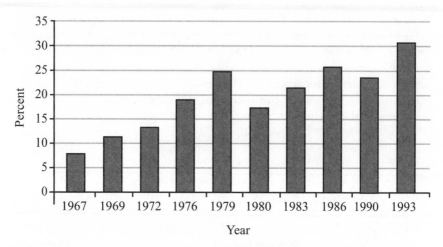

Figure 2.5 Kōenkai membership rates of LDP supporters, 1967–1993 (%)
Source: Analysis of 1972–1993 Meisuikyō data. Data for 1967 and 1969 from Masumi (1995
[1985]), 481) using Kōmei Senkyo Renmei survey results reported in Miyake (1977, 295).

Furthermore, it is important to keep in mind that in these early years
the LDP did not even promote kōenkai as part of its electoral mobilization
strategy.[9] To the contrary, both at the very outset of the LDP in 1955 and at
several points in the early years, the LDP made a concerted effort to establish local party branches that would subsume kōenkai. These efforts were
fairly consistent. In addition to the examples in 1955 and 1956 already mentioned, in 1960 the LDP announced a Plan for Organizational Activities
(Soshiku Kkatsudō Hoshin), in which party activists were to be educated at
party headquarters to learn how to discipline a variety of groups in the local
municipalities (Adachi 1960, Kayano 1960). The same type of reform was
announced again in 1961 but with no meaningful result (*Asahi Shimbun,*
May 29, 1961, 2). All these early efforts failed (Nonaka 1995, 51–55).

Again, the sequence of events is critical here; had the LDP emerged as a
large, unified conservative party to contest the 1947 election, the development of kōenkai and party branches would plausibly have taken very different courses. But in reality the kōenkai developed first, and *then* the Liberal
Party and the Democratic Party merged (and not without some ill feeling).
Thus, the merger occurred after kōenkai had already developed to some
extent (to mobilize votes), and as it turned out, these kōenkai severely
restricted the ability of the newly merged party to achieve a strong local
party branch system. The LDP merger after a nearly a decade of electoral

9. Indeed, as late as the 1970s, LDP members were less likely to be in a kōenkai than
were supporters of the JCP, DSP, or CGP, polling ahead of only the JSP and New Liberal Club
(NLC). Of course, we could argue that the kōenkai of legislators of other parties were different in nature from LDP kōenkai.

competition solidified the hold that kōenkai had on the electoral mobiliza-tion function of the party. Kōenkai were not the inevitable, or even logical or natural, choice to solve the problem of vote division. Instead, they were a second-best response to the struggles between entrenched incumbents with their own organizations, which had been developed to cultivate the personal vote during a period when party labels were weak.

Another important factor during this period was the growing power of factions. Factions are a critical complementary institution of kōenkai (see chap. 1). In chapter 4, we trace the origin and development of factions. For our present discussion, note that the late 1950s and early 1960s, when factions really became entrenched in the LDP, was also the time when fac-tions and kōenkai began to reinforce one another. The increased factional rivalry spurred competition in the districts among the LDP Diet members, including strengthening their kōenkai. Faction leaders were keen to get a leg up on the competition by sponsoring new candidates. These candidates were often unrecognized by the party, and so they relied heavily on build-ing up their kōenkai. In this way, factions sought to extend into the districts via the kōenkai. The heating up of the factional competition also made the prospect of unified local party branches less likely. Instead, as factions con-solidated into an institution, they reinforced kōenkai.

The Development of Kōenkai

The Liberal Democratic Party Failure to Control Kōenkai in 1963

In 1963, Prime Minister Hayato Ikeda led a movement to reform the LDP and strengthen the central party. The Organization Research Committee (Soshiki Chōsa Kai) spearheaded these efforts. A famously "clean" politi-cian, Takeo Miki headed the committee to give it greater legitimacy, and it was strongly supported by Hirohide Ishida, chairman of the National Organization Committee. Because local party organization was a glaring weakness, the committee moved swiftly in that arena. In October 1963, the LDP announced its final proposal. The proposal called for a new pol-icy charter and the establishment of "political ethics," but its centerpiece was a plan to strengthen local party branches (Liberal Democratic Party 1987, 478–89; see also *Asahi Shimbun*, August 17, 1963, 2; Masumi 1964, 59; Thayer 1969, 105). The plan was a clear attempt to centralize party control. Understanding the attempt and the reasons it failed is critical to understanding the development of kōenkai. The new arrangement re-quired, among other things, the local party branches to report directly to party headquarters. The plan also called for integrating kōenkai members into the party, with "as a transitional measure . . . the leading members of a kōenkai and at least five hundred [others to] register with the local branch and be asked to cooperate positively in party activities" (Miki Commission report, cited in Masumi 1995 237; see also *Yomiuri Shimbun,* October 18, 1963, 1).

Within a few months, this second major initiative in eight years to build local party organization was as dead as those that had come before it. Opposition from within the party killed the effort (*Asahi Shimbun,* January 5, 1964, 2). The LDP then went to an alternative backup scheme in which the LDP would create a liaison council between the kōenkai and local branches. This council would distribute the party press releases and engage in some election activities. This retreat to a minimal role for the local branches represented acquiescence to a political defeat (*Asahi Shimbun,* January 5, 1964, 1; Masumi 1967, 1995).

Nonaka (1995) views this event as a turning point. The LDP had struggled for almost the entire first decade of its existence to abolish kōenkai, launching effort after effort. After the 1963 defeat, the LDP abandoned the fight and switched to the strategy of coopting kōenkai to serve in place of the local branches. This was unmistakably a choice the LDP made not as a desirable strategy but in recognition of its inability to achieve its preferred strategy of party branches.

The 1978 Party Presidential Primary

Another important change came when, for the first time, the LDP party presidential election in 1978 employed a primary (Nonaka 1995, 51–55; Satō and Matsuzaki 1986, 238–39).[10] New rules allowed the mass membership a vote at one stage of the electoral procedure for the first time. LDP membership swelled from a few hundred thousand to nearly a million and a half. Most of the new members were kōenkai members who had been registered wholesale by their Diet members, sometimes even without the members' knowledge. This reform, introduced by Takeo Miki (who came to power after Tanaka's disgrace left the LDP in need of a "clean" image), was meant to allow LDP party members to choose their own leader and avoid the smoke-filled-room politics of the past. But the election failed to achieve its aims. Instead, it had the unintended consequence of further intertwining the factions and kōenkai, a development that Miki surely abhorred (see chap. 4).

As competition for the job of party president heated up, contenders vied for ways to influence the vote. The tactic they hit on was to enroll their kōenkai members as LDP party members en masse so they could vote. Masayoshi Ōhira was reportedly the most energetic candidate in this

10. To be eligible to vote in the primary, an individual had to be either a party member (*tōin*) or "party friend" (*tōyū*). To become a party member, an individual had to pay the party membership fee for two consecutive years. To be a party friend, an individual had to donate 10,000 yen (about $100) to the People's Political Association (Kokumin Seiji Kyōkai), a political fund agent of the LDP (Iwami 1978). The party membership fee was set at 1,500 yen (roughly $15). Later Miki criticized this price as being too cheap and allowing easy vote buying (*Mainichi Shimbun,* October 29, 1978, 1).

(*Asahi Shimbun*, February 13, 1978, 1). He was hardly alone, however. One kōenkai official reported that "we plan to make 20 percent of our kōenkai members join in the party" (*Asahi Shimbun*, February 13, 1978, 1). Local assembly members took advantage of this movement because it was help-ful for expanding their own kōenkai as well (*Asahi Shimbun*, February 13, 1978, 1). Although some kōenkai members were willing to support their factional leaders—their success in the primary would ultimately lead to the promotion of their local bosses—most kōenkai members were mobilized just through personal and territorial networks (*Asahi Shimbun*, August 9, 1978, 2; August 11, 1978, 2). Some firms even made their employees join the LDP because the connection with a particular LDP politician would be beneficial, especially in getting public works contracts (*Asahi Shimbun*, August 10, 1978, 2; *Yomiuri Shimbun*, November 12, 1978, 23). Because of the low party membership fee (1,500 yen—about $15)), many politicians paid the fee for voters directly to increase their voting base in the party presidential election (*Asahi Shimbun*, August 14, 1978, 2). In some cases, the Diet members' staff would circulate ballots to voters but request that the ballots be returned with the name of the candidate selected left blank; the staffers would then fill in this name themselves. In other cases, kōenkai members brought the blank ballots to the kōenkai office. Usually, the Diet member considered it enough to simply make his endorsed candidate known to kōenkai members (Tsurutani 1980, 853).

Even after Ōhira's easy victory in the election, newspapers continued to criticize the nature of the primary as factional bosses' buying votes from the members of factional followers' kōenkai (*Asahi Shimbun*, August 26, 1978, 1; *Mainichi Shimbun*, October 23, 1978, 2; *Yomiuri Shimbun*, November 28, 1978, 2). According to an *Asahi* survey, more than a half of local assembly members estimated that at least 70 percent of voters were influenced by factions when deciding whom to vote for (*Asahi Shimbun*, September 23, 1978, 1–2). Another survey by *Asahi* showed that more than 90 percent of the kōenkai members of Fukuda's faction would vote for Fukuda and that 83 percent and 73 percent of the kōenkai supporters of Ōhira's and Tana-ka's factions would vote for Ōhira (*Asahi Shimbun*, November 10, 1978, 3). Masaharu Gotoda (1998, 369), politically savvy, acknowledged the negative aspect of the primary; he knew factional politics would diffuse across the nation. Factional rivalries had played out through the prisms of the kōenkai (and vice versa) for years (*Asahi Shimbun*, November 9, 1963, 1; August 29, 1970, 4), and the massive scale of the 1978 party presidential election fur-ther strengthened the relationship between the factions and kōenkai.

Kōenkai in Other Parties

What about kōenkai in other parties? The JSP ran multiple candidates in many districts in its early years (ninety districts in 1947, vs. ninety-eight for the liberals and ninety-nine for the democrats; and ninety-six in 1958), but it began to build kōenkai only after the 1963 election, when it ran multiple candidates in just over half of the electoral districts (Kitaoka 1985, 53). For the JSP, membership in kōenkai rose through the 1970s, even though the number of districts in which multiple JSP candidates ran dropped; this again undermines the assumption of a strict causal link between SNTV and kōenkai.

What about the parties that *never* ran multiple candidates in a district? After all, if a need to divide the vote created the kōenkai as distinct from the party branches (as the assumption of a causal link suggests), then we would expect that parties that did not needed to divide the vote would not have kōenkai. But both the CGP and the JCP had vigorous kōenkai. And, despite their kōenkai, no party shared the extreme organizational weakness of the LDP at the local level. A study of local party organization in Hyogo Prefecture showed that "[a]ll parties, except the LDP, have some intermediary organizational units between their Hyogo prefectural offices and the lowest level of party organization. They are labeled variously *kurengokai* (DSP), *sou-shibu* (JSP and KOM [Kōmeitō or CGP]), and *chiku-iinkai* (JCP)" (Foster 1982, 845).

Having strong kōenkai in addition to party branches for parties that did not divide the vote seems anomalous; the logic of a causal link with the electoral system holds for these parties only rather weakly. If kōenkai existed primarily because of a need to divide the vote, there would be little reason for parties that did not run more than one candidate in a district to have kōenkai. The CGP would need few kōenkai, but in fact it had the greatest ratio of kōenkai members to party supporters of any Japanese party. And perhaps the party least likely to develop kōenkai would be the JCP. After all, the party never attained significant success in legislative elections; moreover, the JCP also had a famously centralized and hierarchical structure, as well as a powerful ideology. It must be counted somewhat surprising, then, that the JCP did develop an extensive network of kōenkai in parallel to its party branches. As Peng Er Lam notes, the JCP "kōenkai membership is larger than the party membership and not surprisingly the JCP cannot win its elections by relying on the party organization alone" (1996, 362; see also Lam 1999).[11] Communist parties competing in other democracies, primarily in Europe, did not develop kōenkai, so there is little reason to believe that the nature of the party or its ideology are causes.

JCP documents direct party members to adhere to the Four Basic Points as the most essential daily activities: offering consultation services to the masses, driving up readership of the party newspaper (*Akahata*), carrying out mass publicity, and expanding party and kōenkai organizations

---

11. In his excellent *Green Politics in Japan*, Lam (1999) also describes the struggle of the Seikatsu Club and its green party, the Network Movement (NET), to avoid creating kōenkai. Although the party achieved success, winning 123 seats in prefectural, city, ward, and village assemblies (Lam 1999, 8), and abhorred kōenkai on principle, it failed in its attempt to create a new mobilization network and then capitulated by creating kōenkai.

(Japanese Communist Party Central Committee 1984, 499, cited in Lam 1996, 369). The JCP also urged its members to funnel their family, neighbors, and friends into these political machines (Lam 1996, 371). The JCP was aware of the ticklish ideological issues raised by supporting kōenkai, but found this an effective strategy nonetheless. In July 1959, the JCP approved the development of kōenkai at the Sixth Central Committee of the Seventh Party Congress (Lam 1996, 371). JCP sources in 1991 put membership in JCP politicians' kōenkai at nearly three times membership in the party, or around 1.5 million (Fuwa, 1991; "Presidium Report," *Akahata*, May 19 and 20, 1991, cited in Lam 1996, 370).

What are the JCP kōenkai activities? Whereas the LDP kōenkai have late-night drinking parties and trips to the hot springs, perhaps the JCP activities are no more thrilling than heated discussions of Friedrich Engels. Although the reader might be forgiven for harboring such a suspicion, in fact JCP kōenkai activities (like those of the kōenkai of other parties) are primarily social and not ideological in nature. The range of activities includes bazaars, New Year's parties, flower arrangement classes, chess, bowling, hiking, legal sessions, travel, and barbecues (Wahara 1990, 160, cited in Lam 1996, 371).

In a fascinating contrast to other parties, however, twenty-one years after endorsing kōenkai, the JCP *was* able to transform the nature of its kōenkai from being devoted primarily to the individual candidate to becoming really "party kōenkai," meaning they became very much like party branches. Lam provides a good account of this 1980 development:

> Prior to 1980, most of the *kōenkai* of JCP candidates were named after the candidate and not the party. In November 1980, [party leader Kenji] Miyamoto in his speech on "new electoral policy and *kōenkai* activities" proposed a name switch from personal candidates to a party *kōenkai*. In both name and substance, *kōenkai* must be a party *kōenkai* rather than a personal candidate *kōenkai*. (Lam 1996, 371)

JCP kōenkai membership plummeted after 1980. Before then, membership in JCP kōenkai as a proportion of party supporters was *higher* than the LDP or the JSP! After 1980, however, membership was nearly halved (see figure 2.1).

JCP leaders were motivated to make this move by the change in the House of Councilors electoral law that gave voters a PR vote at the national constituency. Party leaders feared that kōenkai members might not be faithful to the JCP with their PR ballots and took steps to correct this (Lam 1996, 371–72). The JCP revisions to its kōenkai show the importance of the electoral system, to be sure. In addition, they cast new light on the failure of the LDP leadership to accomplish the same thing in 1955, 1963, and—when the parallel of an electoral system change is very close indeed—after 1993.

The successful change by the JCP is worth keeping in mind as we review what happened to kōenkai in the LDP and other parties after the electoral reform of 1994 changed the House of Representatives system from SNTV to MMM. It also shows that the transformation of the kōenkai *was* possible, and this forces us to reevaluate events after 1994. Although we do not examine the JCP in depth here, the evidence about the JCP kōenkai constitutes additional within-case evidence bolstering our argument about institutional change.

Historical Institutionalism and the Kōenkai

Far from eagerly embracing kōenkai as an efficient means to divide the vote for the party, the LDP leadership on two occasions in its early history mounted major efforts to build up local party organizations and eliminate the kōenkai—these were serious efforts, not just lip service. Various other attempts at change at the national and local levels also failed, including Yasuhiro Nakasone's 1986 Karuizawa lecture advocating the end of kōenkai (Lam 1999, 51) and an energetic push by the Kanagawa Prefectural LDP to establish local policymaking organizations to replace kōenkai (Lam 1999, 52–59). Whatever the merits of the kōenkai as a solution to the problems presented by the electoral system, it appears that the party leaders were unpersuaded. The resistance of party leaders alone should give us pause in accepting kōenkai as an inevitable and efficient outcome of the SNTV MMD electoral system. As a party, the LDP never embraced kōenkai as a strategy.

How, then, should we properly understand the origin and development of kōenkai? The electoral system and the incentives it creates to divide the vote are clearly a critical factor. But the existence of kōenkai in the JCP is a puzzle for divide-the-vote explanations, even though JCP kōenkai are responsive to electoral system change (and more responsive than the vote-dividing LDP kōenkai after 1994). More centrally for our argument, the role of the electoral system in shaping the institution of the kōenkai has been misunderstood. Drawing on insights from historical institutionalism, we contend that our understanding of kōenkai is enhanced when we recognize the importance of sequencing, positive returns, and institutional complementarity.

Kōenkai emerged as a successful institution due in part to the historical accident of sequencing—the LDP formed as a party after several elections in which conservative candidates had built up rival kōenkai that later could not be subsumed into a single local party organization. Kōenkai did not spring up immediately after the 1947 introduction of SNTV MMD; rather, they spread slowly across the archipelago, with significant variations in different regions but, generally, all gaining strength. By the time of the LDP merger, conservatives from the Liberal Party and the Democratic Party had formed rival groups, and these groups could not easily be merged despite the strong party push.

Note that we do not claim that the electoral system was irrelevant to the formation of kōenkai; of course, the electoral system was also an important factor. Had the LDP merger taken place under an SMD system, it is likely that the significant barriers to merging the local party organizations would have been overcome (but also keep in mind that the 1955 conservative party merger was not an inevitability simply because of the electoral system). Nevertheless, the electoral system alone is not sufficient to explain the existence of kōenkai. Rather, it is the sequencing of a party merger after several elections in which kōenkai were developed.

In addition to sequencing, we see the phenomenon known as positive returns, which tracks events on to certain paths. LDP candidates who relied on party branch support lost; the victorious had put their trust in kōenkai. This created a positive feedback loop—winners built kōenkai, which in turn built winners. In consequence, the chance of party branches being built lessened, and so negative externalities were created for politicians who relied on party branches—rendering such a strategy untenable.

Once Diet members had built up strong kōenkai, they were loathe to relinquish them. After all, these Diet members faced heated competition in the next election under SNTV MMD, and they abhorred the idea of doing so bereft of their kōenkai. Strong kōenkai also meant more independent Diet members, who could, in a pinch, run as liberal democrat independents (LDIs, conservatives without official LDP endorsement; Reed 2009) with a strong chance of victory. In a way, the weakness of the party label contributed to the inability of the party to strengthen its party label with a more vigorous local organization. Put another way, once kōenkai existed, they created positive reinforcement for a weak local party organization and strong kōenkai. This is the second key reason for the failure of the LDP to centralize its local party organization.

The pattern of increase in kōenkai membership over time is consonant with this explanation. In contrast, a pattern that showed an immediate jump in membership after 1955 (and, later, an immediate drop after 1994) would have been strong evidence supporting the purely electoral system argument. Figure 2.5 shows the increase over time in the percentage of LDP supporters who were also kōenkai members. The initial numbers seem very low for effective vote division. The gradual increase, again, seems to reveal that kōenkai membership is responsive to factors that change over time.

The third critical factor was the institutional complementarity that kōenkai developed with the campaign rules and the factions. The tight campaign restrictions that were in place under the Occupation no doubt frustrated many politicians. Once elected, however, these same politicians enjoyed a considerable incumbency advantage due precisely to these restrictions. A short campaign period with highly restricted activities gave the advantage to the incumbent, especially an incumbent with a healthy kōenkai. There was a virtuous circle at work here.

Kōenkai also grew to mesh quite well with the factions that developed, and this contributed to the defeat of the LDP centralization efforts. As Masumi argues regarding the early attempts to build local party organization, the

LDP "established a system of local organizers modeled on that of the British Conservative Party. But the LDP prefectural federations were riven by local factional conflicts and personal feuds that the party headquarters could not control. In the end, these efforts to strengthen the party's local organizational structure proved ineffective" (1995 [1985], 5). In Masumi's view, this also spelled the demise of the centralization efforts in 1963:

> Ultimately, it was the efforts of individual Diet members and candidates that contributed most to the defense of the LDP's *jiban*. They poured money and energy into fortifying their personal *jiban* in their home districts, which were weakening in the face of the newly emerging mass society. Personal support associations (*kōenkai*) proliferated during the 1958 general election. Organized and permanent, they frustrated efforts to strengthen the party's prefectural organizations. When regional developments began, the *kōenkai* served as [a] mechanism for channeling public works projects and heavy and chemical industrial plants to local electoral districts....As LDP Diet members strengthened their *kōenkai* to compete with other LDP Diet members running in their districts, they became even more tightly aligned with the factions at the center. (1995 [1985], 5)

In 1978, an attempt to eliminate factions was beaten back due to the strength of kōenkai, and even backfired and strengthened the link between the two.

Of course, this link had been present for years. Factions bankrolled the kōenkai of new candidates (*Asahi Journal* 1967, 1972a; Asahi Shimbun Seijibu 1968). To create a kōenkai, a first-term Diet member named Hajime Tanaka remarked in 1970, "you have to get monetary support from party leaders, or the power of a faction" (*Asahi Shimbun,* January 14, 1967, 1). Note that factions are also not the inevitable result of SNTV MMD (see chap. 4). Because of the importance of factions as a complementary institution, this extra layer of contingency matters for our understanding of why kōenkai exist.

Although the peculiar SNTV MMD electoral system is important for our understanding of kōenkai, kōenkai did *not* first came about because of the need of a dominant party to divide the vote. Instead, the historical record shows that kōenkai in their archetypal form predated the merger of the LDP. In fact, it is the existence of kōenkai *before* the need to divide the vote among candidates of a majority party that caused the rise of the kōenkai in the LDP. After the merger, the kōenkai that had developed over nearly a decade were not so easily brushed aside, despite the earnest efforts of the party. In a positive feedback loop, politicians embraced them and built them up to the point that the politicians had to go all out to defend their investments against the 1963 centralization efforts of their own party. The complementarity of kōenkai with other features of Japanese political life, such as factions and election campaign laws, also contributed to their persistence. The factions and kōenkai reinforced one another.

Chapter 3

The Kōenkai Today

Institutional Change

The LDP minus *kōenkai* equals zero.
Shigezo Hayasaka, chief of staff for Kakuei Tanaka
(quoted in Kitaoka 1998, 36)

How have kōenkai fared since the electoral reform that analysts predicted would eliminate them or, at least, transform their role and relationship to the party branch? How has the LDP organization changed after electoral reform? Here we examine the current state of kōenkai through several different lenses, including detailed case studies. We find that kōenkai have suffered a decline since 1994 but that they continue to thrive as a widespread organizational form in much the same shape and playing much the same role that they have for decades. Moreover, party branches have not taken up the slack from the weakening kōenkai, as predicted. At the end of the chapter, we discuss the reasons behind this somewhat surprising state of affairs.

Electoral Reform and Kōenkai

Many analysts have argued that one of the key factors affecting the development of the kōenkai was the SNTV electoral system (see chap. 1). Japanese reformers thought that changing the electoral system would curtail "money politics" (*kinken seiji*) spurred by the demands of intensely cultivating the personal vote. The decline of the personal vote and pork politics that fueled kōenkai would portend a shift to electoral campaigns in which parties dueled over policy platforms and away from money politics and the over-reliance on the personal vote that obscured policy-based competition. After all, PR puts parties in the spotlight, and even SMD winnows the field (usually) to two candidates from opposing parties. No longer would LDP politicians have to compete in the same district with another LDP candidate, the putative reason that kōenkai were necessary from a systemic perspective. Observers could be forgiven for seeing the days of kōenkai as numbered. For our part, we stress here (as we did in chap. 1) that we believe this logic is sound and that we do not seek to ridicule it. Indeed, many of the predictions of the electoral scholars about how electoral reform would change campaigns and parties were correct.[1] We are not surprised by this, because, in general, we strongly believe in the importance of the electoral system in shaping politics and the quality of scholarship by researchers in this subfield. However, in this book, we are concerned with some specific political party organizational features such as institutions (and the evidence in these cases points toward a weaker than expected effect of electoral systems). Our intention is to provide an answer for why these expected developments did not take place so that we can refine our understanding of institutions and institutional change.

Indeed, although some scholars argued that the electoral system change might make the kōenkai "unnecessary and even irrelevant," although they might survive for a while (Fukui and Fukai 1996, 285), not all political analysts saw kōenkai as doomed. Their survival confirms the prescience of Abe, Shindō, and Kawato (1994) prior to the electoral reform. They warned that the kōenkai were not necessarily going to disappear and pointed to commonsense reasons that we should not have expected kōenkai to disappear: "the fact that politicians who do not run against others from the same party have also built their own kōenkai and that the kōenkai perform valued functions for both MPs [members of parliament] and citizens, suggest that changes in the electoral system alone will not immediately affect the role of the *kōenkai* in Japanese politics" (Abe, Shindō and Kawato 1994, 180–81).

In the short term, however, politicians had to adjust to new district boundaries. Many also had to alternate in districts with another incumbent, each taking a turn running in the SMD election while the other rotated to PR election. This was a temporary measure, known as the Costa Rica system.[2] Politicians also had to figure out how the PR system worked in practice and how it affected their electoral strategy. The "surviving for a while" mentioned earlier highlights some of the difficulties of transition.

These difficulties should not be underestimated. Consider an LDP politician who had invested years, if not decades, laboriously cultivating personal networks and allegiances in his district, using the methods and techniques described in chapter 2. Now, imagine this politician being told that not

---

1. The rise of "manifestoes" has something to do with the increased value of the party label (Kollner 2009). Although tight fiscal times and mergers of local governments may play a role, there is also evidence that the distribution of pork has changed as a result of electoral reform. And of course the number of parties, while in flux at least from time to time, seems to be another area where electoral scholars mostly got things right.

2. By our calculations, there were ten Costa Rica agreements in 1996, twenty-four in 2000 (when New Frontier Party, NFP, incumbents joined the LDP), sixteen in 2003, ten in 2005, and five in 2009.

only has part of his assiduously tended constituency been moved to another district and that the new lines being drawn dump into his electoral district a swathe of territory containing people with whom he has only a slight connection, many of whom might have been deeply loyal for years or decades to a political adversary of his. This kind of wrenching transition would seem to provide a stimulus for his immediate change in kōenkai. After all, this is a chance to start over from scratch in at least part of his territory. But it is at this moment that the temptation to rely solely on the party branch and party label for electoral success must surely have been strongest. Nevertheless, as our case studies show, politicians forwent this possibility and instead concentrated on spreading their kōenkai to the new territory, even if they were running for the first time in 1996.

In fact, despite the expectations of some observers, kōenkai weathered the electoral reform fairly well. Overall, there appears to be a pattern of slow kōenkai decline, but they remain a quite prominent feature of the electoral landscape. They also continue to affect the relationship between party leaders and backbenchers.

A Worm's Eye View: Case Studies of the Kōenkai

Examining how kōenkai reacted to electoral reform through case studies is very valuable. Of course, case studies are not our only means of gauging the strength of kōenkai. In some ways, the aggregate data introduced here are more reliable because of their representativeness, but the trade-off is the lack of depth in analyzing exactly how kōenkai are functioning on the ground.

We interviewed dozens of Diet members about their kōenkai activities and visited the kōenkai (especially during electoral mobilization) of several Diet members. Here we focus on two case studies: the kōenkai of Yoshinori Ohno and that of Katsuei Hirasawa. Of course, such a small number of cases cannot constitute a representative sample; but, we chose cases that varied along several important dimensions.[3] We chose one urban and one rural case (we also did field work in a suburban district, and found results consistent with what we present here, but did not feel access was sufficient for us to write a full case study). We also chose kōenkai of Diet members who were and who were not hereditary politicians, as well as of Diet members with varying experience in the Diet and varying backgrounds. We have compared our in-depth findings with information from our interviews and also with secondary sources. Although the number of published recent case studies of kōenkai is surprisingly small, we do have a few to draw on. Hideo

3. Because our research methods require the active cooperation of the Diet member, it is likely that our selection is biased; Diet members with strong kōenkai were probably more likely to agree to have their kōenkai studied.

Otake (1998) analyzes a kōenkai in Tōhoku, Masaki Taniguchi (2004) studies kōenkai in Shizuoka, and Cheol Hee Park (1998, 2000) and Jean-Marie Bouissou (1999) have provided two good Tokyo case studies. All in all, although we recognize that each kōenkai is unique in its history, attributes, and context, we feel that our detailed case studies are fairly representative, or at least illustrative, in some important ways.

The Conservative Kingdom in Kagawa:
Yoshinori Ohno's Kōenkai in Kagawa 3rd District

We discuss in depth first the kōenkai of Yoshinori Ohno in Kagawa Prefecture in Shikoku. At several points in our discussion, we refer to our other case studies or to secondary sources to indicate how Ohno's case is representative or exceptional. Both authors interviewed Ohno several times over several years (2003–2009) in Tokyo and visited his kōenkai offices in Kagawa. One author spent a week in Kagawa just prior to the 2003 election and several days just before the 2009 election, allowing us to observe the kōenkai at the height of its electoral mobilization and also to observe how it changed over time. We conducted interviews with local politicians, Ohno's staff and kōenkai officers, and journalists. In this case study, our focus is on how the kōenkai adapted to electoral reform.

Yoshinori Ohno was born in Kagawa in 1935. He graduated from high school in the prefecture before attending the University of Tokyo and joining the Ministry of Finance in 1958. He married the daughter of a prominent national Diet member from Kagawa. He failed in a bid for the Kagawa governorship in 1978, but was elected for the first time to the Diet House of Representatives in 1986. The 2009 election inaugurated his eighth term in national office. He served as minister of state for defense from 2004 to 2005. Ohno boasts an elite resume—University of Tokyo and Ministry of Finance background, fluent in English and French, and a Cabinet portfolio under his belt—but in Kagawa he is as comfortable talking about noodles with a local fisherman as arcane policy matters with local representatives. A tireless campaigner, he endlessly circulates in the district seeking opportunities to serve and connect with his constituents.

October 16, 2003, saw the opening of Ohno's election campaign headquarters (*senkyo jimusho*) in Marugame City, Kagawa. A few hundred people attended and listened to a string of short feisty speeches. A Shinto priest officiated at the opening ceremony, praying not just to purify the office but also for votes and specifically for Ohno's electoral victory. Standing near the back, one author discussed the unfolding event with a national newspaper reporter. The reporter engaged in a bit of Kremlinological analysis, remarking on not just who attended but who did not attend and in which order speeches were given. This kind of analysis could strike the layman as excessive, but it is valuable because politicians understandably script their political events as much as possible.

For example, just one day previously, there had been a meeting in Ohno's Marugame City kōenkai office to plan the mobilization for Ohno's campaign. The head of the Marugame campaign office (*sentai buchō*) was there to make sure things went smoothly. But, of course, it was Ohno himself who ran the show. In addition to the four elected officials or campaign staff, there were twenty-eight kōenkai members in attendance, mostly older folks. These were the people who get out the vote for Ohno. The discussion centered on how many people to get to each of the several events that precede the election. For example, it was decided that the "departure to the front" ceremony (*shutsujin shiki*) on October 28 at 11 a.m. should have 500 people, Ohno's speech the next day at 6:30 p.m. should have 1,500 people, and the opening rally (*kekki taikai*) should have just over 1,000 people. After these desired numbers were fixed, the attendees were allocated on a quota system for each ward of the city for each event. For example, Ward A would have to get fifty people out to the opening rally, seventy-five to Ohno's speech, and so on.

The dedicated activists were at this meeting. They were taking notes and preparing to go back to their neighborhoods and mobilize. These were among the hard-core supporters that Ohno can count on not only to vote for him but to devote their time and energy to his kōenkai to turn out the vote for him. Politicians often have a mental map of the concentric circles of their supporters, from the most passionate and loyal (the primary constituency) to the least devoted. These kōenkai members were a good example of dedicated supporters.

This meeting is also a good illustration of the realities of campaigning because it shows the overlap among the LDP activities as a party, Ohno's electoral campaign activities, and Ohno's kōenkai activities (see figure 3.1). Kōenkai fulfill their purpose when they are mobilized for election campaigns. Formally, however, they are distinct from the party, and the longevity, function, and personnel of the kōenkai and campaign organizations can be distinguished. One of the unusual characteristics of the kōenkai is that they are continuously active (see chap. 2); election campaign organizations, in contrast, are transitory. During an election, when the kōenkai are focused on campaigning, the two share a purpose. But once the campaign ends, the election campaign organization vanishes, whereas the kōenkai continues with the types of nonelectoral activities illustrated earlier.

In terms of personnel, there is considerable overlap between the election campaign organizations and the kōenkai, but they are, again, distinct. At the foot soldier level, it is the kōenkai that provide the manpower; for example, Ohno would like to have 30–40 activists (*kanbu*) in a town of approximately 10,000 (Interview, Yoshinori Ohno, Tokyo, October 5, 2007). But election campaign organizations have a number of top officials, added for strategic electoral reasons, who do not necessarily have intimate prior involvement with the kōenkai. For example, the Marugame branch of Ohno's campaign is headed by a local politician named Kagawa. He is a

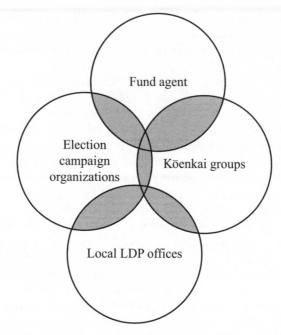

Figure 3.1 Overlap of kōenkai, campaign, and LDP organizations

member of Ohno's kōenkai but not an official in it. In addition, he is the head of the Marugame branch of the LDP. Moreover, Kagawa is also an elected official in his own right, a city councilman in Marugame. So, this same man fills multiple positions in the local LDP: city councilman, head of the Marugame City LDP branch, Ohno kōenkai member, and Ohno election campaign official. Local city council members and prefectural assembly members may be brought in to lead part of the election campaign organization for a number of reasons. For example, Ohno explained at the opening of his election campaign headquarters that he had chosen as the head of his overall election campaign the head of the prefectural assembly because he could in turn mobilize the prefectural assembly members. The choice of top leadership logically differs between kōenkai and election campaign organizations.

The kōenkai can be distinguished even more clearly from the local LDP in terms of personnel and membership. The prefectural branch of the LDP, which is located outside Ohno's district in Takamatsu City, has only four full-time employees. In other words, there are no LDP employees in Ohno's district, only Ohno employees. Ohno keeps a permanent staff of ten. Four of them work in Marugame, three in Kannoji, and three in Tokyo. Although Ohno maintains twenty-five or so contact offices (*renrakusho*), these are not actually staffed. During election campaigns, he employs around a score of people full-time, not to mention a large number of volunteers. In addition, Ohno's kōenkai membership handily outnumbers the official LDP

TABLE 3.1
Yoshinori Ohno Kōenkai membership by locality, 2003

Location	Population	Voters		Kōenkai Members	
		Number	Percentage	Number	Percentage
Marugame City	80,804	65,312	80.83	18,132	27.76
Zentsuuji City	36,058	28,546	79.17	5,852	20.50
Kanonji City	44,449	36,125	81.27	11,842	32.78
Kotonan Town	3,134	2,767	88.29	835	30.18
Mannoo Town	12,829	10,851	84.58	2,239	20.63
Kotohira Town	11,329	9,436	83.29	2,017	21.38
Tadotsu Town	23,661	19,662	83.10	4,863	24.73
Nakanan Town	4,740	3,926	82.83	1,408	35.86
Takase Town	16,798	13,707	81.60	7,510	54.79
Yamamoto Town	7,630	6,337	83.05	2,994	47.25
Sanno Town	9,702	8,095	83.44	3,784	46.74
Oonohara Town	12,798	10,657	83.27	3,449	32.36
Toyonaka Town	11,805	9,877	83.67	5,419	54.86
Takuma Town	15,276	12,759	83.52	3,351	26.26
Nioo Town	6,961	5,918	85.02	4,307	72.78
Toyohama Town	8,827	7,400	83.83	3,830	51.76
Zaida Town	4,597	3,926	85.40	1,693	43.12
Total	311,398	255,301	81.99	83,525	32.72

Source: Yoshinori Ohno, personal communication.

membership (see table 3.1). For example, the LDP only counts a few hundred members in Marugame. In the electoral district as a whole (with a population of 220,000), the LDP had only a few thousand members. When the LDP prefectural organization is pressed to sign up new members, it has no choice but to turn to the kōenkai of its politicians. Organizationally, the LDP is weak; in Ohno's words, "the party's shadow is faint on the ground" (Interview, Yoshinori Ohno, Marugame City, October 14, 2003).

The faintness of the party's shadow implies that Ohno's shadow had better be very dark on the ground for him to win reelection. In fact, Ohno is in constant motion during the campaign period. He works incredibly long hours, moving from one meeting to another without a break. On the phone to his staff, he complains about the flab in his schedule; he asks for ever more events and a brisker pace. He plans on giving ten speeches in every city in the district. He also leads the morning greeting (*chōrei*) at two or three companies every day. Ohno values these morning greetings because it allows him to meet the younger people who are working and thus not home during the day (Interview, Yoshinori Ohno, Marugame City, August 9, 2009). When the banks close their doors at 3 p.m., Ohno is there for another greeting. In many cases, Ohno's office approaches the company and requests the chance to greet the workers. He would like to do even more.

Electoral campaign laws are so strict. I can't make any key chains or t-shirts in my name, for example, and pass [them] out to voters. I cannot do anything in my name that I don't do personally. If I go to a funeral and give money, I can put my name on the envelope. But if my secretary goes, he cannot put my name on it or my office's name on it. I cannot buy food or drink for people. There are so many limitations that I have to use my *kōenkai* to reach the voters. (Interview, Yoshinori Ohno, Marugame City, October 14, 2003)

Ohno chafes at the restrictions of the electoral laws, but he is always scrupulous about respecting them. In Ohno's strong electoral position, an inadvertent miscue is one of the greatest threats to him (Nyblade and Reed 2008).

Ohno is also very detail oriented. He is not one to just let his staff plan the schedule; he is intimately involved with all the details. He also has a keen knowledge of the district and his connections there. In his car, he carries in the pocket behind the driver's seat a laminated sheet with the electoral results for the past several elections, broken down by location. At one point, as he glanced over it, one of us heard him wonder aloud about why his vote total in one particular village had gone down slightly in the last election. In his kōenkai work, Ohno feels and acts as though he is chasing every single vote in the district one by one.

Ohno's kōenkai does not go into hibernation when the election is over. Naturally, the frenzied pace of activities slackens, but there is still a steady stream of activity. The continual nature of activity is characteristic of kōenkai (see chap. 2). Ohno holds two large fund-raising parties, with the funds going to his fund agent. A December party takes place in Tokyo (for companies headquartered in Tokyo that do substantial business in Kagawa), and a February gathering takes place in Kagawa. Even outside the campaign, he is very active. A favorite event of Ohno, and of many other Diet members, is to report on doings in Nagata-cho to his constituency. This simultaneously puts the Diet member in a powerful light, connects the Diet member to his constituency, and serves the democratic purpose of letting the Diet member see how constituents feel about major and minor issues of the day. Ohno typically labels such meetings "Diet Report Meeting under the Sponsorship of the Yoshinori Ohno Kōenkai and the LDP Local 3rd District Branch" (Interview, Yoshinori Ohno, Tokyo, October 5, 2007).

Ohno's kōenkai is itself not a single organization (see chap. 2). Rather, it is a coalition of a large number of groups. Some of these groups are based on occupation. Consider, for example, the Kensetsu Dōyūkai of Kannonji; Ohno paid a visit to talk to forty members of this group two days before the campaign office opened. This group brings together workers and employers in the construction industry. Thus, it is a functional or occupational group, and most of the people in the audience were construction workers. And each group also tends to have multiple local chapters, rather than serving the entire district through a single organization. For example, a Zentsuji meeting that same day brought together the heads of local construction firms and local representatives of larger firms. Overall, most groups are based on geography, whether or not they also have a secondary organizing principle. There are a number of women's groups (*fujinkai*) spread throughout the district; Marugame alone boasts three. Other groups bring together long-time or dedicated Ohno supporters, part of a circle much closer to Ohno. The Kōyūkai in Kannonji is such a group. The same evening as the Kensetsu Dōyūkai meeting, Ohno stopped by this small group. Fewer than a dozen members belong, but they include a prefectural assemblyman affiliated with Ohno. In general, this group offers Ohno unwavering support, and when Ohno visits, it is not to make a speech or convince them to turn out to vote for him. He already has their votes. Instead, he comes for a serious, frank discussion of what is going on in the district. This group is not a brain trust, but Ohno engages in strategic discussions with the members to some extent.

Ohno himself divides his kōenkai into three main categories: local, vocational, and special. Local groups are based on geographical proximity and follow administrative units (although after the merger of many local governments in the early 2000s, Ohno kept his kōenkai organized along the old administrative lines). Vocational groups link people in the same industry. Special groups vary widely, but prominent ones include those bringing together age cohorts (as in the Hashimoto kōenkai example discussed in chap. 2, some of these "young stars" might be in their sixties) (Interview, Yoshinori Ohno, Tokyo, October 5, 2007).

Ohno also visits LDP organizations as part of his electoral mobilization. For example, the day before opening his election campaign office, he visited the LDP officers' meeting in Mannō. The head of the LDP in Mannō is also a prefectural assemblyman. Ohno visits each LDP office once, but usually only once, at the start of each campaign to personally ask for its support. Because the LDP does not have physical offices, these meetings take place in venues selected by the local LDP head. Of course, even if they existed, the LDP local offices could not legally so much as put up Ohno posters. So, the mobilization effort is really directed at the local LDP members and spearheaded by a local elected official. National Diet members typically have close connections with the prefectural and local representatives. Indeed, the connection is so close that the prefectural and local legislators are usually classified as being part of the "conglomerate" (*keiretsu*) of one of the national Diet members (Desposato and Scheiner 2009).

Under SNTV, national Diet members created networks of local representatives as allies (Fukui and Fukai 1996; Scheiner 2005). The local representatives were crucial assets in electoral struggles, and national Diet members struggled over their loyalties. Now, however, national Diet members do not have to compete for the allegiance of these local representatives. Whereas each national Diet member has, perhaps, dozens of local representatives in his district, the local representatives only have a single national Diet member. As one city council member told us, "Under the old system, Diet members competed for and stole each other's local city council supporters.... Under the old system, 1–10 percent of local Diet members would change during an election....The power relationships have definitely changed to the detriment of the local representatives" (Interview with local elected politician, Marugame City, October 13, 2003). No longer are they wooed. Their help is still valuable, especially in competitive districts, but it is no longer essential (Interview LB, October 16, 2003). The city council member noted, "Rather than change the allegiance to another Diet member, the local Diet members just now have the threat of working less hard to get out the vote for the Diet member during the election" (Interview with local elected politician, Marugame City, October 13, 2003). But this can be insufficient because the Diet member and the party (which naturally wants to win the seat) can return the threat of noncooperation. The local representatives still can help turn out the vote; they can also help solidify the national Diet member's kōenkai.

In election campaigns, Ohno gives many talks at the kōenkai meetings of prefectural assemblymen and other local politicians (*mini-shūkai*). The typical format is for the local politician to introduce Ohno with a warm-up speech, and then for Ohno to give a brief version of his stump speech. While Ohno is giving this talk, the local politician slips out to warm up the crowd at the next meeting. In this way, Ohno can visit four meetings of likely voters in only two hours. The local assemblyman explained:

> My main form of supporting Ohno is to invite him to my *kōenkai* and the groups I know and introduce him. During the election, we can't visit individual homes, but at other times we do. Another way I support him is to persuade people to join his *kōenkai*. I only do this when Ohno requests me to do it. He will give me a quota and I fill it. Over the past year, I brought in 600–700 people. We had our own election in April so I was busy with that, though. Another way I support him is to attend various events and show my face in the audience when he gives a speech or has a rally. These things are no different from under the old electoral system. But, now it is easier in fact. The old system featured two LDP Diet members. It was hard to balance demands to support both of them. Even just attending the events for both of them was difficult. (Interview with local elected politician, Marugame City, October 13, 2003)

Nevertheless, tensions remained after the electoral reform. In the process, the district boundaries themselves were redrawn, and new districts were created. Some of the new districts contain territory from more than one old electoral district. In such districts, candidates must create new kōenkai organizations and local ties with people who were not formerly their constituents. Such is the case for the newly created Kagawa 2nd District, which combines parts of the Old Kagawa 1st District and Old Kagawa 2nd District[4] (see figures 3.2 and 3.3). The Old Kagawa 2nd District was represented by

---

4. For clarity, we refer to the old districts as Old (Place Name) District and the new districts as New (Place Name) District or just as (Place Name) District.

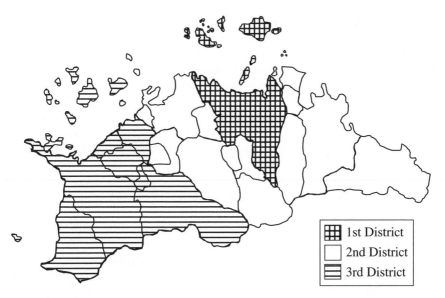

Figure 3.2 Kagawa Prefecture: Three electoral districts under the new electoral system
Note: Kagawa 3rd District is Ohno's new district.

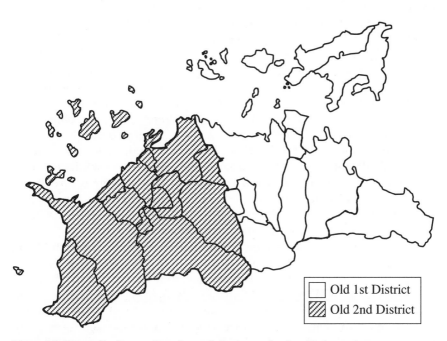

Figure 3.3 Kagawa Prefecture: Two electoral districts under the old electoral system
Note: Old Kagawa 2nd District was Ohno's district.

Yoshinori Ohno and Hajime Morita, also an LDP politician and former Prime Minister Masayoshi Ōhira's son-in-law and former secretary.

The question became, who would run in the New Kagawa 3rd District, Ohno or Morita? This would be the easiest district for either man because it was only a subset of their old district, without any added territory. In the end, Ohno emerged as the SMD candidate for Kagawa 3rd District. Of course, there were still transition costs. Ohno was forced to shift his geographical center of operations. Under SNTV, Ohno's headquarters were in Sakaide City, in central Kagawa and to the east of Marugame City. Sakaide is where Ohno's father-in-law, Tsunetaro Katō, had based his kōenkai. Ohno inherited the Kato kōenkai and, naturally, kept it centered there. In the redrawing of electoral districts, Sakaide was placed in New Kagawa 2nd along with some territory from the Old Kagawa 1st District, where Ohno had no presence. So, although Ohno was fortunate to run his first campaign under MMM in 1996 in a district where he was already known, he did have to largely rework his organization. First, he needed to choose a new base of operations. Ohno's hometown of Toyohama Town is in the extreme west and also is small in population, so it was not a good choice; the logical choice was Marugame City. Marugame is the biggest city in the district, having approximately one-quarter of the district population. It is also near Zentsuji City, which is another large population center for the district. Ohno moved his headquarters to this city, however, only after the 1996 election. He also established a secondary base in Kannonji, a one-room office that he inherited from the kōenkai of Hajime Morita (who had represented the Old Kagawa 2nd District along with Ohno). Morita also shared his kōenkai membership rolls with Ohno.

This brings us back to our Kremlinology. At the opening ceremony for Ohno's campaign headquarters, the reporter and one of us discussed who was there and who was not. Even though he was electorally quite strong and would go on to be named to the cabinet soon after this election, Ohno's relationships with the local legislators have been haunted by the ghost of former Prime Minister Masayoshi Ōhira. In 1980, a serious heart attack took Ōhira's life during an election campaign. But, even years later, he remains enormously popular in Shikoku, particularly in his home prefecture of Kagawa. One local legislator told us, "I don't know what I can say to make you understand how important the influence of Ōhira is here" (Interview with local elected politician, Marugame City, October 13, 2003).

Hajime Morita, Ōhira's son-in-law, went on to become a successful LDP politician and comfortably won reelection in Kagawa for years as a national Diet member. Table 3.2 lists the electoral results for the last few elections under SNTV, in which Ohno and Morita competed head to head. Note that Morita earned more votes than Ohno in the elections in which they ran head to head. In 1990, for example, Ohno squeaked through to reelection by only 735 votes while Morita's margin was over 14,000 (see table 3.2).

TABLE 3.2
Election results in Kagawa District, 1986–2009

	Old Kagawa 2nd		
	1986 Election		
Candidate	Party	Votes	Results
Hajime Morita	LDP	78,583	Elected
Yoshinori Ohno	**LDP**	**65,788**	**Elected**
Shigeaki Tsukihara	LDP	65,394	Elected
Ken Fujii	JSP	50,932	Lost
	1990 Election		
Candidate	Party	Votes	Results
Hajime Morita	LDP	74,761	Elected
Shigeaki Katou	JSP	68,612	Elected
Yoshinori Ohno	**LDP**	**61,189**	**Elected**
Shigeaki Tsukihara	LDP	60,454	Lost
	1993 Election		
Candidate	Party	Votes	Results
Shigeaki Tsukihara	NRP	74,801	Elected
Hajime Morita	LDP	69,059	Elected
Yoshinori Ohno	**LDP**	**62,338**	**Elected**
Shigeaki Katou	JSP	46,886	Lost
	New Kagawa 3rd		
	1996 Election		
Candidate	Party	Votes	Results
Yoshinori Ohno	**LDP**	**79,870**	**Elected**
Shigeaki Tsukihara	NFP	62,468	Lost
	2000 Election		
Candidate	Party	Votes	Results
Yoshinori Ohno	**LDP**	**90,690**	**Elected**
Kenji Okuda	DSP	37,759	Lost
	2003 Election		
Candidate	Party	Votes	Results
Yoshinori Ohno	**LDP**	**84,803**	**Elected**
Kenji Okuda	DSP	23,087	Lost
Touru Yamamoto	DPJ	22,091	Lost
	2005 Election		
Candidate	Party	Votes	Results
Yoshinori Ohno	**LDP**	**107,726**	**Elected**
Kenji Okuda	DSP	39,177	Lost

(continued)

Table 3.2—(cont.)

	New Kagawa 3rd		
	2009 Election		
Candidate	Party	Votes	Results
Yoshinori Ohno	**LDP**	**73,379**	**Elected**
Haruhiko Maida	DSP	53,822	Lost
Takeshi Manabe	Hiranuma Group	32,963	Lost

Source: Kokkai Binran, 1986–2009.
Note: Candidates receiving fewer that 15,000 votes not shown. Results for Yoshinori Ohno appear in boldface. DPJ, Democratic Party of Japan; DSP, Democratic Socialist Party; JSP, Japan Socialist Party; LDP, Liberal Democratic Party; NFP, New Frontier Party; NRP, New Renaissance Party.

Various suppositions circulate as to why Ohno got the nod for the SMD instead of Morita. Some Morita supporters say Morita's personality was better suited to policy issues and made him a natural for the PR election. Ohno loyalists suggest Morita feared losing in SMD to Shigeaki Tsukihara (who after all had topped Morita's vote total by more than 5,000 in 1993) and instead preferred the security of a guaranteed high ranking in the PR election. Of course, only Morita himself knows for sure. Nevertheless, it is widely acknowledged that, had Morita wanted the SMD nomination, it would have been his for the taking. Yet Ohno has clearly flourished as the lone LDP candidate in recent elections. In the elections of 2000, 2003, and 2005, he received more than double the vote of his nearest challenger. And in 2009, despite the disastrous results for the LDP generally, Ohno won his district.

Nevertheless, as the sole holder of the number one spot on the LDP PR list for Shikoku until he retired in 2005, Morita was guaranteed victory. He also remained a LDP representative from Shikoku. In a sense, then, he was still the representative of the voters in New Kagawa 3rd District, and many of them still nurture affection for him. After one of us attended a LDP local chapter meeting in Kagawa with Ohno at which the tepid reception was palpable, Ohno explained that this chapter was composed of diehard Morita loyalists. So, although many erstwhile Morita supporters have wholeheartedly thrown themselves on to the Ohno bandwagon, a number remains tightly connected to Morita. It is the nature of the Japanese MMM system that such divided loyalties can persist because both men represented the people of the district.

And there are many signs that the rivalries of the SNTV have not completely vanished but lurk just under the surface. For example, in Ohno's hometown, Toyohama, Ohno's former political secretary ran for mayor. It is common in Japanese politics for some political secretaries to run for office after a sort of apprenticeship as a staff member. Many analysts of hereditary legislators (nisei giin) count as hereditary transitions those cases in which a political secretary succeeds the politician for whom he or she served. It is also common for the secretary to run for some other elective office in the district. Such was the case for Ohno's secretary, who ran in Toyohama. Running for office in the hometown of a successful national Diet member brings several advantages. Chief among these is the candidate's ability to use the networks that the national Diet member has established, along with campaign visits from said Diet member. Nevertheless, Ohno's secretary lost his election bid. This caused some observers to wonder about Ohno's political strength and popularity. Rumors were rife that the Morita loyalists had not thrown their support behind the candidacy. Next, the winning candidate was arrested for violations of campaign laws, and the election was contested again. But, even then, Ohno's secretary lost. Similarly, Ohno supported the losing incumbent in the April 2003 Marugame City mayoral election against a challenger who was perceived as weak. Again, accusations flew that the Morita loyalists had thrown their support behind Ohno's candidate's rival. It is difficult to prove conclusively, even though circumstantial evidence seems to support the thesis. Assuming the accusations are true, however, it is speculated that this was part of Morita's plans to have his son run in the Kagawa 2nd District as the SMD House of Representatives candidate. But Ohno may also want his son to succeed him. If so, it would not do, from Morita supporters' perspective, to have the mayoralty dominated by Ohno supporters. In other words, these local connections are so important for the kōenkai and electoral victory that politicians make very long-term plans regarding them. This consequently influences how national politicians structure their local alliances.

In 2008, the Ōhira shadow fell over the district again. Takeshi Manabe, a potential challenger to Ohno, began to hold rallies in the district. His father, Kenji Manabe, was a LDP House of Councilors member representing Shikoku from 1977 until his election loss in 2007. The elder Manabe had close ties to Ōhira as his secretary, and his son played these up in attempting to drum up support in Kagawa. Ohno had been instrumental in securing the renomination of the elder Manabe by the LDP—who had been out of favor with the party because he had opposed postal privatization in 2005—in the House of Councilors race in 2007, which he then lost. In 2009, the younger Manabe ran against Ohno in Kagawa as an independent. Although he was handily defeated, the very fact that he could mount a serious candidacy in the face of a strong DPJ and SDP headwind and against a powerful incumbent like Ohno demonstrates the deep roots of Ōhira loyalty in the district.

Morita had transferred his office and membership lists, key assets for any kōenkai, to Ohno, but in some sense the transition was incomplete. Many LDP activists in the district remain Morita loyalists. Nevertheless, even if he does not command fervid loyalty from the Morita supporters, Ohno is very secure electorally, as his enviable margins of victory in recent elections demonstrate.

The fact that Ohno is now the only LDP candidate in the district has changed many things, including the national Diet member's relationships with interest groups and with local politicians. Agricultural interest groups headed by Nōkyō are a prime example. Shortly before the official election campaign period began, Ohno met with the local Nōkyō representative. This alone is not unusual, even though before electoral reform Ohno did not have a close relationship with this group. Now the terms of trade have changed. Nōkyō support could have been essential, or perhaps sufficient, to elect someone who needed 20 percent of the vote, but it certainly cannot get a candidate 50 percent of the vote. Moreover, Nōkyō can no longer play favorites among the LDP candidates but must lump it with the single LDP representative in the district. And the behavior of Nōkyō has changed accordingly. For the first time in this district, Nōkyō escorted a national Diet member to its organization members. These kind of home visits (*kobetsu hōmon*) are considered to be quite effective forms of electoral mobilization and loyalty building, but they are time consuming. Before 2003, Ohno made them only to the construction industry and postmasters; in 2003, he added Nōkyō to that short list. The visits took place near Zentsuji City, where the main crops are onions, *mikan* (tangerines), and garlic. The Nōkyō representative accompanied Ohno to the doors of the ten Nōkyō division chiefs[5] to make a personal introduction and reinforce the Nōkyō endorsement of Ohno. Of the ten house visits, only three were to people who were already members of Ohno's kōenkai, so it seems likely that the visits will bear fruit in terms of future membership and strengthening the organization, as well as in electoral mobilization. It is a sign of the changed relationship between interest groups and national legislators that Nōkyō felt compelled to go to these lengths to court Ohno.

The 2009 election was characterized by the defection or demobilization of traditional LDP support groups, with many postmasters supporting the DPJ, for example. The Japan Medical Association (JMA) endorsed the DPJ candidate in Ibaraki Prefecture. In Kagawa, however, the JMA was solidly behind Ohno. Visiting small clinics and hospitals in the district represented a mainstay of many of Ohno's campaign days. For example, between 10 a.m. and noon on August 10, 2009, Ohno visited fourteen small clinics and hospitals in Marugame and Zentsuji. In each, Ohno greeted the doctors, staff, and each patient who could be spoken to. Ohno took the opportunity to shake hands with every patient able to grasp his hand, greeting each one individually. Later that afternoon, from 2:30 to 5:30 p.m., he visited another eighteen clinics and hospitals using the same methods. With 145 medical facilities in Marugame, Ohno seemed determined to visit each one before election day; he saw doctors as valuable supporters who were difficult to meet without these visits. Thirty-two visits in five hours constitute a tremendous display of stamina and speed, to be sure, but even more interesting

5. The divisions are organized by crop, so there is a garlic division chief (*ninniku buka-ichō*), for example.

is that Ohno was accompanied on each visit by a JMA official. Similarly, on a series of visits to fishermen's cooperatives, a pair of cooperative officials and a local seafood wholesaler accompanied Ohno. These organizational figures reinforce to those being visited that the organization stands behind Ohno, making his visits more effective and persuasive. The mobilization of interest groups through kōenkai still operates in much the same pattern that it has for decades.

Three things should be borne in mind here. First, there is the inter-generational dimension. The asset specificity and value of the kōenkai make politicians want to pass the organization along. Many politicians seem also to be playing not just for their own reelection but possibly also to set up their relatives to succeed electorally (by succeeding them) in the future. Second, even though SNTV has been replaced and even if Ohno and Morita do not consider one another rivals any longer, local politicians continue to take sides and the 2009 candidacy of Takeshi Manabe shows that the old rivalries and divisions die hard. The old rivalries permeate the relationships that the national politicians have with local politicians from both sides, affecting how local politicians align themselves and also how national politicians forge local alliances. Third, the story of the adaptation of the Ohno kōenkai to electoral reform cannot be understood without knowing about these webs of loyalty, providing an excellent illustration of institutional change.

The Liberal Democratic Party in Downtown Tokyo: Katsuei Hirasawa's Kōenkai in Tokyo 17th District

The second case study we present is that of Katsuei Hirasawa, the LDP representative from Tokyo 17th District. We interviewed this Diet member on multiple occasions over several years (2002–2009); visited his district with him a number of times, including during an election campaign; and interviewed several members of his staff as well as local elected officials.

Born in 1945, Katsuei Hirasawa grew up in the village of Shirakawa in Gifu Prefecture. He graduated from the University of Tokyo (where he served as private tutor to a young Shinzō Abe for two years)[6] and then joined the National Police Agency. He left this position in 1995 to make his first and successful bid for the Diet in 1996, when he was the subject of an excellent scholarly case study of the campaign of a first-time LDP Diet member (Park 2000). The 2005 electoral victory began his fourth term in office. He appears frequently on serious national television news programs and more frequently on variety shows, where he engages in political discussions with a mixed group of other politicians and celebrities. His forthright speaking style has won him fans throughout his district and, without exaggeration, across the country.

---

6. http://www.hirasawa.net/profile/index.html (accessed August 24, 2008).

As his biography indicates, Hirasawa had scant connection to the Tokyo 17th District, which encompasses the Katsushika Ward as well as part of Edogawa Ward and has approximately 420,000 voters and 540,000 residents. The district, although just across the Sumida River and so technically outside of the ancient boundaries of *shitamachi* downtown Tokyo, is commonly thought of as part of shitamachi. As a place name, shitamachi resonates among Japanese as the home of friendly, outgoing, no-fuss people overflowing with a sense of human connectedness (the immensely popular film series *Otoko wa tsurai yo* was set in Katsushika). It is a densely populated ward of Tokyo and so not at the top of anyone's list of hospitable districts for the LDP.

Parachuting in from the outside into a tightly connected district put Hirasawa at an immediate disadvantage. He knew this and moved decisively to build ties in the district through a powerful kōenkai (Interview, Katsuei Hirasawa, Tokyo, July 9, 2002). As an unknown, his first steps were to borrow the mantle of established politicians.

> Mr. [Masaharu] Gotoda [a famous ex-police officer turned politician], my mentor, asked ward assembly members to support me. He came to Katsushika so many times, 20 or maybe 30 times. The LDP was very strong in the ward assembly. It was my first election. Seiroku Kajiyama, then chief cabinet secretary, and other big names came to my district. And, Ryūtarō Hashimoto also came. The local people thought "we don't know this Hirasawa, but he must be good." They thought that because I had such connections, I might be able to do a great job. (Interview, Katsuei Hirasawa, Tokyo, June 29, 2004)

In addition to appearances at campaign events, Hirasawa worked hard to use his connections to build ties to the local community:

> When I first became a candidate, I had absolutely no connection to the district. I asked local politicians and influential people to go with me to introduce me to their circle of acquaintances. At the same time, I also asked Mr. Gotoda, my college classmates, friends, acquaintances, and retried police officers to help me by introducing me to various corporations, groups, alumni associations, etc. (Hirasawa 2007, 26)[7]

From the start, Hirasawa's instinct was to cultivate the personal touch.

Hirasawa's first campaign was under the new electoral system, so he did not face Ohno's problem of having to move his base. There were, of course, incumbents who had previously represented the district (then, Old Tokyo 10th District). Forging positive relationships with them was crucial to Hirasawa's early success.

---

7. All translations from Hirasawa (2007) by authors.

Before I got the party nomination, we had the multimember district system, and when single-member districts were introduced, the Tokyo 17th District emerged out of the old multimember district. The area was a part of the electoral base of two politicians, Yoshinobu Shimamura and Hyosuke Kujiraoka. Thanks partly to Masaharu Gotoda's effort, Shimamura introduced me to his *kōenkai* members and told them, "you cannot vote for me in the Tokyo 17th District, so vote for Hirasawa." Because of that, the former officers of Shimamura's *kōenkai* [living in the 17th District] later became members of my *kōenkai*. . . . Kujiraoka asked the members of his *kōenkai* [in the 17th District] to switch to my *kōenkai,* thanks partly to Gotoda's request. (Hirasawa 2007, 51–52)

As we have seen in the Kagawa case study, voters' loyalty to another politician who no longer represents the district can linger and undermine the enthusiastic conversion to a new politician's kōenkai. Park cannily points out that Shimamura's and Kujiraoka's support was perhaps not completely wholehearted:

Shimamura introduced Hirasawa [to his *kōenkai* members] at his *kōenkai*'s New Year's parties. He explained that they cannot vote for him in the 17th District and requested they help Hirasawa instead. So, the former officers of the Shimamura *kōenkai* became new members of the Hirasawa *kōenkai.* . . . On the other hand, Kujiraoka could not actively assist Hirasawa because he was serving as the vice chairman of the House of Representative at the time. . . . So, he instructed his veteran secretary of 25 years, Mitsumasa Ōyanagi, to introduce his *kōenkai* members to Hirasawa. . . . However, Shimamura and Kujiraoka never handed over their *kōenkai* member lists to Hirasawa . . . and even after Hirasawa received the party's nomination for this district, the *kōenkai* members maintained strong affiliation to their old Diet members. (Park 2000, 75–77)[8]

It is especially striking that Shimamura and Kujiraoka never handed over their kōenkai lists to Hirasawa; recall that Hajime Morita handed his rolls over to Yoshinori Ohno in Kagawa.

Hirasawa also continues to work hard to build a kōenkai up over "every inch" of his district, conceding nothing (Park 2000, 79). "We have to make kōenkai throughout Katsushika Ward like a spider web with multiple layers and leave no open space" (Interview, Katsuei Hirasawa, Tokyo, October 5, 2007). This pays off at the ballot box, and Hirasawa grew his vote total in every election from 1996 to 2005, when it more than doubled the 1996 level (see table 3.3).

---

8. All translations from Park (2000) by authors.

TABLE 3.3

Election results for Tokyo 17th District, 1996–2009

1996 Election			
Candidate	Party	Votes	Results
Katsuei Hirasawa	**LDP**	**73,726**	**Elected**
Natsuo Yamaguchi	NFP	63,732	Lost
Akira Sugie	JCP	34,662	Lost
Kumiko Yoneyama	DPJ	33,667	Lost

2000 Election			
Candidate	Party	Votes	Results
Katsuei Hirasawa	**LDP**	**95,606**	**Elected**
Natsuo Yamaguchi	Komeito	74,633	Lost
Kumiko Yoneyama	Independent	42,882	Lost
Junichi Mikoda	JCP	41,083	Lost

2003 Election			
Candidate	Party	Votes	Results
Katsuei Hirasawa	**LDP**	**142,916**	**Elected**
Atsushi Nishikouri	DPJ	65,269	Lost
Katsusuke Kanno	JCP	22,316	Lost

2005 Election			
Candidate	Party	Votes	Results
Katsuei Hirasawa	**LDP**	**161,324**	**Elected**
Atsushi Nishikouri	DPJ	67,300	Lost
Sachiko Kojima	JCP	27,597	Lost

2009 Election			
Candidate	Party	Votes	Results
Katsuei Hirasawa	**LDP**	**138,512**	**Elected**
Kumiko Hayakawa	DPJ	106,892	Lost
Sugio Arai	JCP	21,448	Lost

Source: Tokyo Election Commission, http://www.senkyo.metro.tokyo.jp/data/data01. html (accessed September 16, 2008); Ministry of Internal Affairs and Communications, http://www.soumu.go.jp/main_content/000037488.pdf (accessed October 25, 2009).

Notes: Candidates receiving fewer than 15,000 votes not shown. Results for Katsuei Hirasawa appear in boldface. DPJ, Democratic Party of Japan; JCP, Japanese Communist Party; LDP, Liberal Democratic Party; NFP, New Frontier Party.

This tenacity is reflected in Hirasawa's decisions about the organizational structure for his kōenkai.

There were two reasons why I made a hard effort to establish my *kōenkai*. First, my district is located in an urban setting, even though it is in shita-machi. Urban districts have many swing voters, but I thought it was necessary to secure solid supports. Second, I had no connection in the Tokyo 17th District....I first tried to build an organization that covers all the areas in the district. Under the SMD system, you cannot win by relying only on certain areas. You need to have a *kōenkai* system that covers the entire district just like the web of a spider. So, I divided the district into seven blocks and asked LDP ward assembly members to take charge of each block. Also, to strengthen and expand my support bases, I tried to make a *kōenkai* system that is well connected with trade associations. I asked *kōenkai* members to help me approach persons of high standing in various industries and areas. I asked people from different areas to become facilitators of my *kōenkai*. Those areas include agriculture, commerce, medicine, education (the retired principals' association), alumni associations, prefectural associations, hobby clubs, sports clubs, and the like. I then connected these people to expand the network.... My *kōenkai* currently has 60,000 members. (Hirasawa 2007, 52–54)

Intensely focused on the local area, Hirasawa has tried to tie his small, hyperlocal kōenkai firmly into the local community. "For instance, in Katsushika Ward, we divided the ward into smaller areas. I divided it into a dozen or so areas and made *kōenkai* in each area. We ask the president, vice president, or another important member of the neighborhood association to become core members of these *kōenkai*. Or, we ask the head of shrine parishioners" (Interview, Katsuei Hirasawa, Tokyo, October 5, 2007). This focus on the local district permeates Hirasawa's activities as a Diet member.

I go to all neighborhood associations, especially when they have small meetings with 10 to 20 members. If there is a meeting of more than 100 people and there is a smaller neighborhood association meeting elsewhere, my delegate attends the big one. If I go to small ones, it makes the participants happy, and they become my fans. If I make a speech at big meetings, they think it is nothing special. It is the same with funerals. People get happy when I go to the ones with 10–20 people. If I do, they will continue to support me even after I die myself. But, if I go to a big funeral, no one cares. Everyone is making a mistake. Diet members too. They think they need to go to big ones and ignore small ones. That's opposite. You should go to small ones. (Interview, Katsuei Hirasawa, Tokyo, October 5, 2007)

I spend almost all my free time in my district. Whenever I drink, eat, get my hair cut, I do it in my district. I do it strictly in the local shops. When I go shopping, I can build my local network in various locales. Another reason we do well in elections is because we use funerals wisely. I just went one in this morning. I never fail to go to funerals. (Interview, Katsuei Hirasawa, Tokyo, June 29, 2004)

I buy necessities strictly at local shops. *Ochūgen*, *oseibo*, suits, shirts, shoes, drugs, stationery, dictionaries, and so on. Whenever I have time, I drop by at local shops or convenience stores.... I try to go to ones I have never been before as much as possible. That way, I can tell if the store owners know me or not. If they don't, I can tell that our campaign is not good enough there.... I get my hair cut at local barbers.... there are about 300 barbers in my district, but I try to choose the ones I have never been to before as much as possible. (Hirasawa 2007, 23–24)

Hirasawa describes his daily routine:

> Whenever I am in my district, my day starts with meeting people. It starts at 5 in the morning [with meetings with religious groups]. They meet in offices in Shinto shrines or community halls. They meet every day between 5 and 6. Then, I join radio calisthenics at 6:30 a.m. And, I stand in front of train stations and speak to commuters. That's called *asadachi* [morning standing]. Everyone is busy, so all I can say is "good morning" or "have a nice day." But, it helps to get my face known. (Hirasawa 2007, 27–28)

> There are some kinds of events in my district throughout a year.... From January to March, there are New Year's parties. I usually go to about 500 every year. Then the time for graduation ceremonies and new school enrollment ceremonies comes. In the summer, it is the season for bon-odori. They are sponsored by neighborhood associations, local commercial areas, children's associations, elder care facilities, and so forth....I go to about 300 of them. Sometimes, I go to 15 or 20 in one evening. In the fall, we have emergency drill, elders' meetings (*rōjinkai*), athletic meetings, festivals, and the like. In the winter, we have year-end security drills, and I try my best to attend them too. And, throughout the year, there are weddings, funerals, hobby groups' meetings, and other parties. (24)

He continued to explain the traditional kōenkai emphasis on funerals:

> We send condolence telegrams and other telegrams all the time. Many people like to receive telegrams. I attend 6 or 7 [funerals] every week....The question is how to obtain information [about funerals]. This is so important. Sometimes, they tell us. But, everyone is busy, so we sometimes do not hear. In such cases, we made a deal with funeral companies. They give us information. Only a few have the funeral at home. Funeral companies take care of them. I need to check information. I will definitely go to funerals for people to whom I owe a favor, people I have met before, or people who helped me in an election. (Interview, Katsuei Hirasawa, Tokyo, June 29, 2004)

As Hirasawa deepened his ties to his district, he began to attend more funerals: "I attend 2 or 3 funerals a day, so about 700–800 a year now....I've been active as a politician in my district for more than a decade, so I've been to about 10,000 funerals" (Interview, Katsuei Hirasawa, Tokyo, October 16, 2008).

This geographical emphasis implies a loose confederation of local kōenkai. Hirasawa coordinates them through frequent meetings:

> We often hold meetings with the heads of my *kōenkai*. My *kōenkai* are decentralized, and basically there is no interaction among them. We just had another meeting of *kōenkai* heads recently with more than a hundred people

assembled. We do this about two or three times a year. If a House of Councilors election, for example, is coming up, then I meet them to ask them for support. It is too difficult to gather all the members, so I only assembly the heads of *kōenkai*. Then, the heads tell their members. If I speak to the 100 or so *kōenkai* heads, they speak to dozens of their fellow members. So, when I gather 100 or so *kōenkai* heads, I can communicate with tens of thousands of members in no time. For ordinary communication, we don't have a meeting but I use faxes and the like to communicate with the *kōenkai* heads. (Interview, Katsuei Hirasawa, Tokyo, October 5, 2007)

Hirasawa's strategy emphasizes geography, one of the core organizing principles of kōenkai (see chap. 2). This does not mean he has abandoned other types of kōenkai. He has worked hard to build kōenkai that link people who are in the same occupation, such as real estate agents, barbers, and medical doctors. He has also created a set of kōenkai that pull in enthusiasts of the same hobby, from folksongs to haiku, and those who share the same college ties (and here Hirasawa works with many schools, not just his alma mater) (Interview, Katsuei Hirasawa, Tokyo, June 29, 2004; see also Park 2000, 80, 140–45). Hirasawa explains his strategy:

we create trade-specific *kōenkai*—for example, tax accountant associations. There are many organizations that automatically support the LDP, such as the Japanese Society of Judo Therapy [orthopedic therapists] and the Food Sanitation Association. They support the LDP, no matter what. Some organizations support the LDP, Komeitō, and the DPJ at the same time. They let members decide which party to support. In those organizations, my personal supporters establish *kōenkai* within the organization, for example, "the Tax Accountants' Hirasawa Kōenkai." Another kind is *kōenkai* based on certain activities such as hobbies. There are dance circles or baseball teams, right? The members of such groups get together and make my *kōenkai*. Also, there are associations for people from other prefectures [in my district]—the Yamanashi Prefecture association or the Gifu Prefecture association, for example. Not all members support me, but those who do support me in such groups will establish my *kōenkai* within their organizations, creating, for example, the Gifu Prefecture Association Hirasawa Kōenkai. There are three types of *kōenkai*: to repeat what I said, there are *kōenkai* in each area, trade-specific *kōenkai*, and *kōenkai* based on other groups such as hobby or prefecture. Within each framework, those who support me create *kōenkai* and we connect them like a spider web. So, membership sometimes overlaps. [Some people] belong to more than one [Hirasawa] *kōenkai*. (Interview, Katsuei Hirasawa, Tokyo, October 5, 2007; see also Hirasawa 2007, 52)

Hirasawa's kōenkai total over fifty and are roughly evenly divided between geographical kōenkai and trade or hobby-based kōenkai, with the number of the latter types growing over the years and the number of territorial groups remaining more or less constant (Interviews, Katsuei Hirasawa, Tokyo, June 29, 2004 and August 13, 2009).

In addition to kōenkai in his district, Hirasawa has created a nationwide kōenkai for supporters who live outside his district. This group meets once a year in Tokyo, and its honorary chairman is Takamasa Ikeda (the brother-in-law of the emperor) (Interview, Katsuei Hirasawa, Tokyo, June 29, 2004).

This brings us to questions of leadership. Early on, Hirasawa found Masaaki Satō, a well-respected figure from the neighborhood, to serve as head of his Katsushika kōenkai (Park 2000, 78). But his strategy for the small, local kōenkai differed from this approach.

> It would be problematic if I chose the heads. So, the head is nominated by local ward assembly members. . . . If I pick someone, it would ruin his relationship with other members. The prerequisite for the *kōenkai* presidents is to have no enemy. You also need to be well respected in the area. If those who have enemies become presidents, people will not vote for me. Someone with no enemy and well respected—that's who I have manage my *kōenkai*. (Interview, Katsuei Hirasawa, Tokyo, June 29, 2004)

Managing the kōenkai is also the work of Hirasawa's staff. He employs about fifteen staffers in his local offices, about eight or nine of those working full-time and the rest part-time (Interview, Katsuei Hirasawa, Tokyo, June 29, 2004).

In addition to the kōenkai built around trade and hobby groups, Hirasawa cultivated links with various interest groups themselves. Park reports that fourteen religious organizations with more than 1,000 local members helped Hirasawa's campaign (Park 2000, 145). Under the SMD, Hirasawa had an easier time than he would as a new entrant in the MMD. In the Old Tokyo 10th District, Kujiraoka and Shimamura had regional bases (the former in Adachi Ward and the latter in Edogawa Ward), but they "also had a mechanism to attract support from different organizations. For example, the Truck Associations supported Kujiraoka, and the Dentists' Federation supported Shimamura" (Park 2000, 75). Hirasawa never had to attempt to carve out a separate interest group base from other LDP members because he was the sole representative for the district. Instead, he could work broadly.

> Hirasawa receives support from the LDP's strong supporting groups. First, local politicians introduced him to business leaders. . . . Also, Hirasawa was given a list of industry groups from the LDP party branch. There were 204 supporting groups listed in the list including 32 food related groups, 62 commercial groups, 42 industrial groups, 16 construction groups, 12 welfare/education groups, 8 tax related groups, 8 medical groups, and 16 environmental groups. . . . For small and medium-sized enterprises, there was a solid organization called KSD [Small and Medium-Size Enterprise (SME) Managers' Welfare Corporation]. . . . KSD Katsushika had 20,000 members, which was about

half of all the SME managers there. (Park 2000, 137–38)

This simplified matters for some interest groups: "KSD Katsushika Ward Branch Director Saburō Shimomura said, 'there used to be two LDP Diet members, so it was not easy to support one of them, but we only have one candidate this time. Things got easier'" (Park 2000, 138).

With the Japanese MMM electoral system, the incentives for specialization through privileged links between interest groups and one of the SNTV district politicians have disappeared. As we have seen with Ohno, Hirasawa is also broadening his range of links. Hirasawa also commented that the strong anti-LDP sentiment in the run-up to the 2009 election altered party–interest group relations. "Some groups now support both the LDP and the DPJ. They play both sides of the fence. It is insurance for them. The groups that strongly support me now, I really appreciate. We can now differentiate between groups that just supported the party in power and the groups that support the LDP. We can see who is sticking by us" (Interview, Katsuei Hirasawa, Tokyo, August 13, 2009). Despite the diminishing of this type of specialization and the shifting electoral fortunes, both Ohno and Hirasawa continue to invest heavily in building up their kōenkai.

Managing relationships with local elected officials is another area that has simplified dramatically under the new electoral system. Katsushika Ward elected two members of the Tokyo Metropolitan Assembly (the equivalent of the prefectural assembly) until 2009, when this was reduced to one seat. In addition to these prefectural assembly representatives, the group of local politicians also comprises ward-level politicians. Hirasawa works to forge ties with as many as he can because they can scratch one another's backs. Hirasawa seeks and gets support not only from LDP local politicians but also from some nonpartisan local politicians. In return, he uses his strong local kōenkai to support these politicians. Nevertheless, his own kōenkai and that of the local politicians remain completely separate, although membership does sometimes overlap (Interview, Katsuei Hirasawa, Tokyo, June 29, 2004). Early on, when Hirasawa divided up his district to pursue his local organization strategy, he asked the (then) fifteen LDP ward assembly members to take charge of these seven areas. Where no LDP ward assembly member was present, kōenkai officers took the lead (Park 2000, 79). Although the mutualistic relationship has developed considerably, at first it was slow going because some local politicians resisted strong pressure and at first did not work very hard. The kōenkai leaders began to threaten not to support the recalcitrants (Park 2000, 106). Hirasawa himself resorted to the same pressure, saying he would ensure victory in the next election in return for cooperation:

> These words were not bluffing or exaggeration. Hirasawa's *kōenkai* members outnumbered theirs, and it would not be impossible for him to make several ward assembly members lose an election. To further strengthen support from local politicians, the LDP branch confirmed that the level of their support for

Hirasawa would be evaluated when they chose the party's candidate in the Tokyo Metro Assembly election in 1997. (Park 2000, 109–10).

In this case, the local branch of the LDP applied pressure to support Hirasawa, but there have also been tensions between his kōenkai and the LDP branch. Hirasawa is in a strong position, however, with his formidable kōenkai. "Even if every other LDP politician in Tokyo loses, I will win my election" (Interview, Katsuei Hirasawa, Tokyo, July 9, 2002). He explained the role of the party branch:

> The party's branches are for Tokyo Metro Assembly members and LDP affili-
> ates to communicate with each other. My *kōenkai* that spread out like a spider
> web has nothing to do with LDP local branch. They are strictly my personal
> *kōenkai*. The members support me no matter what. Some are members of the
> Communist Party, but they support me. They support me personally. We have
> to gather this kind of people. Otherwise, you cannot win elections. (Interview,
> Katsuei Hirasawa, Tokyo, October 5, 2007)

Hirasawa also pointed out that he heads the local LDP branch, which has no staff members and is located in his kōenkai office. He called this branch a façade (*tatemae*) (Interview, Katsuei Hirasawa, Tokyo, October 16, 2008).

Another significant asset for Hirasawa is his celebrity. He is a frequent guest on a variety of TV shows. His trademark no-nonsense speaking style and the strong stands he often takes on issues no doubt contribute to his popularity on the medium. Despite the fact that he is probably one of the best-known politicians in Japan through TV, he refuses to rest solely on his celebrity laurels but instead continues to assiduously cultivate his kōenkai organizational base. "I spend about 100 times as long working my district as I do appearing on TV" (Interview, Katsuei Hirasawa, Tokyo, October 16, 2008). In 2009, he looked back and judged that his strategy had been the right one:

> Those LDP politicians who have kept up with their activities in their districts
> will win re-election. You need to prepare for whatever political winds may
> blow when the election is held. That is your duty, your job as a politician.
> Those who did, will win. Those who didn't, will lose. It is like the ant and the
> grasshopper. It is too late to start building your kōenkai now that the election
> has been called. You need to rely on yourself, not others. (Interview, Katsuei
> Hirasawa, Tokyo, August 13, 2009)

The Surprising Continuity of Kōenkai, Old and New

It is difficult to generalize with any confidence on the basis of such a small number of kōenkai case studies. But we do have some corroboration from other studies. In addition to our own field work in other districts (urban, suburban, and rural), we have secondary sources. Masaki Taniguchi (2004) investigated the kōenkai of LDP and New Frontier Party (NFP) politicians in the 1996 election in Shizuoka 1st District. His avowed purpose is to see whether the new electoral system has transformed the kōenkai and led to a shift to local party branches. He evaluates this transformation on three dimensions: daily activities, electoral mobilization, and funding. He finds little evidence that the party branches are supplanting kōenkai along these dimensions and concludes that the party organization exists mainly on organizational charts (Taniguchi 2004, 84, 87).

On the basis of primary and secondary case study evidence, the kōenkai seem to function in much the same way now as they did before electoral reform. To some extent, their importance in electoral politics can be said to have diminished, especially in some urban areas. Nevertheless, as institutions, they persist. Indeed, it is striking how little kōenkai activities have changed over time. By this, we mean not just the continuity of kōenkai activities before and after electoral reform, but from the dawn of the LDP into the twenty-first century. Recall the 1958 *Asahi Shimbun* article on the spread of kōenkai that described the main electoral strategies as very personal, "sending letters, putting up posters, distributing towels and matches, attending wedding ceremonies and funerals, door-to-door campaigning" ("Kōenkai ō hayari" [Rise of the kōenkai], *Asahi Shimbun* April 15, 1958, 2).

As seen in the case studies, kōenkai activities seem remarkably consistent before and after electoral reform. No one today has a kōenkai to rival Kakuei Tanaka, but a Diet member from Kawasaki apparently gives him stiff competition in attending funerals; Kazunori Tanaka reportedly attends 2,000 funerals every year (Interview N, June 29, 2004). Even DPJ Diet members who have built kōenkai report much the same tactics. For example, one boasted to us that over the past two and a half years he had spent 900 days walking around, shaking hands with about 50,000 people, standing in front of the train station every day, setting a quota of 300 individual meetings per day, participating in every possible meeting in his district, and allowing himself the single luxury of one beer at the end of the day (DPJ Diet member, Tokyo, August 31, 2004). In response to a question about changes in campaigning under the new system, one Diet member responded without bothering to flatter the questioner's profession, "Nothing has changed in the campaign. It's just the stupid political scientists who said it would change. Nothing at all has changed" (Interview N, July 9, 2002).

Voters also join kōenkai for the same reasons they did before electoral reform. National surveys of kōenkai members show that the overwhelming bulk of them join for personal reasons (personal connections, 54.2 percent; connections through work, 25.1 percent). Those who join because of policy are at most 26 percent (and this response category also includes personal characteristics) ("Heisei 12-nenban yoron chōsa nenkan," 2001).

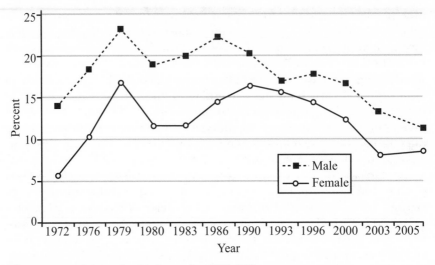

Figure 3.4 Kōenkai membership by gender, 1972–2005
Source: Analysis of Meisuikyō data.

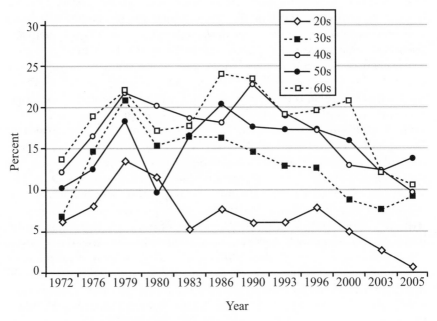

Figure 3.5 Kōenkai membership by age, 1972–2005
Source: Analysis of Meisuikyō data.

The same types of people also still join kōenkai. Figures 3.4 and 3.5 break down kōenkai membership by gender and age.

We are not arguing that nothing has changed in Japanese politics as a result of the electoral reform. Both case studies show that the relationship between politicians and interest groups has been transformed.[9] Similarly, we find that the relationship between the national politician and local politicians have a vastly different character as a result of electoral reform. The reasons for this are similar to those that altered the landscape for interest groups. With a single representative replacing competing representatives, the terms of trade have changed and now the national politician is in a much more advantageous position. Nevertheless, our object of study here—the kōenkai as an institution—functions in much the same way as it did before electoral reform and indeed has changed remarkably little along these dimensions for decades.

A Bird's Eye View: Kōenkai Today

Although kōenkai themselves may act much the same as they have since their inception, they have weakened in membership strength since the passage of electoral reform. We have evidence from several general sources to support our belief that kōenkai remain important in Japanese politics but have declined from their peak of strength.

Membership numbers from individual kōenkai are extremely difficult to obtain. Politicians are naturally reluctant to divulge them. After all, precise knowledge of the strength or geographical distribution of an opponent's kōenkai could be valuable information for those running against him or her. Politicians also have an incentive to exaggerate their kōenkai membership to appear more popular or electorally secure (and to discourage challengers). Moreover, even if membership numbers appeared to be the same, the strength of kōenkai membership would not necessarily be constant because some members are enrolled by their affiliated groups but have only a nominal membership. Unfortunately, just as before electoral reform, we still have few reliable reports of the kōenkai strength of politicians.

But, to augment the case studies discussed here, we can gather evidence from surveys of politicians as well as from voters. In a 1997 fax survey of House of Representatives Diet members, nearly all the 123 respondents said that they "mobilized votes through local organizations and social networks" (Richardson and Patterson 2001, 97). Politicians continue to rely on kōenkai to get out the vote.

Why have kōenkai declined in strength? We again remind the reader that we are not arguing that electoral reform is irrelevant for kōenkai or for Japanese politics but, instead, seeking to refine our understanding of how institutions change and how party organization develops. In the case of the kōenkai, there are multiple possible causes for decline. Electoral reform is certainly one, and we believe it has had an impact, although much less than

9. See also Shinsuke Hamamoto (2007), who analyzes the groups with whom Diet members met before and after election reform and finds evidence of transformed patterns.

predicted. Another possible explanation involves the voters. It is possible that the politicians remain as keenly interested in developing kōenkai as they were prior to 1994 (and some evidence supports this view for many politicians, although not all) but that the voters are now much *less* interested in joining kōenkai. In other words, the cause might not be the "supply side," with politicians switching their strategies to party branch support, but the "demand side," with voters becoming progressively less interested in joining kōenkai, despite the earnest entreaties of politicians. Figures 3.4 and 3.5 show that the decline in membership has been broad-based across both men and women, and people of all ages. The rise of the floating or independent voter is clearly part of the story of the slow decline of kōenkai over the past decade and a half.

We believe this is a partial explanation, although not a complete one. Consider figure 3.6 showing kōenkai membership by party identification for voters and parties since 1972. We see that LDP supporters belong to kōenkai only at about the same rate in 2005 as they did in the early 1970s, with a clear downward trend since electoral reform. Unlike the JCP reaction to electoral reform (see also chap. 2), however, the LDP kōenkai membership decline has been more gradual—although given the weaker strength of identification of LDP supporters with their party compared to JCP supporters, we might have expected the decline to be even steeper. Nevertheless, although it does not control for intensity of identification, this graph clearly shows that kōenkai membership is declining not just in general but even among self-identified LDP supporters.

A fourth possible cause for the decline in membership is the rise of television. In other words, the increased ability of politicians to use television to reach voters, rather than the electoral reform, could be shifting politicians' strategies from a reliance on the kōenkai to a reliance on television. The gradual decline of kōenkai membership may be the result of politicians' selecting new tools in the digital age. Of course, not every politician can become a TV star and garner votes simply through name recognition. Moreover, risk-averse politicians such as Hirasawa could seek both TV fame and a strong kōenkai.[10]

The real influence of television manifests in the resulting increasing importance of the party label. And it is here that the rise of the influence of television presents a challenge for explanations based on the electoral system, although in important ways the two phenomena are intertwined. In other words, electoral reform alone might not have driven politicians to diminish their investment in kōenkai and rely on the party label, but electoral reform

10. Hirasawa cautioned other LDP Diet members to heed his example. "I advised [a new Diet member] as one of the Koizumi children; I told him, 'build your *kōenkai*.' He didn't listen to me. He thought Koizumi's popularity would last forever and win him countless re-elections. Now he's certain to lose" (Interview, Katsuei Hirasawa, Tokyo, August 13, 2009). The Diet member in question lost his seat.

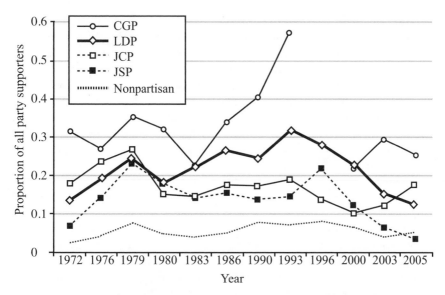

Figure 3.6 Kōenkai membership by party, 1972–2005 (proportion of all party supporters)
Source: Calculated from Meisuikyō data.
Note: CGP did not contest the 1996 election because they had merged with the New
Frontier Party. By 2000, the NFP had broken up and CGP again existed as an independent
political party.

combined with the rise of television seems to have made the party label a more
reliable asset for politicians and thus led to the diminishment of kōenkai.

As we see this transformation in campaign techniques, it is useful to
keep in mind Robert Agranoff's (1978, 232) argument that, in the U.S. context, electoral uncertainty was the factor pushing the embrace of modern
campaign techniques. In Japan, this uncertainty for individual politicians
stems not from the change in the electoral system but from the long-term
decline in party loyalty and the increasing reliance of voters on short-term
factors in choosing for whom to vote—exactly as in the United States.

Remember, too, that some analysts expected the kōenkai not simply to
decline but to be replaced (perhaps immediately) by strong party branches.
We do see evidence that the party branches are playing a more robust role
in electoral mobilization, but, frankly, their role is incomplete. Perhaps
the quotation that opens this chapter should be read not as a description
but as a prediction. In Ohno's case, in an electoral district with a population of over 200,000, the LDP had only a few thousand members. When
the LDP prefectural organization was pressed to sign up new members, it
had no choice but to turn to the kōenkai of its politicians. Organizationally, the LDP remains weak; to repeat Ohno's words, "the party's shadow is
faint on the ground" (Interview, Yoshinori Ohno, Tokyo, October 2003).
In Hirasawa's case, the party leaders (if not the branch office) played a
key role in spurring the local politicians to initially support Hirasawa, but

subsequently Hirasawa has focused on and relied on his own kōenkai rather than the party organization. Recall also that Taniguchi did not discover much evidence that the party branches were supplanting kōenkai along these dimensions and that the party organization existed mainly on organizational charts (Taniguchi 2004, 84, 87). Analyses of financial contributions to politicians suggest that the regulations on political contributions have helped to ensure the continued existence of the kōenkai at the expense of the party branches (Carlson 2007, 134). Although kōenkai have weakened, they have not been replaced by local party branches as predicted. Rather, a subtler transformation is at work.

In fact, some Diet members complain of an old tension: "If I try to make my kōenkai more active, the LDP people get angry," even though the LDP organization is completely inadequate to propel a candidate to victory (Interview B, October 5, 2007). In the past, this conflict was resolved in favor of the kōenkai at the expense of LDP branch offices (see chap. 2). What will happen in the future is an open question, although there are good reasons to expect both the LDP party label and branch offices will strengthen.

The 2005 election offers lessons about the balance between the kōenkai and the party label. Prime Minister Jun'ichirō Koizumi dissolved the House of Representatives after his postal privatization bill did not pass the House of Councilors (which the prime minister cannot dissolve). In the subsequent election, Koizumi stripped the "rebel" Diet members who had voted against postal privatization in the House of Representatives of their party endorsement and then went a step further and dispatched "assassin" (*shikyaku*) candidates from the party to contest the districts of the rebels (Nemoto, Krauss, and Pekkanen 2008). Most of the rebels lost, some won, and the LDP as a whole cruised to its greatest electoral victory ever. So, kōenkai alone are no longer enough to reliably get a Diet member elected, although strong politicians can still win (perhaps for only one election) with their kōenkai alone. The electoral context has changed the power balance between the backbenchers and the prime minister. Still, the lessons of 2005 are not all one way. On the one hand, the election showed that strong kōenkai must struggle to elect their Diet member without the party endorsement. In that sense, it may have taught caution to many Diet members and thus increased the power of the leadership. On the other hand, without the kōenkai, none of the rebels could have imagined victory. And the circumstances of the 2005 election were nearly an ideal case for the party leadership, helmed by a charismatic prime minister and running on a popular issue. The historic LDP success at the polls reflects this. Nevertheless, even under such near-worst-case conditions, kōenkai won fifteen of the battles, and this is another lesson of the election.

Historical Institutionalism and the Persistence of the Kōenkai

Kōenkai remain an important part of the Japanese political landscape. In many ways, they are remarkably unchanged after electoral reform, acting much the same as they did before 1994. And the attraction for kōenkai felt by politicians remains in many cases as strong as it ever was. Candidates with kōenkai won a few electoral battles in 2005 against LDP-endorsed candidates, although that election also showed the new limits of kōenkai potency. Although some candidates now choose to rely on the party label, there are few for whom the personal vote and a kōenkai organization are not valuable. Even politicians running for their first election in an SMD have chosen to invest substantial resources in building a kōenkai.

In addition, most of the Diet members elected in the PR tier of the Japanese MMM run simultaneously in the SMD districts. The LDP has adopted a "best loser" provision to rank PR candidates based on the percentage of the winner's vote that they obtain (see chap. 1). So, Candidate A, who lost narrowly in one district, will be ranked ahead of Candidate B, who lost overwhelmingly in another district. As a result, LDP Diet members almost all have an incentive to cultivate kōenkai in their district, even those who are elected from the PR tier, where the party label should matter more. Only a relatively small number of Diet members run solely in PR.[11]

So, the kōenkai are certainly not dead. Membership in kōenkai after 2003 (a decade after electoral reform) was as high as it was in 1972 (nearly two decades after the first SNTV MMD election). Yet, when we look at the change in kōenkai membership rates among LDP supporters (to exclude the increasing share of floating voters; figure 3.7) over time, we find that kōenkai membership proportions have declined steadily after electoral reform. Still, even though the trend is clear, the rates remain higher today than they were in the 1970s. If we are to avoid cherry-picking the evidence, we must acknowledge both realities: kōenkai are declining but remain vibrant in many ways.

The bigger question is the cause or causes of all this. Contrary to expectations, the kōenkai have not simply been replaced by powerful party branches. This alone should give us pause before we accept a purely electoral cause, although electoral reform is clearly also part of the explanation. The rise of television and the decline of partisanship are also possible factors.

Historical institutionalism also has some insights to offer. Sequencing is an obvious one. Had the Japanese adopted a MMM system in 1947 and then switched to a SNTV MMD system in 1994, we would now see a very different state of affairs. In that case, the LDP might even have realized its long-cherished dream and established powerful party branches that flourished even under SNTV. But, as fate and the Occupation authorities would have it, Japan elected to go with SNTV. This was part of, if not all, the story

11. According to our calculations, there were sixty-eight LDP-endorsed candidates running only in the PR tier in 1996, seventy-three in 2000, sixty in 2003, fifty-six in 2005, and thirty-seven in 2009. Summing these, we find 284 PR-only candidates out of 1,689 LDP candidates during the period. Most of these were hopeless candidates filling up the bottom ranks of the PR list (except in the surprisingly 2005 election, when many unexpectedly won); only a relative handful at the top of the list were serious candidates.

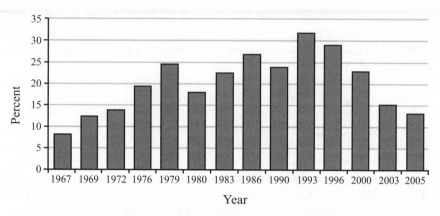

Figure 3.7 LDP kōenkai membership rates, 1967–2005 (% of all supporters)
Source: Analysis of 1972–1993 Meisuikyō data. Data for 1967 and 1969 from Masumi (1995 [1985]), 481) using Kōmei Senkyo Renmei survey results reported in Miyake (1977, 295).

of the postwar origins of kōenkai (see chap. 2); and the sequence of electoral systems adopted in Japan clearly had something to do with the persistence of kōenkai today under MMM. Once a politician has a kōenkai, it is easy to see why he or she would want to keep it. For one thing, running in an election is risky business and politicians tend to want to acquire all the victory insurance they can. For another, kōenkai are flexible instruments, allowing non-party supporters (who might be splitting their vote or otherwise think of themselves as belonging to another camp) to register their approval of a particular politician. In an age when the number of floating voters is growing, politicians are naturally interested in building links with voters who are disinclined to think of themselves as belonging to any particular party. As Ohno remarked, "People support me as a candidate and not as a party representative; people are moved by personal connections in Japan.... Look at the PR vote in Kagawa. My vote is 90,000 and the LDP PR vote is 60,000 in this district. I get the extra 30,000 votes by showing my face, talking to people, and going to meetings" (Interview, Yoshinori Ohno, Marugame, October 14, 2003). Even a DPJ Diet member boasted to us that his kōenkai members (120,000 strong) were not members of the DPJ but of the Suzuki Party (a pseudonym; Interview FF, August 6, 2004). In districts where the LDP party label offers only cold comfort to a candidate, kōenkai are a natural recourse. As one Diet member complained to us,

> My area in [my district] is a very difficult area for the LDP. The DPJ is very strong there. Even in the last election [2005], I won only narrowly despite the LDP landslide. The LDP organization is practically nonexistent. I've had to work hard to develop a *kōenkai*, but I know that I need to do it. I cannot rely only on the party label and the party organization to win. (Interview LL, October 5, 2007)

Perhaps Aesop's fable of the ant and the grasshopper, invoked by Hirasawa, springs to the minds of the Diet members. "If I leave everything in the hands of the LDP organization, chances might be great that I lose the next election.... That is the lesson I learned from the [2007 House of Councilors] election" (Interview B, October 5, 2007).

Complementary institutions are another and perhaps even more important part of the story. Although the electoral system changed, the Public Offices Election Law (POEL) did not; it still handcuffs candidates' efforts to reach the voters. Recall Ohno's complaints about the restrictions (and this from a politician who cruised to victory). Indeed, with kōenkai membership down (but functioning in much the same way it always did) and the party branches not noticeably stronger, we might look more closely at the complementary institution of the POEL as the driver of the role that kōenkai play.

Chapter 4

Factions under the Single Nontransferable Vote System

If a person gathers three people together, he can make a faction.
Former Prime Minister Masayoshi Ōhira (quoted in Mabuchi 2001, 26)

The LDP has always been a fractionalized party (see chap. 1). Most of its national Diet representatives belong not just to the party itself but also to smaller competing groups within the party. Although many political parties in the world can be described as having factions within them, LDP factions are different in some respects. They are far more organized, sometimes seeming almost like mini-parties within the larger party, and the factions in the 1990s and 2000s can trace their lineages back to their predecessor factions of the 1950s (Park 2001, 433).

Moreover, unlike the factions in some political parties elsewhere, LDP factions were not actually formed around or came together because of a core of people who shared similar policy views. In fact, the party factions have had only an indirect influence on policymaking and policy within the LDP, in part because they are usually made up of representatives with very diverse policy views and opinions on the issues (but still within the very broad umbrella of the conservative nature of the LDP). No faction formed around a specific policy position, even when the factions differed in policy nuances on certain issues or had representatives who shared important policy views or goals. Rather, the major goal of LDP factions and the reason for their existence were unrelated to policy—it was to get their leader selected as the LDP party president and, thus, prime minister. Even in Taiwan under SNTV, the party factions rested on "the single main underlying cleavage" in that country—relations with the People's Republic of China and the independence issue—and were therefore unlike those of the LDP (Grofman 1999, 389). Factions in the LDP are, therefore, "factions of interest" based on patronage rather than "factions of principle" based on policy beliefs (Bettcher 2005, 344).

It is widely believed that the LDP factions were a product of the pre-reform SNTV electoral system. But, contrary to the expectations of some analysts and reformers, they have not disappeared after the reform. Why did the electoral reform have only a partial influence on factions? Why do they still exist, and what does their continued existence and functions tell us about their role within the LDP? Can we find the answers to these questions in how factions developed and the way the LDP under the '55 system became institutionalized as a political party? This chapter and the next address these questions and examines how factions originated, developed, and then were transformed (or not) by the 1994 electoral reform.

What Are Factions?

As are legislators everywhere, Japanese national politicians are constantly involved in many overlapping and interconnected worlds and roles with voters, supporters, and colleagues. They make policy, but they are also active in the internal affairs of their party, including the politics of choosing their leader. They try to advance their careers within the party, parliament, and government, and they interact with their fellow legislators both socially and politically. In the case of a governing party, choosing the party leader also chooses the person who will head the government and who may well also have an effect on legislators' careers and on how and how well they can provide services to their constituents and policy to both constituents and the nation.

Belonging to a faction is particularly about the role of internal party politics, although it may have consequences for all the roles a politician plays. Kim Eric Bettcher defines *factions* in political parties as "groups that compete with others for power advantages within parties" (2005, 340). In the LDP in particular, factions are organized groups of LDP representatives who are loyal to one particular senior leader of the LDP who is trying to become the party president and thus the prime minister. The support of LDP Diet members is necessary to attain that post because since 1956 the LDP has chosen its leader generally with a vote in which Diet members have the dominant, although not sole, role. LDP factions are thus probably most fully described as "personal party leadership factions." Members meet on a regular basis, usually at least once per week, with other representatives who are members of the same faction (and who thus share this goal) to conduct faction business, discuss current party and parliamentary issues and process, and interact and communicate with their faction leader and other members. Over time, membership in LDP factions also became exclusive; Diet members could not belong to more than one faction. Factional membership is also quite clear and public; newspapers, guidebooks to the Diet, and other publications print universally agreed-on membership lists, and some Diet members even list their factional membership or factional positions on their business cards.

In many ways, the members of a faction probably have closer social relations with fellow faction members than with other representatives in their own party because of this frequent interaction, and thus factions have a dimension of social cohesion and information-sharing as well. In this sense, the relationship among faction members and between the members and their leader goes beyond a purely exchange relationship.

It is the exchange relationship, however, that lies at the core of factions under the '55 system. Factions existed because a party leader needed support from Diet members in the party to gain the party presidency and thus become the prime minister. In exchange for this loyal support, the leader provided political and financial benefits to his faction members, and thus this exchange was beneficial to both sides. Before electoral reform, the faction member typically gained much from his faction leader in return for his or her loyalty to the leader and service in the faction. Members gained support in being nominated as an LDP candidate in their districts, they received funding twice a year to help maintain kōenkai and more funds at election time beyond what the party provided to all candidates, and the well-known faction leader might visit constituencies to help members get reelected. Members' entire political careers and advancement were also shaped greatly by factions.

The factions were hierarchical. Members' years of service in the faction (i.e., the number of times elected) determined their rank within the faction, and seniority in the faction determined eligibility for posts not only in the faction and party but also in the parliament and government. Each faction leader maintained a list of his members and their eligibility for particular posts to put forward and push the next time post rotation occurred (approximately once per year). From their fellow faction members, they received advice, friendship, and, when necessary, information from the experts among them on how to help respond to their constituents' particular policy requests.

Party personal leadership factions have been the crucial influence on political leadership in the LDP, determining to a large extent who became prime minister; who was selected for the cabinet; and which positions all other LDP Diet members were given in the party, Diet, or government. In this way, they also indirectly influenced the shape of policy. For much of the postwar period, they also played a role in elections, helping to secure nominations and providing funding for candidates. Factions thus had a major role in shaping, to some degree, all the functions of the LDP as a political party: office-seeking, policy-seeking, and vote-seeking. Indeed, as the one party organizational feature influencing each of these, factions may well be characterized as one of the key coordinating bodies linking all these functions within the party. Masaru Kohno, for example, describes them as "the central organizational units within the party" (1997, 91).

Why Are There Factions?

How do we explain the importance of factions in the LDP and Japanese postwar politics, and their somewhat distinctive characteristics—their degree of organization, hierarchy, and seniority-based ranking of members—compared to party factions in other countries? Two explanations have been proposed at various times in the study of Japanese politics, both of which were considered powerful and obvious at the height of their popularity. We find, however, that neither explains the origins and development of factions sufficiently. We therefore offer a third explanation, which we then demonstrate in the rest of this chapter.

Cultural Determinist Explanations

In newspaper coverage and scholarly analysis, for many years the major focus of attention to internal party politics in the LDP was its factions. The origin of the factions, considered to be both the core and most important dimension of party politics, was once attributed to Japanese cultural styles of social organization (Nakane 1967; Hoffmann 1981). In other words, because factionalism tended to fit a more general social pattern in Japanese society, namely the importance of small groups and their tendency to be hierarchically organized with seniority often determining rank within the group, factions within the LDP were assumed to be merely a reflection of this deeper and more general societal organizational pattern.

One problem with the cultural explanation of factions, much as with the urban village explanation of kōenkai, is that it assumes all causal explanation is bottom up (i.e., society determining politics) rather than considering any possible causes that are top down (i.e., the role of the state in politics). Since the early 1990s, in part because political scientists "rediscovered" the state and the role of institutions in shaping behavior, this approach has been fully replaced by a stress on the SNTV electoral system as the prime reason for the existence and persistence of the factions through time.[1] Thus despite Japanese society featuring such characteristics in its social organization, for example, Kohno (1997, 91) argues against the cultural explanations for factions. He finds major changes to the internal attributes of the factions in the last two decades of LDP rule before electoral reform—the development of the very characteristics of LDP factions that made them distinctive, such as their more formal organization, promotion according to a strict seniority principle, and institutional norms of proportionality in appointments—that a constant such as culture cannot

---

1. Others, however, have recognized that "the electoral system was never more than one of several reasons for institutionalized factions within the LDP" (Reed 2003, 185) and that "the greatest stimulus to the growth of the factions in the present conservative party has been the party presidential election" (Thayer 1969, 21).

explain.[2] We agree. Although small personal groups may exist in all Japanese social organizations, the development of the particular organized form of party political factions cannot be explained by culture alone.

A further argument against the cultural approach is that it can neither explain changes in the factions over time nor explain variations across space. Countries with cultural environments totally different from Japan, such as Italy and India, also have had ruling parties for long periods characterized by factional politics, although not of exactly the same pattern (for India, Hoffmann 1981; for Italy, Zuckerman 1979; for a Japan-Italy comparison, Bettcher 2005, 339–58). Even within Japan, other political parties than the LDP have not had the same type of factions.

Electoral Determinist Explanations

It seems to us, however, that both these objections to a constant (culture) being unable to explain change also apply to the explanation centering on electoral incentives, which in the last two decades have supplanted culture as the dominant variable explaining factions. But the incentives of the electoral system did not change during the postwar period from 1947 until 1993. How can an unchanged incentives in an electoral system account for the changes in the factions analyzed by Kohno during this period? And the political systems in India and Italy, for example, also characterized by party personal factions and leadership, had very different electoral systems and consequently political incentives yet somewhat similar political outcomes, whereas parties in Japan under the same electoral system did not. Moreover, the political systems in Taiwan and Korea had a SNTV electoral system similar to that in Japan, but the party factions were somewhat different than in Japan, and the impact of the electoral system varied depending on other government institutions, party electoral strategies, and the importance of overriding policy issues (Grofman 1999, 388–89).

Furthermore, analysts (e.g., Ramseyer and Rosenbluth 1993, 59, 63; Kohno 1997, 92) emphasizing the electoral system as the determinant of factions often seem to make fine distinctions between the causes and origins of factions, on the one hand, and their persistence and maintenance, on the other, but it is unclear why they make this differentiation. Exploring this distinction reveals a difference between electoral incentives as independent and intervening variables.

A Historical Institutionalist Explanation

We agree that the electoral system matters in producing some of the particular ways in which factions operated; but we are skeptical that the electoral

2. Park (2001, 430) notes this and also that political factions have distinctive characteristics from factions in other parts of Japanese society.

system is the sole or even major factor in the origin and development of factions and all the roles they have performed in the LDP. The more we researched the development of factions, the more we discovered that the internal struggles for power among the LDP leaders and between the leaders and the rank-and-file representatives were at least as important and that these struggles then became intertwined with the electoral system, producing the nature and role of the factions under the '55 system.

Here we look first at how the factions and their purported role in personnel and election campaigns developed and became fully established under the '55 system. As in all our chapters, we try to avoid "actor-centered functionalism" (Pierson 2004, 103–32) by not conflating the eventual outcomes with the original intent of the actors who made the decisions that led to those outcomes. We argue that the explanation for factions' becoming a defining characteristic of the LDP as a party and of its leadership, and their importance in all the major functions of the party, was the origin of the party and the unintended consequences of the method of selecting its leader that it adopted at a particular historical time. We demonstrate that the form that the factions took and the way they became institutionalized under the '55 system were the outcomes of internal power struggles for control of the party. Only as a result of these power struggles were the factions' vote-seeking activities and functions adopted, expanded, and linked to the other office-seeking and policy-seeking functions of the factions and the party. And their final institutionalization developed over a long period only after certain conditions had been established. Finally, we show that this explanation for the development of factions allows us to more validly explain the ways that the 1993–1994 electoral reform partially undermined the role of the factions in the party and the ways that it partially did not.

Before the Liberal Democratic Party

Factions existed in prewar Japanese political parties, under both the SNTV electoral system (1918–1925) and the SMD system (1900–1917 and 1925–1938). Although Ramseyer and Rosenbluth argue that the personal vote electoral incentives of the SNTV system after 1918 helped transform the character of the factions, they also acknowledge that factions based more on regional competition among the oligarchs existed prior to the SNTV system and that, even after 1918 when SNTV came back, "membership in factions was small and erratic" (1993, 61). Thus, even though an SNTV electoral system existed prior to the Pacific War, factions were not at all as extensive or the same as after the war.

After one election under a larger multimember district and plural vote system during the Occupation in 1946, Japan reverted to SNTV in the 1947 election. Factions in the form that later became institutionalized under the '55 system did not really exist in the first decade after the SNTV electoral system was introduced. There were pro–and anti–Shigeru Yoshida "factions" within the Liberal Party (Jiyūtō) and later within the Democratic Party (Minshutō), the other main conservative party (recall that these parties later merged to form the LDP). Unfortunately, although the nature of the premerger Liberal and Democratic parties may be crucial to understanding the origins, nature, and development of factions within the merged LDP, only a few have analyzed this.

Factions in the LDP predecessor parties and in the immediate post-LDP merger years existed, but they bore little resemblance to the factions that developed later in the 1960s to 1980s in the LDP. They differed in at least nine fundamental ways:[3]

1. The parties tended to be polarized around two groups jockeying for leadership of the party, with each group having multiple, fluid factions (Reed 1992, 7).

2. Ideology and policy were important in several of these groups and part of the basis for their conflict (Reed 1992, 7). In this sense, as bifurcated groups around a leader and policy issues, these factions originally resembled the "mainstream" and "antimainstream" factions of the Kuomintang Party in Taiwan under SNTV in the transition to democracy (Winckler 1999b, 280), not the LDP factions that developed in Japan later.

3. Factions in these parties did not have permanent and exclusive membership; rather, membership was much looser (Thayer 1969, 20).

4. The factions were not passed on to new leaders when the leader died; instead, they dissolved.

5. The factions did not control personnel allocation; they did not distribute posts in the party or cabinet to faction members.

6. "Factions were not the basis for decision-making in the party in terms of leadership selection or candidate selection" (Sveinstóddir 2004, 29).

7. The influence of these factions, because of their limited political importance in the party, did not extend to the electoral districts. In the Liberal Party, for example, there were often two or three party candidates elected in the same district, but despite this intraparty competition, these candidates did *not* necessarily belong to different factions. Factions did not interfere in the nomination process in electoral districts. Indeed, in the midst of growing tension between Prime Minister Shigeru Yoshida and his intra-Liberal Party rival Ichirô Hatoyama, some in his faction suggested that Yoshida deny Hatoyama faction members party membership and also his endorsement in the next election. Yoshida refused, and even anti-Yoshida members were given endorsements (*Mainichi Shimbun* [evening ed.], September 1, 1952, 1; *Mainichi Shimbun*, September 5, 1952, 1).

---

3. In her excellent dissertation, Sveinsdóttir (2004, 28–140) discusses most of the first eight points. Other confirming or originating authors and arguments are cited in each case as they are discussed.

8. These factions did (as did those in the LDP) distribute financial funds to Diet members, but this role was limited because the parties prior to the formation of the LDP were far more centralized than the LDP in this regard; also sometimes Diet members received financial aid from beyond their own faction.

9. Indeed, these factions did not even perform one of the most (if not *the* most) important functions they were to carry out in the LDP after 1955—selecting the party president (Reed 1992, 6–7).

Hulda Sveinsdóttir argues that "[t]he electoral politics of the Jiyūtō and Minshutō show[s] that the multimember electoral system cannot be said to be the most important contribution to factionalism in Japan" because "the party centre was strong enough to maintain centripetal power" (2004, 134). "The parties' emergence allowed strong leadership and a coherent dominant coalition that prevented factionalism from escalating" (135). It appears that the more centralized nature of party leadership, therefore, shaped the nature of pre-LDP factions and not the incentives of the electoral system. The nature of the LDP factions during this brief pre-LDP SNTV era parallels somewhat the history of kōenkai during the same period—they were in existence but with a slow development, weak and sporadic distribution, and more amorphous form until a sudden increase in numbers, consolidation of form, and importance after the party merger that formed the LDP.

The Formation of the Liberal Democratic Party and the Origins of the Factions

On November 15, 1955, the LDP was formally established after almost two years of complex negotiations between the Liberals and Democrats. Although many have seen the causes of this merger as the merger of the former left and right socialists into a combined party in the same year (Hoshi 2005, 59) and in the pressure from big business based on its fear of the united leftist party, Kohno presents a convincing analysis that neither caused the union. Instead, he sees the "interactive game" and "shadow of the future" of the Liberals' desire to increase the credibility of the offer of the incumbent Democratic Party to form a coalition as leading to the merger. And, rather than external pressure from business, the way the interparty negotiations were "nested" within intraparty power struggles in each party created the basis for the amalgamation (Kohno 1997, 82–88).

At its founding convention, the party decided, as a compromise, to make the initial, temporary leadership of the newly established party collective rather than individual. An Acting Presidential Committee (Sōsai Daikō Iinkai) was formed, composed of two Liberal and two Democratic Party leaders, including Taketora Ogata, a Liberal, and Bukichi Miki, a Democrat, both of whom had been instrumental in bringing about the merger (Hoshi

2005, 59; Uchida 1983, 28). Ogata was slated to become prime minister, but he died prematurely in January 1956. The new LDP acquired its first individual leader, Ichirō Hatoyama, when he was elected party president nearly unanimously at the second party convention in April 1956 (Hoshi 2005, 61; Uchida 1983, 28), receiving 394 out of 413 effective votes cast (Okushima 2006, 26).

Despite the merger, the factions of the original parties did not seem to change much at first. Nathaniel Thayer (1969, 22–23) views factions as becoming a major element in Japanese politics only about two years after the LDP was formed, and Sveinsdóttir (2004, 144–48), similarly, demonstrates that the merger did not begin to change the nature and character of the factions until 1957.

The most important stimulus to the transformation of factions toward their present canonical form was the direct election of the party president. President Hatoyama had essentially run almost unopposed. After he resigned, however, on December 14, 1956, the third party convention witnessed its first competitive election. In this and most of the party conventions in the first twenty years of the party, Diet members constituted the overwhelming majority of those casting ballots (the remainder being a few representatives of each party prefectural federation), and thus candidates had to compete for the support of LDP Diet members if they were to have a chance at winning. The 1956 candidates were Nobusuke Kishi (a former Democrat), Tanzan Ishibashi (also a former Democrat), and Kōjirō Ishii (a former Liberal). On the first ballot, Kishi got the most votes but not enough for a majority, with Ishibashi coming in second. On the third and deciding ballot, Ishii threw his support to Ishibashi who consequently won the election.

Many analysts, beginning with Thayer (1969, 21), agree that this presidential election changed the nature of LDP factions in very important ways. As Steven Reed (1992, 9), for example, says, "The factionalization of the LDP was, in many ways, an event that occurred after the 1956 party presidential election." The participants themselves thought so too. A 1963 survey asked the seven most important faction leaders in the LDP, "Why do you think factions were created?" Most responses (four) favored the LDP presidential election, with one citing the merger of the parties, one saying his faction formed around a particular policy on which the members agreed, and only one mentioning general elections (Jimintō Kishada 1963, 130–51).

First, and most important for the future form and development of the factions, the candidates began to mobilize consistent support from their members instead of accepting a looser, less committed, and less exclusive relationship with their followers. Kenzō Uchida cites the reason for the expansion and institutionalization of factions in the party: "Because this party presidential election was adopted, it made it necessary for the influential people who aimed at the party presidency to gather as many party members and representatives as possible under their umbrella and to 'nurture soldiers' [*hei o yashinau*]" (1983, 28).

Although factions remained somewhat fluid into the 1960s, the competition for support in the party presidential election was a critical component in their development. As Michael Leiserson has noted, up until the party presidential election, the factions were like factions elsewhere and the nature of factions changed only after this "radical innovation (1968, 770)

Now, with the ultimate prize, the party presidency and with it the prime ministership (because the merged LDP now had a firm majority in the Diet), determined by the vote of the party convention with Diet members having the largest share of that vote, leaders realized they needed a more stable and reliable basis of support if they were to have a chance of becoming prime minister. In the 1956 party presidential election, "Factional ties were strengthened during the desperate vote gathering that accompanied this election, and leaders learned that they needed a faction if they were to gain control of the government" (Masumi 1995, 18–19; see also, Sveinsdóttir, 2004, 186; Reed 1992, 9).

The power of the prime minister in the party was much stronger in the 1950s and 1960s. Under the Japanese constitution, the prime minister has the total power to appoint cabinet ministers and the top party leaders. Unlike the later prime ministers of the 1970s and 1980s, when the hardening of the factions, seniority, and factional balancing norms were instituted and a good deal of policymaking was decentralized into PARC, those who held the post right after Yoshida's one-man rule in the early 1950s and the formation of the LDP had not only prestige but a more significant degree of influence than they did under the later '55 system. To attain this coveted prize, once the party presidential election was instituted, it was no longer enough to merely wine and dine Diet members; this never sufficiently ensured their support in the party presidential election.

Now with the new leadership rivalry induced by the selection of the president by the party convention, the presidential candidates needed a more formal and exclusive structure to attain consistency in their drive to become prime minister. Factions became formal organizations with their own offices and staff (Thayer 1969, 22–23), and exclusive membership in a faction was also demanded.

In the rush after 1956–1957 to recruit new and loyal members to their factions, leaders cared little about policy or ideological uniformity (Sveinsdóttir 2004, 167). Timing and the prior existence of kōenkai were important factors in this. Diet members were beginning to mobilize support in their districts through kōenkai and the personal vote. Having an ideological or policy litmus test for membership in a faction was contradictory to the leaders' purpose of forming factions to ensure greater core support in the party presidential election; limiting faction membership to only those with common beliefs would put any leader at a disadvantage compared to those who were unconcerned with policy agreement and frantically mobilizing all those with a strong personal vote. It was more advantageous to maximize the size of the faction by recruiting anyone who was a likely winner in the district (including those who had formed kōenkai). This practice of recruiting new members without regard to policy or ideological proclivities continued through the '55 system and beyond: "[T]he *habatsu* grow by enlisting any promising candidate at election time without any consideration for his policy preferences (if any)" (Bouissou 2001, 585).

On the other side, Diet members' incentives to join a faction also had little relation to policy or ideology. Candidates were mobilizing personal votes, which were not particularly based on ideology or policy, so what was the incentive for them to join a leadership faction based on such considerations? The faction leaders' and their recruits' incentives were aligned—both were more concerned with building up numbers (either faction members or voters) based on personal allegiance than with any ideological or policy considerations. Competition and rivalry for votes in the party presidential election were the main stimuli to the formation of exclusive and well-organized factions. This helps explain why the opposition parties at the time, the JSP and the JCP, never developed the same kind of factions. Factionalized they were, but their factions were based on strictly ideological divisions within the party, in the JSP the left versus right socialists and in the JCP pro-Soviet versus pro-Chinese communist models. Although operating under the same electoral ground rules, the basis for the factions in the LDP and its opposition parties were totally different.

Before the establishment of the LDP and its presidential election, party factions had been fluid, looser, and more informal, often having at least some basis in ideological or policy consensus. Now, however, the more organized and exclusive factions were much more internally diverse in terms of policy beliefs but much more consistent in their loyalty to a particular leader through time and well organized to accomplish the leader's aim of becoming the prime minister. In other words, they had started the first steps toward becoming institutionalized. Leiserson (1968, 771) compares this new emerging structure to a military organization, with a "general" and his "general staff," permanent and public membership, regularized sources of funding, and so on. Hirofumi Iseri (1988, 82–87) succinctly observes that, whatever the other conditions that also helped transform the factions, the party presidential election was the *necessary* condition.

The second important change brought by the 1956 election of the LDP president was that the factional coalitions that resulted were not institutionalized along previous party lines. Ishii, a former Liberal, enabled the election of Ishibashi, a former Democrat; this began a game of factional coalitions to produce LDP presidents and prime ministers that had no consistent influence from previous party allegiances. For example, when Kishi became prime minister in 1957 (after Ishibashi resigned due to a sudden illness soon after his selection), his "mainstream" coalition (the factions that had won and had supported the now-elected party president and prime minister) that brought him to power and his losing opponent's "antimainstream" supporters were both mixtures of former Liberal and Democratic faction leaders and members. "Only a year after the merger, the four factions each of the Liberals and Democrats had become completely mixed up: in the new LDP, mainstream and anti-mainstream factions were formed according to the logic of party leader change" (Uchida 1983, 30) rather than their party origins. Thus, cleavages that existed prior to the party merger were not incorporated into the new party, and the party presidential competition trumped, cut across, and transcended these cleavages in the new LDP, making coalitions among factions in the early years of the LDP highly volatile, unprincipled, and opportunistic.

Another change, which had begun after the war and now intersected with the new competition among leaders for faction members, was financing. Before the war, the two main *zaibatsu* conglomerates had provided much of the political funding, with each aligned with one political party: Mitsui supporting the Seiyūkai and Mitsubishi the Minseitō. Funds flowed to the party leaders to distribute to the representatives. With the dissolution of the *zaibatsu* after the war, factions that formed after 1956 could raise funds from diverse sources (Watanabe 1958, 13–20; Kitaoka 1985, 25–141), some of them legitimate and some illicit (Samuels 2003b, 236–47). By 1960, a large amount of money was being provided to representatives through factions (*Yomiuri Shimbun* 1960, 1).

By the late 1950s, factions were being transformed and consolidated from loose-knit, nonexclusive, and partially policy-seeking groups into the more cohesive, exclusive, and office-seeking party units they continued to be for nearly four decades, although other dimensions of their organization changed greatly over time.

A full decade after the SNTV election system was reintroduced into Japan by the Occupation, because of the method of selecting of the LDP leader, the bare beginnings emerged of the factional form that later developed. The LDP began as a merged party with two sets of leaders who were already competing among themselves for dominance within the previous parties. The addition of an election among mostly Diet members in this context set off a no-holds-barred scramble among these leaders to acquire firm and loyal support from any followers they could recruit. Any leader with aspirations to become prime minister who did not emulate the mobilization tactics of other leaders in this regard found himself without a chance of eventual victory; any Diet member who did not join in the newly formed factions found himself bereft of the major advantages of aid and funding for reelection that factions members enjoyed. These competitive advantages had a great deal to do with the formation of exclusive and persistent factions in the LDP. These factions, however, were still a far cry from hierarchical, seniority-based, and institutionalized organizations that provided electoral nomination and funding and that controlled the careers of their members according to strict factional and party rules and norms.

The Institutionalization of Factions and Factional Norms

If they were not the direct product of the electoral system, why and when did factions ultimately develop into their archetypal form under the '55 system? Only a few scholars have looked at the aspects of the LDP relevant to this question, and they do not always agree (Satō and Matsuzaki 1986, 52–77; Kohno 1992; 1997, 91–115; Kawato 1996a, 933–57; 1996b, 11–145; Bouissou 2001). We can, however, piece together from the evidence they provide a picture of how the factions in the LDP developed over time into their final institutionalized form.

This process was more complex, was multidimensional, and took longer time than observers may have expected or theorists have posited. It seems to have occurred in three stages over a thirty-year period, with the causes of the changes in the different dimensions of factions not always the same but all stemming from party and intraparty leadership competition and leader-follower relations.

The first stage was the development of rigid seniority rules within the factions, making them strictly hierarchical. The second stage was the extension of factional competition into electoral districts, with each faction minimizing the number of candidates it ran in each district. And the final stage was the application of the seniority rules within the factions to the party as a whole and the application of these to the appointment of faction members to various posts within the party, parliament, and government. Of course, these were not always clearly delineated stages—in reality there was overlap and important interactions among them as the factions developed.

Establishing Seniority within the Factions and in Party, Parliamentary, and Government Posts

Three conditions were necessary for a seniority rule to be established as the norm in the LDP. The first was for the LDP to stay unified (not a foregone conclusion in the immediate years after the merger) and stabilize over time so that members could accumulate experience to become senior. The second was for the seniority rule to become established within the factions and then be applied to the party as a whole. The final condition was a rule that posts should be distributed based on seniority (Kawato 1996a, 936).

Factions in the early years of the LDP were not organized hierarchically as strictly by seniority as they later became (Kawato 1996b; Sveinsdóttir 2004, 71–172). One reason for this was the heterogeneous nature of the early LDP after 1955—a combination of "strange bedfellows": prewar politicians who often had served several terms in the Diet before and after the war, former bureaucrats recruited especially by former Prime Minister Yoshida (e.g., Eisaku Satō and Hayato Ikeda), and new politicians elected since the war. It would have been difficult to immediately establish a strict seniority system based on the number of times a leader was elected to the Diet when

many of the most senior and powerful LDP and faction leaders had less seniority than some of the new postwar politicians. By the late 1960s, once the
prewar politicians began to die or resign and former bureaucrats such as
Ikeda and Satō themselves became the leaders of increasingly coherent and
exclusive factions, a more hierarchical structure based on seniority began
to develop in the factions (Kawato 1996b).

The application of factional seniority to the LDP personnel structure
took even longer. In the first decade after 1955, the main division of the
party had been between the "mainstream" and "antimainstream" factions.
In this period after the formation of the LDP, the "mainstream" factions
tended to dominate the party and did not have to worry too much about
the "antimainstream" factions defecting because the party enjoyed such
a large majority in the Diet that the threat was not particularly credible.
The best and most important posts generally were given to old members
of the "mainstream" factions. Factional balance and the norm of giving
out cabinet positions and other posts based on the rough proportion of
the membership of a factions to the membership of all factions had not
been instituted yet, which resulted in often intense internecine conflict.
One of the most salient examples was the factional undermining of Prime
Minister Kishi's administration by intraparty machinations surrounding the
politics of the 1960 U.S.-Japanese Mutual Security Treaty (Bouissou 2001,
591; Packard 1966, 64–81).

The first move in this direction was toward factional balance in the cabinet posts rather than domination of the cabinet by the "mainstream" faction leaders. Some have put the origin of this norm in the early 1960s, with
full institutionalization in the late 1960s during Eisaku Satō's long tenure in
office (Satō and Matsuzaki 1986, 67; Kohno 1997, 97–98, 110–13; Ramseyer
and Rosenbluth 1993, 64; Sveinsdóttir 2004, 172). More extensive analysis, however, now indicates with fair certainty that the distribution of cabinet posts according to proportionally to factions was not really established
until the latter part of the 1970s (Kawato 1996a, 943; 1996b) and that in
some places it was not fully implemented even after 1980s (Bouissou 2001,
593–96). Only when factions had grown larger, as smaller factions disappeared or were incorporated into the larger ones (Kohno 1997, 107–9),
and the LDP share of seats was reduced by the late 1970s to a point at which
the defection of disgruntled factions might cost the LDP power, did the
party as a whole began to distribute posts according to seniority in the faction and roughly for factional balance (Kawato 1996b; Kohno 1997, 97–98).
With the possibility of factional defection that would deprive the party of
its majority, the most dominant coalition of factions (the Tanaka and Ōhira
lineages) gradually gave up its control over the office-distribution benefits
to preserve party stability and power (Bouissou 2001, 291).

The institutionalization of the distribution of other party, parliamentary,
and government posts was a similar story. Satō and Matsuzaki, in their seminal 1986 book about the LDP, identify three types of factional distribution

of these posts. The first was the "faction power proportionality" (*habatsu seiryokuhi*) method, according to which posts were distributed roughly proportional to the representation of the factions in the party. Examples included cabinet posts and the chairmanships of the LDP Executive Council (Sōmukai) and PARC. A second was the "factional representation" (*habatsu daihyō*) method, whereby each of the major factions furnished a representative. This characterized, for example, the deputy secretary-general (*fukukanjichō*) positions in the party and the vice chairs of PARC, the Executive Council, and the House of Councilors Members Committee (Sangiin Giin Sōkai). The third type of post distribution was the "all members participation" (*zenin sanka*) method, in which all LDP Diet representatives were at some time in their careers eligible by seniority rules for the posts of parliamentary vice minister (*seimu jikan*), PARC division chair (*seichōbukaichō*), and, prior to cabinet experience, Diet permanent committee chair (*kokkai jōnin iinchō*) (Satō and Matsuzaki 1986, 63–66). Satō and Matsuzaki see these methods as being institutionalized in the 1960s.

More recent and extensive scholarship by Kawato (1996a, 955), however, finds a very different time frame of institutionalization for all three types. His results strongly indicate that although the "all members participation" method of distribution was established relatively early in the post-1955 history of the LDP, the other two types were not consistently established (in other words, not institutionalized) until the Yasuhiro Nakasone cabinets of the early to mid-1980s.

John Hibbing (1999, 59) has indicated that a member's length of service in a legislative body *before* leadership positions are attained may be a better measure of institutionalization. If this is the case, then the career norms and patterns within the LDP were not fully institutionalized until the late 1970s at the earliest. The role of factions in personnel appointments in the party, parliament, and government did not originate early or evenly within the LDP; the process was checkered and did not settle into the pattern most analysts identify as the typical '55 system until the late 1970s or early 1980s. It is difficult to see how the SNTV electoral system, established in 1947, caused the institutionalization of this pattern in the role of the factions in personnel appointments.

Once factions eventually had developed into the exclusive, seniority-based, hierarchical personal leadership organizations that they did after the selection of the party president by election in 1956, there is no reason to assume that the methods of distributing posts by the various factions necessarily would be incompatible with another type of electoral system, for example, a SMD system. After all, the institutionalization of seniority-based methods for allocating legislative committee executive positions also developed in the U.S. House of Representatives over time (Polsby, Gallaher, and Rundquist 1969). Such a regularized system of career advancement tends to become decentralized in subparty or sublegislative units in countries where the parties themselves are decentralized in their vote-seeking and there is a high personal vote, in both SNTV or SMD systems (Epstein et al. 1997). The uniqueness of this important function of factions in Japan is not necessarily the way the task of making appointments is performed and institutionalized or the norms that govern it but, rather, the fact that the control over the implementation of these duties has been decentralized to units (the factions) within the party instead of being held within the parliament itself. And this, in turn, has more to do with the early LDP organizational consolidation of its competing and fractionalized leadership after the introduction of the party presidential election system than the existence of any particular form of electoral system.

Extending Factional Competition to Electoral Districts

We now turn our attention to the origins of some of the most important functions that factions performed for their members under that system: party endorsement, financial aid, other kinds of help to win elections, and help with constituency services once elected.

Factions did not start linking up to individual Diet members' electoral districts until after the introduction of the party presidential election and the beginning of the faction leaders' rivalry to expand and consolidate their factions. But link up they did. Between 1956 and 1960, when the newly formed LDP tried to organize local branches and train party activists to recruit new voters at the local level, national-level party factional competition and conflict, first of Liberals versus Democrats and then of "mainstream" versus "antimainstream" factions that now extended down to local assemblies, prevented these initiatives from succeeding (Adachi 1960; *Asahi Shimbun,* December 4, 1956, 1; *Asahi Shimbun,* January 8 [evening ed.], 1956, 1; *Asahi Shimbun,* December 29, 1958, 3). This pattern continued in the 1960s. In the 1960 election, some faction members changed factions to avoid running against a member of their own faction, and newspaper articles during this period reported that factional competition at the central party level had already been transplanted to regional politics (*Asahi Shimbun,* November 9, 1963, 1; *Asahi Shimbun,* August 29, 1970, 4). This indicates clearly that central LDP factional rivalry had extended into the electoral districts during the two decades after the founding of the LDP. As Hajime Tanaka, a first-term LDP representative from the Satō faction, said in 1970, to create, maintain, and activate kōenkai, "You have to get monetary support from party leaders, or the power of a faction" (quoted in *Asahi Shimbun,* September 26, 1970, 4).

Beginning with Kakuei Tanaka, factions also began to help Diet members perform constituency services. Tanaka referred once to his faction as a "general hospital" (*sōgō byōin*) (Satō and Matsuzaki 1986, 61; Reed 1992, 14) because so many types of experts and fixers in so many policy areas existed within the faction that these specialists could help their fellow faction members respond to any constituency problem or demand they received.

The pattern of the extension and institutionalization of the factions into the electoral districts due to intraparty factional competition became even greater later, in the 1970s. And factional competition grew fiercer than ever in the late 1970s because of the Daifuku War. In part because of the Lockheed Scandal (in which former Prime Minister Tanaka had been indicted for bribery a few years before), the LDP instituted a primary system among LDP grassroots members in a two-stage nomination process for the party president. After party members voted, a complex formula of prefectural votes would establish the two front-runners, who would then compete in a vote by LDP Diet members. Incumbent Prime Minister Takeo Fukuda, who supported the new primary system to make the LDP more open to the grassroots voter and to show that backroom faction deals would not completely determine the selection of the next prime minister, publicly stated that if he did not win the first-stage primary, he would step aside in favor of the winner.

This new system affected the LDP organization (see chap. 2). Party Secretary-General Ōhira quietly mobilized the kōenkai supporters of the members belonging to both his and the large Tanaka faction to vote for Ōhira. This included a massive increase in the channeling of funding from the factions to their members' kōenkai, much of it illicit (Tsurutani 1980, 853–56). As a consequence of this, factional conflict extended among the grassroots party members and party membership rose dramatically, by a factor of five, to over a million and a half members (Tsurutani 1980, 851–53). It was said that the Ōhira faction members brought the largest number of party entry application forms to their electoral districts (*Asahi Shimbun*, February 13, 1978, 1). To acquire new party members, the kōenkai were extensively used. Right after the LDP headquarters decided to introduce the primary, factional leaders ordered their kōenkai members to mobilize party members, evidently with specific membership goals. As one kōenkai official said, "We plan to make 20 percent of our kōenkai members join the party" (quoted in *Asahi Shimbun*, February 13, 1978, 1). As we have shown in chapter 2, Diet members were quite confident of their ability to deliver their grassroots organization for their faction leader (Tsurutani 1980, 853).

In short, this primary represented the "massification" of the factions by linking their role in the selection of the party leadership directly to the kōenkai. Factional bosses were even reported to be buying votes from the members of factional followers' kōenkai (*Asahi Shimbun*, August 26, 1978, 1; *Mainichi Shimbun*, October 23, 1978, 2; *Yomiuri Shimbun*, November 28, 1978, 2). According to a *Asahi Shimbun* newspaper survey, a majority of local assembly members said that over 70 percent of voters were influenced by factions when deciding for whom to vote (*Asahi Shimbun*, September 23, 1978, 1–2). Another poll showed that more than 90 percent of the kōenkai members of the Fukuda faction would vote for Fukuda, whereas 83 and 73 percent of the Ōhira and Tanaka factional supporters, respectively, would vote for Ōhira (*Asahi Shimbun*, November 10, 1978, 3). One observer criticized the undemocratic nature of the primary because most of the 1.5 million party members were just kōenkai members mobilized by factional followers. Masumi Ishikawa (1979), at the time a prescient young politician who later became a power in the LDP, acknowledged that he knew that factional politics would diffuse across the nation (Gotoda 1998, 369).

The result was a surprising first-stage win for Ōhira. Even though Fukuda probably could have won in the second-stage Diet member run-off, he adhered to his promise and stepped down as prime minister, allowing Ōhira to take his place. This led to protracted conflict and permanent bitterness between the Ōhira-Tanaka factions and the Fukuda faction, producing in 1980 the passage of a no-confidence resolution against the Ōhira cabinet when members of the Fukuda faction and others failed to show up for the vote (Reed 1992, 11; Tsurutani 1980, 857–59).

Even more important for our purposes, the mobilization of kōenkai members in the 1978 party presidential primary was the culmination of the institutionalization of the extension of the factions into the electoral districts (Tsurutani 1980, 856–57). From the late 1950s to the late 1970s, the factions at the center extended and consolidated their role in securing their members' reelection through help with nomination and funding to buttress their leader's chance to be prime minister. With the 1978 primary election, the direction of the connection became more directly two way, with the grassroots support of the kōenkai shaping the intraparty rivalry of the factions for the prime ministership at the center. The continuing linkage between the central factional rivalry and individual kōenkai competition in the electoral districts (which had begun with the mobilization of exclusive factions soon after the founding of the LDP) and the institutionalization of the role of the factions at all levels of LDP politics was now fully established. And, as in the allocation of posts, this process of institutionalization and adaptation was not completed until at least the 1970s. Once again, it was not the electoral system per se that created and institutionalized the factions but intraparty factional competition and leader and incumbent versus backbencher and challenger relations that were extended into the electoral districts and that adapted them to the electoral system over time.

There was also a consolidation of factions in the 1970s and a change in the way they funded their members. One catalyst of this consolidation of several small and medium-size factions into four or five large factions that dominated the LDP was Kakuei Tanaka and the attempt by his faction, after his indictment in the Lockheed Scandal in the mid-1970s, to extend its influence by recruiting new members to prevent any prime minister from coming to power without its support.

Another source of change in the number and size of the factions was the 1975 revision of the Electoral Funds Law, an attempt by Prime Minister Miki (who became the party leader in the wake of the Lockheed Scandal) to divert funding from the factions to the party as a whole. The unintended result of this law, however, was to provide incentives for individual Diet members to raise more funds (often with their faction leader's help) and to rely more on funding from local businesses instead of larger national corporations. The expectations that faction leaders should raise a great deal of funds continued as well, allowing the larger and more successful factions to expand their memberships and become larger still. By the 1980s, the middle and senior faction members, not just the faction leaders, were also supposed to be raising the money for the faction and for some of its more junior members (Curtis 1988, 83–84, 176–87; Köllner 2004, 93). In funding, as in the nomination and allocation of posts, the nature of the factions changed over time and did not become settled and institutionalized into the archetypical '55 system model until the late 1970s or early 1980s. Driving the process were the negative externalities of faction leaders and representatives who feared losing out to their rivals, who had made organizational gains through innovation, the existence of complementary institutions, and exogenous changes in the institutional rules of the game.

Did Factions Support Only One Candidate in a District?

The link between a faction and an election district candidate also raises an important question about the role that the electoral system played in the institutionalization of '55 system factions. One of the most common arguments for an electoral system explanation of development of the factions is the claim that members of the same faction tended not to compete against one another in the same electoral district, thus indicating that the intraparty competition stemmed from SNTV intra-electoral district competition. This argument is made by Thayer (1969, 35–36), for example, and more recently by Park (2001, 435). Even after the merger of the LDP in 1955, however, members of the same faction were still found running against one another in the same electoral district, something that we might expect would happen rarely if, in fact, factions were caused by intraparty competition in the districts. Furthermore, it was not until after the late 1960s, only *after* the factions had begun to develop into their present form and to move into electoral districts to help their members, that we find any movement toward the later factional norms of no more than one faction member per district and competition among members of different factions in the same electoral district.[4]

For example, between three-quarters and all of the factions elected more than one representative in at least one district in the first three elections (1958, 1960, and 1963) after the merger that created the LDP.[5] As figure 4.1 indicates, in these first three elections, between approximately 25 and

---

4. Satō and Matsuzaki (1986, 58) place the change in the late 1960s, but as our data show, even then a substantial proportion of the districts had more than one member of a faction competing against one another.

5. From data provided by Sveinsdóttir (2004, 199–209, including figs. 5-1 to 5-4), and recalculated by the authors.

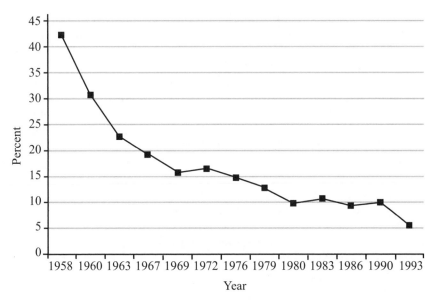

Figure 4.1 Districts with multiple LDP-endorsed candidates of same faction running, 1958–1993 (% of all districts with two or more LDP-endorsed candidates running)
Source: Calculated from data kindly provided by Steven Reed of Chūō University.

45 percent of election districts in which the LDP ran more than one member (which were nearly all the election districts in which the LDP ran a candidate) had more than one candidate from the same faction. That proportion dropped below 20 percent only with the 1967 election and continued to reach 15–20 percent through the 1976 election. By the 1979 election, 10 percent or fewer districts had more than two members of some faction competing; this low rate continued through the end of the '55 system in 1993.

But this analysis underestimates the number of multiple candidates in the same faction in a district because it does not count the conservative independents who did not receive the official LDP endorsement but who, nonetheless, received aid and support from a faction leader, promising to join the faction if elected. Naturally, this would all be done surreptitiously so that the faction leader would not be seen as putting his own factional interests above that of the collective interests of the party—which of course he was! As Reed and John Bolland (1999, 220) have indicated, factions do not have the same incentives as political parties to reduce the number of candidates they run. Unlike the parties, they are unlikely to split their own factional vote because voters do not vote based on the candidate's factional affiliation. Factions thus suffer few negative returns from at least trying to run multiple candidates, unlike a political party, which is likely to split its vote when the vote is based on party identification. For example, when Yoshirō Mori did not get the party endorsement in his first bid for office, he nonetheless went to Nobusuke Kishi, a faction leader, and asked him to come to his district to help. When Kishi agreed and Mori admitted that he did not have LDP endorsement, Kishi replied, "It doesn't matter" (quoted in Iokibe, Itoh, and Yakushiji 2007, 25). Indeed, if we include the independent candidates who were known to be supported by LDP factions, the percentage of districts with multiple candidates supported by the same faction is even greater, especially in the 1970s and 1980s. For example, between 1972 and 1990, including independents increases the average number of districts with multiple candidates by almost 50 percent (to an average of almost 15 percent instead of a bit over 10 percent; Nemoto, Pekkanen, and Krauss, unpublished paper, table 3).

The thesis that the development and origins of factional rivalry lies in the SNTV electoral district competition therefore does not hold up to scrutiny. If the intraparty electoral competition was the cause of factional competition, we would expect the pattern of one candidate per faction per district to be established much earlier than the late 1970s, thirty years after the electoral system was introduced! We think there is a better explanation, one that acknowledges the way that the factions adapted their competition to the electoral system, takes our data into account along with the entire historical development of the patterns of factional competition in the districts, and shows that factional competition drove electoral district competition rather than the other way around.

Why do we see both the largest number of and then the steepest reduction in districts where at least one faction fielded two or more members during the 1958–1963 period? One reason may be the post-1956 process in which faction leaders competed fiercely to recruit new members, whatever district they were from, creating the most multiple candidates from individual factions in 1958. Then, as factions solidified among the incumbent representatives and competition between the factions intensified after 1960, and as kōenkai also became institutionalized within the electoral districts, faction leaders sought to link their factions to those incumbents who could mobilize support in their districts to win, or appear as if they might win, and thus become faction members (Sveinsdóttir 2004, 210–12). And those who sought the nomination began to look to faction leaders to help them secure it or, if not successful at that, at least victory in the election (Sveinsdóttir 2004, 207–8).

A second reason may be that the decline in party nominations led to a limiting of the available candidacies that factions could compete for. For example, Gary Cox and Frances Rosenbluth (1994, 4–16) have shown that after 1958 there was a decline in the number of LDP candidates, particularly nonincumbents, nominated by the party to increase the likelihood of more efficiently maximizing LDP seat totals in the face of a gradual overall decline in the votes it could obtain. And this party policy began to be implemented by the LDP Electoral Strategy Committee (Senkyo Taisaku Iinkai) in 1958— thus the start of the decline in the districts with multiple endorsements of candidates by the same faction after 1960. As the number of endorsed candidates declined, the argument goes, it made less sense for the factions to try to run more than one of their members. They would have little chance of getting multiple nominations through the Electoral Strategy Committee. The reason for the pattern therefore was a combination of the factional cooperation for the collective benefit of the party to reduce the number of nominees over time as well as to preserve the advantages of incumbency and the continued factional competition that determined which factions would win more seats in this arrangement than others (Cox and Rosenbluth 1994, 13–14; 1996, 259–97). Only after 1976, when the LDP majority over the opposition parties became razor thin and there was greater pressure to avoid damaging *tomodaore* ("falling together"), do we see the factional redundancy rate in districts decline to the 10 percent level and below.

Recall, however, that because the party endorsement itself might not prevent factional candidate duplication the causes of decline may be more statistical. As the number of LDP candidates per districts declined, the probability of duplication would decline, even if factional candidate duplication were determined randomly. Even so, there was far more factional candidate duplication than we would expect statistically, given the number of candidates per district and the number of factions over time (Reed and Bolland 1999, 221–23). Therefore, although factional candidate duplication did decline over time, continuing duplication is not merely a statistical artifact. Clearly, there were other reasons for the factional duplication of candidates in districts than the electoral system.

For further clues to the manifestation of factional politics in the electoral districts, let us look at the patterns of candidate duplication for particular factions. Figure 4.2 shows the percentage of districts in each election in which each of the five major factions nominated more than one candidate as a proportion of all the districts (the vast majority) where the LDP nominated at least two candidates in that district. In the figure, the factions are labeled according to their leaders in the 1970s but represent a fairly consistent lineage through their successors. As we can see, the proportion of multiple nominations of faction members varied greatly over time and from faction to faction. Nevertheless, certain patterns stand out. First, as we might expect, the Miki and the Nakasone lineage factions, the two smallest lineages of the big five, were also the factions that consistently nominated multiple candidates in the fewest districts. Second, from 1972 to 1980, the Fukuda lineage faction nominated multiple candidates in the highest proportion of districts, attaining a high of almost 60 percent in 1972. In 1986, the Tanaka lineage faction surpassed it for that and the next election in 1990, before its percentage of districts declined precipitously and the Fukuda lineage faction made a large resurgence, with multiple candidates in up to almost 70 percent of the districts in 1993. The Ōhira lineage faction had fewer and less-steep peaks and valleys than the other two biggest factions, but it still shows peaks in 1963 and 1979, the latter of course around the time of the 1978 party primary election when Ōhira was surreptitiously trying to win over Fukuda.

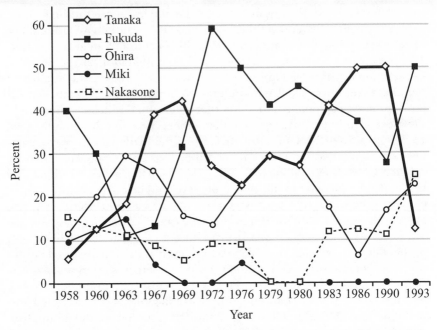

Figure 4.2 Districts in which each of the five major factions ran multiple candidates (including independent candidates), 1958–1993 (% of all the districts where the LDP nominated at least two candidates)
Note: The factions are labeled according to their leaders in the 1970s.

The SNTV electoral system naturally makes this intraparty factional competition in the districts possible—such competition among factions would probably have been intraparty and also interdistrict in a SMD system, unless manifested in a SMD during a party primary—but clearly cannot be responsible for these particular patterns for each faction. What might explain the pattern?

There are several possibilities. First, note that for each faction the major increases the proportion of districts in which it ran multiple candidates took place either around the time or right before the leader of the faction was prime minister. Thus, we see a large expansion in the percentage of districts for the Tanaka faction right before 1972, when Kakuei Tanaka became prime minister. This pattern can also be seen for:

- The Miki faction when Miki was prime minister (1974–1976).
- The Fukuda faction in the mid-1970s, right before Fukuda became prime minister (1976–1978).
- The Ōhira faction when Ōhira was prime minister (1978–1980).
- The Nakasone faction in late 1982, when Yasuhiro Nakasone took the position (1982–1987).

- The Tanaka faction in the late 1980s when Noboru Takeshita (then the faction leader) was prime minister (1997–1989).

Second, we might see a secondary expansion about the time these leaders served as secretary-general of the party, a post usually considered a major stepping stone to becoming prime minister. During 1961–1964 and 1976–1979, when the Ikeda-Ōhira lineage faction held the position, and during 1966–1968 when Fukuda occupied the post, we see sudden increases in the proportion of districts in which their factions supported multiple candidates. Indeed, Cox and Rosenbluth (1996, 259–97) find that nonincumbents in the secretary-general's faction were more likely to receive a party endorsement than nonincumbents from other "mainstream" factions. It may be that both the prime minister and secretary-general take advantage of their positions and are able to exert enough influence in the party to get more of their faction members nominated, including more of their faction members even in the same districts. Another possibility is that, in preparation for running for prime minister, faction leaders make special efforts to expand their factions by putting up multiple candidates in several districts where they think they can win those extra seats.

With our colleague Kuniaki Nemoto, we conducted an analysis (Nemoto, Pekkanen, and Krauss, n.p.) that shows some interesting results that can be used to test these and other hypotheses. Various conditions are correlated with a faction's having multiple candidates running in the same district. For example, districts in which the socialists or the CGP had an incumbent, smaller districts, and elections in which there was certainty about the results tended to have fewer faction multiple candidate endorsements. But when a faction had had a strong candidate in the district previously, raising the prospect of being able to shunt some of his or her votes off for another candidate, the faction was encouraged to run multiple candidates. In terms of our previous speculations, having a leader who was a serious contender for the next party president *did* make a faction more likely to endorse multiple candidates in districts; however, the post of secretary-general had no significant relationship. The competition for party president and prime minister seems very much to be behind the phenomenon of factions having multiple candidates running in the same districts. Finally, the presence of rival factions in a district mattered—factions were more likely to support multiple candidates in those districts in which similarly ambitious factions had strongholds. Once again, intraparty competition among leaders and their factions was the origin of the patterns we found.

Factions before the Reform

As we have seen, factions, both before and after the merger of the Liberals and Democrats to form the LDP in 1955, did not emerge in their final form primarily or directly as the result of the SNTV electoral system or as the straightforward rational choice of LDP party leaders directly in response to that system. Before the merger, the factions in the two smaller conservative parties were not at all like they were to become later. Indeed, they only began to assume their later pattern after the 1955 merger and the installation of the party presidential election system in 1956. Factions did not become institutionalized into the familiar Japanese factional archetype—controlling the distribution of party, parliamentary, and government posts and the electoral district nominations by strict seniority, establishing themselves as the arbiters of who became prime minister, and serving as major funding sources for the candidates—until much later, in many cases not until the late 1970s and early 1980s. This process was shaped all along by the LDP leaders, through their rivalry, competition, and conflict, some of which developed during the early postmerger period, and their incentives to institute greater control and consistency within their factions to enhance their chances of becoming prime minister. It was also shaped by their backbench members, who wanted to enhance their long-term career prospects in the party, Diet, and government.

The final form and function of the factions in the 1980s, at the height of the '55 system, could not have been anticipated, much less designed explicitly, by anyone, least of all the LDP leaders. Several leaders, including Takeo Miki in the early 1960s, when he headed the Organization Research Committee of the LDP (*Asahi Shimbun,* September 29, 1962, 2), and Takeo Fukuda in the late 1970s, when he was prime minister, attempted to eliminate the LDP factions but failed, much as some leaders had attempted to centralize vote mobilization in the local party branches rather than kōenkai (see chaps. 2–3).

Our analysis here casts serious doubt on many of the assertions about the factions that have been made by observers. First, clearly a cultural explanation for the origin and development of factions does not work at all. Japanese culture and social organization cannot explain the fact that political factions of this type did not really began until a decade *after* the war and right after the LDP merger and party presidential election; this could not have been a coincidence. Nor can the cultural explanation account for the factions' not attaining their ultimate '55 system form until almost thirty years after that. Unless the basic Japanese social organizational model fundamentally changed during this period (which would be a contradiction to the basic premise of this approach), we can exclude this explanation.

The effect of the SNTV electoral system is not as easily dismissed. As we have seen, the existence of kōenkai and the personal vote in the SNTV districts probably did have an effect on the form that the factions took, making them non-policy- and non-ideology-oriented. Faction leaders were able to offer incentives to candidates to join and stay in their faction, without regard to their compatibility with the policy views of the candidates, because the personal vote was more important in winning election and reelection.

Factions did play a major role in the politics of elections by helping their candidates gain the nomination and funds. And the new electoral system did weaken the factions because the intraparty competition of the SNTV disappeared as chapter 5 will show.

Yet, ultimately, the SNTV electoral system fails as a full or prime explanation for why and how the LDP factions developed. One problem with this explanation is the same as for the cultural explanation. The electoral system was a constant from 1947 to 1993, and yet the factions changed greatly during this time. They did not really attain even the beginnings of the ultimate '55 system form until after the LDP merger and party presidential election of 1955–1956, a decade after SNTV was reintroduced into Japan by the Occupation. Even prior to that, when they were separate parties under SNTV, both the Liberals and the Democrats ran multiple candidates in almost every district. As we have seen, the factions reached their archetypal form, developing their full roles in nomination, funding, and post allocation, only gradually during the 1970s. A constant cannot explain change.

Furthermore, as we have seen, the argument that, because of intraparty competition in the districts under SNTV, each faction always supported only one of its members in each district is not supported by our data. This type of specialization by the factions in districts also developed slowly during the thirty-five years after the imposition of the SNTV system and never completely developed even then.

As with kōenkai, the leaders of the LDP themselves did not seem to perceive the electoral system as the reason for the factions, as shown by the survey of leaders. Also, some leaders, such as Prime Minister Takeo Fukuda in the late 1970s, made sincere efforts to eliminate or weaken the factions by instituting a primary election in the selection process for the party leadership. Note that Fukuda did not attempt to change the electoral system to accomplish this goal. And this attempt to change the party leadership selection process only ended up linking the factions at the center more closely with the kōenkai in the districts rather than weakening the factions. It makes much more sense to see the electoral system as a contributing, or intervening, cause of the factional forms (but not of their origins or of their development).

What then are the primary variables creating the pattern of factional development in the LDP? Using the historical institutionalist model (chap. 1), we find the primary explanation for the origin of the LDP factions as exclusive nonpolicy groups with members loyal to a particular leader in the adoption by the LDP in 1956 of the election for the party president and in the changes that occurred to that selection system over time. Until 1956, faction leaders were primarily simply the most influential politicians in the party, leaders who could temporarily collect a group of fickle followers based on policy similarities or antipathy to another leader; they did not control post allocations or exercise power over nominations or provide a great deal of electoral funding.

Once these leaders began competing to gain a core constituency to fulfill their ambition to become the elected party leader and then the prime minister, the nature of the factions changed, becoming more exclusive. And the leaders began looking for ways to ensure that their followers belonged to only one faction and were persistently loyal to that leader. They then began to ferociously recruit more members into the faction and, after several years, to offer them incentives such as funds to use to get reelected. In 1978, when the party presidential selection system instituted a party primary, factions finally penetrated into the constituencies in a direct manner. Changes in the electoral funds law in the mid-1970s, which devolved funding tasks down the factional ladder from the leader, also altered the fundraising role of the factions.

Several factors affected the origin of the factions and the development of their shape, process, and functions over time. In this regard, institutional complementarity was important. Most obviously, the election of the party president by a ballot of mostly LDP Diet members was crucial to setting in motion the entire scramble for consistent loyalty among a leader's faction members. Another, less obvious, complementary institution were the kōenkai. If leaders were to maximize the number of their supporters, they could not limit faction membership because of policy or ideological compatibility; they were competing with Diet members, who relied on their kōenkai to mobilize the personal vote (which is not related to policy or ideology) for reelection. Thus, the factions became more diverse and based on neither policy nor ideology.

Note that, had a centralized party system of vote mobilization existed, it would have been much more difficult for the factions to offer much in the way of electoral support and to recruit members and maintain their loyalty. Conversely, when the primary election for the party president was introduced in the late 1970s, had the kōenkai not existed, this new first stage in the process for choosing the party president might well have helped to undermine the factions; instead, it revitalized them by linking them to the grassroots.

Sequencing may be important too; there were signs of this in the earlier premerger factions. It may not be a coincidence that both factions and kōenkai really blossomed in the 1956–1958 period—both leaders and rank-and-file Diet members were simultaneously searching for ways to maximize recruits and votes. For the leaders, new recruits to their increasingly exclusive factions became necessary after the 1956 party presidential selection system was instituted; for the Diet members, increasing their personal vote became more necessary after the 1955 LDP merger pitted former Liberals and Democrats against one another in the same district under the same party label, making the party label and party leadership irrelevant to differentiating themselves. This simultaneous institution of new incentives made their linking up through factions for mutual benefit more likely and thus put factions on to the path to the form that they eventually developed.

Part of another key sequence occurred in the 1956 party presidential election, when Ishii threw his support to Ishibashi in the first real competitive election process. This ensured that the prereform parties would not become the basis for factional coalitions. Imagine if Ishii had supported his prior party colleague Kishi instead. Factional coalitions from that point on may well have formed based exclusively on their leader's previous party affiliation. Almost simultaneously, factions began the quest for loyal and exclusive members without regard to their previous party affiliation. Had the hardening of factional loyalty occurred before the factional coalitions with previous party rivals, coalitions might have been based more on premerger party affiliation.

Finally and perhaps most important in this situation, the competitive advantages for both leaders and members helped stimulate the formation of the factions as faction leaders began to insist on exclusivity after the 1956 party presidential election to gain a relative advantage over their competitors. In exchange, they promised benefits such as funds for elections, support for their members' kōenkai, and help to first-time candidates in securing the nomination in that district. Any faction leader who did not do the same would not have been able to compete for the party presidency with those who had formed exclusive and loyal factions.

What really institutionalized and perpetuated the factions over time, however, were the penalties that were gradually imposed on those who were not members of factions. Eventually, as seniority became institutionalized within the factions over a couple of decades, negative externalities (costs) for LDP representatives who did not join a faction became even worse because over time most of their colleagues did join. Due to factional control over the allocation of posts, as the factions tightened their grip on the nomination process and more and more Diet members became enmeshed in this system, the costs of remaining aloof became severe. Deprived of financial and other support in elections; of any chance of access to the best party, parliamentary, or government posts; and of information and aid on policy matters, those who were not faction members were at a severe disadvantage; only the very stalwart or foolhardy could afford not to join.

By the early 1980s, the factions were embedded within an institutional matrix with the kōenkai of individual Diet members and, within the party, with party, parliamentary, and government positions. Because the asset specificity of the investments of both the faction leaders and their followers has become so great and the social contracts within the factions have become so strong, this system of factional competition is stabilized internally within the faction and externally among them, making alternative possibilities for institutional adaptation almost impossible without a major external shock (Pierson 2004, 148–53). This shock was provided by the electoral reform of 1994.

Chapter 5

Factions Today

Once upon a time it was enough for a prime minister to win over five or six main faction leaders and they could deliver the support of their henchmen. Now henchmen don't hench so easily.
Ronald Dore (2004)

It's factions, eh? They're responsible for the distribution of committee and then [PARC] division [posts]; it's all factions.
Interview M (July 4, 2002)

As with all other perceived iniquities of the '55 system, the factions were a prime target of the electoral reform and campaign finance reform that passed the Diet under the reforming coalition in 1994 (Curtis 1999, 142; Christensen 1994). The new hybrid electoral system was supposed to do away with factions or severely weaken them on the assumption that factions would wither away absent intraparty competition in the districts. The campaign finance reform provided a second attack on factions by making it illegal to contribute directly to factions at all after a five-year phase-in period and by attempting to channel all contributions, now more limited as to amount and source, to political parties and to one individual candidate's fund-raising organization (Christensen 1996, 56–57).

For years, both journalists and scholars had expected the change to an SMD system alone would lead to the demise of factions because they assumed that the electoral system was the progenitor of the factions, especially when combined with a campaign finance reform of this nature. Thus, as early as the 1960s, Japanese newspapers such as *Asahi Shimbun* predicted that the factions would vanish with an electoral system change (*Asahi Shimbun*, February 14, 1966, 2; Cox, Rosenbluth, and Thies 1999, 41; Thayer 1969, 141). And political scientists assumed that factions existed or persisted only (Ramseyer and Rosenbluth 1993, 59) or primarily (Kohno 1992, 385–91) because of the need to divide the vote and the electoral incentives under the SNTV electoral system. LDP officials also expected an end to the factions. "With the abolition of the medium-sized electoral district, there would be a single LDP candidate in 300 districts, and factions were expected to dissolve" (Mabuchi 2001, 202).

Despite this, they still existed in 2009, a full decade and a half after the reforms, although after the huge LDP election loss in August 2009 there have been calls for the complete abolition of factions. Whether this will occur remains to be seen. Even so, the factions continued, albeit in weakened form, long after electoral reform should have buried them.

Note that the intellectual puzzle here is not that the factions lost many of their functions and much of their importance. Rather, the puzzle is that factions continue to exist at all, much less continue to perform any important function. From an electoral determinist standpoint, this is inexplicable.

In retrospect, we can hardly fault the forecasters for these predictions and explanations; they are both rational and reasonable *if* we start with the assumption that the electoral system itself caused the factions and shaped their nature. As the effect of the reforms became clearer over time, however, many political scientists, some of them the same ones who earlier had predicted the demise of factions, have conceded the continued existence of factions while also arguing that factions have been fundamentally transformed from their pre-1993 functions (see Thies 2002; Cox, Rosenbluth, and Thies 1999; Christensen 1994, 603–4). Here, we confirm these postreform analyses. Factions have not completely withered away, despite the electoral change; but their role has changed.

Perhaps the best way to approach an explanation of why factions have persisted and how they have changed and the implications of these developments is to use as a framework the four major roles that the factions performed for members and leaders after being institutionalized under the '55 system. Recall that factions prior to the electoral and campaign finance reforms played three major roles for the faction members:

1. Electoral/nominations: getting nominations for new candidates they wanted to run in a district and making sure their incumbents were renominated.
2. Electoral/funding: providing part of the funding that incumbent and new candidates needed to maintain their kōenkai and run their election campaigns.
3. Managing careers/posts: negotiating with representatives from other factions for party, parliamentary, and government posts for their members, with seniority determining eligibility for particular posts.

A fourth, but secondary, role was constituency response, for example, providing information or aid from fellow faction members when a representative had requests or demands from constituents for which she did not have the expertise or contacts to develop an adequate response.

There was only one major role that the factions performed for their leader—providing a stable, reliable core support of LDP representatives with whom the leader could bargain, with other faction leaders, to try to attain a winning coalition to become party president and prime minister.

Factions and the Election of Members

Let us deal with the two electoral roles first. To a very large extent, after the 1994 reforms, factions lost their importance in helping candidates in elections, first, for the district electoral nominations and, second, with money. In the SMD electoral system, any party consistently denying its one incumbent district representative renomination was committing political suicide over time. So, the only possible roles for factions regarding nomination might be (1) to secure a nomination to challenge an opposition party incumbent in a district; (2) to try to secure for new candidates a place in an electoral district where the incumbent had died or retired; and (3) to help get a higher place on the party PR list for one of its members, thus enhancing his or her chances of getting elected that way.

For the first possibility, however, the dual nomination and "best loser" provisions of the new system mean that, in districts where an opposition party has an incumbent, there is usually already a good LDP candidate who had challenged previously but lost and was still returned from the PR list. The party is more likely to give that person the chance in the district again because he or she probably has name recognition, has been able to do constituency services in the district as a PR incumbent representative, and probably has been preparing for a candidacy again with funding and other contacts. In short, they are "PR incumbents in waiting" for an SMD seat.[1]

Indeed, as we shall see (in chap. 6), the LDP has even adapted its personnel appointment strategies to party, parliamentary, and government positions to provide just such dual-listed PR winners (sometimes called "zombies") with positions with which they can also provide political pork to districts in the regions they represent to prepare the way for eventually winning in their old SMD district (Pekkanen, Nyblade, and Krauss 2006). So even in districts where a vacancy is created, there is usually a ready-made candidate in the wings.

The second possibility, an incumbent dying or retiring, may present the best chance for factions to play some role in securing a seat for a member. Even here, however, with the increasingly large number of hereditary politicians in the LDP who can "inherit" their relative's kōenkai and reputation in the district (Smith 2009), in many cases it is likely that the progeny or close relation of the previous incumbent (who is likely to be from the same faction anyway) will have had the inside track for the new nomination.

---

1. We should note, however, that after the LDP's epic 2009 defeat, its future nomination process and strategies remain to be seen as there are many fewer incumbents but many more former representatives.

Any ability of the factions to influence their members' getting on the PR list or how they are ranked on the list seems to be progressively disappearing as well. We do know that a large proportion of slots for the LDP PR candidates have been reserved for those who also run in the SMDs. For example, in 1996 there were forty-nine representatives elected on the LDP PR list who were not also dual listed (i.e., elected as purely PR representatives), but in 2000 that number dropped to thirty and in 2005 to twenty-six. In the 2009 election, purely PR candidates won only nine seats out of the thirty-seven listed. On the other hand, 64 of the 269 dual-listed candidates won in their local districts, and 47 had to settle for a PR seat. And a majority of the dual-listed candidates were either ranked number 1 or 2 on the PR list: 40 percent were ranked number 1 on the list and another 17 percent number 2.[2]

Other signs of the waning of factional influence in even PR nominations came in the 2005 election. In this election, Prime Minister Jun'ichirō Koizumi faced the challenge of "rebels" from within his own party voting against his pet postal reform bill and then kicked them out of the party. It was Isao Iijima, his top close political aide, and party Secretary-General Tsutomu Takebe who handpicked the new candidates to challenge the "rebels" in their own district. They determined the rankings themselves, often to disgruntlement from others on the list (and undoubtedly from their factions), who found themselves with a lower ranking than they otherwise might have had (source close to Koizumi, pers. comm., September 10, 2005). Factions and local party federations did seem to reassert themselves in determining PR rankings before the 2009 LDP debacle, however.

Finally, in preparation for the 2009 general election, the LDP Election Strategy Committee decided in December 2007 that the party would limit even further the number of purely PR candidates and that all candidates who were dual-listed would be ranked at the same level on the PR lists ("LDP's 'Koizumi Kids' Won't Get Preference," *Yomiuri Shimbun* online, December 13, 2007). Thus, although there may be exceptions to this general rule, all the obstacles to the factions' having influence in nominations for the small districts now also applied increasingly to PR district nominations. It is no wonder, therefore, that some analysts have argued that after reform factions did not play any significant role in determining nominations, either for SMDs or the PR lists (Cox, Rosenbluth, and Thies 1999, 42–43).

In terms of funding, even before the new electoral system was instituted, the role of factions in directly providing money to their members for their elections and kōenkai already had declined—candidates were making their own connections with business to raise funds directly, although those connections were often made with the help of the faction leader (Curtis 1988, 175). The new campaign regulations that first limited and now forbid contributions to any organization except the party further undermined the financial role of the factions in Diet members' elections.

2. Data from J-LOD.

Our more recent interviews with LDP Diet members confirm that they no longer saw the factions as relevant for any sort of electoral help. One former prime minister told us:

> In the age of the old medium-sized district system, factions had several functions. One was money; one more was endorsement; one more was posts, personnel power, eh?; one more was an information network. After it became the small district system, and after that various reforms, it can be said that factions have just about no relation to either money or endorsements and thus posts and information are the remaining functions. (Interview O, July 11, 2002)

Even when it comes to the rankings of candidates on the PR list, on which we would expect factions to have an interest in how their members are ranked, it appears that their role is not as large as expected. According to the same former prime minister, "In deciding on the rankings, it's generally the party executives who decide, and factions in this case are going to help but generally in the case of the order of PR list, it's naturally being decided by things such as number of times elected or influence in the Diet" (Interview O, July 11, 2002). Almost all of those we interviewed after this interview had the same negative view of the roles of the factions in elections after the reform, but very few went as far as the former cabinet minister who said simply, "Their roles have already completely changed. If I say it even further—their roles have disappeared, haven't they?" (Interview SS, October 29, 2008).

This brings us to the remaining two functions: the allocation of posts and mutual support in responding to constituents' demands that the individual representative has neither the expertise nor the contacts to accomplish. These remain fairly viable and important roles for the factions.

Factions and the Allocation of Posts

Factions remained very important in post allocation and thus in career advancement: "the final role of factions—post allocation—seems to have survived intact" (Reed and Thies 2001b, 393). Our interviews also confirmed others' contentions (Thies 2002; Cox, Rosenbluth, and Thies 1999; Krauss and Pekkanen 2004) that this is the one area that still provides incentives to belong to a faction.[3] One LDP Diet member succinctly put it this way:

> So the function of factions now is personnel only. It's the faction that recommends a minister, or me to my past committee. However, Mr. Koizumi didn't do factional nominations for minister; even so, for vice-minister and secretary,

---

3. Cox, Rosenbluth, and Thies (1999) also stress the party management functions of the factions, which they also continue to perform.

it was still faction recommendations. Therefore, it was a really incomplete reform. After that the factions decided all the PARC research committees and divisions and so forth. Thus ultimately only this personnel power is the reason for the continuance of factions now. (Interview G, December 11, 2001)

Several Diet members described and gave examples of the actual process by which faction representatives determined the various posts. For example, the Diet Affairs Committee deputy chairs (*kokkai taisaku-fukuiinchō*) all came from the factions and bargained among themselves and also with the equivalent leaders of the other parties to settle the specific distribution of Diet committee posts. They further elaborated on how the LDP vice secretary-generals (officially, the acting secretary-generals; *fuku-kanjichō*) horse-traded and settled among themselves the division chairs and vice chairs of the PARC, as well as the personnel over one hundred special, issue, and research committees (*tokubetsuiinkai; mondai iinkai; chōsakai*) so that their factional Diet members can go to their constituents bearing many titles in the policymaking apparatus of the party (Interview M, July 4, 2002; Interview T, December 6, 2001; Interview C, December 7, 2001).

One veteran political journalist gave us a graphic look into the process of negotiation among faction representatives for posts:

> For the PARC, Diet, and subcabinet government posts, here's how it works. There are *meibō*, produced by the factions. There isn't one meeting, but the faction representatives take turns coming into the room, making phone calls to the *kanjichō shitsu,* etc. to decide the outcome along with the secretary-general or the vice secretary-general. The *kanjichō shitsu* is where the lists are handed in and calls made, meetings held, etc. for PARC, Diet, and government posts—all of them. It is the number two or number three person from the faction who goes in. Factions all have different names for these positions, but it is this senior number two person who goes in. Factions don't just present the lists once, but many times—there's a lot of back and forth. Sometimes the factions ask for specific posts for the Diet member, citing his or her expertise. Sometimes, they just say "vice minister" or whatever post and leave it at that. Typically, the final list is accepted *in toto* by the prime minister. (Interview TT, October 7, 2007)

Some LDP representatives are quite objective about the process and see the factions' determining the posts as having both positive and negative consequences:

> The "plus/minus" of factions, when it comes to doing personnel accurately among 347 Diet members, is having about five groups like factions first choosing among these. Coordinating like this I think in a certain sense is a rational way of handling it.... This is the merit of factions. The minus is that it becomes rather arbitrary. Depending on the faction, there are factions who do personnel well and those that don't. People who belong to a faction that does

it well are going to get the appropriate posts, eh? Well, they're going to get them unconnected to ability. (Interview A, June 27, 2002)

In the early 2000s, the most vivid testimony to the continued power of the factions in determining the distribution of party and Diet posts, and thus the career trajectories of LDP representatives, came from those who were not members of a faction and thus were discriminated against in the allocation of positions, rarely getting their preferred posts: "I'm not in a faction. The way someone got put into those committees was completely from factional order, and ultimately the nonfaction guys are put into what's left. So, since no one wanted X and Y committees, since there wasn't anyone, in the end I was diverted into these. Well, there's nothing I can do about it" (Interview N, July 9, 2002). Despite this assessment, it turned out that there was something he could do about it—when we met him again a few years later, he had joined a faction.

Factions may have lost many of their roles and functions in nominations and financing, in part because of the new electoral system, but it is no wonder that an LDP party executive intimately involved in this process can tell us that "the function that remains the most is 'posts'" (Interview J, July 1, 2002). In this way, factions have retained their considerable influence over the party, parliamentary, and government (below the cabinet level) career paths of their members.

Factions and Response to Constituents

As we have noted, Kakuei Tanaka considered a faction to be a "general hospital" because its collection of "specialists" in various policy sectors could help one another when constituents wanted something not in the specialized area of their representative; is this still true postreform?

To test this, we looked at members of all factions prereform, at the height of the '55 system (1982–1993), and all factions' members postreform (1996–2007) to determine which percentage of the faction were zoku giin (policy tribe representatives or veteran policy specialists) Diet Members within a particular policy sector. (See chap. 6 for more about zoku giin.) Suffice it to say, for now, that the term refers to those Diet members who have spent enough of their careers in the LDP on PARC divisions, Diet committees, and in cabinet and subcabinet posts to have developed both great expertise and contacts with bureaucrats and interest groups in that policy sector.

We analyzed an eleven-year period both pre-and postreform. Figures 5.1 and 5.2 show the percentage of the members of each of the five major factions who were zoku giin in each policy sector (these reflect the organization of Diet committees, PARC divisions, and bureaucratic ministries and agencies that parallel one another) among House of Representatives members, pre- and postreform. These data should give us an idea of whether and which factions are specializing after electoral reform.

We found, first, that in general there is a fairly consistent average of 3 percent of the membership of each faction who were such policy experts during the prereform period. In the postreform period until the LDP's 2009 defeat, both the extent and the range—4–6 percent—increased. This may not be surprising considering that more LDP representatives who made the transition from prereform to postreform now have had time to accumulate more experience and time in particular posts in a policy area.

But even a quick glance at figures 5.1 and 5.2 also shows that not only was the proportion of zoku giin representatives in each faction larger after the reform but that factions seem to have been concentrating in fewer policy areas more intensively.[4] For example, when we examine the number of upper bars in the graph (representing a higher-than-average percentage of zoku giin in the factions in the policy areas), we find that prereform there were forty-two such cases; however, postreform there were only thirty-two. On the other hand, the number of cases of in which percentage of zoku giin in the factions in the various policy sectors was below the average of their counterparts increased postreform. Taking as an example the Tanaka lineage factions, we see that, whereas prereform it was truly a "general hospital" with a greater concentration of veteran policy specialists in ten areas than the other factions, after reform it had more specialized and surpassed its rival factions in only five sectors. Similarly the Fukuda lineage factions went from surpassing the other factions in terms of specialized members in fourteen areas to surpassing them in only eight. The Miki faction was most specialized both pre- and postreform, although it too becomes more concentrated after the reform; this is because, as the smallest faction, a larger proportion of its members are zoku giin.

To make sure that our data represent a real concentration (specialization) in fewer policy areas after reform, we also used one more measure. The Herfindahl-Hirschman Index (HHI) is a standard measure used by economists and the U.S. government of the concentration of industry in sectors, for example, for antitrust cases.[5] The results are shown in figure 5.3. As we can see, all the factions, and even nonfaction independents, specialized more after the electoral reform, at least as measured by the policy areas in which their share of zoku giin is greater than that of the other factions. If the Tanaka faction and other factions can be considered "general hospitals" prior to electoral reform, it appears that most of the

4. The increased specialization of the factions can be seen, too, in the standard deviations. The smaller the standard deviation, the more the number of factions is concentrated around the mean of policy areas; the larger the standard deviation, the more the sample is dispersed. In other words, each faction seems to specialize in different policy sectors. Because the standard deviations generally increased in the postreform period, this too indicates that factions today specialize in specific areas, distinct from other factions.

5. For more details and an explanation of this measure and its use in determining industry concentration, see http://www.justice.gov/atr/public/guidelines/horiz_book/15.html; http://www.justice.gov/atr/public/testimony/hhi.htm (accessed September 23, 2009). The HHI basically finds the share of the overall market of all the units competing in the market and then sums them.

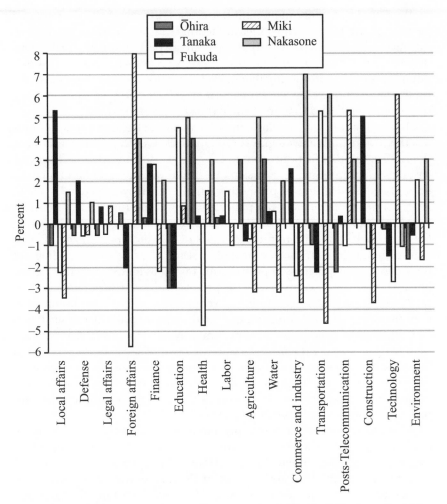

Figure 5.1 Differences between the average percentages of zoku giin in the five major LDP factions by division, prereform
Source: Analysis of 1972–1993 Meisuikyō data. Data for 1967 and 1969 from Masumi (1995 [1985]), 481) using Kōmei Senkyo Renmei survey results reported in Nenpō Seijigaku (1977, 295).

major faction lineages have, postreform, become "specialty clinics" (*senmon shinryōjo*).

Why do we find more division of labor among the factions after reform, with each concentrating more in some policy areas than others? In the prereform period, as each faction member tried to specialize in either a geographical part of the district or a policy sector to differentiate him- or herself from the other members of his party in the district, the division of labor among specialties was more within each faction, thus the "general

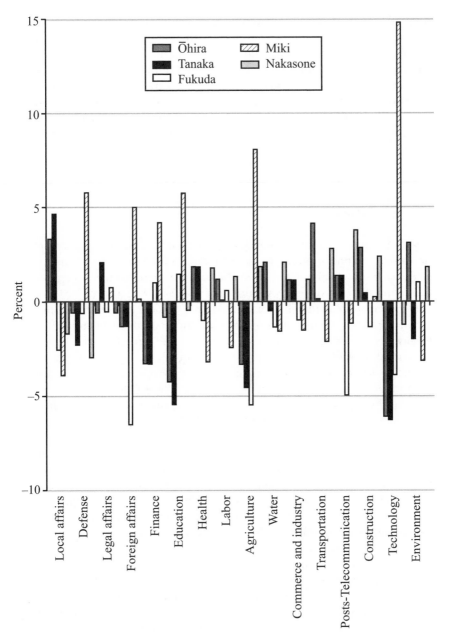

Figure 5.2 Differences between the average percentages of zoku giin in the five major LDP factions by division, postreform

Source: Analysis of 1972–1993 Meisuikyō data. Data for 1967 and 1969 from Masumi (1995 [1985]), 481) using Kōmei Senkyo Renmei survey results reported in Nenpo Seijigaku (1977, 295).

hospital" label. With the introduction of the SMD, specializing in a particular policy area became less important than being a generalist because a member has to respond to a wider variety of demands in the whole district. As a result, more faction members specialized in the sectors that were more important to most of the constituents in their districts and from which they could bring home political pork for the whole district (such as in education, agriculture, transportation, and construction) or the faction members gained the liberty to specialize in policy areas that were important to them or that they believed important to the nation as a whole (such as defense, and science and technology).

Changing Factions Today

The consequences of these changes for the factions and for the party are significant. Most important, because factions can no longer perform as many roles for their members, loyalty to the factions seems to have considerably weakened. Several of our respondents emphasized that loyalty to factions and the personal leadership of the old-time faction bosses that inspired it has disappeared; "Different from the past, there are many factions that lack loyalty," as one of our interviewees (Interview E, December 2001) put it.

The result is obvious in both the cohesion of the factions and the ability of faction leaders to count on their members' support and their faction to help them become prime minister. First, as figures 5.3–5.4 show, after the reform, the five major factions began splitting up. As of 2007, ten factions had emerged from those five (but see Park 2001, 444); in addition two (the Koga and Tanigaki factions) later merged, so there were nine, and more nonfaction members also subsequently joined factions. Second, although the largest faction was the Mori-Machimura faction, part of the Fukuda faction lineage, the second largest group in the party was actually the nonfaction group, not another faction (see figure 5.4). This gives us an indication of the extent to which both factional membership and loyalty to a faction have declined since the reform and Koizumi.

The loss of strict loyalty to the faction leader after the reform has also extended to votes in the party presidential elections, the original and still one of the major reasons for factions to exist. After the reform, however, faction leaders may be able to bring along a majority of their members to vote for a presidential candidate who they wish to win, but not always all their members. Indeed, the race for party president and thus prime minister is far more fluid and not always under the control of faction leaders since the reform.

The year after the 1994 electoral reform, for example, Ryūtarō Hashimoto defeated Yōhei Kōno with the support of LDP backbenchers (Thies 2002, 49–55). In 1998, the Keizō Oōbuchi faction ran two candidates: Keizō Obuchi himself and Seiroku Kajiyama. Most dramatically, in 2001 Jun'ichirō

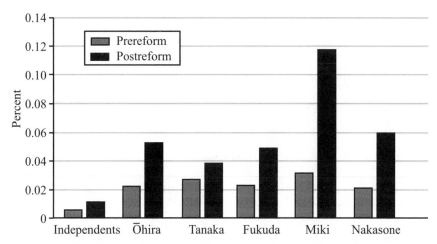

Figure 5.3 Degree of zoku giin specialization in the five major LDP factions, pre- and post-reform, using the Herfindahl-Hirschman Index (HHI)
Source: Analysis of 1972–1993 Meisuikyō data. Data for 1967 and 1969 from Masumi (1995 [1985]), 481) using Kōmei Senkyo Renmei survey results reported in Nenpo Seijigaku (1977, 295).

Koizumi won the party presidency even though the faction bosses were lined up behind another candidate—ironically, Hashimoto this time.

Some Japanese journalists see the selection and administration of the post-Koizumi LDP prime ministers—Shinzō Abe, Takeo Fukuda, and Tarō Asō—as a reversion to the factional political game of the '55 system. In fact, they represent a continuation and manifestation of the changes in factions that we have discussed. Let us look at the selection process of these leaders.

Shinzō Abe was not selected in 2006 as successor to Jun'ichirō Koizumi as a result of his becoming a faction leader through seniority and then cobbling together a winning minimum winning coalition by alliances with one or two other faction leaders through backroom deals. If he had, this would have epitomized the process we have seen under the '55 system; instead, he was chosen through a very different process.

The LDP prefectural vote now plays a much greater role in selecting the LDP president than previously, when each prefecture received only two votes (often influenced by the dominant LDP faction in that district) each. It played an important role, for example, in bringing Jun'ichiro Koizumi to power in 2001, even when he probably would have lost the subsequent vote, taken solely among LDP Diet members (Ehrhardt 2004). Although a similar situation has not arisen since 2001 because the prefectural and Diet member votes have been cast mostly for the same candidate, note that a major factor in the selection of Abe, Fukuda, and Asō was the prefectural votes (Park and Vogel 2007, 30). Even when the LDP has a super-majority in

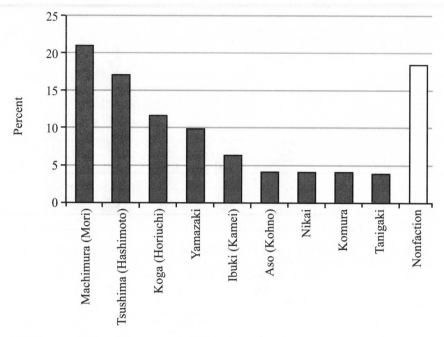

Figure 5.4 LDP factions, 2007 (% of LDP Diet members)

the House of Representatives, as it had in 2007 when Fukuda won the LDP presidential race, prefectural representatives still have approximately one-quarter of all the votes with many of the prefectures holding party member primaries to determine how their representatives will vote (*Yomiuri Shimbun* Online, September 19, 2007), and often their voting results, if consistently for one candidate, can influence how Diet members will vote. After the 2009 election loss, in the September 28, 2009, party presidential election, prefectural party representatives actually outnumbered LDP Diet members by a ratio of 3:2 because so many Diet members had lost their seats in the election ("Shunted Aside LDP Starts Presidential Election," *Asahi Shimbun* Online, September 18, 2009).

Second, faction leaders are no longer the chief contenders for the position. Not since Yoshirō Mori in 2001 has the leader of a major faction been a leading candidate for the position of party president, and none of the successful winners has been. Koizumi, Abe, and Fukuda were not faction leaders, and Tarō Asō became the leader of his small faction only after it split off from the Mori faction a couple of years before he ran and finally won in 2008.

Third, and perhaps most important, as an indicator of how much the selection process is no longer driven by factional bargaining, the faction leader does not even determine how his faction members will vote. An interesting case is the selection of Fukuda in 2007, when eight of the ten

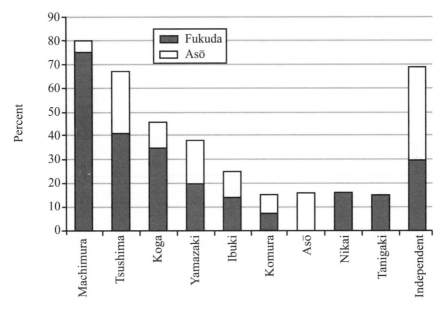

Figure 5.5 Party presidential election votes for candidates by factions, 2007 (%)

faction leaders announced their support for Fukuda versus Asō, his main opponent at the time. Yet a glance at figure 5.5 shows that only Asō's small faction and two other equally small ones (of about fifteen members) delivered all their votes to one of the candidates. All the others, including the independents' group, were split, some nearly 50–50, between the two candidates once the voting took place.

In 2007, faction leaders no longer controlled their members' votes or their bargaining deals the outcome, a far cry from the way the '55 system determined the LDP prime minister by the party. The outcomes of all the party presidential elections since Koizumi were determined by transfactional coalitions of members driven in large part by which leader was seen as most likely to help the party. Factions still counted in influencing who becomes prime minister, but they were no longer the whole game.

The ability of the factions to control the distribution of all the important posts has also diminished. Prime Minister Koizumi refused to allocate the most important posts of all, the cabinet ministers, with regard to the factional balance. This move was cited in some polls of voters as one major reason for his extremely high popularity (Shinoda 2003, 23–24). Although satisfying some of the major factions remained a priority of prime ministers since reform, the institutionalized norm of factional balancing in proportion to the factions' weights among Diet members has weakened since electoral reform. Abe, Fukuda, and Asō all announced that they were not going to use factional balancing in their cabinet appointments.

Indeed, a study we conducted with Benjamin Nyblade, based on all cabinet appointments before the electoral reform (1980–1993) and after the electoral reform (1996–2005) (Pekkanen, Nyblade, and Krauss, n.p.),[6] found that during the 1980–1993 period factional proportionality (measured by the proportion of the members of a faction in the cabinet to their proportion among the LDP House of Representatives Diet members) ranged from 84 to 91 percent. Most of the remaining disproportionality can be attributed to the fact that there were only twenty-one portfolios in each cabinet, so perfect proportionality was unlikely. In contrast, in 1996–2005 only one cabinet—Obuchi's first—ascended even to the low end of this range (85 percent). The bulk of the proportionality scores were between 60 and 80 percent after the reform. The average proportionality dropped from 87 percent in the prereform period to 74 percent in the postreform period. Thus, it is not just Koizumi's ignoring of the factions in choosing his cabinets but a consistent weakening of adhering to the factional proportionality norm across all postreform prime ministers (Pekkanen, Nyblade, and Krauss, n.p.).

In figure 5.6, the trend line indicates that giving cabinet portfolios based on the proportional strength of the factions has continued to decline compared to earlier postreform prime ministers. Prior to Koizumi, proportionality (where 100 percent is perfect proportionality) averaged well over 80 percent, with four cabinets exceeding 90 percent. Since Koizumi (not shown in figure 5.6), 80 percent has been the upper limit with only one cabinet (Fukuda's second) exceeding that, and with four cabinets with percentages between 60 and the low 70s.

The same is true for seniority at the cabinet level—in the prereform period entrance into the cabinet before a member's sixth term was rare, but in the postreform period, even fourth- and fifth-term veterans were likely to be included. And instead of factional proportionality and balance, women, non-Diet member policy experts, and politicians who had relatives who had been in the cabinet in previous years (hereditary politicians)[7] were much more likely to be in postreform than prereform cabinets. In the case of women, this increase was not just because there had been a vast increase in the number of women in the Diet since the reform. Comparing a woman's and a man's chances of being in a postreform cabinet to the proportion of women and men in the Diet shows that a woman's chance was almost five times that of her male counterparts (Pekkanen, Nyblade, and Krauss, n.p., 20–22). Figure 5.7 displays these trends by cabinet in the postreform era. As we can see, there are variations depending on the prime minister and the cabinet, magnified by the fact that after 2001 the size of the cabinet

---

6. The study excludes Mori's first cabinet because Mori ascended to become prime minister on Obuchi's death and did not reshuffle the cabinet.

7. *Seshū-giin* is the generic term for politicians who have relatives who were previously Diet members; they are also called *nisei giin* (second-generation politicians), although some are third- and even fourth-generation Diet members.

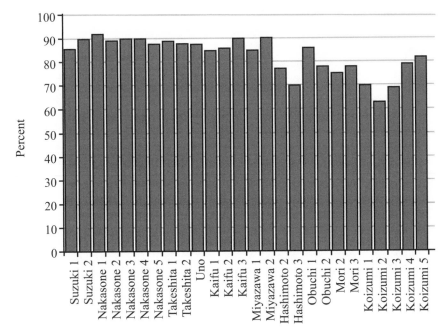

Figure 5.6 Pre- and postreform cabinet faction proportionality indexes (%)
Source: J-LOD.
Note: Prereform = from Suzuki 1 (1980) to Miyazawa 2 (1993). Postreform = from Hashimoto 1 (1996) to Koizumi 5 (2006). Perfect proportionality is 100 percent; perfect disproportionality is 0 percent. The index measures factional proportionality only and thus excludes cabinet seats that go to non-Diet members or Diet members who do not belong to a LDP faction.

was reduced by approximately one-third due to an administrative reform. Yet there is a fair amount of consistency in the large proportion of hereditary politicians, 40–80 percent, and a respectable proportion of women and private-sector policy experts (usually 10–30 percent) in LDP cabinets since reform.

What explains this increase in the numbers of women, nonpolitician policy experts, and hereditary Diet members being appointed to the cabinets in the postreform era? Recall that in the later days of the prereform '55 system period the LDP was almost assured of staying in power against the socialist opposition, vote seeking was left primarily to the individual Diet members mobilizing their personal vote, and zoku giin representatives were the policy experts who dominated the policymaking process in an era of ever-expanding GNP and budgets. The LDP, in other words, was primarily an office-seeking party in that it did not have to concern itself very much with vote-seeking or policy-seeking—these were delegated to the representative level.

Postreform, faced with real competition for power from the moderate DPJ; SMDs, PR districts, and a larger floating vote for which the image of

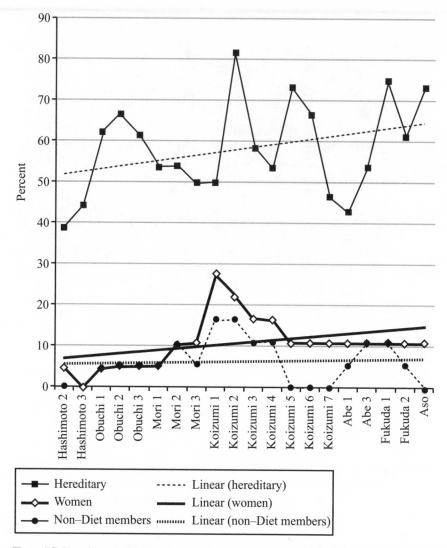

Figure 5.7 Hereditary politicians, women, and non-Diet members in the cabinet, post-reform (%)
Source: J-LOD.

the party and government leadership counted for more in mobilizing the vote; and a long no- or slow-growth period of declining budgets when the influence of policy-tribe experts declined, the party needed a cabinet that was the face of the party and government and could appeal to voters and signal responsible reform policies. Popular women candidates in the cabinet helped a great deal in mobilizing the vote, as did the hereditary politicians who had national name recognition from their family predecessors' being in the cabinet. The latter, along with policy experts from the private sector, also gave the party and government an image of working toward prudent policies to help bring about reform with personnel who knew their business. Using hereditary politicians for their name recognition and possible signal to voters that they understand policy, however, turned out to be a two-edged sword. In the run-up to the 2009 election, the DPJ made this into an issue, deciding before the event to restrict potential hereditary candidates from getting the endorsement of the party in the same electoral district and submitting a similar bill to the Diet (Democratic Party of Japan 2009; Martin 2009).

One former cabinet minister confirmed both the vote- and policy-seeking advantages to appointing a non-Diet member to a cabinet post, responding that the reasons that factions and Diet members accept such appointments are that the appointed outsider is an expert in that policy area and also that it is a means to gain votes:

> It is like a public relations gesture that the government and party are fully flexible and open. So appointing that person advances the image of the government....And then you need more media-oriented ministers than in the past, of course. A segment of ministers will be appointed with those concerns factored in, the others still appointed on a seniority basis, but if you have a few ministers who are all right in the media, then that will maintain the support rate of the cabinet (Interview OO, October 3, 2007).

Interestingly, having a nonparliamentarian in the cabinet also strengthens the power of the prime minister in that policy area against the factions because the nonparliamentarian has no power base in the party (Interview OO, October 3, 2007). Thus, the prime minister's greater autonomy from the determination of his cabinet by the factions has also led to a more functional use of the cabinet to help the party stay in power during the postreform era, as well as providing the party leader with more autonomy from factions in general.

Choosing party leaders and cabinet members whom the public found appealing and responsible took priority after electoral reform, although some of this (for the hereditary politicians) backfired in 2009. The strict institutionalized norms of the '55 system—factional determination of the party leader and the cabinet, factional proportionality in cabinets, and factional seniority for cabinet positions—all had been weakened substantially due to a combination of electoral reform, the party presidential primary, and the influence of the media.

Yet the factions soldiered on and continued to have some influence in the party presidential races, although the factions witnessed a decline in loyalty and cohesiveness and no longer determined outcomes through the bargaining of their leaders. Most important, subcabinet positions, party posts, and parliamentary positions all still remained the purview of factions and constitute their main reason for existence today, despite Koizumi's attempts to undermine even this function. Indeed, for the first time, there was an intentional strategic purpose in maintaining strict seniority rules below the cabinet level, especially for party posts:

> since this has become an era for political appointees [at the cabinet level], the party side has become even more strictly seniority based...in order to balance it out and control the dissatisfaction of loyal party politicians who served in traditional ways....
>
> I wouldn't say [the rigid structure of seniority is] worse, it's more strategically kept. But in the past it was inertia, it was simply an authoritarian sort of rule. Today it's more of a strategic mechanism...to keep party unity. (Interview OO, October 20, 2008)

Prime Minister Koizumi attempted to weaken the factions even further. When the LDP won its overwhelming electoral victory under his leadership in 2005, Koizumi personally urged the over eighty new representatives who came to the Diet as a result, known as "Koizumi's children," to not join factions, and he indicated that he hoped many levels of posts could be distributed without regard to factions. In addition to the electoral system change, Koizumi's tenure in office further weakened the influence of the factions over allocating posts and the management of their members' careers that they still retained.

Furthermore, nonfaction members, including the remaining "Koizumi's children," may no longer be discriminated against as much in the allocation of posts in the government, and it was not uncommon by 2008 for even first- or second-termers to attain cabinet or advisory posts in the *kantei*. Nevertheless, seniority is still "very strong" in the allocation of party positions, and factional membership still counts, although decreasingly so, in the allocation of posts, even after Koizumi's attempts to undermine factions (Interview OO, October 20, 2008).

Many did not join factions, although over time and after Koizumi retired, more eventually did. A comparison of how different 2005 was from previous elections in terms of new candidates' joining factions is shown in figure 5.8.

As we can see, after around 1983 almost all new candidates joined factions, and almost all of them joined a faction either before or right after they were elected for the first time (i.e., those shown as joining a faction in first term in the graph). This accords with our analysis in chapter 4 of when the five major factors became dominant and party rules and norms governing the allocation of posts were institutionalized.

Then in 2003 with Koizumi, there is a drop in newcomers belonging to factions to below 80 percent for the first time since 1985 (these and following statistics are more detailed breakdown of the summary figures shown in figure 5.8). And then there was a second major change in 2005, when

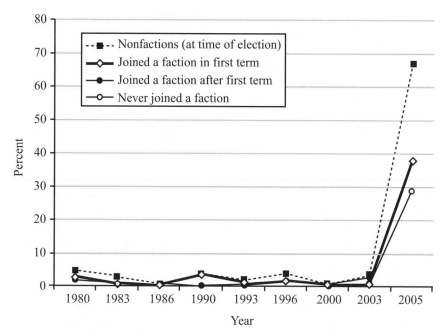

Figure 5.8 LDP freshman Diet members: who joined factions and when, pre- and post-reform, 1980–2005 (%)

for the first time only a small minority of the successful LDP candidates (sixteen out of eighty-three) joined a faction prior to or right after their election (sixty-seven out of eighty-one of the House of Representatives new-comers remained nonfaction). During their first term between 2005 and 2008, however, a majority (approximately 57 percent of those remaining nonfaction after their election and 46 percent of the original total newcom-ers) did join a faction. Only 43 percent of the nonfaction newcomers never joined a faction, representing only a little over one-third of the original newcomers.

These results confirm several of our assertions in chapters 3–4. First, after the institutionalization of factions in the LDP in the late 1970s to early 1980s, the negative externalities of not belonging to a faction were extremely high, inducing new LDP Diet members to join one. Second, these nega-tive externalities continued even after the electoral reform. Only Koizumi's strong stance against the factions and his encouragement of awarding posts not based on factional seniority made a dent in these tendencies. But even Koizumi could not undermine the negative externalities completely, and after his retirement they reasserted themselves, providing incentives for even many of "Koizumi's children" to join factions once again.

We spoke to several young Diet members who were very worried about their decisions not to join a faction. Even those who resolved not to join a faction, such as the first-term member of the House of Councilors who we interviewed, fret about possible damage to their career hopes due to not joining a faction: "It is true that I'm disadvantaged by not joining a faction. I worry about that" (Interview QQ, July 17, 2008). Another member we interviewed was thinking of reversing her earlier decision not to join one: "Without the support of a faction, I can't get good posts. I had decided not to join a faction until I had won my third election, but now I have to reconsider that decision. Factions get us positions. And, without a position, I can't work effectively" (Interview LL, October 5, 2007).

Statistical data can explicate the extent of the change and continuity in discrimination against nonfaction members in obtaining positions. Figure 5.9 shows the extent of the discrimination during the postreform period by year and position. There was less discrimination at the cabinet (minister and vice minister, and particularly in the former position) level, especially during Koizumi's term. The discrimination was more severe in the Diet committee executive positions and most severe in the party PARC executive positions (except for a brief spike in 2003–2004).

Table 5.1 compares the likelihood of faction and nonfaction members' getting major government and party posts (minister, vice minister, Diet standing committee chair and directors, and PARC chair and vice chair), controlling for seniority (number of terms in the party and Diet). Discrimination overall has declined compared to the prereform period; nonfaction members are still at a disadvantage compared to faction members, but the figures indicate that gap has diminished a bit. The likelihood gap between them has declined from about 9 to 7 percent for third-termers, from 24 to 9 percent for fourth-termers, from 27 to 8 percent for fifth-termers, and from 25 to less than 7 percent from before Koizumi to after Koizumi. So discrimination against those who are not in a faction still exists in the distribution of posts, but it is less than before Koizumi's efforts to change this.

The process for allocating posts has changed as well and may be one reason for the relative decline in discrimination against nonfaction members. After Koizumi, Diet members (those who have not been a minister previously and who are expected to serve the party in whatever way it requires; posts such as chair of *chōsakai* are reserved only for former ministers) were given a questionnaire to fill out with their preferences for posts. This went directly to the secretary-general, who decides on the allocation of posts. He might, of course, then have negotiated with faction representatives or leaders before deciding the allocation, but even nonfaction members made representations to the secretary-general who, because the nonfaction representatives were decreasing in number and because the party was afraid of undermining its image of not catering to factions, may actually have discriminated less in the distribution of posts than before (Interview OO, October 20, 2008).

We thus see the decline of factional unity, loyalty, and influence in picking the prime minster; a decline in the amount of attention paid to factions

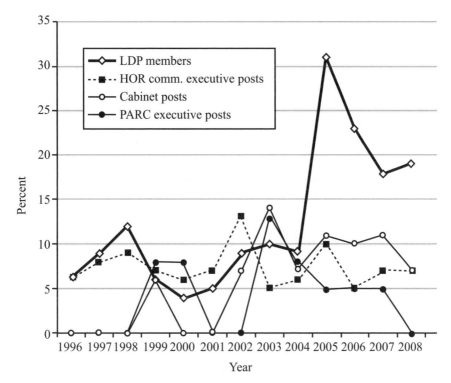

Figure 5.9 Nonfaction Diet members in LDP and in key posts, 1996–2008 (%)
Source: J-LOD.
Note: HOR comm., House of Representatives committee; PARC, Policy Affairs Research
Council.

and factional balance in the allocation of cabinet and other government
posts; and new, more centralized procedures and less discrimination in the
treatment of nonfaction members in the distribution of posts. Yet, for party
positions, a stricter seniority system remained (although reduced in the
number of terms it takes to qualify), and factions could still have some influence on who gets which posts and provide negative externalities, albeit
weaker than previously, for those who prefer not to join a faction.

The Development of Liberal Democratic
Party Factions after Reform

As we have seen, the electoral reform of 1994 weakened the factions and
changed their pattern. It did not eliminate them completely, which is what
we would expect to occur if SNTV were the sole or even primary influence
on factional development. The real intellectual puzzle, again, is that factions continue to exist at all, not that they have changed quite a bit since

TABLE 5.1

Likelihood of an incumbent legislator getting a post (%)

	Faction Member?	
Years	Yes	No
Third-term Legislator		
1996–2001	86.0	67.0
	[82.7–88.8]	[55.1–77.9]
2002–2008	74.4	67.1
	[69.8–78.4]	[58.1–76.0]
Fourth-term Legislator		
1996–2001	77.5	53.3
	73.0–81.6]	[40.3–65.7]
2002–2008	61.9	53.4
	[56.6–67.2]	[43.2–63.6]
Fifth-term Legislator		
1996–2001	63.7	37.0
	[57.0–69.6]	[25.0–50.8]
2002–2008	45.2	37.0
	[39.0–51.3]	[27.8–46.7]
Sixth-term Legislator		
1996–2001	49.7	25.1
	[43.3–56.5]	[15.7–35.9]
2002–2008	31.8	24.9
	[26.4–37.7]	[17.7–33.6]

Note: Posts considered are minister, vice-minister, Diet standing committee chair and directors, and PARC chair and vice-chair. Values in brackets are 95% intervals.

1994. After all, factions changed significantly in almost every decade of their existence, from the 1950s to today; the story of factional change is one of almost perpetual change, not of a shift from one state before 1994 to another after 1994.

So, why did the reformers and many analysts, who correctly predicted that the new electoral system would profoundly change the factions, also think the factions as an organizational form would disappear? They based their predictions and explanations on the assumption that the SNTV electoral system itself had caused the factions. This assumption may rest in the timing of its origins. Interestingly, the calls for electoral reform and the systematic analysis of the LDP under the '55 system all occurred from the late 1980s until the early 1990s, when electoral reform was instituted. These reformers and analysts focused on the LDP during this period and assumed that its organizational forms and processes had always existed since the origin of the party. Following this *a*historical institutionalism, the next logical leap to assuming these patterns arose due to the electoral system. But, as we have seen, it was the constantly evolving dynamics of intraparty rivalry, not the electoral system per se, that determined the LDP factional organization and strategies, just as the factions have also adapted themselves and the nature of their competition first to the SNTV and then to the new electoral systems.

The factions kept their grip on the allocation of posts (at least through the 2009 election), even though they have been eliminated as a force in the selection of cabinet posts and have been weakened for others now that nonfaction representatives are somewhat less discriminated against. The PARC and other party and governmental institutions were complementary to the factions and helped sustain them both before and after the electoral reform. These are the same dynamics we have seen in the example of the Diet member who reluctantly joined a faction after proclaiming his independence. Factional control over the allocation of posts continues to create negative externalities for nonfaction members, and this is the major cause of the perpetuation of factions over time, both before and after the electoral reform. They did not disappear, and the mystery of why they did not is found in how the factional control over the distribution of posts after the 1970s (and continuing today) locked in the costs to representatives who did not join factions. Like the QWERTY keyboard, however appealing the alternative was, the disadvantages of not conforming far outweighed the advantages.

Nevertheless, the factions have become weaker because of the elimination of some of their late–'55 system roles and functions and thus, consequently, weakening the structure of the factions by nearly eliminating their electoral functions and (along with the actions of entrepreneurial actors such as Prime Minister Koizumi, who came to understand the new system) weakening others. The negative externalities for not participating in the system, organizational complementarity with kōenkai and other electoral institutions such as the funding law, and sequencing that had developed by the end of the '55 system were disrupted by the reforms. One of the major roles of factions, funding for the support of kōenkai, saw one of its chief organizational complementarities, the funding law, changed to eliminate that function. And when more prefectural representatives became important for ensuring a member's election as the party leader, as in Koizumi's selection in 2001, the influence of the factions on the process and their ability to determine the outcomes were weakened, as it also was when Koizumi refused to take the factional balance into account in appointing cabinet members.

But the organizational form (although not all its functions or consequences for the party) persisted because of the continued aligned incentives of leaders and backbenchers for office-seeking and career advancement, which remained relatively unchanged (except at the cabinet level) by the reform. The strategies related to the electoral system changed; however, the organizational forms did not because they also fulfilled other needs of the party and representatives that were unrelated to the electoral system, such as the allocation of posts and information sharing. As Park has emphasized, "politicians operate within a complex network of multiple institutions" (2001, 432). And thus the electoral system, although one important influence, was and is not determinative of the fate of the factions.

Sequencing must be considered as well. What if the electoral reform had been imposed in the early 1970s, when Prime Minister Kakuei Tanaka hoped to abolish SNTV in favor of a pure SMD system and before factional norms of seniority and the allocation of posts had been completely institutionalized? It is entirely possible that the factions might never have developed further than their earlier forms in the years after the LDP merger.

Paradoxically, the less cohesive, less loyal, less powerful, and more fluid factions of the LDP today have begun to resemble once again the factions within the Liberal and Democratic parties prior to and immediately after the LDP merger and first presidential race in 1956 (the former under the new electoral system, the latter under SNTV). For example, as we have seen, factions have become more numerous and smaller again; there are now nine LDP factions, nearly the same number as under the Ishibashi cabinet of 1956 (Watanabe 1977, 78) rather than the four or five dominant factions at the height of the '55 system. The factions also may be have begun to acquire more leanings against a particular leader or even policy-oriented hues (Akagawa 2003; *Yomiuri Shimbun* online, September 15, 2007), similar to those in the earlier era. The postal privatization issue and the 2005 election (see chap. 9) indicate a convergence of faction, zoku giin, policy orientation, and coalition interests against a particular leader. The Fukuda versus Asō party presidential election in 2007 also contained a faction-policy convergence in which the two candidates represented very different foreign policy views and received much stronger, although usually not unanimous, support from different factions. These resemblances to the earlier factions reinforce our point about the negative externalities of the factions' controlling posts; it is the perpetuation of that control that allows factions to survive at all, even though in weakened form because almost all their electoral functions have been eliminated.

In the LDP party presidential selection race in 2009, there were many calls by younger and mid-level LDP Diet members and some of the three candidates for the post to abolish the factions. The faction leaders seemed to be resisting, so their ultimate fate remains unclear.

The common denominator seems to be much less institutionalization of the role of factions in the electoral district and the somewhat weakened institutionalization of their role in the control of posts and their members' careers. The electoral system reform did matter in gradually undermining both the cohesiveness and role of factions in the party; however; it was not completely determinative. Under both the SNTV and the new electoral system for a decade and a half, the origins, development, and outcomes of the forms and functions of the factions were, at least partially, unintended by the party leaders and representatives and not fully predicted by the reformers and analysts focused only on possible electoral causes.

Chapter 6

The Policy Affairs Research Council and Policymaking under the '55 System

It can be argued that the council is more important than the Diet because it is in the council where the real deliberations on policy take place.... The role of the Diet as a forum for the making of policy is limited. The council is the seat of the action.
Nathaniel Thayer (1969, 235–36)

However, this thoroughly bottom-up pattern was not because it was there from the beginning.... [and] it was not an intentional systematization.... [but, rather] it was produced inadvertently, due to the conditions in which factions variously competed with each other.
Naoto Nonaka (2008, 186–87)

The third major institutional dimension of the LDP under the '55 system was its Policy Affairs Research Council (PARC; Seimu Chōsakai). PARC was a core organization in structuring both the policymaking process and the roles of LDP Diet members within that process; thus it affected the status; influence; and electoral, party, and governmental careers of the LDP politicians. Even though PARC was an extra-legislative party organization and not a formal part of government or the legislature, PARC divisions had more influence over the final shape of legislation that the government introduced and the Diet approved in any given policy area than did the parliamentary committees and arguably as much influence as the government ministries that often formulated bills. Over the years, it has been variously credited or blamed by scholars, journalists, and the public for being the primary cause of the highly decentralized and fragmented policymaking process under the '55 system; for providing the expertise to LDP politicians that enabled them to hold their own or master the bureaucrats in that process; and for being a key means by which the LDP provided pork-barrel benefits, mobilized the vote, and maintained its electoral superiority in the face of the challenges of the multimember SNTV electoral system. In this chapter, we analyze the complex origins and development of PARC before the reforms of the 1990s to identify which variables determined its nature, role, and function within the LDP and Japanese politics.

What Is the Policy Affairs Research Council?

Every political party in democratic polities has some means of formulating its policies and programs. In Japan, since the founding of the party in 1955, the PARC was the major policymaking body within the LDP. Its members were the LDP representatives in both legislative houses, and it was the basic forum in which the party discussed, negotiated, and decided party and, because the LDP was the governing party for so long, government policy. Although its emerging policy proposals still had to get approval from party executives and the cabinet before being introduced in the Diet for discussion, debate, and passage, PARC essentially was the organ that had the most influence in shaping legislation.

Sometimes in parliamentary systems party policymaking is done prior to elections and enshrined in the party manifesto in the form of promises to voters of the policies that the party will pursue if and when it is in office. In some democratic polities, such as the United States, no one really expects the party platforms cooked up during election campaigns to necessarily represent what will happen once the party actually takes power. In other parliamentary regimes, however, these promises are taken very seriously as a form of contract with the voter, and voters may punish the party for reneging when in office on its fundamental pledges.[1]

Of course, general promises about the overall contours of policies that a party will pursue do not specific legislative bills or policy proposals make. The actual implementation of these general election promises in Westminster systems, such as the United Kingdom and New Zealand is usually left to the cabinet and prime minister, who converts them into specific legislation. Because these individuals are also the leaders of the governing party, they obviously also helped shape the party electoral manifesto and promises, even before taking the reins of government. In New Zealand, for example, the Cabinet Office invites the government ministers to propose legislation for the government legislative program for that parliamentary session; part of the cabinet and then the full cabinet approve the priority bills before they become the legislative agenda for that parliamentary term (Palmer and Palmer 2004).

In Britain, as Curtis Martin and Bruce Stronach write, "There is, unlike Japan, no formal machinery for processing legislative proposals for

---

1. This happened in New Zealand in the 1990s when voters punished both the major parties for reneging after they were in office on their basic economic promises that had been in their manifestoes; it also was one of the most important causes of voters' ratifying the change in electoral systems in a subsequent referendum (Nagel 1994, 527).

government within the parties, and no formal consultation procedures among government, MPs [members of Parliament], and party in the generation of legislation" (1992, 255). Backbenchers have some input in terms of communicating their preferences to the party leaders and cabinet through party committees and a parliamentary caucus made up of members from that party in the parliament and led by the party leader, through the formation of the electoral promises and manifestoes, and through the party whips. The whips transmit the representatives' sentiment up to the leaders and cabinet, but also serve to "cajole, bully, or conciliate the potential dissident" (Kavanagh 2000, 166) to adhere to the line of the party and party leadership on important legislation and to vote accordingly once the bill is introduced to Parliament.

This is strikingly different from the manner of policymaking in the Japanese '55 system. Policymaking in the more textbook model of parliamentary cabinet government involves strong cabinet leadership and coordination in setting the legislative agenda, with backbenchers (a majority of MPs in the United Kingdom and a minority in New Zealand) having input into policymaking through rather less influential, more informal, and more dispersed channels than those in the cabinet. In Japan under the '55 system, the reverse was the case. Representatives who were not in the cabinet were often the other pivot of policy through their formal roles in PARC. PARC, in consultation with bureaucrats and interest groups, already had input into policy before the cabinet and prime minister or upper party executives could shape it further.

PARC was organized primarily on functional lines, with divisions as the major units within it that generally paralleled the bureaucratic agencies and the committee structure of the Diet. For example, there was a Commerce and Industry Division of PARC that paralleled the Ministry of International Trade and Industry and the Commerce and Industry Committees; an Agriculture and Forestry Division that paralleled the Ministry of Agriculture, Forestry, and Fisheries and the Agriculture, Forestry, and Fisheries Committees; a Communications Division that paralleled the Ministry of Posts and Telecommunications and the Communications Committees; and a Cabinet Division that paralleled all the agencies within the Prime Minister's Office and the cabinet committees. At the height of PARC in the 1980s, the general rule was that every LDP member of both houses belonged to up to three divisions. In addition, because LDP representatives were appointed to two committees in their legislative house and because they were automatically assigned to the parallel divisions in PARC, they could be approved for up to two divisions of their choosing in addition to their committee-related ones that were automatically assigned. Thus, if a Diet member belonged to the Agriculture, Forestry, and Fisheries Committee and the Transportation Committee in the House of Representatives, she might belong to both the PARC division on Agriculture and Forestry and on Transportation and still could choose up to two others of her preference, for a possible maximum total of four (Inoguchi and Iwai 1987, 103–4; Ramseyer and Rosenbluth 1993, 31–32). At its height in the mid-1980s, PARC had as many as seventeen divisions.

This, however, was only the beginning of the PARC specialized, complex structure. At its height, each PARC division also had subcommittees within it composed of some of the members of the division. And in addition to the divisions, PARC had separate research committees (*chōsakai*) and special committees (*tokubetsu iinkai*), both with additional subcommittees (*shoiinkai*) also that were focused on specific policy issues, for example, an Oil Issues Research Committee and a Housing Counter-Policy Special Committee. LDP representatives could be in up to sixteen such units in addition to their maximum of four divisions (Ramseyer and Rosenbluth 1993). PARC was a highly organized, complicated, and specialized body of Diet members, which in the mid-1980s had 121 separate specialized units within it and another further 144 subcommittees within those.[2]

The divisions were the chief policymaking bodies, however, and no piece of legislation could be introduced into the Diet without going first through the PARC divisions, even if the draft of the legislation had originated within a bureaucratic agency, as many bills in the postwar period did. Here LDP Diet members scrutinized the prospective bill, discussed it, and amended it to accord with the needs and interests of the representatives, the party, and their constituencies. The divisions were, as Takashi Inoguchi and Tomoaki Iwai aptly put it, the "frontline of interest coordination" and the place where the individual interests of the representative and his supporters in society and the collective interests of the party and its supporters in society were integrated (1987, 101–3).

Most of the decision making of the divisions, however, was done by the executives of the divisions—the chair and the various vice chairs—although in the early years the role of the chairs was more to coordinate the different interests and disagreements among the vice chairs and the Policy Advisory Council (*seimu shingikai*) (Seisaku Geppō 1964, 142). Later, the norm was that executive decisions were made unanimously and that, if there were strong objections and the executives were divided, the proposed bill would be shelved but not rejected (Inoguchi and Iwai, 101–2). It was known that there was a fixed seniority in the posts within the PARC divisions and house committees. A politician became a member of a division and of a committee after his or her first election, became a committee *riji* (director) and vice chair of a division after being elected three times, and was eligible to become a division chair after five elections (121). Appointments to the divisions and the executive posts were made at the same time as cabinet shake-ups, about once per year on average.

Above the divisions within PARC was a body called at various times the Policy Affairs Advisory Council (Seimu Shingikai) or the Policy Advisory

2. For a chart of PARC units by type and year, see Satō and Matsuzaki (1986, 263).

Council (Seisaku Shingikai), made up of veterans of the PARC whose ostensible job it was to screen the policy bills that came out of the divisions before they went to the Executive Council (Sōmukai) and its party leaders. From there policy bills went to the cabinet for final approval and, finally, to the cabinet secretariat to be put into the final form for introduction to the Diet as cabinet-sponsored legislation, which constituted the majority of all bills introduced and most of the bills that passed the Diet. Thus, the PARC and its various components, especially the divisions, were the fundamental source of the policies that would go on to become law in Japan. In the process, the LDP representatives who made up the PARC were able to study, discuss, and learn about the details of policy for the particular areas on whose divisions and various committees they served, and thus PARC also served as a policy training ground for LDP politicians. In addition, PARC was a major stepping stone to higher offices in the party, Diet, and government—it was from, and interspersed with, their division service that representatives worked their way into positions as house committee chair and director and in the subcabinet and cabinet.

Thus, in addition to playing the central role in LDP policymaking and, thus, given the long-term LDP majority in the Diet, also in the Japanese government, PARC performed important socialization, training, and career-structuring functions for both the party and government. And in these roles and functions, it was an almost uniquely powerful party organ among the parties of parliamentary democracies in the industrialized countries.

Why Is There a Policy Affairs Research Council?

How did PARC originate and develop into a major policymaking organ for Diet members within the LDP? How did it perform its important functions for the party and LDP Diet members, and how influential was it compared to the party leaders during the various stages of the growth of the LDP as a dominant party? Why did the process of policymaking involving a nongovernmental party organ develop in such a unique way in Japan? And what changes, if any, has the electoral reform brought to PARC? These are the questions to which we devote the rest of this chapter.

Let us explore first some competing (non–historical institutional) hypotheses about the origins of PARC and its development. First, as usual in Japan, there is the cultural explanation for PARC and the decentralized policymaking process within the LDP. We might, for example, point to the tradition of *ringisei* ("bottom-up system of making decisions") instead of top-down decision making and the Japanese cultural penchant for consensus instead of formal-legal and conflict-prone processes as manifesting themselves in PARC and its role in LDP policymaking (Ward 1978, 71–72).[3]

---

3. More sophisticated and recent examples include (Martin and Stronach 1992, 244–47).

In contrast, we agree with Ramseyer and Rosenbluth's (1993, 2–3) general critique of cultural explanations as tautological, and especially so when applied to PARC. To explain why the LDP uses a decentralized, bottom-up form of relatively consensual intra-PARC decision making by saying that Japanese culture contains preferences for bottom-up and consensual decision making is no more an explanation than to say that the LDP is a Japanese organization and that LDP politicians are Japanese. We do not consider this an insightful or useful explanation. Further, LDP policymaking was less decentralized in the prewar and early postwar years, was more centralized at the height of the '55 system, and is more centralized again today. That is, PARC was a very different body in the late 1950s and early 1960s than it was by the 1980s, much as we have seen that kōenkai changed greatly over the same period. Does the influence of Japanese culture vary that much? But according to the usual definition, such cultural value and behavior patterns should be fairly constant over time and not display such variation.

The second competing explanation is a much more powerful one and has become fairly dominant among some political scientists. Ramseyer and Rosenbluth (1993, 32–34; McCubbins and Rosenbluth, 1995, 48–52) portray PARC and its operations primarily as a response to the SNTV electoral system. Comparing Japan to Britain, the argument is that these differences were due "primarily to the electoral rules that underpin the two systems" that pitted LDP candidates in the same district against one another. Therefore, "To facilitate the necessary vote division among these candidates, the LDP allows its members to use the policymaking process to secure private benefits for their constituents to a greater degree than is customary in Britain" (Ramseyer and Rosenbluth 1993, 30–31). These authors elaborate on this argument further and provide some empirical evidence to support their case. "PARC committee assignment patterns show evidence that systematic care is take to separate the committee assignments of LDP members from the same district" (McCubbins and Rosenbluth 1995, 50). They conclude from their subsequent empirical analysis[4] that in eighteen of the twenty-six cases examined there was either no overlap or only one overlap and that, therefore, this could not be random. Thus, intentional differentiation among PARC division assignments is supported (51). Masatsugu Yoshioka even sees the whole PARC structure and decentralized policymaking process as an intentional rational calculation by which by which the party achieves "universal distribution of welfare" that aids in party unity (2007, 11).

We agree with these authors that in the '55 system the SNTV electoral system provided great incentives to cultivate a personal vote and also that PARC ultimately served the interests of LDP Diet members well in this

4. Using a sample of twenty-six randomly selected 1990 districts, they first compute the odds that assignment overlap will occur and conclude that it is close to zero "with the number of district LDP seats greater than three and average assignments per member also greater than three" (McCubbins and Rosenbluth 1995, 50). In looking at their data sample, they find that thirteen of the twenty-six districts had no overlap and that five districts had one overlap only among two LDP members.

regard; we also agree that LDP Diet members' differentiating themselves by specialization in the PARC divisions is certainly logical. There are reasons to be skeptical that the electoral system *alone* is a sufficient explanation for the origins and development of the PARC structure and process in the LDP under the '55 system.

First, zoku giin even developed in sectors that had less vote appeal than the usual pork-barrel sectors, for example, Defense policy, which had none of the ostensible electoral advantages of votes or money. And Education policy had a bit more voter appeal than Defense, although not as much as the pork-barrel areas, yet there were policy tribes in this area as well (Schoppa 1991). Why were there policy tribes of specialists in these policy areas if the electoral system and differentiation from fellow LDP representatives for dividing the vote were the primary causes of specialization (Yuasa 1986, 48; Inoguchi and Iwai 1987, 126–28)?

Other doubts about this explanation are based on comparative and historical cases. First, even in Taiwan, which had one of the few other SNTV systems, the long-ruling Kuomintang Party never developed such a decentralized, specialized, policymaking body within it. Rather, its policymaking process was far more centralized, even after the introduction of an SNTV system, although it did introduce more democratic procedures (Cheng 1989, 495–96). Further, the pay-offs of private-good policymaking were limited at the constituent level, and they were not channeled through the party organization itself but, rather, through the local elites and even then were channeled mostly to local elites and not to constituents (Winckler 1999a, 340–41). The U.S. congressional committee system of specialization; differentiation; credit claiming; and the "iron triangles" of politicians, bureaucrats, and interest groups, however, bears a striking resemblance to Japan, with the PARC divisions substituted for the U.S. House of Representatives committees. One reason for this may be that both U.S. and Japanese vote mobilization share an emphasis on the personal vote rather than the party vote. But Britain and the United States both have SMD systems, and British politics did not develop such features. It is difficult to find a great deal of consistency between party organizations and policymaking that can be explained solely by the type of electoral system, even just comparing the two SNTV systems of Japan and Taiwan and the two SMD systems of the United States and Britain.

There are also puzzling historical anomalies. Japan had a SNTV system for part of the prewar period, and the conservative parties also had policy-examining bodies that resembled the postwar LDP PARC in process and organization. Yet none of these prewar precedents had anywhere near the importance in legislative policymaking (because of the greater role of the bureaucracy in its formulation during that period) or the differentiation and specialization of the postwar LDP PARC.[5] Even in the postwar, although

5. For example, the prewar Seiyūkai was divided only into divisions dealing with policy issues such as administration, finance, economics, foreign policy, and education (Murakawa 1984, 46).

the SNTV system was reestablished in 1947, PARC could not and did not begin performing its major policy role or assume its ultimate policymaking and specialized policymaking roles until after the LDP was established; only thereafter did PARC assume its major roles in the 1960s.

Moreover, these competing analyses are based on actor-centered functionalism (discussed in chap. 1), which assumes rather than demonstrates that outcomes determine origins by intentional design.

A more historical institutionalist approach to the origins and development of PARC reveals a deeper, more logical, and more empirically valid story than either the simple cultural or electoral explanation alone. In our analysis of PARC, pre- and postreform, we also look closely at the circumstances of its origins and development and also the argument that the LDP allowed or even encouraged specialization among its representatives in the same district for vote mobilization.

The Early Development of the Postwar Policy Affairs Research Council: 1955–1960s

Prewar conservative parties had PARC-like organizations, but they were not as important in policymaking or as differentiated by policy specialization. The form of the current PARC does not begin to take shape until after the war, and at a quite specific point in postwar development. Unlike in the prewar Diet, the postwar U.S.-supervised constitution installed an extensive permanent committee system in the Diet; as a result, the Liberal (Jiyūtō) and Progressive (Kaishintō) parties established PARC divisions for each committee to carry out legislative activities (Murakawa 1984, 48). In other words, the postwar antecedents of the LDP PARC assumed its current form due to the establishment of a diverse and wide-ranging formal and permanent committee system in the Diet. In addition, the reorganization and broadening of the postwar bureaucracy, which shaped the Diet committee structure, also played a role.

After the end of the Occupation in 1952, the Liberal Party, especially, strengthened the role of its PARC but not in response to any electoral factors. Rather, because the fifth Yoshida cabinet in 1953 was a minority one and had acquired a reputation for failing to keep control over bills in several policy areas, the Liberals decided to reinforce the role of its PARC. An important contributing factor, as well, was that, as a minority cabinet, the Liberals had difficulty getting the budget passed without the cooperation of the Progressives; as a result, influential younger Liberals, such as the future LDP Prime Minister Eisaku Satō, were pushing for better policy coordination of the Liberal Party PARC with the Progressive Party PARC. This became one of the most important functions of the Liberal Party PARC, and it was, indeed, a step toward the merger of the two parties and the renaming of the Progressives as Democrats just two years later.

The strengthened Liberal Party PARC, working with the Ministry of Finance, also functioned to restrain Diet members' demands for greater expenditures (*Asahi Shimbun,* May 27, 1953, 1; June 5, 1953, 1). This theme of party leaders, the government, and the bureaucracy all searching for ways to limit their backbenchers from making excessive additional budget demands, particularly for constituency pork-barrel and credit-claiming purposes, runs through the entire history of the LDP and its antecedent conservative parties during this period. Such issues were not a major problem when the Occupation enforced budget restraint on the Japanese government, but very soon after the end of the Occupation they became more of a problem. As early as 1953, the House Management Committee recommended that Diet members' bills should be limited to be more in accord with the budget proposal of the government and Ministry of Finance (*Mainichi Shimbun,* December 18, 1953, 1).

In 1955, to cut down on the number of government and opposition party individual member bills, especially on important matters such as the budget that were seen as being the province of the government, the Diet Law was revised to require a minimum of twenty Diet members in the House of Representatives (ten in the House of Councilors) to introduce a bill and, in the case of bills related to the budget, a minimum of fifty in the House of Representatives (twenty in the House of Councilors) (Kawato 1999, 481).

The merger of the Liberal and Democratic parties into the LDP in 1955 led to a transition period within the party, but the newly merged LDP quickly established its own PARC as well as a policy affairs advisory council (*seimu shingikai*) to screen the bills that came out of the divisions. Indeed, even at this time the new LDP already had a party rule (Article 30 Clause 2) that required any bill that the party adopted as policy to go through PARC before it could be submitted to the Diet (Jiyūminshutō 1987, 32). We can see the impact of the formation of the LDP and the raising of the minimum number of sponsors needed to introduce a member bill in figure 6.1. The largest increase in the number of cabinet-sponsored legislation occurs during this period, after which the proportions more or less stabilize into the 1970s.

In general in the years after the merger, even the new LDP PARC seemed to have only nominal influence compared to the party executives, with the divisions and research committees holding infrequent meetings but the Advisory Council holding three times as many (Satō and Matsuzaki 1986, 84–85, 88–89). Even after several years, the PARC structure had fifteen divisions, but only six research committees and special committees (*Asahi Shimbun,* September 12, 1957, 2), a far cry from its far more complex and specialized structure later on. At this time, PARC was hardly a highly specialized, decentralized, or influential body. Indeed, Michio Yonezawa, a young Finance Ministry bureaucrat who later became an LDP Diet member, labeled the PARC discussions during this time as "amateurish," and Hajime Iwao, his senior, stated PARC had had very little influence (in Satō and Matsuzaki 1986, 90).

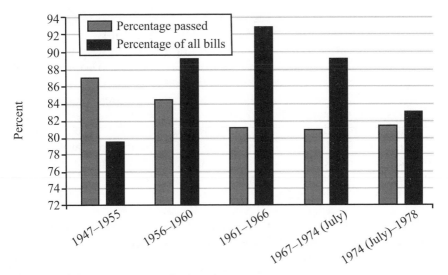

Figure 6.1 Prereform cabinet-sponsored bills passed, 1947–1978 (%)
Source: Mochizuki (1982, 110).

A book on the LDP written at the time by an influential political journalist familiar with the party even claimed that both the Executive Council
and PARC positions were filled by those who could not get cabinet posts,
often by those who were from the antimainstream factions of the party and
were trying to gain some influence; as a result they were just "lowly posts"
(*hiyameshi posuto;* literally "cold rice posts") (Watanabe 1958, 53–57).

Influential bureaucrats often did not consult with PARC even on some
policies for which there were the divisions actively trying to influence policy,
although the most active members of these divisions were representatives
who were former bureaucrats and who still had close contact with their
erstwhile colleagues in the ministries. In extreme cases, PARC did nothing
more than convert the bureaucracy proposals directly into approved bills,
and even when they did not, PARC divisions and research committees had
to accept the bureaucrats' revisions. Lacking staff, expertise, and financing,
the PARC subdivisions could not compete with the ministries. The PARC top
executives were chosen with regard to factional balance and representation,
augmenting the bureaucratic influence because former bureaucratic politicians controlled the factions (*Asahi Shimbun,* September 12, 1957, 2)

Further, there were continuing and almost constant conflict and struggle between the backbenchers with the government and party leaders over
such key policymaking issues as prior decision power on budgets. Even
right after its formation, a segment of the LDP, as well as the bureaucracy,
thought that PARC was trying to usurp the right of the government to
form the budget and argued that the party should think more about collective interests such as the people's tax burden than about the demands

of individual Diet members, even though the PARC had less influence than the party executives (*Asahi Shimbun,* December 27, 1955, 1).

Therefore, in October 1957, the LDP top executives decided that any bills whose content made budget measures necessary had to be proposed by the government, not the Diet members; this was to protect against such bills being introduced solely to enhance Diet members' popularity in their districts in anticipation of the House of Representatives dissolution and election. Six months later, party executives again implemented a policy to restrain any bills or resolutions proposed by Diet members that might undermine the budget; bills "aimed at election" that had emerged from committees had recently created a stalemate in Diet procedure (on this process after the mid-1950s, see Kawato 1999, 505–12; *Asahi Shimbun,* October 30, 1957, 2; *Asahi Shimbun* [evening ed.], April 4, 1958, 2).

Clearly, ever since the establishment of postwar democracy under the Occupation and through the 1950s, there was a constant attempt by the backbenchers to divert government resources to their districts. This is not surprising—in any electoral system, SMD or SNTV, that has local constituency representatives, this is often the case. But there is no evidence that these efforts were in any way mostly accomplished through specialization of the PARC divisions, and the party leaders constantly struggled to contain and control these demands and did not use PARC to fulfill them for electoral purposes.

Rather, there is probably some inverse institutional complementarity at work here. With their constituency demands for political pork and other benefits being restrained, individuals, especially those in the antimainstream factions who were shut out from any real policy influence on the relatively weak and ineffectual PARC, turned their attention to building up their personal support bases in the district through kōenkai rather than by trying to provide policy benefits to their district. It is probably no coincidence that kōenkai expansion really begins during this same period of the antimainstream factions' being shut out of power and a weak PARC (see chap. 2).

These conflicts continued in the late 1950s, with bureaucrats and former bureaucrats continuing to dominate PARC and the government establishing rules to ensure it kept control over the most important bills, such as the budget, which it considered within its purview, not the party's. These conflicts between party leaders and backbenchers over expenditures and policymaking power came to a head in the early 1960s.

In 1960 the LDP Executive Council laid down the requirements for bills to be submitted to the Diet. These included that any bill submitted by a Diet member first had to be approved by the Executive Council, the Executive Council chair, the PARC chair, and the Diet Strategy Committee chair. Another requirement was that any bill submitted by a Diet Member that would require the further revision of the budget was prohibited (Kawato 1999, 505–12; Murakawa 1989, 162).

The party leadership during the first years after the formation of the LDP was attempting both to establish a regularized procedure for bills introduced by Diet members and to ensure that such bills did not affect the decision power of the government over expenditures. Interestingly, Sadafumi Kawato credits such internal LDP rules as doing more to eventually solve the problem of myriad member bills in the 1950s than the revision to the Diet Law in 1955 (requiring a minimum number of representatives to introduce the bill) that was intended to accomplish this (Kawato 1999, 505–12, 533).

By 1961, PARC had grown to sixty units (divisions, research committees, special committees, etc.) and become more specialized. But it was still far from the powerful policymaking body it became later. Party leaders criticized it for being little more than the agent of the interest groups, spending more time on petitions to government agencies on their behalf than on policy discussions, and being administratively inefficient; some even called for its abolition or, at the least, its reorganization (*Asahi Shimbun,* July 24, 1961, 2).

Thus, in the early years after the formation of the LDP and almost two decades after readoption of the SNTV electoral system, few institutionalized norms or rules existed concerning many aspects of the policymaking process and the party remained divided on policymaking procedures and on how much the government and party could afford to use the budget for electoral purposes. LDP leaders, far from encouraging the development and use of PARC for electoral purposes, were constantly trying to maintain its control over the policymaking process to protect against too many bills meant to bring benefits to individual Diet members' districts, especially concerning any items that might impact the budget.

The Rise of the Party and the Rise of the Zoku Giin: Late 1960s–1990s

The stage was set for the transformation of the PARC in the 1960s. The atmosphere created by the 1960 U.S.-Japanese Mutual Security Treaty crisis, in which both the Diet and the country were polarized in the conflict between the LDP and conservatives, on one side, and the leftist parties and anti-Treaty forces outside the Diet, on the other, meant a more difficult policy process within the Diet, providing more incentives to institutionalize the process within the LDP. In 1962, Munenori Akagi, the Executive Council chair, sent a memo to Chief Cabinet Secretary Ōhira demanding that, before government bills were submitted to the Diet, they should be referred to the Executive Council; Ōhira accepted this, although his motivations for doing so are unclear. Ōhira might have understood that this was a win-win move for both the government and party leaders and also the backbenchers. Now *all* bills, not just those proposed by individual Diet members, would go through the party before the cabinet could propose them in the Diet. This meant individual members' bills could be restrained by being vetted in PARC (government win) but also that the backbenchers had a more institutionalized channel to get their demands into policy (backbencher win).[6] Some scholars and journalists see this memo as a turning point and as the beginning of the party- and PARC-based policymaking system that ultimately characterizes the '55 system.[7] For the first time, intraparty organs had influence in shaping government-sponsored legislation, including the budget.

It is from this point forward that PARC gradually became a much more influential LDP institution, and now LDP politicians could promise to provide their constituents, especially those in the kōenkai that they had been building up the last few years, with concrete policy benefits. A collective discussion by all eight of the PARC chairs in 1955–1964 indicates that by the mid-1960s many of them saw PARC as becoming primarily concerned with the narrow sectarian concerns of Diet members trying to respond to their constituents' demands (Seisaku Geppō 1964, 136–58). Along with the LDP's now having been in power over a decade, we see the germination of the important role of PARC in policymaking under the '55 system.

Around this time as well, the quality of personnel in PARC was improving. Under Hayato Ikeda (1960–1964), up-and-coming LDP party leaders who eventually became prime minister—such as Takeo Fukuda and Kakuei Tanaka, who both became chair of PARC—and his successor Eisaku Satō, and more specialists who were former bureaucrats, took over the division chairs and the beginnings of an "agricultural tribe" could be seen among LDP Diet members who were trying to get rice prices set higher in the regulated Japanese system to help their farm constituents in the rural areas (Hoshi 2004, 415).

And, thus, we see by the late 1960s a change in PARC as the first signs of the zoku giin appear, quietly getting their ducks in a row (nemawashi) in the divisions, and the Agriculture, Construction, and Transportation tribes already show influence (Kosugi 1967, 152–59). Now, as an indicator of the rising importance of PARC in policymaking, LDP representatives began coming to division meetings every day to learn about policy and hear about pressure group requests (Watanabe 1981, 34–40).

In 1966, the chair of the LDP Organization Research Committee told the party executives that he wanted to *strengthen* bills introduced by Diet members to develop legislative politics further. Because most bills introduced by Diet members were now submitted by the opposition parties, and therefore the chief role of LDP Diet members was say "no" in Diet committees, few of these bills passed. This worked to the advantage of the

6. We are grateful to Professor Sadafumi Kawato for this insight (pers. comm., October 6, 2008).

7. For the complete text, see Hoshi (2004, 412–13).

government and the bureaucrats. Instead, the LDP Organization Research Committee chair wanted the number of bills introduced by LDP Diet members and their role to increase (*Asahi Shimbun*, May 28, 1966, 2). Instead of party leaders and governments' viewing PARC and its divisions as nothing more than agents of the interest groups trying to bust the budget, and then working to restrain the demands of these backbenchers from access to government expenditures, leaders now came to see PARC as a potential agent of the party, training and using party policy experts to allow the party to play a greater role in policymaking vis-à-vis the bureaucracy. Kakuei Tanaka, in a 1983 newspaper interview concerning PARC, acknowledged the "shallow" roots of legislative politics in Japan and that PARC was not powerful enough, touted its role as the means to establish real legislative politics in Japan as a form of greater democratization (Nihon Keizai Shimbunsha 1985, 194–95).

Indeed, Tanaka continued the trend under Satō of placing talented young politicians in PARC to activate it and allow these representatives eventually to become zoku giin. Tanaka's aim, however, was not to displace either the bureaucracy or interest groups but, rather, to link them through these Diet members, thus allowing the party to become the key pivot and using the bureaucracy to cater to interest groups to accomplish party and political goals. It was Tanaka who deserves much of the credit, or blame, for establishing the zoku giin structure—and its consequent "structural corruption"—that was to come to characterize the 1980s (Hoshi 2004, 414–16; Johnson 1995, 222–23).

Much of this change in both the perception and actual role of PARC was due in no small measure to the changed economic environment in Japan. In the 1950s, when Japan had still not completely recovered from the war and the "pie" available for the government to distribute was limited, the governments were naturally concerned about curbing wasteful expenditures (in addition to keeping control of them). Beginning in the 1960s, however, and through the 1980s, the tremendous rapid Japanese economic growth meant the pie was constantly expanding and that a great deal more could be distributed, preferably at the discretion and coordination of the LDP itself rather than just by the government and the bureaucrats. One other condition that made this possible (and that also, self-fulfillingly, helped establish that condition) was the longevity of LDP rule combined with the incumbency advantage enjoyed by those LDP representatives with strong kōenkai in their districts. This allowed the development over time of politician specialists who had the expertise and the bureaucratic and interest group contacts to become influential in policymaking in that area.

The third condition, and in many ways the most important and a precondition for the others, was the mitigation of the conflict between the mainstream and antimainstream factions. This had led to the mainstream domination of the cabinet and Executive Party posts, but also the antimainstream members' using PARC as a base to gain some influence and attack the mainstream. The end of this division and the beginnings of PARC as a true all-faction policy organ came with the institutionalization of the seniority rule in factions and then in the party as a whole (see chap. 4). As we have seen, the all-faction participation model was institutionalized fairly early in the LDP, including appointments to the PARC division chair. Once all the factions began to have a stake in the PARC divisions and could use them so that their members could respond to their constituency demands relatively equally, and as gradually the other seniority rules were institutionalized over time, the conflict between mainstream and antimainstream, and thus the use of PARC as a tool in that struggle, was eased. By the early 1980s, Yoshirō Mori, an up-and-coming Fukuda faction politician and a future prime minister, could state that "In PARC, policy is the priority not factions" (Nihon Keizai Shimbunsha 1985, 123), an indication of how routinized and non-conflictual PARC factional politics had become compared to its earlier history, when it had been an area for mainstream and antimainstream rivalry.

With the compromise between the leadership and backbenchers and the mainstream and antimainstream factions in the Akagi memo that forced even government bills to go through the party and PARC, the larger and ever-expanding pie of resources, the gradually increasing leverage of LDP rule, and the institutionalization of rules for PARC personnel appointments, this became a win-win situation for everyone and was soon institutionalized: bureaucrats got bigger budgets; politicians helped ensure their reelection by bringing the goodies home to their constituents and key interest groups; and interest groups, in return for financial contributions or votes, made more money. The famous "iron triangle" had come to Japan, with the PARC divisions as the Japanese equivalent of the U.S. congressional committees. And now, instead of an inverse relationship between the kōenkai and PARC and the LDP antimainstream politicians, who had as little influence on policy as in the late 1950s, we see a symbiotic complementary relationship as politicians used both the local geographical strategy of mobilizing votes and the pork-barrel policy strategy of bringing home the bacon to those very constituents. This can be seen in the custom that developed among the politicians who won their first election in the late 1960s and in the 1970s (described in their autobiographies as the *kinki karai*, or "go home Friday and come back [to Tokyo] Tuesday") strategy—returning to their districts on Friday to show the flag among their local constituents and kōenkai supporters and then returning to Tokyo by overnight train on Tuesday morning to participate in the PARC division meetings (Watanabe 1981, 43–45; Gotoda 1998, 379–81).

This development of zoku giin began with little fanfare or public knowledge in the 1960s and early 1970s. Indeed, as we have seen, the term *zoku giin* itself does not seem to have appeared in the newspapers until the late 1960s and then again in the Lockheed Scandal, which fittingly was wrapped up with the godfather of these tribes, Kakuei Tanaka. In one of the first important newspaper references to the term, the *Asahi Shimbun* analyzed the scandal for what it revealed about the existence of an "airline tribe" within the LDP (*Asahi Shimbun,* May 3, 1976, 18). Academics began to take note in the early 1980s, especially of how the growing expertise of Diet members in PARC was allowing the LDP for the first time to have as much influence in policymaking as the bureaucrats (Muramatsu and Krauss 1984, 126–48; Satō and Matsuzaki 1986, 92). Surveys of bureaucrats conducted by Michio Muramatsu in 1986 indicated that bureaucrats perceived the zoku giin to be the most powerful influence on their ministry or agency in policy formation and implementation, even higher than the prime minister and far higher than the top party leaders and others in the LDP or other ministries (Muramatsu 2005, 159).

There are many ways of defining who qualifies as a zoku giin. Satō and Matsuzaki (1986, 264–65), for example, find four definitions in the literature, but reject several because they are too wide or do not include an important characteristic of zoku giin—that they have strong connections to the specific bureaucratic agencies in that policy area. They finally settle on the following definition: "Persons who are, prior to their first entry into the Cabinet or first term ministerial experience (you can say that these are largely mid-level representatives), among those representatives who are exercising a strong daily influence concerning policy areas that are compartmentalized with the bureaucratic agency as the basic unit" (Satō and Matsuzaki 1986, 265).

Inoguchi and Iwai, however, include all those whom Satō and Matsuzaki do and also compile a list of such representatives in each policy area from journalistic and other sources. In addition, they construct charts of the posts these people held during their careers and the number of PARC divisions and Diet committees they served on. Key in these charts and in the careers of the zoku giin are the posts of PARC chair and vice chair and, secondarily, the posts of legislative committee chair and director (the equivalent of a vice chair) (Inoguchi and Iwai 1987, 293–304, 123–24). Inoguchi and Iwai also develop a points system for ranking the levels of the posts, which they use to confirm their identification of zoku giin membership. Ultimately, the definitions used by Inoguchi and Iwai and by Satō and Matsuzaki's are broadly similar, including generally the pattern of career posts already described, with only some differences in the cases of a few individuals.

By the 1980s, PARC had become an enormously complex organization. In addition to the divisions, there were myriad research committees and special committees established in PARC from the beginning of the LDP to investigate and discuss policy on specific contemporary salient issues. In 1955, there were only three of the former and fourteen of the latter. By 1987, they had grown to thirty-two research committees and seventy-two special committees. But this does not completely account for the scale of the PARC subdivisions because each of these committees also had subcommittees. For example, there were ninety-nine subcommittees of the research and special committees in 1987. The number of divisions, themselves, remained fairly constant (at between fifteen and seventeen) over time (Satō and Matsuzaki 1986, 263). In addition, the number of meetings of the general divisions were decreasing by the latter part of the 1970s, suggesting that the zoku giin were having more informal meetings to make the decisions that used to be made more formally in the divisions (Satō and Matsuzaki 1986, 93).

How did Diet members get appointed to particular PARC and other posts? Who determined specifically which individuals got which posts varied with the positions? LDP party vice secretary-generals (*fukukanjichō*) negotiated and decided who was appointed to the PARC positions, including the division chairs, vice chairs, the key personnel in the myriad special, issue (*mondai iinkai*), and research committees;[8] the deputy chairman (*kokkai taisaku fukuiinchō*) of the Diet Affairs Committee decided on distribution of the Diet committee posts (Interview M, July 4, 2002). In effect, however, those who decided these personnel decisions were acting as the representatives of their factions and the decisions were made by bargaining among the factions. The subcabinet posts were determined along with the cabinet positions by the prime minister and party secretary-general, who also took the factional balance into account in making such governmental appointments (Thayer 1969, 183–206;[9] Kawato 1996a, 1996b). Thus, the careers of LDP Diet members and their ability to become zoku giin were crucially determined by factional membership and seniority within the factions. Indeed, some scholars (e.g., Inoguchi and Iwai 1987 26–27; Kohno 1997) consider the adoption of the seniority rule in the appointment of posts within the LDP to be one of the key factors in the origins of zoku giin.[10] This change undermined the prior advantages of former bureaucrats in obtaining posts based on their backgrounds as policy experts. Instead, now nonformer bureaucrats could gradually acquire expertise in a policy area by acquiring seniority and then serving in posts in that policy area within the party, Diet, and government.

Because the PARC, Diet committee, and subcabinet positions were rotated each year, along with the cabinet posts, and because Diet committee positions brought with them automatic appointments to PARC divisions, no LDP Diet member usually served in the same position, or necessarily even in the same area, for two years in a row. To become a zoku giin, therefore, required repeated elections and long service to acquire seniority and

8. Note, however, that appointments to the research and special committees may have been based more on considerations of expertise and potential career advantages to the appointee than on factional seniority as the division appointments (Nonaka Naoto, pers. comm., October 6, 2008).

9. At the time Thayer was writing, the number of cabinet posts that a faction obtained was not automatically determined by its strength within the party; later, the LDP institutionalized such norms for all PARC, Diet committee, and government appointments.

10. Another key factor, they think, is the gradual decline of the LDP vote, which began in the 1960s and which made LDP representatives more interested in forging connections with the interest groups to help them gain reelection.

also eventually to occupy the key positions that were thought of as being prerequisites.

By the 1980s, the career ladder through PARC, parliamentary committees, and government subcabinet and cabinet positions had become relatively standardized, and the zoku giin had become institutionalized. In large part, this was because the long-term rule of the LDP by this time had created the opportunity for LDP representatives to serve in PARC, Diet, and cabinet and subcabinet positions long enough to acquire the expertise and contacts to make them influential in a particular sector (Satō and Matsuzaki 1986).

The Origins of the Policy Affairs Research Council: Dividing the Vote?

Was the main purpose of PARC to divide the vote under the SNTV electoral system by allowing LDP representatives from the same district to specialize in different policy sectors to claim credit to different interest groups, thus leading to the zoku giin?

Masahiko Tatebayashi (2004) and Tatebayashi and Margaret McKean (2002) conducted an extensive data analysis, in which they hypothesize a more complicated scenario of specialization strategies. Rather than only dividing the vote based on the policy specialization to allow a representative to differentiate herself from party rivals in a MMD, they assume one strategy of dividing the vote based on geography and another based on policy specialization. The former, they argue, was designed to bring political pork benefits to a subregion within the district, whereas the latter was designed to bring specialized benefits to the entire district:

> In districts with equilibrium based on geographical division of the vote, politicians tended to focus on delivery of specific pork-like services to their own sub-region in the electoral district. On the other hand, in districts with an equilibrium based on policy issues, LDP politicians who each became a policy specialist in his or her (different) policy fields could, taken together, actually cover a wide range of policy issues on behalf of their constituents. (Tatebayashi and McKean 2002, 4)

Using data from five prereform elections and the entire universe of LDP representatives in the House of Representatives, they find that, indeed, representatives whose vote base was concentrated geographically in a specific part of their district tended to get pork-barrel PARC division assignments; those who specialized in a policy sector did not particularly gain pork assignments.

We decided to follow up on the Tatebayashi and McKean analysis and investigate this question more thoroughly using our J-LOD of LDP representatives from the 1980s to the present (although here we use only pre-reform data). McCubbins and Rosenbluth (1995) exclude from their sample members of the *gosanke* ("Big Three")[11] divisions of Agriculture and Forestry, Construction, and Commerce and Industry and, to their credit, imply that it is in the non–*Big Three* divisions of PARC in which specialization may be most acute. If we are interested in whether division membership was used to divide the vote, however, it seems to us that excluding a priori the three most popular divisions for a representative's doling out concrete benefits to a district does not make much sense, given the credit-claiming basis for the hypothesis, which may stack the deck in favor of the specialization hypothesis. Thus, we include these divisions in our analyses and, indeed, find that it is in these divisions that overlap is most frequent.[12]

Our initial analysis measured the simple extent of overlap (i.e., more than one LDP representative from the same district serving in the same division) in several prereform years (assignments that immediately followed a general election). The results are shown in table 6.1. As we can see, around one-half of all districts had no overlap in representatives from the same district appointed to the same division. But approximately one-half did.

Yet even this simple analysis actually greatly underestimates the extent of overlap. First, it includes several LDP districts that had only one representative—clearly, there could not even be a chance of overlap in those! Second, it includes LDP cabinet ministers and party leaders, who were not members of PARC divisions. These alone affect approximately 20 percent of the districts (and constitutes nearly 10 percent of LDP members of the House of Representatives), decreasing the probability of an overlap. We therefore ran the same analysis again, this time excluding single-seat LDP districts and the individual LDP cabinet ministers and party leaders (i.e., those members who could not possibly overlap with any others), as Mc-Cubbins and Rosenbluth also did in their sample. The results are shown in table 6.2.

Once we have excluded the districts that could not possibly have any overlap and those higher leaders who were not given posts in PARC, the results appear even less supportive of the specialization to divide the vote hypothesis. Now, only between 12 and 37 percent of the districts, depending on the election, had no overlap, with the average being only about 20 percent. Further, overall about 40 percent of the districts had two or more overlapping memberships.

How do we know, however, that these results are any greater than we might expect from a random distribution of positions in the divisions?

---

11. "Big Three" is a loose translation of gosanke. A more precise translation might be the "three great houses" and comes from the three branch families of the Tokugawa House. It is applied in many contexts by Japanese to refer to the most powerful or popular units or individuals in an organization.

12. McCubbins and Rosenbluth also used a lower standard for nonoverlap specialization—both no overlap and "only one overlap" 1995, 51). In our analysis, we consider specialization to be no overlap only.

TABLE 6.1

Districts with nomination overlaps, 1980–1993

		Districts With				
Year	Total Number of Districts	No Overlaps (%)	One Overlap (%)	Two Overlaps (%)	Three Overlaps (%)	Four Overlaps (%)
1980	130	49.2	26.9	14.6	6.2	3.0
1984	124	46.8	24.2	19.4	8.1	1.6
1986	129	37.2	26.4	19.4	13.2	3.9
1990	129	51.9	19.4	17.8	7.8	3.2
1993	122	53.3	24.6	13.9	7.4	0.8
Total	634	47.6	24.3	17.0	8.5	2.5

Source: J-LOD

TABLE 6.2

Districts with nomination overlaps, excluding single-member LDP districts and party leaders not in divisions, 1980–1993

		Districts With				
Year	Total Number of Districts	No Overlaps (%)	One Overlap (%)	Two Overlaps (%)	Three Overlaps (%)	Four Overlaps (%)
1980	83	20.5	42.2	22.9	9.6	4.0
1984	75	12.0	40.0	32.0	13.3	2.7
1986	92	12.0	37.0	27.2	18.5	5.4
1990	86	27.9	29.1	26.7	11.6	4.7
1993	75	37.3	40.0	17.3	5.3	0.0
Total	411	21.7	37.5	25.3	11.9	3.6

Source: J-LOD.

McCubbins and Rosenbluth (1995, 51) compare their results to random distribution to test this, and we must do the same. We used our J-LOD data on division assignments by district for the years 1980, 1984, 1986, 1990, and 1993 (in other words, the period after factional norms of seniority and so forth had been institutionalized and for each year after a general election at the height of the '55 system). We then divided the 411 districts in the sample where there was an LDP representative after these five elections into the 54 separate possible combinations of LDP legislators and the number of divisions that those legislators joined. In other words, the first combination of number of legislators and number of division assignments consisted of only one legislator who joined one division, the second consisted of one legislator who joined two divisions, and so forth, up to four LDP representatives, two of whom joined four divisions each and two of whom joined five each, the maximum combination in our sample.

We then calculated the expected value of each of these combinations based on random probability and compared that to the actual extent of the overlaps in districts with each combination.[13] Finally, for each combination we compared the number of actual no-overlap districts to the expected value for that combination. For each combination, if the number of overlaps in actuality was the same or lower than the expected value based on random probability, then the specialization hypothesis was considered confirmed for that combination. If it was higher, then our hypothesis of more overlaps than random probability can explain was confirmed.

We found that, out of the fifty-four possible combinations of representatives in a district and their division assignments, only in four were the number of overlaps lower than the expected values based on random probability; and all of these were districts in which there were only two representatives and one of them was assigned to only one division, thus of course decreasing the odds of an overlap. On the other hand, fifty showed a higher number of overlaps than might be expected from random distribution.

Thanks to our J-LOD, we were able to test on an extensive set of data. McCubbins and Rosenbluth's were limited by the data available to only a small sample of districts in snapshot of time. Our results show a strong confirmation of the nonspecialization hypothesis. Of course, there are other, far more complex ways of calculating overlaps and specialization that should be done in the future. For now our results here, combined with Tatebayashi's analysis (2004), give us reasons to question the hypothesis that specialization by sector was the norm.

Encouraged by this test showing the overlap was not random, we conducted a few more simple analyses. In perhaps the most important, we broke down the division data by type of policy sector: distributive (those that have generally been used in the distribution of particularistic benefits to constituencies), high-policy (high-profile nondistributive sectors), and public goods (low-profile nondistributive sectors).[14] We found a clear relationship between type of sector and extent of overlap or specialization in the districts. LDP Diet members in the same district do not tend to specialize at all when it comes to distributive (pork-barrel) sectors—they all wish

13. Specifically, we then calculated, first, the total number of districts with each combination of representative and division assignments and, then, the number of overlaps in division assignments and nonoverlaps for each district. Finally, we calculated the random probability of no overlaps (the mathematical probability of no division overlap based on the assumption that such assignments were random) and calculated the expected number of no-overlap districts from the total number of districts with each combination of legislators and division assignments and the random probability of no overlap. For example, if there were eighteen districts in which two members each joined four divisions, then mathematically the expectation is 5.41 overlapping districts

14. *Distributive sectors* include the following issue areas: Construction, Transportation, Trade and Industry, Agriculture, Local Affairs, House Budget, and Posts and Telecommunications. *High-policy sectors* include Finance, Foreign Affairs, Legal Affairs, Defense, Cabinet, Tax, and Basic Policy. *Public goods sectors* include Environment, Science, Labor, Social Affairs, Education, Youth, and House Management. For a similar use of these policy-sector categorizations, see Pekkanen, Nyblade, and Krauss (2006, 189).

to feed at the trough. There is more specialization in high-policy and public goods sectors, confirming Tatebayashi's (2004) and Tatebayashi and McKean's (2002) (as well as McCubbins and Rosenbluth's) conclusions that specialization was much more likely in the non-pork sectors. This, of course, raises an interesting question for the specialization to divide the vote hypothesis: If the purpose of specialization was to differentiate LDP representatives from the same district for the purpose of dividing the vote, we would expect this differentiation in the more constituency service–oriented sectors; yet it is exactly in these pork-barrel areas, of most direct relevance to voters in the districts, where it is least common!

A more detailed if preliminary analysis of the relationship between the type of district and the number of overlaps reveals further interesting information. We ran the extent of specialization overlap in division membership of LDP representatives in the same district (again, of course, excluding single-seat LDP districts and higher party leaders, who are not in any divisions) with five distinct variables: (1) the number of LDP representatives in the district (2–4); (2) the district magnitude, measured as the number of seats in the district (2–6); (3) seniority, measured as the average number of terms served in the district (categorized as 1–4, 4–8, or 8 or higher); (4) the strength/weakness of the LDP in the district, measured as the average share of LDP votes in the district divided by the Droop quota; and (5) the urban/rural nature of the district, measured by the "Densely-Inhabited Districts" (DID) measure index[15] (categorized as very rural, rural, urban, or very urban).

The results are a bit surprising for the specialization to divide the vote hypothesis but also somewhat consistent across the variables. First, specialization (low overlap) *decreases* with the number of LDP representatives in the district and also with the district magnitude. In other words, more LDP representatives tend to be in more of the same divisions the larger the number of LDP representatives in their district; perhaps this was unforeseen if we expected that the greater the number of competing LDP representatives, the greater the need for specialization. We do not know, of course, whether this result is merely a statistical artifact—the greater the number of representatives, the greater the probability of overlap.

Second, the higher the average seniority in the district, and the stronger the LDP is in the district, the greater the tendency to specialize. Thus, the more LDP representatives from the same district in the same division, the less senior they are and, depending on the year, the more electorally vulnerable the district is to the LDP. The specialization to divide the vote hypothesis might have led us to expect the reverse—the less senior and less secure the district for the LDP representatives, the more they should need to specialize and divide the vote more efficiently.

---

15. The DID index is a measure of the density of population in the district area.

Third, the more urban the district is, the more overlap of Diet members in divisions and the less specialization. Because the LDP has been stronger in rural and semirural areas and weakest in urban and metropolitan areas, we might have expected the greatest need for specialization to divide the vote to appear in more urban areas, and not our actual result. This analysis, however, is also consistent with the electoral strength and seniority findings in that rural areas are where LDP representatives probably have the longest tenure and also the greatest capacity to mobilize votes.

To test the validity of these simple and preliminary findings, we then conducted a multivariate analysis, presented in table 6.3. The table shows substantially the same results, with all the variables being mildly to strongly significant except for district magnitude (which has positive results but is not significant). The most consistent and significant correlations are (1) an increase in overlaps when the number of LDP members in the district increases and (2) a decrease in overlaps with increasing seniority. Less consistent but still significant overall are the correlations for declining overlaps with the LDP vote share and with the degree to which the district is urban.

Given how logical the specialization hypothesis seems, how can we explain these results? Our results make sense once we look more closely at PARC, the electoral credit-claiming functions division membership might perform for a representative in his or her district, and how members are appointed to particular divisions. First, the most popular divisions of PARC are Agriculture and Forestry, Construction, and Commerce and Industry—the "Big Three." Each of these three divisions attracted over one hundred LDP representatives per year at their peak in the 1980s. With that much popularity, it stands to reason there would be more overlap in these divisions. Two of these—Agriculture and Forestry, and Construction—have the most political pork of the sectors, whereas Commerce and Industry has the strongest connections to big business, which was the major supplier of funds to LDP politicians and factions. Being assigned to these divisions would be particularly important for junior, electorally vulnerable representatives who were in the most competitive (with more LDP incumbents running) and larger districts, especially in the rural areas where constituents expect their representative to deliver a great deal of political pork. In these districts, a LDP Diet member would be a fool (and probably a fool with a short political career at that) not to join one of these divisions, whether his fellow LDP representatives in the district were on it or not. Indeed, not joining these divisions would lead to increasingly negative relative returns over time. Thus, the more urban, secure, senior LDP politicians in larger districts were freer to specialize in non-pork divisions than their counterparts in very different political situations.

Even regarding non–"Big Three" divisions, recall that assignment to divisions is automatic for those appointed to the seventeen or eighteen permanent committees in each legislative house, and add to this that in many of the least popular divisions most or all of the members are the chair and

TABLE 6.3

Ordered logit estimates for the likelihood of PARC division overlaps, excluding single-member LDP districts and those who did not belong to any divisions, 1980–1993

	Years					
	All Years	1980	1984	1986	1990	1993
Number of LDP members in district	1.96*** (0.22)	1.28** (0.55)	1.10** (0.53)	2.17*** (0.48)	2.50*** (0.55)	2.76*** (0.60)
Seniority	−0.095*** (0.017)	−0.067* (0.038)	−0.083** (0.039)	−0.10*** (0.034)	−0.10** (0.041)	−0.096** (0.043)
Strength of LDP in district	−12.85* (7.01)	−34.48** (17.51)	−10.66 (16.77)	−18.45 (15.80)	−2.23 (20.99)	−30.70 (19.74)
Urban nature of district	−1.20*** (0.50)	−1.64 (1.27)	−1.25 (1.28)	−0.72 (1.08)	−1.23 (0.98)	−2.61* (1.48)
District magnitude	−0.15 (0.12)	−0.31 (0.30)	−0.21 (0.29)	0.071 (0.27)	−0.37 (0.31)	0.18 (0.28)
Cutpoint 1	−0.49 (0.96)	−4.78 (2.68)	−2.92 (2.49)	−0.29 (2.23)	1.18 (2.32)	0.26 (2.44)
Cutpoint 2	1.56 (0.95)	−2.57 (2.63)	−0.76 (2.47)	2.27 (2.21)	2.71 (2.32)	2.73 (2.44)
Cutpoint 3	3.18 (0.97)	−1.17 (2.63)	0.95 (2.47)	4.06 (2.25)	4.57 (2.38)	4.54 (2.50)
Cutpoint 4	5.06 (1.01)	0.18 (2.67)	3.01 (2.55)	6.05 (2.31)	6.42 (2.50)	7.32 (2.81)
Cutpoint 5	6.59 (1.11)	0.96 (2.73)			7.32 (2.59)	
Cutpoint 6	7.31 (1.22)	1.68 (2.82)			8.10 (2.69)	
N	411	83	75	92	86	75
LR chi-square	127.71***	20.20***	7.55	43.99***	34.74***	38.21***

Source: J-LOD.

Note: *** indicates $p < 0.01$; ** indicates $p < 0.05$; * indicates $p < 0.1$. Values in parentheses are standard errors. Variables: Number of LDP representatives in the district (2–4); Seniority, measured as the average number of terms served in the district (categorized as 1–4, 4–8, or 8 or higher); Strength/weakness of the LDP in the district, measured as the average share of LDP votes in the district divided by the Droop quota; Urban/rural nature of the district, measured by the DID index (categorized as very rural, rural, urban, or very urban); and District magnitude, measured as the number of seats in the district (2–6). DID, density in district; LR, likelihood ratio; PARC, Policy Affairs Research Council.

Results:

• If a district has more members from the LDP, the higher the likelihood of overlaps.

• If a district has senior members, the lower the likelihood of overlaps.

• The LDP's electoral competitiveness lowers the likelihood of overlaps; if LDP members are more electorally vulnerable, the higher the likelihood of overlaps.

• The more rural a district, the higher the likelihood of overlaps.

• The larger magnitude tends to lower the likelihood of overlaps but is the only one statistically insignificant.

• These tendencies vary over time.

those forced to be in the division because of their parallel committee assignment (Inoguchi and Iwai 1987, 134–35). It seems possible that the greater specialization we find in non-pork policy sectors is most likely the result of the need of the party to widely distribute representatives to staff Diet committees and their parallel divisions. Legislative committee assignments spread representatives out, even against their wills, to link policy formation within the party to policy formation within the Diet, and this in turn might account for some (or even many) of the cases of specialization.

In other words, although we agree that credit claiming and vote mobilization were certainly behind the assignments that Diet members and their factions sought in trying to get PARC division assignments, we find little evidence that representatives usually tried to specialize by seeking to be placed in divisions in which their fellow LDP representatives in the same district were not members to divide the vote in the district; especially they do not appear to have done so in the divisions that were most important to constituents in that they could provide votes or funding. Although there were undoubtedly such cases, our evidence does not indicate that doing this was anywhere near universal or even common in districts where more than one LDP member competed.

Instead, we find the same phenomenon we might find in SMDs with regards to committee assignments in legislatures—representatives seeking to be on the committees that might most help them with their constituents or the suppliers of political funding without regard to what other representatives were seeking. Explanations relying on pitting members of the same party against one other in SNTV district elections (the pure electoral system explanation) for PARC are not supported by our analyses here.

The Multiple Roles and Functions of the Policy Affairs Research Council

If PARC specialization is not solely the direct response by the LDP qua party to the need to divide the vote under the SNTV electoral system (even though it does perform some vote mobilization and credit-claiming functions), then to what can we attribute its origins and development? The functions it performed for the LDP and the roles it played in the political process prior to electoral reform can provide us a road map for understanding what electoral reform changed and what it did not and why. Conversely, the changed electoral system and its consequences may give us further insight into other origins and purposes of PARC than just the electoral system.

As we have described, before the electoral reform PARC had developed into a very complex organization performing many functions roles under the LDP-dominated '55 system. Some of these were for vote-seeking, as Ramseyer and Rosenbluth emphasize. PARC subunits enabled LDP representatives to specialize in non-political-pork areas that could aid particular interest groups and other specific groups of constituents throughout their districts, such as health (and the powerful doctors' and dentists' associations in that sector), education, environment (in urban constituencies especially), and even labor. Or many representatives served, even if not specializing in these policy areas, in the gosanke divisions and the related committees of construction and agriculture or the small and medium enterprise committee in Commerce and Industry that brought pork-barrel benefits back to the subregions of their districts, especially in those parts of their districts where their kōenkai members were concentrated. In some instances, the former vote-seeking purpose allowed representatives to differentiate themselves from their fellow LDP rivals in the same district but not always; these divisions and committees were so popular and so many representatives joined that even those from the same district could not afford not to. The thing that distinguished the latter type of appointments to PARC by the LDP from, for example, party appointments to committees in a parliament under an SMD electoral system was that the party allowed so many representatives to join some divisions, not specialization to divide the vote.

There was another important vote-seeking goal that is often forgotten, however, by analysts who concentrate their attention solely on the direct interface with voters—election fund-raising. Maintaining the personal vote in Japan was a very expensive proposition. Although representatives received partial support from the LDP, the party itself could give no representative an advantage over any other in the same district, and so it distributed money equally. This support, however, paid for only part of Diet members' needs at most, given the great expenses needed to maintain kōenkai and so forth. As we have seen, faction leaders provided another part of the necessary funds, although decreasingly so under the '55 system, which Gerald Curtis (1999, 179) attributes to the passage of the 1975 law regulating political funds. The rest had to be raised by the Diet members themselves. Serving in some PARC divisions was an excellent way to become useful to interest groups who could provide that funding. Thus, serving in construction-related divisions and committees was not necessarily done solely for vote-seeking directly; construction firms were the second-highest contributors to the LDP (Krauss and Coles 1990, 337). Financial institutions such as banks were the highest contributors, and thus service in the Commerce and Industry division (which regulated the banks) was useful. It is no coincidence that two of the three most popular gosanke divisions for LDP Diet members to join were Construction and Commerce and Industry; they provided not only the ability to bring benefits to several strata of constituents in their districts but also connections to interest groups that could provide funding to maintain constituency services.

For the individual Diet members, of course, there were additional benefits that provided them with incentives for serving in PARC divisions, not all of which were related to seeking votes. One was a way to achieve their policy-seeking goals, many of which were related bringing benefits to their constituents or raising money but some of which might not. The fact that approximately one-quarter of all LDP Diet members under the '55 system were former bureaucrats[16] means that they had both expertise and interest in their chosen policy area, whatever the constituency benefits it could provide. There were even individual Diet members who, because of their background or personal interest, chose to serve in divisions or on committees that could provide few constituency-related benefits, such as Foreign Affairs, Defense, and Justice. Finally, individual Diet members sought to attain both the vote-seeking and policy-seeking offices that would enable them to become zoku giin in a policy sector and the office that was the pinnacle of prestige sought by most Diet members (and was attained by one-quarter of postwar Diet members)—a position in the cabinet as a minister.

From the perspective of the party and its leaders, PARC served other useful roles in all areas of vote-seeking, policy-seeking, and office-seeking. The provision of constituency benefits by representatives, and their competition to do so, helped maintain the party in power by inducing loyalty to individual Diet members and thus, possibly, increasing the party majority in the next election. As Ethan Scheiner (2006, 64–107, 215–17) and others have emphasized, control over the distribution of policy goods and LDP clientelism was a major factor enabling the LDP to maintain its dominance under the '55 system.

Frequently neglected, however, have been the crucial policy- and office-seeking functions that PARC also enabled the LDP to perform as a governing party. PARC provided a means by which Diet members could accumulate policy expertise and connections to bureaucracies and interest groups that could enable the ruling party to make informed policy decisions that would be beneficial to the country or to the party. As we have seen, in the early stages of the LDP this was particularly beneficial, allowing party politicians to compete with the well-informed and expert bureaucrats who dominated policymaking in the 1950s and early 1960s. The gradual creation of politician-experts by their advancement through the LDP seniority system, ultimately culminating in the zoku giin, allowed the party both to govern with the aid of the bureaucracy and to become well-integrated into it by the 1990s while not being dominated by it (Muramatsu and Krauss 1984, 126–48). This also aided the party vis-à-vis the opposition parties in the Diet. Having an internal and complex body of specialized divisions paralleling the ministry sectors meant that policy experts and influential representatives could fashion bills efficiently and effectively. Once put into final form by the party leaders and cabinet, these could then be presented to the Diet, where usually only tinkering to satisfy opposition party complaints was necessary. To the information advantage of being the governing party using the bureaucracy as staff was added the additional information advantage

16. In 1983–1993, 24.7 percent were ex-bureaucrats. The ratio was remarkably consistent, varying only from 23.5 to 26.2 percent in the thirteen prereform years, 1980–1993 (based on our calculations from the J-LOD).

of the bills' being processed by intraparty policy experts with close connections to the key interest groups in that sector.

A closely related function of PARC was as a training ground for higher posts for the younger, less senior LDP politicians. Service first as members, then as vice chairs, and as parliamentary vice ministers introduced junior LDP members to the party, the Diet, the government, and the policy-making process before they assumed more responsible roles in each of these.

Another important party role for PARC that has been almost neglected by analysts is that it served as a structural mechanism for party discipline, overcoming the coordination problem of wide-ranging and diverse party interests. By delegating policy initiation to the PARC divisions, the LDP decentralized the agenda power to the PARC divisions at a relatively early stage of policymaking.[17] In so doing, it effectively made it very difficult, if not impossible, for LDP representatives who were not in that PARC division to have any influence on bills in that policy sector. Indeed, because the deliberations of the PARC divisions were pro forma, with most important matters related to a bill that had been decided in advance just among the executives of the division (i.e., the chairs and vice chairs), it was very difficult for anyone but division executives and party leaders to shape legislation. Once the bill had emerged from the PARC division and passed muster among the party leaders, of course, it was impossible for any other representative to oppose the bill on the floor without violating party discipline. Naturally, to remain in a PARC division and to advance to the executive ranks at which bills were shaped within the party, a representative had to have, or acquire, similar interests and perspectives on policies in that sector as the existing executives.

In effect, mavericks or opponents of the policies and interests of those who ran the divisions either never joined that division or, if they did, soon found themselves either kicked off or isolated without influence among the ordinary members of that division and without a prayer of advancement to the influential ranks of the executives. Because every faction was represented among the vice chairs of a division and because the factions determined appointments and advancement within the divisions, this was not difficult to accomplish. It is no coincidence that, among major parliamentary parties, the LDP is unusual in having no clearly labeled equivalent of a whip (Krauss and Pekkanen 2004).[18] The franchising of agenda power in particular policy sectors to the executives of the PARC divisions made such a role irrelevant and unnecessary—the structure and processes of PARC usually ensured there would be no backbencher rebellion against the policies

17. On agenda power and on decentralized vs. centralized and early vs. late agenda power, see Cox (2005, 16–17).

18. The chair of the Diet Strategy Committee (*kokkai taisaku iinkai*) may perform some of this role for some bills in his capacity as overseer of the party's handling of legislation especially in terms of priorities and relations with the opposition party, but he is not designated as a "whip" nor is this his primary function.

that veterans in that policy area wanted, and those policies, perhaps with some revisions by party leaders, became the policies of the party as a whole and then of the government, once they had been passed in the Diet (Krauss and Pekkanen 2004, 1–34; Yoshioka 2007, 3).

PARC also performed other policy-seeking goals for the party. In a party riven with factional conflict and competition for offices, the LDP had a huge coordination problem. PARC helped the party to overcome this problem by delegating policy over individual policy areas to decentralized specialized divisions whose members were selected from, and by, all the factions. By pushing coordination down into these bodies and institutionalizing it in an organization in which representatives had a common interest (for electoral, policy, or office reasons) in that sector, the potential for overcoming factional coordination problems was greatly enhanced. Remaining issues could be resolved at the higher levels of PARC, the party, and the cabinet, where the factions were also represented.

Finally, and most obviously, in terms of office-seeking, PARC provided faction leaders with the ability to reward their ambitious followers for their loyalty. It more efficiently delegated the distribution of posts below the cabinet level in the party, Diet, and government to separate personnel representing the factions rather than having to decide these massive personnel questions at the level of top party (faction) leaders.

Development of the Policy Affairs Research Council: From Discord to Synergy

Perhaps the clearest conclusion to emerge from our empirical description and analysis of the development of PARC before the reform is that, although its primary purpose ostensibly was to make policy, it always served all the major LDP party goals simultaneously. PARC catered to the party incentives to seek votes and win reelection for its representatives, rewarded its members' ambitions with offices, and formulated policies to govern. This multi-functionality is key to why PARC existed, why it became institutionalized the way it did, and why it continued to exist even after electoral reform.

It is also clear that the function of vote-seeking by dividing the vote among its candidates in MMDs probably has not always been, if it ever was, among the primary reasons for the existence of PARC. Clear instances of dividing the vote in districts using PARC post allocations does not exist empirically or historically. The use of PARC posts for influencing policies to benefit representatives' constituents and for representatives to become influential within one or more policy sectors certainly clearly have motivated individual representatives from the beginning of PARC and throughout its development. These were achieved, however, without necessarily specializing in different divisions to divide the vote in particular districts; and they were functions shared by non-SNTV systems with specialized committee structures in parliament or in the party as well.

Furthermore, the goal of using PARC to allow representatives to bring benefits to their districts and claim credit there was *not* always completely shared by party leaders. During its early years, PARC was not at all influential in policymaking decisions, and a bit later on, party leaders attempted to restrain the use of PARC for allocating political pork through policy. Indeed, the development and institutionalization of PARC seem very much intertwined with and determined by intraparty battles between party leaders and backbenchers and, later, between politicians and bureaucrats for influence on policy.

Severe mainstream versus antimainstream factional conflict and mobilization were occurring in the seven years after the formation of the LDP. At first, the backbenchers and antimainstream factions were the main, but not very influential, users of the LDP PARC to push for allocations of political pork to their constituencies and to influence policy and maneuver for intraparty power. As we have noted, party leaders adopted various methods to restrain such demands and keep the control over budgets and important policies in the hands of the government.

The factions were a complementary institution to PARC; indeed, the development of PARC from its origin to the present is integrally bound up with the nature of the LDP factions. After the merger creating the LDP, the emergence of exclusive, powerful, and competing leadership factions within the LDP and the institutionalization of the seniority rule to help control conflict among them were crucially linked to how LDP representatives were appointed to PARC and why they were apportioned the way they were. It is no accident that PARC also became increasingly important and began to be institutionalized during the same 1955–1962 period as the kōenkai and factions. The mitigation of conflict among the factions, as we have seen, was a major contributor to enabling the PARC divisions to assume their roles of allocating political pork and producing policy experts with strong connections to interest groups and bureaucrats, the zoku giin.

Our analysis indicates that the multifunctional PARC had a very different path of development than the widely accepted characterization of its having sprung full-blown from the SNTV electoral system for the purpose of dividing the vote among competing LDP representatives in a district. Indeed, PARC did not develop into its archtypical '55 system form (as represented in much of the literature) until the 1970s. Its progression also indicates a deep and important connection between it and the kōenkai and factions.

The dominance of policymaking by the mainstream factions through the cabinet and the influence of the bureaucrats in the early days of LDP led PARC to become a not very influential refuge for the antimainstream factions. This seems to have led antimainstream politicians to attempt to expand vote mobilization through the building of kōenkai rather than through the delivery of policy benefits not under their control. Thus, factional conflict and the nature of PARC helped feed the expansion of the kōenkai.

Note that the SNTV electoral system was important. For example, because of its incentives to cultivate a personal vote, it undoubtedly contributed to the demands from backbenchers in the 1950s and early 1960s for greater influence in the policymaking process, which eventually helped induce Akagi and Ōhira, with Tanaka behind the scenes, to grant these demands and make all bills go through the party, even the government bills, which led to the ultimate development of PARC under the '55 system. But, without the other institutions and variables that the SNTV system combined with, such as the factions, it is unlikely that that development would have occurred the way it did. The complementary institutions were crucial to the development of PARC.

The severe campaigning restrictions on candidates also constituted a complementary institution. They provided incentives for members to participate in PARC divisions, influence policy, and provide benefits thereby, especially pork-barrel benefits, to constituents because, other than kōenkai (through which the representative could provide discrete, individual services, practical and social, to its members), representatives had very few other ways than by claiming credit through PARC to motivate voters to vote for them. Indeed, as we have seen, the kōenkai themselves were a complementary institution; they made it more likely that LDP representatives would be reelected and thus accumulate the seniority to become zoku giin through their long-time service in the PARC divisions.

Yet another complementary institution was the Diet committee system and bureaucratic jurisdictions. Without a specialized committee system in the Diet after 1947 (which, in turn had been shaped by the new bureaucratic structure), there would have been no reason to functionally differentiate PARC into divisions (which became the means of allocating personnel to PARC). Indeed, that system may have as much to do with the creation of PARC structure and its development of policy experts as the SNTV electoral system. The paralleling of PARC divisions with the Diet committees and the bureaucracy also enabled the close integration of the former with the bureaucrats over time.

Any representative who was not a member of the "Big Three" PARC divisions of Agriculture and Forestry, Construction, and Commerce and Industry experienced a severe competitive disadvantage. Any representative from a rural area who did not belong to the Agriculture and Forestry division was at a severe disadvantage compared to other members who were, especially those other members who were rival LDP representatives in the district. Similarly, employees and their families in the construction industry were an important voting bloc in every district as well as influential financial contributors; not belonging to the Construction division was a disadvantage. Being on the Commerce and Industry division gave representatives influence over bank and big corporations, another major source of political funding. For LDP Diet members, the disadvantages of not belonging to these divisions were far more important to which PARC divisions they joined than was specializing in different divisions than their rivals in their home district.

The Akagi memo functioned somewhat as the QWERTY keyboard in the development of PARC. Once backbenchers had institutionalized their influence in the policymaking process and the all-faction participation in PARC through the seniority rules they developed, time served in divisions led to experience and expertise. These, in turn, helped the politicians mobilize votes in their district and influence policy. As the PARC system solidified, it became the only way in which representatives could wield influence over policy and legislation. As alternative routes to exercising policy influence became more and more difficult, if not impossible, politicians who did not serve in one or more PARC divisions had no influence on policy at all. These negative externalities provided a major incentive for all representatives to follow this career pattern; this in turn provided increasing returns for those who were successful at it and greater incentives for them to push to maintain the influence of PARC and its divisions on policymaking.

Over time, the value of developing expertise and influence on policy in one or more divisions, to become a zoku giin, increased as well. Those who did not join the "Big Three" divisions, or who did not specialize geographically or in at least one policy sector, were at a disadvantage compared to those who did, not only to those in their own districts but also to others in the party; they had less influence in policymaking and could not provide their constituents with the concrete benefits that they demanded and saw other Diet members providing their constituents.

The factions, too, were forced to compete by these same dynamics. They had to push their members into useful divisions and key positions in PARC, so that their new members could gain experience, expertise, and win reelection and seniority. Winning reelection meant their faction could maintain its power and even grow, aiding their leader's desire to become prime minister. In contrast, individuals not in a faction were at a great disadvantage in their careers and in gaining key posts. And factions that did not colonize the important divisions of PARC with their members to provide political pork for their constituents did not participate in these benefits and weakened.

Party leaders derived increasing returns from PARC. They could use PARC to increasingly solve both policy and personnel coordination dilemmas. The number of bills that the leadership had to deal with was reduced, and the bills that eventually came to it from each policy sector had already been at least partially coordinated among the veterans and backbenchers and among the factions. The equilibrium established after 1962 continued to provide positive reinforcement to the party leaders and backbenchers, and it especially helped resolve the coordination problems faced by all parties in each of their major goal areas. PARC helped representatives and the party gain votes and thus seats in constituencies, provided a clear and established system for allocating offices without creating conflict among the factions, and ensured that policy-seeking for effective governance and co-ordination among many competing policies in a diverse party was attained by training representatives in policy and creating a system in which veteran experts controlled the initial stages of policymaking.

The first stages of LDP development (late 1950s and early 1960s) re-flected intense factional conflict following the merger of the Liberals and Democrats and the institution of a party presidential election. The expan-sion of the kōenkai was aided by the losing factions in those elections turn-ing increasingly to vote mobilization at the local level because they had little influence in policy.

In the second stage (1960s to early 1970s), the party leaders failed to centralize vote mobilization in the party once the kōenkai were well estab-lished, the locus of policymaking was successfully moved from the cabinet to the party with the Akagi memo, and intense factional conflict was di-minished through the adoption of seniority and all-faction participation rules for personnel decisions in filling the key party and PARC (and later in parliamentary and government) posts. Simultaneous with the last was Kakuei Tanaka's push to link LDP politicians in PARC and the bureaucracy to deliver benefits to the constituents of zoku giin and to the kōenkai.

In the third stage (late 1970s and early 1980s), the factional allocation of posts in PARC through seniority was linked with the rise of the zoku giin and their connections to interest groups and the bureaucracy, which pro-duced the culmination of PARC under the '55 system. The role of PARC by the 1980s had turned 180 degrees from its early years of conflict be-tween leaders and backbenchers, among factions, and between the party and bureaucrats. Now politicians, kōenkai, interest groups, and the bureau-cracy were in a synergistic relationship of increasing returns for all involved through PARC and its divisions. The ultimate form of PARC owes much to these complementary institutions and to path dependence.

Sequencing again plays a critical role here. Had the mainstream-anti-mainstream conflict in the early days of the party not been as severe, the Akagi memo compromise giving the party first review of even government bills probably would never have been written. Had the Akagi memo not been written or not been written until after the institutionalization of the party and the factional seniority and participation rules, PARC might have looked similar to its current form but its jurisdiction would have been only over backbencher bills not government bills. The mainstream factions and the bureaucracy would have continued to be the major influences in pol-icymaking through government bills and the zoku giin influence would have been minimal, confined only to backbencher bills. Had the Akagi memo gone into effect earlier, at the time of the formation of the LDP, it might have helped dampen the mainstream-antimainstream rivalry and the latter's need to create *kōenkai*. this would have allowed the creation of party branches and, thus, a more centralized party for vote mobilization, although still with a decentralized policymaking process. Had any of these alterations in sequencing surrounding the Akagi memo occurred, the LDP would now look like a very different party organizationally and the process of policymaking in the party and government could well have been more centralized than it became.

Observers of LDP policymaking processes in the mid-1980s to the early 1980s saw only the culmination of this complex process. Based on their workings then, PARC and its divisions could be perceived to have arisen through the wisdom of party leaders, who allowed LDP representatives to specialize in different policy sectors to more efficiently divide the vote in their districts and thus solve the problem of coordination in SNTV MMDs. This is an intellectually elegant explanation for the role of PARC in the policymaking process, but it is an erroneous one. As we have seen, PARC evolved through the historical development of institutions to cope with both the horizontal discords of LDP factional rivalry and the vertical conflicts of the party leaders versus the backbenchers.

Chapter 7

The Policy Affairs Research
Council after Reform

Until now in the medium-sized districts, there were people who specialized in, for example, agricultural tribes and social-labor tribes or medical or welfare. But now one person, one seat, so one person must be
a generalist, and therefore one individual is a policy department store;
until now he was just a boutique.
Interview SS October 29, 2008

As we have became an opposition party, our manner of engaging in
policy deliberation will change from the past.... Policy deliberation and
Diet strategy have aspects which go together, and using the image of
combining the Directors of the Diet Committee with the Division Chairs
of the party PARC—that's a "Shadow Cabinet."
**Sadakazu Tanigaki, LDP president, in a NHK interview (*NHK Nyuusu,*
October 1, 2009)**

One of the major goals of the reformers when they changed the Japanese electoral system in 1993 was to reduce the power of special interests.
The main expression of this power, other than through big-business funding of the LDP, was PARC. The "iron triangles" connecting the LDP policy tribes in PARC, the special interests, and the bureaucracy were seen as
having captured policymaking in the LDP, protecting vested interests that
disregarding the public interest (Curtis 1999, 53–55, 142). Both the reformers and some of the U.S. political scientists who studied Japanese politics
saw the electoral system as undergirding this system because SNTV pitted
LDP candidates against one another, forcing them compete to deliver concrete (figuratively and literally) benefits to constituents (especially of the
pork-barrel variety) and to claim credit for those benefits to mobilize votes.
To do this, each LDP representative specialized in particular policy areas
on PARC; accumulated seniority; and, with their experience, knowledge,
and connections to vested interests and the relevant bureaucratic agencies,
gradually became major power wielders at the heart of this system.

Given the understanding that a main role of PARC was to allow specialization for dividing the vote, it was natural that some political scientists predicted that if SMD and party lists were instituted, "PARC committees would grow relatively inactive, as members lost their need to scramble for budgetary and regulatory favors for their constituents" (Ramseyer and Rosenbluth 1993, 197). Others acknowledged that prognosis was dangerous but ventured to predict the possible outright demise of the organization: "If it is true that the *raison d'etre* of the PARC committee structure is to aid in district-level vote division, then we should expect to see nothing short of its demise" (Cowhey and McCubbins 1995, 257–58).

In response to the 1994 electoral reform, there were changes in PARC to reflect a deemphasis of all LDP members participating in the PARC divisions' decision making. Nonetheless, PARC, its divisions, and its other committees still existed and were still active. Indeed the policy tribes (zoku giin) based on these divisions, were the basis, even more than a decade after the reform, for the fierce resistance to some of Prime Minister Koizumi's attempted policy reforms in their areas (see chap. 9).

The answer to why PARC continued its existence despite electoral reform and what the consequences of its continuance were for the LDP and Japanese politics is embedded in our historical analysis. Specifically, analyzing the extent to which electoral reform changed (or did not) the specific roles and functions of PARC under the '55 system and the extent to which the organization adapted to the new incentives of the MMM electoral system, can tell us not only why but how PARC continued and what its roles and functions were under the new system. We can thus gauge in concrete ways the impact of changed electoral incentives on party organization and politics.

The Policy Affairs Research Council, Constituency Benefits, and Claiming Credit

As described in chapter 3, the new MMM electoral system retained a personal vote incentive in the SMDs tier and, thus, also an incentive for individual incumbents to retain their kōenkai and for new candidates to form one. The fact that the campaign restrictions also remained unchanged added to the incentives for candidates to try and reach voters through both the provision of constituency services prior to elections and the provision of benefits to the district while in office. And local representatives of the party, whose electoral systems were unchanged, continued to expect the LDP national Diet representative in whose district they were located to bring benefits to their subregion of the Diet electoral district in return for mobilizing votes for the Diet member.

Furthermore, because of the revival potential of the dual-listing rule of the PR system and the imposition by the LDP of a "best loser" rule for determining which dual-listed candidates would be "resurrected" after losing in the SMD tier, there was an additional incentive for both SMD losers and revived PR representatives to continue to strive for a personal vote. If they strove to provide constituents with services (through a kōenkai) and, while still an incumbent (thanks to the PR list), to work to bring benefits to the SMD district they had run in, they might be able to come back in the next election to unseat the SMD representative of one of the opposition parties.

In short, all LDP representatives and the party could still use PARC for these purposes. Recall again, however, that as we have shown, candidates' distinguishing themselves from their fellow LDP rivals under the SNTV system was not necessarily the major purpose of PARC, especially in political-pork areas such as agriculture, construction, and transportation; representatives in the same district did not necessarily specialize in different policy sectors. So, having only one representative instead of multiple representatives in a SMD did little to change the utility or purpose of PARC to the individual politicians, the factions, or the party. If the main purpose of PARC, as some had argued, really was to allow such differentiation among LDP representatives in the same district, then indeed, PARC might have disappeared after electoral reform—but it was not, and it did not.

This is not to say, of course, that the new electoral system changed nothing with regard to how the LDP strategically used PARC for vote-seeking. By the time the LDP returned to power in 1996 (the first election under the new system), it had amended its own rules regarding membership in PARC. Previously, LDP representatives could belong to only two PARC divisions, unless they were on a legislative committee or two, in which case they were automatically additionally placed on the parallel PARC division. Now, under the new system, they could belong to as many PARC divisions as they wished.

The reason for this change was the incentives of the new electoral system. Previously, when a candidate could win in a SNTV district of multiple seats with only 10–20 percent of the vote, attaining expertise and influence in a policy-sector niche was important and could contribute mightily toward that electoral victory. But under the MMM system, with only one representative from a local district, representatives had to cater to a much wider and more diverse constituency to win an election (see chap. 3). An LDP representative succinctly described the change:

> If you don't become a generalist you don't become a representative in the Single Member District (*shōsenkyo-ku*). Up til now, it was that person is transportation-related, this person is economy-related and commerce-related, this person's agriculture-related. Generally, it was largely divided into three. Now, you have to be a representative of all groups. (Interview M, July 4, 2002)[1]

---

1. This point was made by several of our interviewees. Among many examples, a staff member from LDP Headquarters described the shift to representing a more diverse constituency: "In

Research based on Diet committee minutes also reveals that LDP representatives now not only spoke more often than before the reform, they tended to make remarks in different committees rather than concentrating on a few, as before the reform, behavior consistent with the broader participation required to become more of a generalist (Hamamoto 2007). Probably the quotation from a former LDP cabinet minister presented at the beginning of this chapter about the change from boutique to department store representatives sums it up most felicitously. The LDP adapted its PARC membership rules so that LDP representatives could learn more about the many fields of policy they now needed to know about to serve their more diverse constituencies.

It should also be remembered that under the new electoral system not all Diet members had less need for specialization. Those elected from the PR portion might well have needed to specialize for specific, widely dispersed interest groups, and thus in specific policy areas, exactly because their constituencies were now wider than in the SMDs. A party can gain votes in the PR district by catering to specific, larger groups that cut across and have numerous members in the larger regional PR districts:

> The PR representatives are nationwide. The PR representatives also, indeed, increasingly, are variously specialized! For example, a person in the past might have done something to help a specific postal branch, but increasingly with just a special connection to post offices, they could have the votes to win and so they're going to somehow strengthen that. (Interview PB June 27, 2002)

Thus, whereas there are incentives under the new system for SMD candidates to specialize less because of the increasing diversity of their smaller constituency, for those on the regional party list (the PR tier) there are incentives to specialize more across a wider geographical area. Further, one study indicates that those who were in the Diet prior to reform tended to continue to specialize on the committees they did prior to the electoral change, whereas those who were elected after reform tended to focus on the most popular committees (Hamamoto 2007).

A second way in which the LDP adapted its strategy to the new electoral system was to begin to tailor particular types of posts to particular types of representatives, depending on how they were elected and how electorally vulnerable they were under the new system. In research with Benjamin Nyblade (Pekkanen, Nyblade, and Krauss 2006), we analyzed all the PARC

---

the case of the single-member district, increasingly you have to gather [votes] equally from both agriculture and small and medium-sized enterprises in the district. Hitherto, to give an extreme example, you could win with one-fifth of the votes in a five-person choice.... [Now] over half is necessary. But there aren't nearly enough votes for that in one organization. So you depend on various sources and become an 'almighty expert' in everything. In a single-member district, you can't win without obtaining the support of several strata, several occupations, several industries" (Interview PB, Tokyo, June 27, 2002).

posts held by all LDP members in the House of Representatives since 1996. Dividing the sample categories depending on how they had been elected—for example, those who ran only in PR (PR Only), those who ran only in SMDs (SMD Only), those who ran in both and were elected in the SMD (SMD Dual), and those who ran in both but lost in the SMD and were "brought back to life" by being elected in the PR tier (zombies). We found that there was a relationship between the manner in which representatives had been elected and the type of PARC, Diet committee, and governmental leadership posts (minister, vice minister, House of Representatives committee chair, and PARC committee chair) they were allocated after the reform. We categorized these posts as distributive, high-policy, or public goods. As in chapter 6, distributive posts are those that have generally been used in the distribution of particularistic benefits to constituencies, such as agriculture and construction (roughly 40 percent of posts were in distributive policy areas). We divided the nondistributive posts into high-policy posts (high-profile; 37 percent), and public goods posts (low-profile; 23 percent).[2]

We found that representatives who lost in the SMD election but were revived in PR election (the zombies) were much more likely to hold distributive posts than single-listed winners in the SMD election, pure PR winners, and even SMD winners who had been dual-listed. Furthermore, in distributive posts the weaker the electoral strength of the Diet member, the more likely she was to receive a leadership post. Putting together the type of electoral victory and electoral vulnerability, we also found that the strongest revived representatives to PR seats—those who lost by a handful of votes in the local districts—were almost twice as likely as the weakest SMD incumbents to receive a high-policy post (20.5–10.5 percent). In addition, they were nearly as likely as strong SMD incumbents to hold a high-policy post—SMD incumbents who won by 40 points in their district had a 23 percent likelihood of holding a high-policy post. Thus, those who had a chance of recapturing a SMD seat next election were given access to pork-barrel policymaking, whereas strong zombies (to give them greater visibility and thus a better chance of winning the next time around) and relative secure and more senior SMD Diet members (who were and were going to be the main face of the party and could enhance the party label) received the high-policy positions.

Although we did not separate out the PARC leadership positions from other types in this analysis, it is clear that after the reform the LDP has used all types of posts, including the chairs of the PARC divisions, quite strategically both to aid those who were more electorally vulnerable with the kind of positions (distributive) that could help them gain votes in the next election and to allocate high-policy positions that enhanced the party label to

2. The results in subsequent analyses were robust to minor coding variation. See chap. 6, n. 14 for lists of policy areas involved for each.

those who were electorally more secure. Thus the LDP adapted PARC to the requirements and incentives of the new electoral system.

Breeding Specialization and Policy Tribes

In contrast to the adaptation of the LDP to the declining need for specialization for vote-seeking in the SMD election and the tailoring of positions to the incentives of the new electoral system, other dimensions of PARC remain relatively unchanged. Most especially, while accommodating to its representatives' need to become generalists (to respond to the new constituencies of SMD), PARC still also trained politician-experts through the seniority system to serve its need to be a governing party making policy. Although any LDP member could now join any PARC division and attend its meetings—no records were kept of who joined or attended—the executives of PARC (the chairs and vice chairs of its divisions and the chairs of its many committees) still were chosen through interfactional negotiations in which eligibility depended on seniority (within the faction and party). These executive ranks of PARC committees still maintained restrictive and exclusive rosters, unlike for ordinary members. And, as one LDP representative indicated, specialists in any case were necessary and inevitable even under the new more open participation rule: "In fact, the divisions of the LDP have pretty much been opened, but to the extent that you can't attend them all, there is specialization responding to your own interests" (Interview EE, August 6, 2004).

From the LDP perspective, PARC remained a means to develop future party leaders and policy experts who were knowledgeable and influential in particular policy sectors and could govern effectively. From the Diet members' perspective, PARC retained important benefits for career advancement. PARC was an important policy training ground for Diet members to learn about the wider diversity of policy areas that they need to know under the new electoral system and also for them to begin training in a few specialized areas if they wished to move up in the party and become zoku giin.

As a result, even after the electoral reform, the zoku giin type of representative remained in many of the same policy sectors that they had been in before: "Even now the specialist *zoku giin* exist and are strong" (Interview A, November 30, 2001). Indeed, in areas such as roads and postal issues, they fiercely resisted Prime Minister Koizumi's attempts at reform and ultimately provoked a major crisis for the LDP and a critical election (see chap. 8). Further, appointments to PARC, Diet committees, and subcabinet-level posts were still selected the same way as before the reform and remained the only crucial function performed by the factions (and thus the primary reason they survived after electoral reform; see chap. 6).

Even as there was a movement toward more generalization, the need for specialization also remained: "It's necessary to have an eye out for all fields with the small electoral districts just as in America. Beyond that, there are places where you have to establish these specialties" (Interview H, December 12, 2001). And, even though PARC division meetings were now open to any LDP politician who wanted to attend, it was particularly important for aspiring zoku giin to be there:

> And those *zoku,* for *zoku,* it is very important for them to come to *bukai* and listen to what bureaucrats have to say, the government has to say. Or to show you their new policy agenda. And they will speak out at the *bukai,* and they call it the kind of party guidance to the government right? So it's an opportunity for them to express their views and if you have accumulated seniority and if you are an active participant of the *bukai,* then there is a good chance you become the leaders of the *bukai,* and then you become a real *zoku.* (Interview OO, October 20, 2008)

The opening up of the divisions to participation by any member only widened the potential pool of those who attended with aspirations to become a member of a policy tribe.

Further, the PARC divisions as a whole retained their influence in the policy process, even though the process became more top-down than previously. Asked about this more top-down process with coalition government, a relatively young former cabinet minister replied, "It's a fact that they (divisions) can't take all the work. Still when they move negatively, they are still terribly strong." When we followed this up with the observation that they thus essentially become one veto point in the process, the representative responded, "in that sense, when they move negatively *bukai* still have a tremendous impact" (Interview C, December 7, 2001).

A Training Ground in Policy?

Under the old electoral system, in effect, the LDP maintained a "two-tiered system combining both seniority and expertise" (Epstein et al. 1997, 992). Through service on the parallel tracks of PARC executive positions and House of Representative committees and through seniority within the factions, a pool of talented and knowledgeable leaders was created. From this pool, appointments to, first, subcabinet and, then, cabinet positions were made. Over time in the postwar period, these leaders managed to learn enough about policy in their areas of expertise to ensure that the bureaucracy remained responsive to the needs and desires of the party and its constituents.

We conducted simple analyses of who became the division executives (chairs, vice chairs, and acting chairs), one of the major stepping stones on the way to become a zoku giin, before and after the electoral reform (see figure 7.1). After the reform, there were more women in these positions,

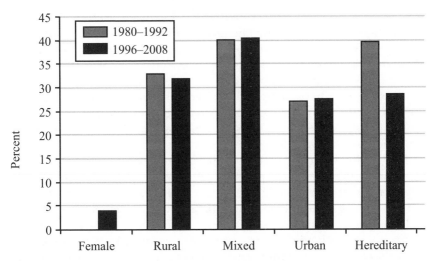

Figure 7.1 Female, urban/rural, and hereditary SMD PARC division executives before electoral reform, 1980–1992, and after electoral reform, 1996–2008 (%)
Source: J-LOD.
Note: Excludes PR representatives. Division executives = chair, vice chair, and acting chair.
PARC, Policy Affairs Research Council; PR, proportional representation system; SMD, single-member district.

which was not difficult because there were no women executives before reform (similarly, the proportion of women in the cabinet increased; see chap. 9). Interestingly, even though the number of urban LDP representatives increased, especially after the 2005 election, there was very little change in the number of division executives who come from rural, mixed, and urban areas; there was only an almost imperceptible decrease in rural representatives compared to those from urban and mixed districts. Because most of the increase in LDP representatives occurred only in the 2005 election, clearly there had not been enough time for them to accumulate the seniority they needed to become a division executive. There was a noticeable decline, however, in the number of hereditary representatives (those who had inherited their kōenkai and their districts from a close relative who had been a major LDP politician previously). The reasons for this are unclear; however, the number of hereditary politicians being given cabinet appointments, even without seniority, increased after the reform. It may be that these politicians skipped the stage of division executive in their careers, perhaps because their family backgrounds already gave them more policymaking knowledge than other representatives.

In a study with Benjamin Nyblade (Pekkanen, Nyblade, and Krauss 2007, 1–26), we found using a broader sample of parliamentary committee executives and members, as well as PARC executives, that the number of policy-tribe specialist representatives decreased after the electoral reform; however, the extent of decrease was due solely to the reduction after the reform of the overall seniority of the LDP (on average, decreasing by one term). In other words, because representatives were more junior after the reform, there had not been enough time for as many of them to achieve the key posts necessary to be considered a member of these policy tribes. The same analysis found that the wider constituencies of the electoral system may have motivated LDP representatives to choose a wider variety of issue areas in which to concentrate their efforts and attain executive positions, indicating less specialization overall (although some did continue to specialize).[3]

In any case, it is clear that some specialization continued but probably less than in the prereform period. LDP Diet members continued to receive training they needed in a wide variety of areas so they could respond to their diverse constituencies in SMD and in PR regional bloc districts and thus be reelected, especially in their first few terms; they also continued to receive, through advancement to the executive ranks of the PARC divisions, the specialized training they needed to participate in more important policymaking roles. Overall, therefore, the zoku giin were perpetuated, although in smaller numbers because of the lower seniority of the party overall; nevertheless, there was still specialization. Cowhey and McCubbins's (1995, 257–58) prediction of a decline in specialization after the electoral reform proved to be correct in essence but not in form; on the other hand, their prediction of the demise of PARC due to less need for specialization has not been borne out. In part this is because they based their prediction on the assumption that PARC existed primarily for dividing the vote among representatives of the same district; but also in part because some specialization, and the expertise of zoku giin, was still needed for the policymaking that a governing party requires.

There probably had been a partial decline, however, in the margin of advantage over the opposition parties provided by having policy tribes. With the need for specialization reduced after reform, becoming a zoku giin provides somewhat less of an advantage for LDP Diet members elected from SMD elections compared to their opposition party counterparts (although it probably remains an important one for those elected from the PR tier). Furthermore, the decline in seniority within the party (and thus the nominal decline in zoku giin) may have further reduced that advantage. With the LDP now out of power and LDP representatives both reduced in number and having their influence on government policymaking eliminated, the

---

3. Pekkanen, Nyblade, and Krauss's (2007, 1–26) statistics seem the best available thus far on this comparison. Trying to use simpler statistics to ascertain specialization is difficult because of the many changes in context between the pre- and postreform periods. On the one hand, after 2001 there was a decline in the number of PARC divisions due to adjustments to parallel the reduction by the administrative reform in the number of ministries and legislative committees, and thus there were simply fewer division executive positions compared to prereform. But there was also a decline over time in the number of LDP representatives on average after the reform.

advantages enjoyed by specialized Diet members will decline even further. Because, even as the opposition party, the LDP will need policy specialists to come up with counterproposals and strategies vis-à-vis the DPJ government, their value to the party in its policy-seeking role will remain, even though their electoral advantage is much decreased.

Party Policy Discipline

After the reform, with Diet members able to participate in the meetings of any division, the party policy discipline function was loosened somewhat. Nevertheless, with the directors, vice chairs, and chairs of each division (the zoku giin and zoku-giin-in-training for future careers in the party and Diet) still in charge of the division, they could control the bills that come from below to some extent and manage opposition to them. This could help the prime minister if he got the support of the zoku giin and other party leaders behind his bills; but it could also serve as a means of resistance to his policies and provide leverage to force him to compromise if he did not (George Mulgan 2002, 191–95).

As before the reform, those who were not in the relevant division had little say on or input into the bills in that policy area. Even if they were in the division, new members of a division having policy ideas that differed from those of the ranking leadership of that division (the zoku giin) leadership could and would be booted off the committee. In fact, this happened to one of our interview respondents (Interview G, December 11, 2001; also see Krauss and Pekkanen 2004, 21).

And members who were not members of a faction had little chance of gaining good posts, and if they did, they had little power once on the PARC divisions compared to those in the influential factions. Even though the faction independents had a vice chair of the divisions to represent them when the vice chairs met to decide who was going to be selected for which posts in the division, their vice chair had little power compared to those representing the factions: "There are one or two Vice-Chairs (*fukukaichō*) who represent independents like us. But no power, no power. Diet posts, there is the Diet Strategy Vice-Chair (*kokkaitaisaku fukuinchō*) for independents, but no power" (Interview I, July 10, 2002).

Also, because factions controlled the allocation of posts, independents could be kicked off their positions for factional reasons that had nothing to do with policy or seniority: One representative complained that he was about to be kicked out of even a minor PARC division: "But 'X'-faction, they tried to kick me out of this post, 'Y' division. Probably to give this post to a younger member of that faction" (Interview I, July 10, 2002). Thus, the PARC structure continued to guarantee that only legislation favored by and approved by the division executives went to the top leaders of the party for approval.

Party and PARC executives also could informally block any bills proposed by backbenchers, even though Diet law allowed bills to be proposed with the support of any twenty members. This was due to a precedent that went back to the Yoshida era, when the chair of the House Management Committee deemed that ruling party members could submit a bill on their own only after approval from the Secretary-General, the Chair of PARC, the chair of the Executive Council, and the chair of the Diet Strategy Committee of the party. When maverick LDP members tried to submit a bill on their own without such signatures, this pre-LDP precedent was reaffirmed by the LDP and cited by the House of Representatives Secretariat (Shūgiin Jimukyoku) as the reason for not letting it go further. Even threats to take the issue to the courts because of its violation of party rules did not help because the Supreme Court had once ruled in such a case that it would not intervene in an internal Diet matter (Komiya 2005, 149; Interview G, December 11, 2001).

Thus, the PARC personnel structure and the LDP requirement that all bills must be sanctioned by the appropriate PARC division and party executives ensured a form of party discipline on legislation even before a bill was introduced into the Diet for deliberation. This implicit function of PARC continued, but with some modification, after reform. The opening up of division meetings to all interested LDP representatives meant that anyone could now come and object to a policy proposal. And because the norm was that unless the proposal was adopted unanimously by everyone at the meeting that day it could not proceed to higher levels and eventually the cabinet (Interview OO, October 20, 2008), gaining passage became a much more complex and subtle process in which the chair of the division played the crucial role. If there were comments at the meeting from those attending and the bill had to be rewritten to accommodate them, he had to convince those at the meeting to delegate the power to rewrite the text after its passage so that those attending that day would not clap their hands in objection:

> So if the head of the *bukai* (division) fails to get that delegation, you will have to hold *bukai* again. And if you fail to do it the second or third time, that particular bill or whatever the text, will have a very hard time....So if you were the manager of the *bukai*, it is very important for you to accumulate your relationship with the members, all members, because you never know who'll come. You have to get respect so that once you say, "May I be delegated," then nobody will clap.... (Interview OO, October 20, 2008)

When someone was recalcitrant, the chair might go to that member and persuade him or her, for the sake of getting the proposal passed, not to voice the objection again. So much depended on the skill and personality of the division chair.

Objections that were very difficult to resolve at the division meeting, which tended to be the more ideological ones rather than those in which the difference could be split, sometimes could be resolved at the combined meeting of the division with the relevant research or special committee on that issue. This was because the chairs of the latter had more seniority generally (usually they were former cabinet ministers) than the division chairs and were more expert; therefore, they had more authority to persuade everyone to go along. In other words, the PARC divisions and committees still served as a substitute for a real party whip to gain consensus on policy, but after the reform the process was much less heavy-handed, more open, and more consensual than it was prereform.

Reinforcing the Factions

Nothing changed after the reform when it came to the factions and appointments to posts below the cabinet level. Koizumi did change the rules for cabinet appointments, breaking the prior norms of seniority and factional balance (see chap. 9). But below the cabinet level, in PARC and legislative appointments, and even at the subcabinet level,[4] the factions and factional negotiations continued to completely determine such personnel appointments.

Indeed, when it came to party posts, including the important ones such as the executives of a PARC division, factional control and seniority norms seemed to *increase* after the prime minister had the authority to name his cabinet without such considerations. Indeed, for the first time there was now an intentional strategic purpose in maintaining strict seniority rules below the cabinet level, especially for the party posts, as an LDP representative told us:

> since this has become an era for political appointees [at the cabinet level], the party side has become even more strictly [by] seniority...in order to balance it out and control the dissatisfaction of those loyal party politicians who served in kind of traditional ways. I wouldn't say [it is more rigid]; it is more strategically kept. In the past, it was inertia—simply an authoritarian sort of rule. Today, it is more of a strategic mechanism...to maintain party unity. (Interview OO, October 20, 2008)

Therefore, faction leaders were still able to reward their followers and control their career advancement—indeed, this became their chief remaining function, as we have seen. Because of this, at least part of policymaking remained a coordination problem, which factional bargaining and appointments to PARC and other subcabinet positions helped solve. PARC

---

4. These were appointments to the new positions of deputy minister and secretary, which had succeeded the prior subcabinet post of Diet vice minister after the administrative reform of 2001.

remained a delegated policymaking organ. Nevertheless, other changes broke some of its policy initiation powers, and it had to share them with the prime minister and cabinet in a mixed top-down and bottom-up process.

Historical Institutionalism: The Policy Affairs Research Council and Reform

Electoral reform partially disrupted and altered—but did not break and, in some cases, even reinforced—many of the previous patterns found in PARC. Complementary institutions remained vitally important for explaining why many things did not change despite the electoral reform. Restrictions on campaigning, for example, continued to provide incentives for LDP representatives to become active in PARC and influential in at least one policy sector to provide benefits to their constituents and ensure the personal vote. The altered campaign finance reform that accompanied the electoral reform, by channeling campaign contributions through the party and especially by allowing them to go through local party branches over which the now lone Diet member usually presided, meant that the more constituency benefits the representative brought back from his influence in PARC in policymaking and the more credit claiming he could do, the more likely special interests would contribute to him or to the local LDP chapter.

The new electoral system itself emerged as a complementary institution in specific ways. The SMD portion perpetuated a personal vote even after the end of SNTV, and the PR portion and the adoption by the LDP of a "best loser" rule guaranteed that those who lost in their local SMD election but were "revived" in the PR portion wanted to continue to cultivate PARC for the benefits they could bring to constituents in the hopes that they might win in the next SMD election. As we have seen, the LDP even adapted its strategy of allocating posts to aid such members and the more vulnerable SMD winners by appointing them relatively more frequently to pork-barrel positions in PARC, the Diet, and the government to aid their and the LDP SMD seat quest.

The weakening of the factions after the electoral reform (due to the loss of two of their three major functions; see chap. 5) did not change PARC very much because the seniority rules and factional allocation of party posts remained. Indeed, the strict following of factional seniority for such positions became even more important in helping temper more senior LDP representatives' dissatisfaction with losing their automatic access to cabinet posts through their seniority. And as we have seen, the ability of PARC to manage internal policy conflict in the divisions was somewhat enhanced by the greater seniority of chōsakai chairs (the former ministers) in the combined meetings of the divisions and their research committees.

What the electoral reform did cause was the need to cater to a wider and more diverse constituency, inducing the LDP to change its membership rules and, subsequently, reinforcing and even enhancing the function of PARC as a policy training ground for younger LDP representatives.

The negative externalities and, thus, path dependence of nonparticipation in PARC and becoming a zoku giin continued unchanged for Diet members. Even with SMDs, representatives' not being able to "bring home the bacon" in terms of political pork and other benefits to their districts and to claim credit through policy influence (well known in the United States), hurt them and possibly made them vulnerable in the next election. Thus, incentives to do so and to become an elite member of a policy tribe continued relatively unchanged after the reform, especially for PR-level representatives but also for electorally vulnerable SMD representatives and strong zombies). Indeed, the broadening of participation in PARC to all LDP representatives may have actually *increased* the negative externalities of nonparticipation in PARC because, while it continued the incentives for some specialization in policy areas, now if representatives did not also participate in PARC meetings to learn about diverse policy areas to serve their wider constituency, they would be at a disadvantage electorally.

The timing of the reform, not until the 1990s, also played a role. What if the reform had been introduced in the early late 1950s or early 1960s, before the Akagi memo? In this case, it is more than likely that policymaking would have become much more centralized because government bills would still be controlled by the party leadership, especially the mainstream factions; MMM would have reinforced that, as would the lack at that time of institutionalization of factional seniority and other factional post distribution norms and rules. Very possibly there would never have been an Akagi memo, and the policymaking process and the role of PARC in it would look very different today, perhaps much more like the reformers and some political scientists expected. At best, PARC probably would have remained a minor party organ primarily concerned with screening and controlling the less important bills introduced by backbenchers rather than the much more important government bills at the cabinet and top party levels. In short, Japan might resemble a more Westminster system with cabinet government than it does today. Sequencing matters.

With the defeat of the LDP, the DPJ government seems intent on introducing exactly such a Westminster system into its policymaking (see chap. 9). Will the LDP reorganize itself to do the same in response? Very soon after his selection of in 2009 as the first postdefeat LDP president, Sadakazu Tanigaki took the first steps in that direction. As the quotation at the beginning of this chapter indicates, he combined PARC and its division chairs and the Diet Strategy Committee and its related Diet committee directors into something resembling a shadow cabinet to formulate policies for the LDP in opposition (*Mainichi Shimbun* Online, October 5, 2009). This change is the most significant LDP reorganization of PARC and its functions since the Akagi memo of the early 1960s.

Why should PARC potentially change more now than it did with the introduction of the new electoral system? This is difficult to explain for those who see electoral systems as determining everything. This development, however, is entirely comprehensible in our historical institutional development approach (see chap. 10). Moreover, PARC was not an institution set up within the LDP to satisfy the electoral-system needs of its representatives; it was an institution that gradually developed after the Akagi memo as the main policymaking organ for the long-governing LDP. The unfamiliar oppositional role of the LDP means that the PARC close "iron triangle" relationship with bureaucrats and the special interest groups will severely weaken. It is likely, as the Tanigaki quotation indicates, that it will become more of a policy strategy organization, helping the party develop policy ideas and ways of responding to the initiatives of the DPJ government. If combined with the Diet Strategy Committee, it can bring about a more unified and streamlined organization that is better geared to parliamentary government. And if this truly results in PARC's being be closely tied in the future to the party president and secretary-general, combined with its party whip discipline functions, this may potentially result in a more Westminster-style LDP as well. Whether the LDP moves even further in this direction to emulate the intended DPJ top-down and cabinet government style is a key question for its organizational future.

And if, as it seems to be doing, the LDP moves toward a more centralized top-down system of policymaking, the theoretical and practical implications are significant. First, theoretically, it implies that defeat may have been a greater stimulus to change in the LDP organization than the change of the electoral system itself (see chap. 10). Some may argue that such change is still just a delayed adaptation to the electoral reform, and they may be partially correct. Nevertheless, as we have consistently argued, this is not a very satisfactory social scientific explanation—it does not tell us why it took so long for the LDP to adapt; why it did not emulate its newer, more centralized party rival earlier; and why it took a defeat to reduce or eliminate the role of PARC.

Second, if the LDP adopts this organizational change while in opposition, but then if and when it returns to power reinstitutes the PARC in its older form, that too has large implications. It would imply that the pre-defeat development of PARC owed as much to the long stint of the LDP in power as to any electoral system format and that its prereform legacy trumped any adaptation to its 2009 defeat. Either way, the future of PARC will tell us much about which variables, other than the electoral system, can help explain the LDP organizational development.

Chapter 8

Party Leadership in the '55 System

When coalitional and factional politics coincide, then, the emergence
of "grey", insipid prime ministers becomes almost a certainty; the position of chief executive will be filled by individuals who command no
particular authority with voters or within their own party. Inevitably,
this "greyness" carries over into governmental politics. Lacking authority, prime ministers become at best one of several important players in
the political game.... Their predicament is perfectly illustrated by the
Japanese experience....
Anthony Mughan (2000, 14)

The Japanese prime minister, by the standards of most other countries,
is seen as a weak and passive leader.
Kenji Hayao (1993, 202)

So far, we have looked at how the three most important institutions of
the LDP—the kōenkai, the factions, and PARC—developed under the '55
system and why. We also saw how the new MMM electoral system brought
about some changes, although in many cases not as many as theorists
had predicted it would and should, and how the actual change and continuity that exist were related to the historical development of these LDP
institutions.

In the same way, in this chapter and the next we analyze the top positions of the party—its leadership and, particularly, the party president
who became prime minister. Examining the development of the LDP party
president from a historical institutional perspective is vital for understanding both the party as a whole and each of its other institutional components. First, the prime minister is the head of the party and the person to
whom each of the other institutions is, at least nominally, accountable and
the party president is integrally related to each of the other institutions;
they cannot be fully understood without examining the development of
party president. Second, as we have seen, relations and conflicts among the
party leaders and between the party leaders and backbenchers have often
been at the heart of the development of the other institutions. Here we

look explicitly at these relations and conflicts again but from the perspective of the most important party leadership institution—the party president who became the prime minister.[1] As before, we are interested in how this institution evolved over time, both pre- and postreform.

In our previous chapters, the reader may have noticed the possibility of an inverse relationship between the kōenkai, the factions, and PARC, on the one hand, and the party leadership, on the other. Under the '55 system, when the power of the first three institutions increased over one of the key party functions, the party president's influence decreased; the more the party president acquired influence in one of these party functions, the less the corresponding subordinate institution had. At times, the party leadership and one of the other institutions were in overt conflict; at other times, they interacted in a relatively integrated, although not seamless, process. The role and influence of the party leadership are at the core of the issues of how centralized (or decentralized) the LDP has been as a party and how the party operated during various periods of its history.

Of course, there is one major difference between the party leadership and the other three institutions—some theorists predicted that all the other three would disappear or diminish greatly with the electoral reform. No one predicted that the prime minister's role as party leader would disappear. If the predictions of many theorists had actually been correct, perhaps there would be less to explain about the growing power and influence of the party leadership and the greater centralization of the party. As we have seen, however, the other three institutions still exist and perform important functions for the party even after the reform. Yet the party is also somewhat more centralized today and the prime minister's role is greater than it was at the height of the '55 system, before the electoral reform, although there also has been great variation since the reform (Tiberghien 2007, 42–43, 120–21). In an earlier period under Yoshida, under SNTV, the party was even more centralized and the leader's role even greater. How do we explain these variations in LDP institutional development?

The main questions of this chapter are, therefore, why and how the role of the party leadership has ebbed and flowed at various times in its history and how that ebb and flow are related to the development of the kōenkai, the factions, and PARC. If the role and institution of the prime minister and party leadership are integrally linked to and sometimes inversely related to the other three party institutions, how did this relationship develop and change over time? We must raise these questions for the periods both before and after electoral reform because the exercise of leadership was not consistent after the post-'94 system was in place (see chap. 9). These variations lead us to expect, as with the other party institutions, that historical

---

1. We sometimes include the secretary—general of the party along with the party president because he is appointed by the prime minister and is his chief lieutenant—and under the '55 system also sometimes his rival for leadership—in administering the party.

development and factors other than the electoral system might be at play here and that the answer to these questions may lie in the complex relationship of the party leadership to these other institutions over time.

Because this book is concerned with the LDP *qua* party and not as a governing party per se, we focus this chapter on the prime minister and other party leaders and their relationship to the party rather than delving into the much larger subject of the prime minister and party leaders in their role in government and governance. When the party leader's role in policymaking involves his governmental role as prime minister, however, we bring the latter into the discussion.

Much as with our other LDP institutions, there have been both cultural and electoral approaches to the study of LDP leadership and the prime minister. Some researchers taking the cultural approach have seen the source of the relative weakness of Japanese prime ministers under STNV as residing in the generally noncharismatic, nondirective, facilitative, and consensual style and pattern of Japanese leaders in a group-oriented society such as Japan (Ike 1978, 51–54; Reischauer 1988, 291). The problem with this interpretation is that, for a phenomenon to truly be an expression of a pattern of Japanese culture, it has to be nearly universal. But, in fact some Japanese leaders, notably Prime Minister Shigeru Yoshida in politics and Sōichirō Honda in business, were quite top-down, individualistic leaders, and Daisuke Ikeda, long-time president of the Sōka Gakkai Buddhist religious organization, was often treated among the adherents of that faith as charismatic.[2] Furthermore, there has been large variation in the influence of the prime ministers, even just in the last quarter century, that a culturally determined approach cannot explain.

Many others, taking an electoral approach, have seen the relatively weak role of the Japanese prime minister as a second-order consequence of the SNTV system. In particular, having the kōenkai rather than party branches serving as vote mobilization organizations, the role of strong LDP factions in choosing the prime minister and creating a more collective than individual party leadership, and the importance of PARC in the policymaking process are seen as having undermined the prime minister's influence.[3] We find there is truth to this argument. Nevertheless, as we have seen, these institutions were not entirely the product of the SNTV electoral system but, rather, a result of their own historical developments, including factors other than the electoral system. This leads us to suspect that the development of party leadership might also have been influenced by factors other than the electoral system and that, if party leadership's

---

2. Martin and Stronach (1992, 249–51) see the traditional style as the norm and the prime minister's behavior as limited by "the traditional social and political bonds that restrain their behavior," but they also see individual prime ministers as being capable of breaking out of that style occasionally.

3. This is generally the approach and explanation taken by Hayao (1993), the most comprehensive study to date of the Japanese political leader.

influence and role were undermined to some extent by the power of these other LDP institutions, that using historical institutionalist approaches will offer us insights.

Before the Liberal Democratic Party: Shigeru Yoshida and Party Leadership

Kenji Hayao has detailed the factional, party, and bureaucratic influences in the policymaking process that has led Japan to be characterized more by a "dispersion than a concentration of power" and the prime minister consequently to be see as "not play[ing] a particularly activist role in the policy process," making him appear "relatively weak and passive when compared to other heads of government" (1993, 200–201). Others have referred to Japanese politics and leadership as an un-Westminster system (George Mulgan 2003) because of the lack of centralized leadership in LDP and government compared to the far more concentrated power in the ruling party and government leaders' hands in other parliamentary systems, such as the United Kingdom. Japan, instead, is thought to have had a systemic "political leadership deficit" (George Mulgan 2000) in the long-term governance of the LDP. This was the conventional wisdom on Japanese and LDP leadership prior to the electoral reform.

The Japanese prime minister operates under constitutional constraints that the prime ministers of United Kingdom and New Zealand do not. There is a contradiction between cabinet government and parliamentary supremacy in the Japanese system that gives the Diet more influence on policy than in the Westminster-style systems of the United Kingdom or New Zealand (Kawato 2005, 2006, 7). The Japanese prime minister also does not control the daily agenda of the Diet; instead, the party does (Tiberghien 2007, 44–45; 125–27). He also is made more vulnerable because of the frequency of electoral cycles in Japan (Tiberghien 2007, 45–46).

Nevertheless, there was a time, early even under the constitution and SNTV electoral system, when the party and governmental leadership was much more concentrated and influential than presented in this stereotype. Shigeru Yoshida, leader of the Liberal Party and prime minister for seven years (1956–1947 and 1948–1954), is known primarily for his formulation of the foreign policy course of allying Japan with the United States for its defense and providing it with bases but also maintaining defensive limits on its own armed forces and concentrating on economic growth to become a great power again in the postwar world, called the Yoshida Doctrine (e.g., see Samuels 2003b, 197, 200–211, 223–24). His individualist and top-down leadership style earned him the sobriquet of "One Man Yoshida" (Samuels 2003b, 197). On the other hand, Douglas McArthur is supposed to have privately regarded him as "monumentally lazy and politically inept" (quoted in Dower 1993, 211), despite their ostensibly good relationship, and Yoshida is rarely thought of as having played a major role in political party development. Recent scholarship (Komiya 2005), however, has cast a new light on both the style of Yoshida's party leadership and its importance in setting the pattern for the LDP leadership structure that developed after he retired from office.

When Yoshida took over the reins of the Liberal Party after Ichirō Hatoyama (its previous leader) was purged by the Occupation, the organizational structure of the party closely resembled the structure of its prewar predecessor, the Seiyūkai. Directly below the president of the party was the Executive Council.[4] The majority (fifty-six members) of the council were elected proportionally by region from among the party representatives, and ten members were appointed by the party president. The secretary-general of the party was appointed by the president, but he administered the decisions made by the Executive Council; so, the executive (secretary-general) and the decision-making body (the Executive Council) remained undifferentiated, with the secretary-general subordinate to the council on the party organizational charts, and the chair of the Liberal Party PARC was even lower, below the secretary-general. The chair of the Executive Council was considered able to replace the party president in an emergency, thus seemingly making that position second only to the president (Komiya 2005, 113–19).

Yoshida changed all this. He had good reason to try because, despite his advantage of being backed by the Occupation, there was a relatively large group of Liberal Party representatives loyal to Ichirō Hatoyama, the former party leader, and resentful of Yoshida's bureaucratic background and haughty style. Indeed these anti-Yoshida groups contributed to the fall of his first cabinet in 1947.

When he returned to power in 1948, he embarked on his campaign to gain control over the party. In addition to cultivating the anti-Hatoyama politicians in the party and thus splitting the former politician's group, one of his major moves was to recruit talented bureaucrats to join the party and run for office, especially in the 1949 election, when several were elected for the first time. The most famous of Yoshida's ex-bureaucrat protégés were of course Hayato Ikeda and Eisuke Satō, who later were to dominate the party themselves as prime ministers for over a decade (1960–1972). Beyond that, he then carefully placed them in key party positions. He explained, "I want to give a political party education to ex-bureaucrats, and an administrative education to those nurtured in political parties.... Thus, I elevate those raised in the party to Minister and Vice-Minister, and I set the ex-bureaucrats as party officials" (quoted in Komiya 2005, 128).

For example, he placed many of the ex-bureaucrats, including at various times Ikeda and Satō, into the position of chair of the Liberal Party

---

4. Sōmu iinkai or Sōmukai, literally General Affairs Committee but usually translated Executive Council.

PARC, a move that was generally (although not completely) accepted because the ex-bureaucrats were considered experts on policy. By doing this, however, Yoshida was also elevating the position that, up until then, had been relatively unimportant and considered subordinate in policymaking to the Executive Council, and was quietly taking control of party policymaking through his coterie of ex-bureaucrats.

The same technique worked for the even more important position of secretary-general, whose influence and functions were relatively vague at that time and, again, supposed to be subordinate to the Executive Council. Prewar, the secretary-general of the party was not particularly involved in elections or in fund-raising for them; however, gradually under Yoshida the secretary-general came to be highly involved in party election campaigns and fund-raising. In the allocation of posts, especially cabinet appointments, Yoshida increasingly relied on the advice of his secretaries-general; he also delegated the picking of the party division chair posts to them and had them represent the party increasingly in interparty negotiations. While raising the status and influence of this post, Yoshida generally ignored the Executive Council. Thus, under Yoshida, the secretary-general gradually assumed the mission of managing party operations. It should be noted that in doing this, Yoshida skirted Article 4 of party rules, written to establish Executive Council centrism (Sōmukai chūshinshugi). In 1950, although the council was supposed to be in charge of the operations of the Diet committees, it lost this function as well when the Diet Strategy Committee (Kokkai Taisaku Iinkai) was established to perform this role for the party. In only one way was the role of the Executive Council improved under Yoshida—its chair, which previously had been a temporary position, was made permanent (Komiya 2005, 121–34).

These changes were institutionalized and the new roles clarified in a revision of the party rules in 1953. The Executive Council became a decision-making body in which party affairs such as accounts, personnel, and policy were discussed. But the secretary-general now clearly had been made the assistant to the party president and was chosen by him exclusively; he was in charge of party business, including party personnel. And by this revision, both the secretary-general's and the PARC chair's positions were divorced from the Executive Council. In addition, the president's authority to expel party members was made clearly absolute (Komiya 2005, 144–49).

As Hitoshi Komiya (2005, 151) concludes, "In the process of the conflict which is labeled the Yoshida-Hatoyama struggle, the managing of posts, the organization, and the authorities of the postwar conservative party were completed." The organizational structure and functions for the Big Three executives of the conservative parties—secretary-general, PARC chair, and Executive Council chair—was born; this was then incorporated into the LDP in 1955 and has been maintained until the present. Yoshida also established the strong primacy of the president within the party, a precedent, in contrast, that was not consistently maintained in the LDP.

After Yoshida: Party Leadership Power and Its Decline

After Yoshida, the merger of the liberals and democrats to create the LDP put the status of party leadership into a period of flux. Two contradictory groups fought for control of the party. The first was the leadership of the coalitions of the new mainstream factions, which usually included those ex-bureaucrat disciples of Yoshida such as Ikeda and Satō who, because of their control over the party presidential selection at the party convention, could impose at least some form of central control over the party, albeit now a collective one. On the other side were the backbenchers, notably those of the antimainstream factions who had been relegated to subordinate and minor roles in the party, who struggled to make the leadership more responsive to their needs and demands (see chaps. 4 and 6). We thus see a partial diminution of the relatively centralized leadership control that Yoshida had attained; leadership was now more collective, with the prime minister's constitutionally sanctioned monopoly on cabinet and party appointments and his party-sanctioned monopoly on party appointments now shared with the mainstream faction leaders. Yet, although collective, the mainstream leaders as a group could still exercise moderately strong leadership of the party.

What happened next, however, emerging from the rivalry of the factions and the conflicts between the party leaders and backbenchers, was a gradual erosion of this leadership power. We can see these struggles played out in all the major dimensions of the party—vote-seeking, office-seeking, and policy-seeking—from the late 1950s until the institutionalization of the '55 system in the late 1970s or early 1980s, when the compromises forged during these struggles gradually resulted in a relatively decentralized party with relatively weaker party leadership.

Party Leadership and the Attainment and Maintenance of Power

Party leaders attain influence within political parties through various means directly related to the goals that parties pursue. For example, in parliamentary regimes, especially those that are centralized and majoritarian, such as the Westminster system in Britain, a party leader can obtain her intraparty influence through various means related to the collective incentive of her party and the individual incentive of each politician to seek votes to win seats. First, there is the persistent implicit threat that the party leader(s) could deprive a candidate of the nomination, the virtual prerequisite for obtaining or maintaining her seat.[5] A second, more subtle but no less potent weapon becomes available to a prime minister in a centralized party when the party label or the appeal of a particular leader

---

5. The best example of the influence of a party leader over nominations is concisely and metaphorically expressed in the quotation from British Prime Minister Harold Wilson that begins chapter 9.

matter greatly to the fate of individual representatives' chances for re-election. If voters vote to a large extent based on the stable identification with a particular party, support for its policies, or the appeal of the image of its leadership, then representatives depend on the party leaders for their own seats and can be expected to defer to the party leadership. The party leaders may also hold intraparty power if the party organization, of which the party leader is the head, matters greatly in both financing the campaigns and helping to mobilize the constituents to vote for the party candidates. The ability of the party to provide key financing or personnel to aid individual candidates gain or retain their seats makes them more dependent on the party and, thus, on its leaders both during and after elections. All of these make backbenchers dependent on the party leader for their seats and, thus, more amenable to his or her influence within the party.

One of the greatest resources that the party leader may have to gain leverage over fellow leaders and the backbenchers of her party is the allocation of party, parliamentary, and government posts. She can reward or punish rivals in the leadership and the party representatives by the judicious and selective use of appointments, beginning, of course, with cabinet appointments and continuing on to the usually more numerous subcabinet posts such as vice minister and secretary, parliamentary leadership positions, and important party posts.[6]

Finally, party leaders in parliamentary regimes have major influence in shaping the policies of their party. They are, after all, both the face of the party and its policies to the electorate and the spokespeople in the parliament for those policies that must be publicly defended. Party leaders keep control over the shaping of policy because they have influence deriving from their vote-providing and office-providing power within the party. They also keep control over policy because the backbenchers know that, for the party to be successful collectively (and thus indirectly for them individually), good policies have to be sold to the electorate and defended against the opposition by the party leader and need to be crafted by (policy and public relations) experts who are usually found at the higher reaches of the party or in the government cabinet. In short, in the ideal type of strong central party leadership, the interests and incentives of the leader are aligned nearly perfectly with the interests and incentives of the backbenchers for the collective interest of the party.

6. In Westminster systems of strong cabinet government, such as the in the United Kingdom and New Zealand, the prime minister can also determine the order of preference, a largely honorary ranking of the priority individuals in the cabinet that confers prestige to those on the top of the list. The ranking is not fixed or directly related to the ministry involved but is purely a recognition (or if an individual drops down on the list, a potential punishment) that the leader can use to indicate favorites and people she considers close and important in the government (Hennesy 2000, 63–65; also, Nemoto, et al., forthcoming).

The Intraparty Weakening of the Leadership
of the Liberal Democratic Party

As the LDP developed in the 1960s and 1970s, nearly all these potential central party leader capacities eroded. Once the factions consolidated after the 1955 merger of the LDP and after the 1960 crisis, the mainstream factions began to yield more to the antimainstream factions to maintain party stability and district nominees were decided through intense factional bargaining. Nevertheless, as we have seen, this did not prevent factions from supporting independents to run in several districts.

In addition, neither the prime minister nor the secretary-general could maintain control over a seat in which a retiring or deceased incumbent had a close relative or aide ambitious to succeed him. The kōenkai often emerged decisive as a selectorate in such cases (see chap. 2). If the relative or aide was the favorite of the kōenkai to succeed the incumbent and the inherited support organization and name recognition of the successor gave that candidate a major advantage over others in retaining the seat, it was almost a foregone conclusion that the party would nominate the hereditary politician. The faction to whom the predecessor, and most likely the successor, belonged could make a very strong argument to the party, and the party leadership would not, and would have been foolish to, oppose this succession (in part, because each faction leader was going to face or had faced the same situation with some of his own faction members' successions).

The kōenkai, the factions, and PARC, once they were established in the party, also curtailed the Diet members' dependence on the LDP president for the party label, policy formulation, and party and leader image. Not only was the personal vote through the kōenkai significant in Japan under the '55 system, but habitual voting, in which people tended to vote for the same party every election whether or not they had a party identification, and party image were as important as the party label in determining the voters' choices.[7] Cold War polarization contributed to this by making the LDP the only viable choice for conservatives. Even if a portion of voters cast their ballots because of habitual party voting, party image, or party identification, the question remains whether these party variables were influenced by the image of the party leader. There is evidence that this was probably not the case, at least until the mid-1980s.

Organizationally, the dependence of the party on the kōenkai to mobilize the vote meant that the candidates' electoral fates rested as much with themselves as with the party. This provided a large degree of potential

---

7. Richardson (1988) emphasizes that his findings show the importance of habitual party voting, party image, and party identification as influencing voters' choices (as they might well, especially in the Cold War ideologically polarized party system). He neglects, however, (1) that the voter still had a choice among LDP party candidates, which would have probably made the second-order choice must more of a personal vote, and (2) to differentiate between LDP versus opposition party supporters in his findings.

independence from the party leadership; whatever the image or popularity of the party at any given election, each candidate might still win his or her seat with good local personal-vote gathering through the kōenkai. Here the early failed attempts by some party leaders to replace kōenkai with local party branches become salient. Had these attempts succeeded, with vote-gathering (and even possibly greater campaign financing) becoming more centralized in the party, LDP candidates might have become more dependent for their seats on the party organization and thus on its leadership. Such, of course, was not to be the case (see chap. 3).

Nor were candidates particularly beholden to the party or its leadership for financing. The party did provide some portion of the financing, but it provided only a percentage spent by candidates and provided the financing *equally* to all candidates (in part no doubt to avoid making decisions that could lead to factional warfare). The remainder of the needed financing had to be obtained from the candidates' faction leaders or raised on their own. Again, all this lessened the loyalty of candidates to and their dependence on the party leader—but increased them to their faction leader.

The party leader also began to lose any great influence in the distribution of posts, both in cabinet and subcabinet positions and in parliamentary or party positions. Immediately after the party merger that formed the LDP in 1955, the coalition of mainstream factions that won the party presidential election dominated the party (see chap. 5). These factions were given the best of all the posts in the early years of the new party; there were at that time no seniority rules in place to limit the pool of candidates for these positions. During these years, the party leader may have had a fair degree of leeway in rewarding individuals with posts, except, of course, that he was limited by the need to satisfy all the other mainstream faction leaders and their followers. Indeed, although consultation by the leader with veteran politicians and friends had always been the case, even prewar, before a cabinet was named, the process became much more formalized in the late 1950s under Prime Minister Nobusuke Kishi because of party factionalism. The prime minister first chose his chief cabinet secretary, then the secretary-general, and the chairs of the Executive Council and PARC. These posts were given to members of his own faction or of factions in alliance with his (i.e., mainstream factions). And these men would then serve as his cabinet formation staff (*sokaku sambō*); together they decided on the members of the cabinet (Thayer 1969, 183–84). Despite the president's having discretion over certain posts, in general, the prime minister's leverage on cabinet appointments was constrained even in the early years of the LDP by factional considerations, and the appointments were more a collective than an individual choice.

Within the party, from the mid-1970s to the mid-1980s, the party president lost even the right to appoint his own secretary-general, a power, as we have seen, that was crucial to Yoshida's asserting his control over the party in the 1950s. Prime ministers had always appointed someone from their own faction to that key party post until the last Kakuei Tanaka cabinet in 1973. When Takeo Miki became prime minister, he assigned the post of secretary-general to someone from the Ōhira faction, and Fukuda continued that practice. When Ōhira became prime minister in 1978, however, he appointed someone from his own faction, perhaps because he well understood the dangers of having a factional rival run the party because he himself had just used that post to undermine his predecessor Fukuda. He met with resistance from the antimainstream factions, however, and had to compromise by appointing a different person from his own faction.

Thereafter, prime ministers under the '55 system reverted to the practice of separating the secretary-general post from their own faction (*sō-kan bunken*), and this became established as a norm. There also was a tendency after that to disperse the other major party posts (the PARC and Executive Council chairs) among the factions not represented by the two top party positions (Satō and Matsuzaki 1986, 70–73). The prime minister had lost control over the top party personnel positions.

When it came to other posts, as we have seen, with the increasing establishment of the seniority and proportionality rules for the distribution of cabinet and subcabinet positions, for example, and then the application of the all-faction distribution rules to other posts (a process complete by the mid-1980s; Kawato 1996a, 955), the sphere of leadership discretion in the distribution of posts gradually became even more constrained, and the process became even more formalized. With these rules increasingly being applied, the prime minister and his advisory group had to choose from among the lists of party executives and cabinet member candidates based on seniority. In short, the factions now determined who could even be considered for a cabinet position. The other party and parliamentary positions were essentially not decided by the prime minister but, rather, by representatives of factions.

Thus, from the late 1950s until the mid-1980s, the leeway of the party and government leader to use his position to reward or punish representatives (which had been wide under Yoshida) became increasingly narrow due to the factions, the institutionalization of the norms and rules governing allocation of posts, and the decentralization of the party over time. Depicted graphically, this range of discretionary power would resemble a funnel with a fairly narrow end at the height of the '55 system in the mid-1980s.

The failure of the various attempts to eliminate the factions through the years also had huge implications for the power of the LDP leader. The most significant of these, as we have seen (see chap. 5), was Miki and Fukuda's push in the mid-1970s, which resulted only in their greater extension into the electoral districts. The continued viability of the LDP factions throughout its prereform development was not so much a delegation of this leadership power to control and manage office-seeking in the party as a gradual abdication, resulting in the further institutionalization of a weak leader and decentralized party.

Conflict was constant within the infant LDP. When it came to policymaking, in the years immediately following the LDP merger, the party leadership constrained spending and the constituency-oriented bills of the backbenchers, imposing party rules and Diet procedural bills to limit them, especially concerning the budget (see chap. 6). Further, PARC was a weak body, a dumping ground for antimainstream leaders who lacked personnel support, prestige, and influence, and was dominated by the policy preferences of the government bureaucracy. Consequently, the party leadership had greater influence in the early days, although it was collective, in the form of the mainstream faction leaders and its Yoshida School ex-bureaucrats who worked well with the ministries to develop policy proposals.

Two things changed all this and led to the archetypal pattern we find in the '55 system. The first was the Akagi memo of 1962 and the development of the zoku giin in the 1970s. For the first time, *all* bills, even government-sponsored bills that had been developed in the bureaucracy and by the party leadership, had to go through the party before the government could introduce them to the Diet.

The result of the Akagi memo and the development of zoku giin by Kakuei Tanaka's attempts in the 1970s to build up PARC to link the interest groups and the bureaucracy through knowledgeable PARC veterans within a policy sector, was very consequential. Instead of the party leadership either formulating policy as in a Westminster system or at least being the major shaper of policy even if it had been first formulated in the bureaucracy, interest groups' and citizens' demands and the party interests became aggregated in and many policies shaped by PARC and its divisions. In effect, the rigid "iron triangle" of the PARC divisions, key interest groups in a sector, and the relevant government ministry now essentially determined policy. The party leadership's role was limited to a final check and tinkering before the bill went to the cabinet for final discussion before its introduction to the Diet. Once more, as this system had developed by the 1980s, the party leadership was forced to abdicate one of its key functions to other parts of the party.

We see this very clearly in the surveys of bureaucrats conducted by Michio Muramatsu and his colleagues in 1987 at the height of the '55 system. Bureaucrats were asked: "Who had the greatest influence on your ministry's or agency's policy formulation and implementation?" The results show the relative perceived influence of the party leaders compared to PARC and the zoku giin (see figure 8.1). As this graph indicates, the prime minister's perceived influence on policymaking is less even than that of the interest groups; it is the least of all the party and governmental entities mentioned. Even if we combine responses for the prime minister and Big Three party leaders (the secretary-general and the chairs of PARC and the Executive Council), their perceived influence does not equal that of bureaucratic agencies and their affiliated advisory councils or of zoku giin and PARC. Indeed, the latter is clearly seen as the single most influential choice of all

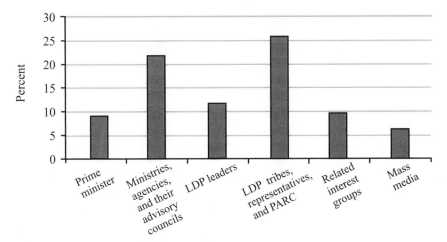

Figure 8.1 From the 1987 Bureaucrats' Survey: The greatest influence on your ministry or agency's policy formation and implementation (%). All four choices combined.
Source: Data from Krauss (2007, 70).

those mentioned. Clearly, influence over policymaking had devolved by the 1980s to PARC and its policy tribes.

This loss in influence over the policymaking process also deprived the LDP leader of another of his powers—party discipline. As in most parliamentary parties, according to the LDP rules the leadership (as we have already seen in the discussion of Yoshida's changes) retained the ultimate sanction of expelling representatives who did not vote with the government on the bills it introduced. What is significant about the LDP is how infrequently even the prospect for such discipline appeared. Given the decentralized nature of the party, the independent bases that representatives had created for vote mobilization, and the wide diversity of policy preferences that the party represented, from far right to moderate or even liberal centrist, the lack of problems under the '55 system with party discipline on policy was nothing sort of extraordinary. This is even more extraordinary when we recall that the LDP is one of the few governing political parties in the democratic world in which there is no clearly designated party whip, the representative of the central leadership whose role is to cajole, threaten, persuade, and otherwise make sure that backbenchers vote on policy and bills the way that the party leadership wishes them to. But under the '55 system PARC and the factions performed those disciplinary functions, making unnecessary and irrelevant the party leader's exercise of them (Krauss and Pekkanen 2004, 21).

As we saw in chapter 6, because all policy went through the PARC divisions for approval before going up to the party leadership, the executives of these divisions, frequently the zoku giin, effectively decided the shape and content of policy because they controlled the process as it went through their division and also could expel any mavericks who opposed the policy.

Building a consensus on policy in the division was therefore not difficult. Once the division had approved the policy, no other backbencher had any say regarding the form or content of the resulting bill because the party as a whole never considered it—it was sent up to even more veteran legislators in the Executive Council and ultimately the cabinet.

Given the size of the factions, opposition in the cabinet of any given faction or coalition of factions could endanger any new policy or bill. But such a pattern of opposition was unlikely because the factions, as we have seen, were heterogeneous in terms of policy and ideology. Furthermore, there was a strong norm requiring cabinet decisions to be unanimous, in part to ensure that no faction could block cabinet decisions on policy to embarrass or undermine the prime minister and the current party leadership or to strategically disclaim responsibility for an unpopular decision. This norm solved the factional collective action problem in the cabinet that the party was unable to solve with nominations, as we have seen.[8] With PARC executives self-recruited, mavericks precluded from influence within PARC, backbenchers outside PARC bereft of influence on policy bills, and factions unlikely to either be coherent on policy grounds or impose their will on the cabinet, party discipline did not require a strong whip.

Negative externalities, complementary institutions, and sequencing, which we have examined in the previous chapters, in combination with legal and established practices within the party and government, over time constrained the party leader to a mere first among equals in a collective leadership of factional bosses.

The Prime Minister's Intragovernmental Leadership

Within the governmental policy process, as already mentioned, there were additional constraints on the prime minister's influence, including the lack of legal authority to initiate policy proposals, the norm of unanimity in the cabinet, and legislative authority constitutionally divided between the cabinet and the legislature (Kawato 2006; Tiberghien 2007, 44–45, 125–27). Furthermore, the national bureaucracy formulated most of the cabinet-sponsored legislation, often initially with the advice of their ministerial advisory councils of societal experts attached to each ministry and agency. Thus, policy proposals initiated by the ministries and advisory councils, having wound their way up through the PARC divisions and committees and then to the LDP Executive Council, only came to the prime minister and cabinet at the last stage of the process. Indeed, even in the cabinet the prime minister was not legally mandated to initiate his own policy proposals until an administrative reform that went into effect in 2001! He was not

---

8. See also Pekkanen, Krauss, and Nemoto, "The Collective Action Problem under SNTV: The Case of Factional Overnominations in Japan" (Unpublished paper) for an analysis of how factional competition affected candidate nomination.

prevented in law from doing so, but nowhere was there a legal mandate entitling him to do so either. This too weakened his ability to exercise leadership on policy.

Kenji Hayao (1993) has exhaustively detailed the weaknesses of the position of prime minister in Japan. This Japanese leader was not, however, totally powerless. Had he been, there would have not been as great a competition for the privilege of serving in this position as there was among LDP leaders. For example, Hayao (1993, 200–201) notes that there was one primary means for the prime minister to have a real influence on the process—he could select among the bills already on the agenda that had backing to bring particular policies to fruition ahead of the others.[9]

One specific area in which the prime minister had a major influence was the budget. By working with the powerful Ministry of Finance, which operated as something like a "super-ministry" when it came to the budget process (Campbell 1977),[10] the prime minister could divert some of the political pork and other policy proposals that had wound their way up from PARC.

Another policy sector in which the prime minister was less constrained by the '55 system process was foreign policy, especially U.S.-Japanese relations. Foreign policy was one policy sector in which there was almost no domestic constituency and no real zoku giin clamoring for goodies to be distributed to their districts; indeed, there was very little interest among LDP representatives in foreign policy, and so in this area the prime minister's ultimate legitimate position as representative of Japan to the outside world was accepted.

Because Japan prior to the 1980s was almost exclusively dependent on the United States both for its economic prosperity and its military security, the premier foreign policy issue facing the country was U.S.-Japanese relations. The prime minister was expected, by both the public and his party, to manage that relationship in the best interests of Japan and to preserve and, if possible, expand both the markets and protection that the United States provided. An indication of the importance of the United States to Japan and its leader is that, from 1960 until 1982 (the bulk of the years of the '55 system), 42 percent of all trips made by the prime ministers abroad were to the United States; this was a greater percentage than to any other region of the world during this period, approximately 25 percent more than to other Asian countries, and almost double the visits to Europe and Russia (Krauss 2007, 62).

So, these were the exceptions to the powerlessness of the prime minister: in foreign policy, especially U.S.-Japanese relation; in the budget process, in

9. Takayasu (2005) also argues that, even in the 1970s, prime ministers had sufficient legal and constitutional resources to exercise leadership and that any weakness in their position stemmed from political factors.

10. Campbell and Scheiner (2008) argue that the model of weak prime ministerial power is a great exaggeration, but almost all their examples of prime ministers' wielding power come from the budget policy process.

which the prime minister could exercise more influence than in any other policy arena; and in pushing a particular issue that already had wide support. In other respects and policy areas, the Japanese prime minister was the "missing leader" (Massey 1976, 21, chap. 2)[11] when it came to policymaking.

"The Dog That Didn't Bark..." and Then Did

There is one significant factor that we have not yet mentioned—the role of television. In most democratic political systems by the early to late-1960s, television had become a major double-edged resource for party and government leaders. On the positive side, the increasing importance of television in democratic countries meant that the image of the party leader began to count more and more in the electoral fortunes of the party in parliamentary regimes and in who became the party and governmental leader in presidential systems. Even in the highly decentralized U.S. party system, for example, the 1960 Nixon-Kennedy debates are generally held to have ushered in the television age in presidential politics (Druckman 2003, 559–71). In the United Kingdom, the impact of television on the image and role of the prime minister began in the mid-1960s and increased especially in the 1980s (Mughan 2000, 39–51). On the negative side, a poor television image or unskillful management of the medium could also result in a premature end to careers or governments.

The point here is not that television images necessarily result in stronger or weaker party leaders but, rather, that it *can* become a prime resource, and increasingly has become so in many democracies, in centralizing leadership in the hands of skillful leaders. There are two major reasons for this. First, a party leader's increased popularity due to his or her television image may help the party he or she leads in the next election, thus increasing the leverage that the leader has on the backbenchers—their electoral fates increasingly depend on their party leader's television image. Second, especially in a party in which the leader feels stymied by decentralized and pluralist power centers, a television image can provide a pulpit for an "end-run" to gaining influence because a more popular leader is more likely to get his or her way on policy.

This tendency, however, did not even appear at all in Japanese politics until the mid-1980s and only became more frequent in the 1990s and 2000s (see chap. 9). Why did the influence of television on party leadership politics come so late in Japan?

We believe the answer lies in the way the complex relationship among governmental, political, and media institutions developed. The government had for a long time strictly regulated the media in election campaigns. For

11. Massey finds in his surveys of Japanese youth that societal perceptions were that the prime minister was quite weak compared to the presidents and prime ministers of Western countries and that, with increasing age, respondents perceived him as increasingly incompetent, unlikeable, and dishonest.

example, although television advertising in election campaigns was allowed by law for the first time after 1967, the way it was implemented was extremely restrictive. Only political parties could buy advertising time; individual candidates could not. The number and production of the free television commercials allowed individual candidates was also strictly regulated so as to give no candidate or party an advantage (Curtis 1970, 860–62). In fact, according to election surveys, the number of voters who found television useful in making their voting decisions in either the House of Representatives or House of Councilors elections barely increased from 1970 to the mid-1980s, remaining only in the 10–15 percent range (Krauss and Nyblade 2005, 362).

Moreover, the ads themselves did not emphasize the leader's image because of the nature of media institutions. Television is not only an independent variable influencing the party leader's image but simultaneously a dependent variable that is, in turn, influenced by the nature of the political institutions. Where political institutions are centralized and majoritarian, as in Britain, television is more likely to promote the "presidentialization" of the party and government leader; where they are decentralized and coalition or factional politics prevail, "'grey,' [and] insipid prime ministers become almost a certainty," as in Japan and Italy, and television is much less likely to foreground them to personalize politics for viewers (Mughan 2000, 14–17). Where political institutions are fragmented and segmented as they were in Japan by the late 1970s, leaders tend not to be very mediagenic or have much popular appeal; when such "grey" leaders are common, television tends not to focus on them, making them even less likely to have popular appeal.

This vicious circle was supported and exacerbated in Japan by the nature of media institutions. Not only did the television campaign ads neglect the uninteresting prime ministers manufactured by backroom deals of the factions, television news did the same all year-round. Television news had surpassed newspapers as the main source of news for most Japanese as early as the late 1960s. The unchallenged, dominant television news station from the mid-1960s until the mid-1980s was NHK, a huge public broadcasting network. Rival commercial broadcasting networks had essentially abandoned putting resources into reporting the news because of the overwhelming superiority of NHK in personnel and resources. The NHK news was the most trusted in Japan, and NHK itself was the most trusted institution in Japanese society, according to polls at that time.

The main NHK news program at 7:00 p.m. emphasized public affairs news that differed from its equivalent stations in other countries in its attention to and portrayal of the national government bureaucracy and the policies it formulated rather than the political actors. Indeed, the prime minister was the least covered of all the actors involved in government and policymaking.[12] And all political news was covered in a staid, undramatic,

---

12. In part this was because of the "reporters' club" system, in which every major governmental and societal institution had specialized journalists consistently covering it, ensuring that many institutions got air time and not just the leadership of the country.

nonvisual fashion without attention to individual personalities (Krauss 2000, 23–52). With this type of coverage, it was difficult for the LDP leader to create a popular image through the media that was separate from that of the LDP; this, in any case, represented a fairly accurate portrayal of a leader who was almost entirely the product of a factionalized decentralized party.

With the factions determining who became prime minister, having popular media appeal was not a necessity for attaining office. With PARC determining most policy, the party leader could not use the policy agenda to appeal through the media to the public except in limited ways. And with the personal vote (through the kōenkai) providing, along with the habitual LDP vote, the stable vote for LDP candidates in the electoral districts (Richardson 1977), there was only a limited "floating vote" that the party leader could try to influence with his own personal image, an image that both lacked personal appeal and was not enhanced by the dominant news media (see chap. 3 for how television affected kōenkai). Thus, the complementarity of the political institutions, media institutions, and government regulatory regime produced a prime minister who was unlikely to need, have, or be able to obtain the type of television image that might appeal to voters. This lack deprived him of an independent and powerful means to counteract the decentralized power centers and institutionalized procedures within the party that undercut his influence. No wonder the dog provided nary a whimper, much less a bark.

It is one of the great ironies of Japanese political history that just when this decentralized party system was finally stabilized, following the chaos produced by the consequences of the Lockheed Scandal and Prime Minister Tanaka's resignation, the LDP barely clinging to a majority of seats amid the internal "Daifuku wars" between the Ōhira and Fukuda factions, and then a caretaker leader such as Zenkō Suzuki in the early 1980s, the most influential prime minister since Yoshida appeared—Yasuhiro Nakasone.

Nakasone: Television and the Advisory Councils

Yasuhiro Nakasone came to power in December 1982. The leader of the fourth smallest LDP faction at the time, he was relatively young (in his early fifties) for a Japanese prime minister under the '55 system. He owed his ascension to power completely to the factional politics of the LDP and the support he received from the largest faction by far in the LDP, that of Kakuei Tanaka, who was under indictment for bribery in the 1976 Lockheed Scandal. Indeed, pundits actually dubbed the Nakasone cabinet the "Tanakasone cabinet" because of Nakasone's dependence on that faction and its "shadow Shogun" leader, Tanaka. There was thus nothing in Nakasone's background, rise to power, or administration that would lead us to believe he might begin undermining of the '55 system constraints on LDP leaders. Yet that is what he proceeded to do.

Nakasone's surprising influence, however, was not a result of the intra-party and intragovernmental system that had weakened the party leader and prime minister's power but, rather, a confirmation of it. Even while relying on the former Tanaka faction to both come to power and main-tain it, Nakasone skillfully used two new techniques to make an "end run" around the limitations on leadership and attain a somewhat more autono-mous influence in the party and government. The first technique was his pioneering use of television to make himself popular with voters and thus indispensable to the party; the second technique was his innovative use of the advisory councils (*shingikai*) within the prime minister's office to coun-teract the lock that PARC and the bureaucracy had on policymaking (Mu-ramatsu 1987, 207–8). Nakasone recognized that, given the weakness of his own faction in the party and his dependence on Tanaka, he had to provide himself with an autonomous personal base so that the party and the other faction leaders would be unable to displace or control him. He found the formula to do that in combining television coverage and foreign policy, especially U.S.-Japanese relations.[13] He knew that the Japanese public, at a time of increasing trade friction pressure from the United States, wanted reassurance that their leader could manage U.S.-Japanese relations and be capable of coping with the U.S. pressure, despite the Japanese dependence on the United States.

He also was the first LDP leader to recognize the growing influence of television in Japanese society. Tall and statesmanlike, he cultivated the tele-vision medium and the photo opportunities that G-7 summits and his visits to Washington provided, especially the coverage of his developing a first name "Ron-Yasu" relationship with President Ronald Reagan. It worked. Sadafumi Kawato (1988) finds that Nakasone's popularity and image won votes for the LDP in its great 1986 electoral victory. Because he was so per-sonally popular and had no obvious successor of equal talents, the LDP broke its two two-year term-limit rule and allowed Nakasone a third term, of one year, as LDP president. These five years in the position made him the longest serving prime minister since 1972. Nakasone was the first LDP post-war leader to develop a television image, providing himself with a resource to transcend the constraints of the factionalist politics of the '55 system (Curtis 1988, 105, 169; Krauss 1996, 262).

The enhanced role of Japan in the world in the late 1980s, as it became an economic power, also helped the prime minister capture increasingly more media attention, as Nakasone realized. The number of trips abroad increased dramatically starting in this period, as did the number of for-eign dignitaries visiting Japan, each giving the Japanese leader a chance for media, especially television, exposure (Krauss 2007, 58–61). Even though

---

13. Nakasone did have some views on security policy different from "typical" '55 system leaders after Kishi. See Samuels (2007) for an excellent discussion of the security approaches within the LDP.

his immediate successors reverted to the "grey" faction leaders, the genie of television influence on politics had been released from the bottle. And it was soon to grow bigger and bigger.

Nakasone's second innovation was to form comprehensive policies from the top down rather than just waiting for the bottom-up process of the bureaucracy and PARC to bring bills to his office for his approval. He formed major public and private (i.e., informal, within his office) advisory councils and commissions (as well as headquarters and promotional groups for less important issues) to tackle major policy reforms, such as administrative reform and opening up markets to foreign trade. To these, he appointed private-sector, bureaucratic, and academic actors. The activities of the public councils became the center of the news, which helped politically legitimate in advance the policies being proposed. Forming an alliance of top LDP leaders, the Ministry of Finance and the other economic ministries, and major business interests, he managed to bypass the segmented bureaucracies and PARC divisions that might have resisted and blocked individual bills in their jurisdiction to push through these more comprehensive policies (Muramatsu 1987, 206–10, 214–15; Samuels 2003a).

By using television and the new ways of pushing his policy agenda through his governmental role, Nakasone managed to overcome some of the established constraints on leadership that had developed within the LDP and the government after Yoshida. His innovations, however, did not survive his administration; his successors reverted to the more typical faction leaders, fell in scandals (Noboru Takeshita), were well meaning but not powerful temporary expedients (Toshiki Kaifu), and then split the party over electoral reform (Kiichi Miyazawa), leading to the first loss of power by the LDP since 1955.

The Limitations of Party Leadership under the '55 System

Under the '55 system, the LDP president and the prime minister became weaker over time. By the early 1980s, the well-ensconced kōenkai of the individual representatives and candidates were the prime vote mobilization organizations; factional bargaining dominated the appointment of posts within the party, parliament, and government according to fixed party rules and norms while factions negotiated the limited range of new endorsements in the electoral districts; and the PARC divisions and their "iron triangle" of bureaucratic and interest-group relations were the major influences on policymaking.

The party leader and prime minister held limited powers. Although he was the face of the party in elections, he was limited to trying to skillfully choose particular personnel for his cabinet from among the candidates advanced by the factions according to seniority, conducting foreign policy and influencing the budget process, and selecting particular policies to advance from the pool of already well-supported issues bubbling up from the decentralized policymaking process.

The developing complementary institutions of the kōenkai, the factions, and PARC (with its zoku giin) clearly constrained the power and influence of the party leader prior to the electoral reform. Indeed, it was exactly the institutionalization of these key LDP components that gradually took the prime minister, a more powerful leadership position when held by Yoshida, and made him into the "missing leader" by the 1980s. The institutions were in, and continue to be in, an inverse relationship with the party leadership, even though some of their functions are now partially merged with that of the leadership, as in the case of PARC.

The Constitution's dividing legislative power between the cabinet and the parliament constrained the power of the prime minister. Similarly, his lack of institutional authorization to initiate policy in his own cabinet deprived him of the leadership capacity to exert more control over his party. These were important complementary institutions limiting the leader's power, which might have been circumvented before the institutionalization of the kōenkai, the factions, and PARC, as Yoshida showed. But they were added constraints after these were institutionalized. Indeed, if the fusion of executive and legislative powers is England's "efficient secret" (Cox 1987 and 2005), the developed separation of powers between the prime minister-cabinet and Diet-LDP was Japan's inefficient secret.

Facilitating the decline of the party leader's power was his not having any power base among the public independent of the party organization and its institutionalized decentralized procedures and norms. Not elected by direct vote, he lacked a president's mandate. More important, the leaders that were created by the increasingly institutionalized '55 system did not need external public support to gain power; they were the result of factional coalitions and bargaining and their seniority within their own faction. Nor did they need public support to maintain power, also because of factional considerations and a fairly fixed, stable LDP vote mobilized by the personal vote of the kōenkai and the habitual voting of the nonleftists during the Cold War. Variations in prime ministers' accomplishments as leaders, such as Nakasone's, nonetheless depended on sufficient legitimacy to drive change (Tiberghien 2007, 45).

Nakasone managed this by using his television image. But even if the other incumbents had tried to use their personal public image to enhance their power within the party, they would have had a difficult time. The use of television by Japanese politicians to create an image separate from the party was in its infancy. In that sense, the media, especially television, which was dominated by the NHK and its lack of attention to the prime minister in favor of a bland coverage of the bureaucrats, was a complementary institution as well.

The leaders produced by the LDP recruitment systems needed seniority and bargaining skills, not skill at managing a media persona. A faction leader who did not pay attention to the game of the factions, nurturing his own faction and rising through the ranks through seniority, experienced competitive disadvantages compared to his colleagues who did and probably never made it to the top. Nakasone was unusual and unique, a forerunner of things to come, in that he was a faction leader and also understood how to use the new power of television. Had he not been the head of one of the weakest LDP factions, however, he might not have had any incentive to do so.

Sequencing mattered in the relative decline of party leadership from the early 1950s under Yoshida. Had television or a different form of political coverage been a major force as early as the mid-1950s, before the kōenkai, the factions, and PARC were fully institutionalized, prime ministerial leadership might have been much different. Even after the factions began to assume their more organized and rigid form, in the early 1960s before the Akagi memo, if television had been a more potent force the power of the part leaders might have developed differently. This pattern of gradually declining party leadership, with Nakasone as the exception, was directly linked to the following sequence of events: the institution of the LDP party presidential election and the congealing of the factions, the spread of the kōenkai, the Akagi memo and the development of PARC, and the rising importance of television.

We may ask: Was the decline of the power of the LDP leadership the result of the development of the kōenkai and PARC arrangements within the party, or were these made possible by a leadership that was weak and ineffectual to begin with? As we have seen, the weak leader was neither inevitable nor the unavoidable consequence of the electoral system. Indeed, under Prime Minister Yoshida, the party leader was a strong individual figure. Later, even the collective leadership of the mainstream faction coalition exercised more power within the party than it and the prime minister did by the late 1970s and early 1980s. Rather, the weakening of the prime minister was due to the gradual dilution of the party leader's power as, first, the kōenkai and the factions and, then, PARC (after the Akagi memo) gradually institutionalized the vote-seeking, office-seeking, and policy-seeking functions of the party below the leadership level between the late 1950s and early 1980s; this process was aided and abetted by a media system that tended to deny prime ministers even the most minimal of extra-party resources to compete with the intraparty power centers.

A subsequent question might then be: Why then did party presidents not fight these trends and try to hang on to their power rather than giving it up so willingly through these compromises? The answer is simply that each individual prime minister was concerned only with attaining and maintaining his own power without concern for the long-range implications of these compromises with the party. None saw or could see the cumulative ultimate future results of these compromises—each thought that by making each individual compromise he was actually buttressing his control of the party by creating greater intraparty stability. Indeed, to put it another way, there were small costs for the prime ministers in allowing Yoshida's central control to be eroded step by step, but given the fierce internecine factional rivalries of the 1960s and 1970s, they could not afford the higher cost to fight to preserve them.

In the next chapter, we examine whether and how the electoral reforms or other factors changed the party leader's role and influence.

Chapter 9

The Changing Role of
Party Leadership

All I say is "watch it." Every dog is allowed one bite, but a different view is taken of a dog that goes on biting all the time. If there are doubts that the dog is biting not because of the dictates of conscience but because he is considered vicious, then things happen to that dog. He may not get his license renewed when it falls due.
Harold Wilson, British prime minister, March 5, 1967 (quoted in Rose 2001, 142)[1]

The Liberal Democratic Party will endorse only candidates who were for Postal Privatization.
Prime Minister Jun'ichirō Koizumi, 2005 (quoted in Iijima 2006, 273)

After Nakasone stepped aside, the LDP and its leadership seemed to revert back to their older patterns of decentralized decision making and relative leadership weakness. The 1994 electoral reform was supposed to bring about the end of many of these patterns: eliminate the factions, centralize party vote mobilization and thus reduce or eliminate the role of kōenkai, and reduce the influence of narrow interest groups and their zoku giin allies in PARC. Other important goals for the reformers were reducing the influence of money in politics and bringing about the end of LDP dominance and the onset of alternation in power. Had the former patterns actually occurred, the natural consequence would most likely have been more centralized parties under stronger party leaders. Instead, the LDP held power an additional fifteen long years and, as we have seen, the kōenkai, factions,

---

1. Wilson was speaking to his party's parliamentary conference; from a March 5, 1967, *London Times* news story.

and PARC with its zoku giin have persisted even longer. And, except for one brief moment in the mid-2000s under Prime Minister Koizumi, when the party leader appeared to have real power and to have centralized LDP functions, the LDP party leadership seemed not to have changed much at all. The traditional faction leaders became the leaders prior to Koizumi, and after him his revamping of the party seemed to have been squandered or undone by his successors.

Nevertheless, in this chapter we show that the LDP leadership did change significantly although not completely—neither the view that Koizumi was an aberration, with everything coming after him reverting to what came before, nor the view that Koizumi and the reform changed everything is valid. Electoral reform was part, but only part, of the significant but incomplete changes that transformed the potential (but not necessarily the actuality) for LDP leadership. Although the LDP leadership had been gradually diminished in power by the development of the three party institutions (see chap. 8), several later exogenous changes (and some intentional ones under Koizumi) gave some power back to the leader. Leaders were, nonetheless, still constrained more than they were under Yoshida, in part because the party organizational institutions persisted and in part because of the way the institutions combined with these other changes. The story of LDP party leadership is intimately and inextricably linked to the development of the other three party institutions—the kōenkai, the factions, and PARC.

Providing Potential

The first cracks in the '55 system were not produced by the 1994 electoral reform but by the changing mass media (see especially chapters 3 and 8). Major changes in television programming, audience popularity and taste, and political party identification were then followed by major revisions in the party system and by electoral and administrative reforms; these provided the prime minister with new potential leadership capabilities.

Television and Floating Voters

In 1985, with Nakasone in the middle of his five years as prime minister, a new type of television news show was introduced by one of the commercial networks, Asahi TV. Hosted by an entertainer, Hiroshi Kume, the program communicated the news in a plainspoken way, using more visuals and even hand puppets and other props to tell the news stories, particularly political news stories. More important, its host went beyond the dry factual reporting of NHK to toss off cynical remarks that often undercut the message that the government and its leaders had been conveying. Political party leaders and politicians were also portrayed in a very personal, individualistic manner. The program, *News Station,* soon caught on with viewers, especially with younger urban viewers younger than thirty, who were the target audience of the program, and gradually over the next few years it began to rival NHK news in audience share (Krauss 2007, 206–11, 219–39).

The importance of this program should not be underestimated. It broke the near monopoly of NHK on the news; spawned several imitators on other networks with even more opinionated, often oppositional, commentators; and over the long run may have helped to stimulate at least two decades of pressure for reform and a more cynical public when it came to politics (Krauss 2007, 206–11, 219–39). And political leaders, including prime ministers, were now subject to far greater individual and critical evaluation by the television medium if they did not know how to manage it or transmit a popular appealing image along with the message of reform.

The changes in news affairs programming also, however, offered politicians a new vehicle for reaching parts of the public previously uninterested in politics or politicians. *News Station* stimulated other, even "softer" news-oriented programs, called "wide shows," that mixed information with entertainment to increase their political coverage; these were very popular in daytime programming, especially among housewives and others normally considered apolitical (Kabashima and Steel 2007, 96). Thus, the two styles of television programs began to blend—news programs began to adopt the style of the wide shows and the softer news programs took up political issues more frequently (Taniguchi 2007, esp. 164).

The 1993 election illustrated another television trend: in addition to "News Station" and "wide shows" devoting more attention to interesting political figures, a gaggle of new television public affairs interview shows also became popular in the early 1990s and had an increasing influence on leadership developments. For example, Prime Minister Kiichi Miyazawa, a smart and able politician but also a veteran faction leader and product of the '55 system, was trying to pass an electoral reform through his divided party and the Diet. On a public affairs interview show, he was repeatedly asked by the experienced host if he would move political reform through in the current Diet session; pressed repeatedly to answer, Miyazawa finally relented and promised that he would. But he failed to do so when parts of his own party proved recalcitrant, and the image of the prime minister's promise and his failure came back to haunt him. In the end, a vote of no-confidence passed the Diet with the aid of LDP defectors, and Miyazawa was forced to call an election. The circumstances that created the election; the effective use of the television medium by several reformist opposition leaders, in stark contrast to its use by the '55 system LDP leaders; and the important role of television led to the 1993 election being called the first Japanese television election (Altman 1996, 172–75).

In the 1993 election, the LDP won the most seats but lost power to a disparate coalition of parties, marking the LDP's first exit from power since it was formed. After coalition negotiations, Morihiro Hosokawa emerged as the first non-LDP prime minister since 1955. A young, dashing former-LDP governor who had broken with the party, Hosokawa had run for the Diet and, with other maverick LDP politicians who championed electoral reform, formed new parties for the 1993 election.

As the scion of one of the oldest families in Japan, grandson of a prewar prime minister, and former journalist, Hosokawa understood not only politics but the importance of managing the media, and he was extremely image conscious. He was a good illustration of the new imperative beginning to emerge in Japanese politics—a successful political leader now had to be telegenic and understand how to communicate using this powerful medium (Kabashima and Steel 2007, 96–97). He was the second prime minister, after Nakasone, to become a popular leader through the television media, a precedent that outlived his tenure in office—he had to resign over a prospective scandal, and the reformist coalition fell apart soon thereafter. Before dissolving, however, this coalition managed to pass an electoral reform bill and a campaign finance reform bill.

The growing influence of television and the success of Nakasone and then Hosokawa in using it to increase the popularity and leverage of the prime minister coincided with another growing trend during this period— the increase in the number of floating voters. Prior to 1993, such voters constituted perhaps one-quarter to one-third of all voters; this approximately doubled in the decade that followed (Tkach-Kawasaki 2003, 109). Whether the changing media structure and style contributed to this trend is unknown, but there is no question that the phenomenon was synergistic with the new use of television to portray leadership image. Party leaders could now go over the heads of other party leaders and representatives and cultivate a personal following among not only party supporters but also the increasing mass of nonaligned voters who tended to cast their ballots on the basis of issues and the leaders' images.

This is shown quite clearly in data that Krauss and Nyblade (2005) analyze from monthly public opinion polls in 1960–1993 comparing the respondents' support for the LDP as a party with their support for the cabinet (a widely accepted stand-in for support for the prime minister). The results are shown in figure 9.1. From the 1960 Hayato Ikeda administration through and including the 1982 Zenkō Suzuki administration, support for the LDP and support for its leader were almost completely coterminous. This is because, as we have seen, the leader was the absolute creature of the party. Note, however, that with Nakasone the two support curves diverge greatly for the first time and thereafter they do not converge again in the preelectoral reform era.

The two curves do tend to go in the same direction; we can assume that an unpopular prime minister will drag support for the party down, whereas a popular one will increase it. But after Nakasone these are clearly two separate kinds of support. This is the consequence of the increasing importance of the party leader's image in the television era combined with the increasing number of floating voters who now constituted a greater proportion

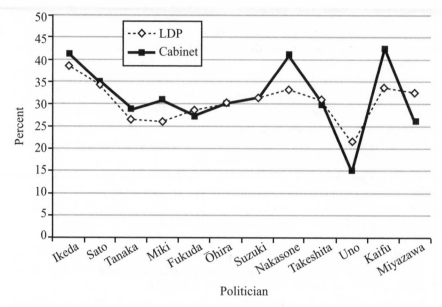

Figure 9.1 Average monthly support ratings of cabinet and LDP for administrations in 1960–1993 (%)

Source: Data from Jiji Press monthly opinion polls, 1996–2008 (updated from Krauss and Nyblade 2005, 366, using Jiji Press poll data from 2001–2008). Used by permission of Jiji Press and acknowledged with thanks. Updated data are from Central Research Services, an affiliate of Jiji Press and acknowledged with thanks.

Note: Cabinet support is used here as a measure of prime ministerial support.

of the electorate and were swayed by television images of the leaders. The party leader now had an independent source of vote-seeking leverage and power with his party if he could effectively cultivate and use it.

Recall from previous chapters that the '55 system LDP (with kōenkai, factions, and PARC) became fully institutionalized only by the late 1970s or early 1980s, within a few years of the beginning of the influence of television in politics (mid-1980s to mid-1990s) and before the number of urban floating voters increased dramatically. What would have happened if a prime minister in the mold of Nakasone had come to power a decade earlier and had used television the same way and if a program like *News Station* had also appeared to compete effectively against the NHK television news? Would the LDP leader have had greater resources and capabilities to assert himself, weaken the emerging institutionalization of the kōenkai in party vote-seeking, of the factions in its office-seeking, and of PARC and the zoku giin in its policy-seeking endeavors, and create more dependence on his leadership in the party? We return to this point later. As it ensued, the further undermining of the '55 system LDP and its partial transformation had to await a changed party system, electoral reform, and a leader who understood the new capabilities that political reform and the new age of television provided.

The End of the Cold War and the Changed Party System

Other profoundly important exogenous changes in the environment of the LDP affected the nature and vagaries of the LDP leadership. The first was the end of the Cold War. Under the '55 system, the parties could be depicted on the continuum below:

Left	Center	Right

JCP   JSP   CGP   [DSP   LDP   ]

The communists were ostensibly the far left, although some elements of the JSP were actually even farther left while other elements were closer to the CGP, in the left of center. The DSP was a socialist party that was quite centrist, and some elements of this party were at least as far to the right on defense issues, the most defining issue cleavage of the '55 system, as the LDP. The LDP occupied a wide spectrum from the center to the extreme right (its ideological space is represented by the underlining within the brackets); as we have seen, it was a diverse party in terms of ideology and policy.

The JSP was by far the largest opposition party, occupying from one-third (in the late 1950s) to approximately one-fifth (by the early 1990s) of the seats in the House of Representatives. The other parties each held between approximately 7 and 10 percent of the seats. The LDP always gained a majority once it added the independents postelection or went into a coalition with a small splinter party from its ranks (which is did in 1976–1986). But after 1969, the LDP never again had a majority in the popular vote. The malapportionment of the electoral districts, often over 3:1 in favor of the rural versus the urban and suburban districts, helped it maintain its seat majority.

In any case, no single opposition party even came close to being able to capture a majority because none ran anywhere near enough candidates to do so. To come close to taking power, the opposition parties would have had to combine, an option made impossible by the ideological and party identity bases for each of the parties. The fundamental cleavage in the party system was caused by the ideological divisions of the Cold War, in which the meanings of *left* and *right* in Japan were related to the position of each party on anticommunism, defense issues, and the alliance with the United States.

Several things changed this system in the early 1990s. The end of the Cold War allowed the old polarized cleavages of left versus right over defense and foreign policy to dissipate, allowing party reformation and many new possibilities for combination and recombination. Then, following the end of Cold War ideological cleavages, the LDP split in 1993, which helped bring about the reformist coalition of all the previous opposition parties, plus the new splinter parties from the LDP, which in turn allowed the passage of electoral reform.

Three events further radically altered the political game and the party system. The first was the electoral reform. Soon after this, the DPJ was formed from some of the former LDP breakaway elements and the remnants of the NFP (including the former socialists) after its break up.

The second event was the breaking away of the JSP from the New Frontier Coalition in 1994, several months after electoral reform was passed, to form a new government coalition for the first time with its erstwhile "enemy" the LDP. The JSP gave up many of its defining principles (it had been anti–Self Defense Forces and anti–U.S. alliance) in exchange for the prime minister's office in that deal. This looked like pure opportunism to JSP core leftist supporters, who dropped away from the party in droves; in addition, its holding only five cabinet posts returned policymaking to the hands of the LDP and left moderates unimpressed with the JSP leaders' acumen. Meanwhile, it was just at this time that the new electoral system with its SMD portion was first used in the 1996 election. This meant that a diminished JSP (now known as the Social Democratic Party of Japan, SDPJ) constituency could not expect to win many seats in the local district election and would be confined to a few in the PR portion. It soon became a small and ineffectual party.

The third event was that the CGP moved from its previous left-of-center positions on defense and foreign policy to a somewhat right-of-center position in the 1980s and 1990s; it also entered into a coalition with the LDP in 2000 and for the next several years. Once again, the new electoral system had an impact because the PR portion made it more difficult for the dominant party to win an outright majority—because the smaller parties such as the CGP could win seats there—and therefore it might need to create a coalition with a smaller party and coalitions also could be necessary to gain a majority in the upper house. For most of the 2000s, this important role of coalition partner was filled by the CGP, which until 2007 provided the LDP with the extra seats it needed for the government to have a majority in the House of Councilors and the CGP could provide the same in the House of Representatives if the LDP lost many seats in the next election.

The position of the socialists as the largest opposition party was taken over by the DPJ. But this was a very different opposition party from the old prereform socialists. Although the leftist parties remained, they were much diminished in the number of seats they controlled (the JCP also could now win seats only in the PR portion). The DPJ now occupied the moderate left-of-center portion of the spectrum, whereas the CGP (now more center-rightist) joined the LDP in a coalition. The LDP continued to occupy the entire rightist portion (again represented below by the solid underline in brackets). The new party system on an ideological continuum now looked like this:

Left		Center			Right
JCP	SDPJ	DPJ	[CGP	LDP	]

For the first time in the postwar era, the LDP faced a larger moderate centrist opposition party, one that could mount a real challenge against it in the local SMDs.

The Democratic Party of Japan

The current DPJ was the 1996 creation of three well-known politicians, both formerly of the LDP via the Sakigake Party, a splinter party that itself was formed only in 1993. Yukio and Kunio Hatoyama were the grandsons of 1950s Prime Minister Ichirō Hatoyama, and Naoto Kan had served as the minister of health in the LDP coalition government with Sakigake. When four other smaller parties joined the Sakigake Party in 1998, including some representatives who had been former JSP members, the current DPJ was born (Itoh 2003, 166–73; Hrebenar 2000, 157–59; Shiota 2007, 86–97; Köllner 2004, 96–97).

For the first several years, the DPJ had difficulty establishing an identity, going back and forth between being a "constructive opposition party" (cooperating with the LDP) and a "wholesome opposition party" (resting its identity on confrontation with the LDP and its policies). These differences reflected the diverse political backgrounds of the leaders and portions of the party and an ambivalence over strategy that plagued the party for years (Itoh 2003, 198–200).

After the NFP broke up in 1998, the DPJ became the second largest opposition party. It had a rocky start due to internal leadership struggles and differences within the party regarding policy—especially between former socialists and former LDP representatives over security policy and between older and younger Diet members—and the strategy issues already mentioned. But by 2000 the DPJ had begun to look like a real alternative to the LDP, especially given the unpopularity of Prime Minister Mori and his government in 2001. But, then, the dumping of Mori by the LDP and Koizumi's taking power changed that calculus, and the LDP, despite predictions to the contrary, won the 2001 House of Councilors election.

In 2003, the DPJ got two big boosts. First, the Liberal Party, now led by Ichirō Ōzawa, former leader of the LDP and then of the abortive NFP, merged with the DPJ. Second, the DPJ won large increases in both the 2003 House of Representatives and the 2004 House of Councilors elections. Indeed, in the 2003 House of Representatives election, the DPJ surpassed the LDP in numbers of votes and seats in the PR tier and increased its share of seats in SMD to approximately 37 percent (Yomiuri Shimbun Tokyo-Honsha Yoron-Choōsabu 2004, 50–53). In the 2004 House of Councilors election, Koizumi's popularity had declined and the DPJ won more seats than the LDP (fifty to forty-nine for the LDP) (Scheiner 2004, 70–71).

The floating voters (those without organizational ties to the LDP kōenkai or without a strong party identity or affiliations) seem to have been especially attracted to the DPJ banner. As we have seen, although floating voters had been around since the 1970s, in more recent years this group had grown to become a majority (or close to a majority) of the voters in the largest cities. Their nonpartisanship since the late 1980s had been reinforced by the more diversified television media, such as Kume's *News Station* and other popular news shows containing more cynical, or even oppositional, commentary. Their deconstruction of the LDP-led state had found sympathetic eyes and ears among a growing urban electorate that did not have organizational or psychological ties to any particular political party. Among these groups, especially, the DPJ message of reform and opposition to the LDP status quo found its most fertile ground.

The viable potential challenge of the DPJ to LDP dominance had important repercussions for LDP leadership in ways that no one fully appreciated until 2001. By then, other reforms had buttressed the potential for the prime minister to exercise greater influence.

Administrative Reform

Beginning in 1996, the first LDP prime minister since 1993, Ryūtarō Hashimoto, began a push for major administrative reform, forming a Council on Administrative Reform with himself as chair. Unlike previous reforms, notably under Nakasone, which had concentrated mostly on privatizing public corporations such as the National Railways, this one focused more on the reform of the government.[2] Hashimoto moved the process forward despite resistance from bureaucratic agencies and successfully passed a law outlining the reforms. He resigned after the LDP lost the July 1998 House of Councilors election. His successor, Prime Minister Keizō Ōbuchi, passed the reforms in July 1999, to be implemented on January 1, 2001 (Shinoda 2000, 183–98; Kaneko 1999, 4–5).

The reforms focused on streamlining the bureaucracy and cabinet from twenty-three ministerial-level organizations to twelve (mostly by combining former bureaucratic agencies) and replacing the Prime Minister's

---

2. Postal privatization proposals were also considered, but the political battle over these was too fierce and they were not included in the final reforms, leaving them to be revived later under Koizumi.

Office with a new Cabinet Office. Yet this administrative reform also was to change the capabilities of the cabinet and have significant consequences for prime ministerial leadership, another of its major aims. First, for the first time the prime minister was given the explicit authority by law to initiate basic policymaking. Second, and this turned out to be perhaps the most consequential reform, the new Cabinet Office was to contain within it advisory councils to the prime minister on economic and fiscal policy, financial services and administrative reforms, consumer affairs, and population and gender equality issues, with cabinet-level appointees made by the prime minister from both within and outside the government. Third, the staff of the Cabinet Office was increased to support the more active prime minister and cabinet. Fourth, more subcabinet level political appointee positions were created. The post of political vice minister was replaced by up to three deputy vice ministers and several secretaries, all Diet members, who were given the task of supporting the minister and thus bringing more political leadership to bureaucratic agencies (Kaneko 1999, 5–8; Shinoda 2003, 23–28).

There were other reforms as well, but these were the ones with the most direct implications for prime ministerial influence. As we will see, especially the new advisory councils within the Cabinet Office (used well by Koizumi) could be a tool for the prime minister to exert greater political leadership, and the buttressing of the cabinet with both political and support staff also enhanced the roles of the cabinet and the ministers in policymaking. All of the changes in television, the floating voters, the party system, and administrative reform were in process even before the electoral reform, but, in combination with the latter, they helped change the potential for party and governmental leadership in Japan.

Electoral Reform

The political reforms of 1994 provided contradictory incentives for the LDP to both centralize the party under the leader and maintain its decentralization in mobilizing votes. Campaign finance reform also exhibited some of these contradictory centripetal and centrifugal pressures. The new campaign finance law that was passed along with the electoral reform was intended to channel more contributions through the political parties. This should have helped centralized funding and thus the influence of the party leadership with its backbenchers. Unfortunately, there was a loophole big enough to drive a Toyota truck through—contributions could be made to local chapters as well as to the central party. And who was often the head of the local chapter and thus able to use those funds to her own preference? The single LDP representative in the district!

More important, the continuation of the draconian campaign restrictions, the decreasing number of voters who cast ballots based on party identification, and the increasing floating vote especially in urban areas meant there was a continued need for a personal vote in many constituencies (see chaps. 2–3). Indeed, the SMD portion of the election allowed for, and even required, a continuation of mobilizing personal votes and kōenkai because one LDP candidate could not mobilize enough votes to win in the expanded diverse proportion needed under SMD by relying solely on votes for the party. Then there were the implications for split-ticket voting, whereby constituents who supported opposition parties could cast their ballots for their preferred party in PR but might vote for the local incumbent LDP candidate in SMD because he brought benefits to the district, they liked him personally, or the party they supported did not have much chance of winning in the district.

On the other hand, Masahiko Asano has hypothesized that the SMD system strengthened the power of party leadership in the area of endorsements. Although some of his centralization hypotheses do not seem fully validated (Asano 2006, chaps. 4–5), he does present evidence that new endorsements after the reform favored the factions of the prime minister and the secretary-general (chap. 3). An interview by one of the authors with a senior LDP Diet member confirmed this. When asked his impression of whether the power of the prime minister and secretary-general in the policy process had become stronger, he replied:

> More than becoming stronger on policy, after the small electoral districts the party has come to have large power on things such as endorsements. Before, in the age of medium-sized districts, the factions had the power. Factions got weaker and the parties came to have the power, and the president or secretary-general have endorsement rights, so their power has emerged. (Interview N, October 16, 2008)

Furthermore, the closed-list PR portion of the election meant voters now cast one ballot of their two for a party, decreasing some of the incentives to mobilize a personal vote. The images of the party and party leader became decisive in the PR portion and more important in the SMD portion than under the SNTV system. As we have seen, a candidate could win an election under SNTV with as little as 10–15 percent of the vote in the MMD. Now, she probably had to mobilize between one-third and one-half plus one votes (depending on how many other parties ran in that district). With one representative per district, the LDP candidate had to mobilize a wider variety and larger proportion of voters. In short, the constituency span (or standard deviation) of the support needed to win increased (see chap. 3; Krauss and Pekkanen 2004, 24–25). With only one representative of a party running, the importance of the party label and image of the party leader to mobilizing support increased as well, especially in the enhanced television age. This meant the individual representative was now somewhat more beholden to the party and its leader's image for securing his seat (for the first time or again) than previously. One of our interviewers put this concretely, estimating that under the new electoral system the difference in leadership image meant over a 20 percent movement in votes for candidates: "Under the Single Member District system, about 20 percent of votes shift depending on who is the leader of which party" (Interview A, June 27, 2002).

The effects of these changes were hard to see in the first few years after the electoral reform. The first LDP and government leaders after reform—Ryūtarō Hashimoto and Keizō Ōbuchi—seemed to epitomize the old factional politics. Both were veteran LDP politicians of the Takeshita (formerly Tanaka) faction, the largest in the LDP. Both had worked their way up the faction ladder by seniority. And both came from rural prefectures.

Under the surface, however, there were signs of change brewing. At first, Hashimoto was a popular politician with good media appeal and a good image, in part stemming from his unusually youthful appearance with his trademark sideburns and in part from his reputation as a shrewd negotiator as trade minister during the trade friction with the United States. He was considered to be the savior of the LDP after it had declined in popularity and had had to endure ceding the office to Tomiichi Murayama, a Socialist, right after it came back to power after the electoral reform by joining with its one-time rival. But economic policy mistakes, such as sponsoring a rise in the very unpopular consumption tax that many felt may have even aborted an incipient recovery in the long Japanese economic recession, soon made Hashimoto unpopular, and he resigned after the LDP suffered a setback in the 1998 House of Councilors election. His successor, Ōbuchi, was definitely not a politician with media appeal or charisma. He was even labeled as having the appeal of "cold pizza" by the Western media. But he wisely used this to foster an avuncular image and to deconstruct his own image (e.g., he appeared on the cover of *Newsweek* holding a cold pizza!) and became mildly popular before he suffered a stroke and died in 2000.

No one could accuse Yoshirō Mori, Ōbuchi's successor, of having even that much media appeal or savvy. Head of the former Fukuda faction, he was jovial enough but hardly charismatic or attentive to managing his media image. He almost immediately made huge media gaffes that drastically and permanently damaged his image and diminished his already low popularity,[3] causing his support rating to plummet to approximately 8 percent, a postwar low. Further, as Ikuo Kabashima and Ryōsuke Imai (2002, 94) clearly show based on an extensive analysis of the 2000 election, the voters' evaluation of Mori had a major influence on their party choices in

---

3. He was caught by the media referring to Japan in a speech as "a Divine Nation" (French 2000), a prewar term associated with the era of military rule and Shintoism as the established religion, and he then destroyed whatever domestic image he had left by continuing to play golf even after being told that Japanese students had been lost in a freak collision of a tour boat with a U.S. submarine off Hawaii (Reitman 2001).

that election, especially in the PR portion, with a negative evaluation of Mori leading to less likelihood of voting for the LDP, even when controlled for party affiliation. Finally, as the party realized how important this leader's image was to its electoral fortunes, it successfully pressured him to resign in spring 2001 because of the fear of a disastrous LDP defeat in the upcoming summer House of Councilors election.

Both Ōbuchi's ability to manage media image despite his lack of charisma and Mori's inability to do so, and the important role this dimension played in the success or failure of both these leaders and of the LDP fortunes during this period, were hints of the major changes under the surface that the now large influence of television and the electoral reform had brought about. The LDP had become dependent on the television image of its party president to stay in power. Clearly, the dumping the popular Hashimoto once he became unpopular and lost an election and, even more so, the forcing out of Mori for fear that his image alone would cost the party dearly in upper house seats in the next election illustrate this, at least in retrospect; at the time, the pundits and observers continued to believe this was all just prereform factional politics at usual. Succeeding events punctured that misperception very dramatically.

After Mori's forced departure, the LDP needed to select a new leader. It looked like one of the same old processes would be used again—either a selection just by LDP Diet members or a primary race such as occurred in 1978 among LDP party members, but one in which LDP Diet members would have more resultant votes and again the final decision. Either way, bargaining and coalitions among the faction leaders would essentially determine the outcome. But so great was the rebellion and pressure (supported by the media) from LDP prefectural chapters petrified that the party would suffer a disastrous defeat in the House of Councilors election—especially from the Tokyo chapter because the Tokyo Metropolitan Assembly was facing an election that spring—that it forced party leaders to change the process. They allowed more votes, although still fewer than Diet members would get, to be allocated to the winner-take-all prefectural primary results for most prefectures and scheduled this vote to take place prior to the Diet members' votes (Estévez-Abe 2006, 643–44; Kabashima and Steel 2007, 101).

This provided a crucial opportunity for Jun'ichirō Koizumi, the maverick challenger to heavily favored former Prime Minister Hashimoto. Using the mass media effectively, catering to a public delighted to find an unusual, telegenic candidate promising the reform of his own party, and taking advantage of coverage on the wide shows, Koizumi swept to a first-round victory in the primary prefectural votes. LDP Diet members now felt enormous pressure to vote in the same way their own prefectures and the grassroots of the party had voted, and Koizumi won even the Diet member round to become prime minister (Kabashima and Steel 2007, 101–6). The more competitive party system and the importance of party leader image in the media in the 2000s had, in effect, caused the LDP to ditch its own leader and in a scramble for survival turn to an outsider who had a chance of saving the party.

During his five-and-a-half-year tenure in office, Koizumi went on to provide the strongest postwar leadership of any LDP prime minister since Yoshida. He changed the way cabinet appointments were made (without consideration of factional balance), used the media and new media to great advantage, made policymaking more top down, managed to force through his party some economic reforms bitterly opposed by its zoku giin, and attained and retained the highest postwar favorable support ratings among the public. Finally, he led his party in 2005 to its greatest electoral victory of the postreform era.

The Changed Leadership Capabilities: Explanations for the Koizumi Phenomenon

Koizumi appears to be an "aberration" among the postwar prime ministers in his leadership style. Nevertheless, his style was based on using the fundamental structural changes that had taken place in the electorate, the LDP, and the government that had increased the potential for a stronger, more centralized political leadership.

How prime ministers become the leaders of their parties matters. If factional bargaining among the faction leaders no longer determines who heads the party and government but, instead, prefectural federation votes and occasional primaries among members and the individual choices of faction members regardless of their leader's preferences have more influence, the victor has a "greater legitimacy and independence" to impose his personnel preferences and policy campaign promises on his cabinet and other party leaders (Estévez-Abe 2006, 644). Note that, with Koizumi's greater independence from the factions, he was able to change the method of appointing people to the cabinet, ignoring the factions and considerations of factional balance, and was able to place pro-reform individuals in key positions in the cabinet, in the new advisory councils in the Cabinet Office, in the post of secretary-general, and in other key party positions.

Of the administrative reform changes, by far the most important proved to be the establishment of a Council on Economic and Fiscal Policy (CEFP) in the Cabinet Office. Isao Iijima, Koizumi's closest political advisor and the head of his executive assistants while he was prime minister, attributes Koizumi's ability to carry out executive leadership to the administrative reform and most especially to the CEFP, which Koizumi used as the main tool of his reform program. The council met 187 times under Koizumi, and he attended and chaired each meeting (Iijima 2006, 20–21). And when Koizumi made it clear that the budget decisions of the CEFP, not those of the Finance Ministry, which had dominated the process, had his backing, bureaucrats and their connected zoku giin and interest groups knew he was serious about top-down leadership in the future (21–23). Like Nakasone and Hashimoto before him, Koizumi used councils under the jurisdiction of the prime minister, in this case new ones created by the administrative reform, to go around PARC and the bureaucracy.

Koizumi also dared to change procedures when necessary. When postal privatization passed the Executive Council of the LDP, it was by simple majority not unanimity, as had usually been the case in the past. In the 2005 election, Koizumi took advantage of his authority as the party president to expel people from the party, thus denying the postal "rebel" incumbents the LDP nomination and endorsement.

The electoral reforms also mattered. The PR portion potentially can strengthen the hand of party leaders if, as Koizumi did, they take a more active role in determining the ranking of the candidates on the PR lists. This can give the prime minister and party leaders more leverage with the backbenchers, both the candidates running solely in PR and those running in the SMD districts who want to be dual-listed in the PR system as insurance.[4]

In the 2005 election, Koizumi targeted the burgeoning urban floating vote through television and by stressing policy issues and his own image during the campaign. Koizumi was the first LDP president to fully comprehend the transformation that the media, new electoral system, and changing voter identities had wrought during the thirty years since Nakasone and to use these changes skillfully. Figure 9.2 illustrates this well. This is a continuation of the graphing of the measures of party and cabinet support presented in figure 9.1 for the postreform era until 2008. As in figure 9.1, generally the lines indicating support for the prime minister (as shown by cabinet support) and for the party diverge, but even more so in the postreform era. The most significant difference between them appears for Koizumi, indicating his personal popularity through the media. The image of the prime minister now had become a crucial determinant of the party fortunes. Note that the general support rate for the LDP is fairly flat, barely changing at all, during the postreform era, despite the variations in electoral results, indicating this dependence on the party leader's image.

Other changes also enhanced the influence of the prime minister. The PR portion of the electoral system almost ensured that coalition governments would often be formed to attain majorities in the Diet, as indeed tended to be the case since 1994. This indirect consequence of the electoral system provided Koizumi, his cabinet, and the party leaders with another way to enhance their leverage in policymaking at the expense of PARC and

---

4. In an article with Kuniaki Nemoto, we explore the relationship between the two electoral tiers and the candidates' incentives and disincentives for being dual listed. See (Krauss, Nemoto, and Pekkanen, forthcoming).

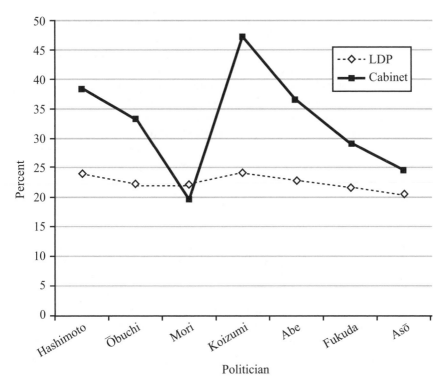

Figure 9.2 Average monthly support ratings of cabinet and LDP for administrations in 1996–2008 (%)

Source: Data from Jiji Press monthly opinion polls, 1996–2008 (updated from Krauss and Nyblade 2005, 366, using Jiji Press poll data from 2001–2008). Used by permission of Jiji Press and acknowledged with thanks. Updated data are from Central Research Services, an affiliate of Jiji Press and acknowledged with thanks.

Note: Cabinet support is used here as a measure for prime ministerial support.

zoku giin. Coalition governments required more top-down decision making than the bottom-up kind that was prevalent under the old SNTV system. Some legislation was initiated by party leaders and this gave the prime minister a way to exert pressure on his own party to pass the legislation he favored (Gaunder 2007, 124). In addition, those issues on which the coalition parties had differences, in content or priority, had to be reconciled at the highest levels of leadership—the cabinet. Thus, near the end of its long tenure in office, the LDP had achieved a less bottom-up and more top-down influence in policymaking than it had had since at least the 1950s.

A similar logic worked for the party manifestos that became popular with and important to voters in the 2003 election; these were introduced by the DPJ and were soon copied by the LDP. The prime minister, as the party leader, now had additional leverage to press the party to allow him to carry through on the policies in the party manifesto because he was the face of the party to the electorate and ultimately responsible for what had been promised (Gaunder 2007, 645–46). Indeed, there are signs that this was exactly what happened immediately following the first "manifesto election" on November 9, 2003. Plans were announced to implement a change in policymaking procedures that would create a more top-down process, with a PARC umbrella committee responsible for planning and drafting policies. The head of that committee, PARC Chair Fukushiro Nukaga said that the reorganization was necessary to increase efficiency in the policymaking process and also the capacity of the LDP to "implement important policies raised in our manifesto." The reorganization was "designed to promote policies that incorporate the prime minister's political vision" (*Nikkei Weekly,* November 24 2003, 2).

The combination of the consequences of these changes—primary elections for the party leader, the new electoral system, manifestos and new LDP policymaking procedures especially for issues in the manifesto, television and the floating vote, coalition government, and administrative reform— strongly implies that the spirit, if not the letter, of the Akagi memo had been partially undermined by the time Koizumi took power. All bills still had to go through the party and the government still had to pass its bills through the party, although not necessarily after the party and PARC initiated them. It seems party leaders and the prime minister were more capable of taking the initiative in policymaking and also at least partially of determining the priority, timing, and process of policies even before they went to PARC.

Systematic data from surveys of bureaucrats confirm a perceived, general, more long-term increase in party and governmental leadership policymaking power at the expense of the zoku giin and even the bureaucracy, whatever the results of specific cases. For example, longitudinal data from Michio Muramatsu and his associates indicate that between 1987 (under the '55 system) and 2002 bureaucrats themselves clearly saw a major increase in the prime minister's influence over their own ministries and a decline in the influence of the zoku giin and PARC and of the ministries and their advisory councils (see figure 9.3).

Data from this same survey also indicate that, within a ministry itself, between 1987 and 2002 the perceived relative influence on the bureaucracy of the upper levels of the bureaucracy (the bureau chief) and the cabinet ministers changed greatly; whereas in 1987 the bureau chief was perceived to have two to three times the influence of the minister, by 2002 the minister was perceived to have almost double the influence of the bureau chief (Krauss 2007, 72–73).

Was the prime minister's enhanced influence seen in all policy areas or only in selective ones? Figure 9.4, based on the same survey of politicians in 1987 (under the '55 system) and 2002, combines particular policies (which, after all, had different priorities in different periods) into the more general categories of distributive, welfare, defense and foreign policy, economic, and

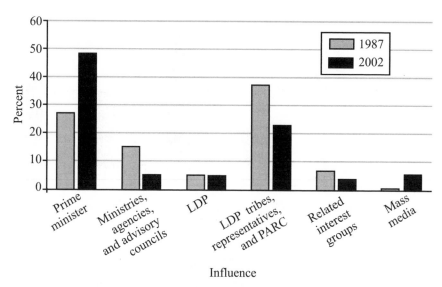

Figure 9.3 Bureaucrats' 1987 and 2001–2002 Surveys: Bureaucrats' perceived greatest influence on policy formation and implementation in their ministry (%)
Source: Data from Muramatsu et al. project; reproduced from Krauss (2007,71).
Note: First choice only. PARC, Policy Affairs Research Council. Fig. 8.1's and this figure's differences in percent is due to fig. 8.1 representing combined scores of all four choices; this figure is first choice only.

political reform policies.[5] We see from the figure that the prime minister had always had great influence in foreign policy and defense but that there were even greater increases after 1987 across the board in all types of domestic policies. The extent of the change by 2002 varies by area, but in no case was there less than a doubling of the party leader's perceived influence.

On balance, by the time Koizumi became prime minister there had been a notable increase in the resources and capabilities of the office and of the party leadership and cabinet on policymaking since the '55 system. Among the changes that brought about a resurgence of leadership power were the 1994 electoral reform and its direct and indirect consequences. The other variables creating at least a partial recentralization of the party included the rise of and changes in television broadcasting, the precedent of Nakasone's and Hosokawa's use of television to create an independent media image, the LDP primary system for selecting its leader, the administrative reform,

5. The distributive category was the issue of rice price decisions in 1987 and public works in 2002; the welfare category was health insurance in 1987 and general welfare policy in 2002; the defense and foreign policy was defense budget decisions in 1987 and general defense and foreign policy in 2002; the economic policy was deregulation in 1987 and general economic policy in 2002; and the political reform policy was electoral law revision in 1987 and general political reform in 2002.

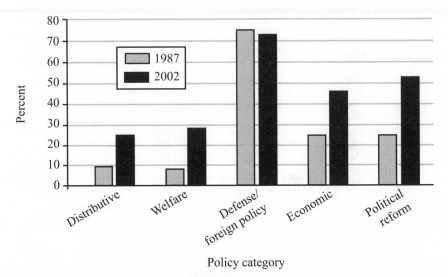

Figure 9.4 Bureaucrats' 1987 and 2001–2002 Surveys: Politicians responding that the prime minister had the most influence, by policy category (%)
Source: Data from Muramatsu et al. survey project, reproduced from Krauss (2007, 70).
Note: First and second ranks combined.

and the precedents and changes Koizumi made during his administration to take advantage of the new resources available.

Our historical institutional concepts can help us understand how these changes came about. One institutional complementarity is between the party leadership and the media institutions. The dominance of NHK TV news and its treatment of politics, even after television became widespread in Japan in the 1970s, allowed for and reinforced the lack of resources available to the party leader to counter the institutionalization of his rival power centers within the party. Even Nakasone's initial use of television to buttress his external popularity was only moderately effective in enhancing the leadership role—it led to no long-term deviation from the path-dependent trajectory and positive feedback processes of the now institutionalized LDP '55 system.

Until the effects of the new style of television news represented by *News Station* came fully into play in the 1990s, and then was combined with the second exogenous institutional change—the growth of an urban floating vote that was amenable to the appeals of a different, critical media view of the LDP and its leadership—could a Koizumi base his attack on the '55 system institutions on that new view and voter base.

The third exogenous change in institutional complementary was the imposition of the new electoral system, which magnified the effects of the image of the party leader and the floating vote in the new majoritarian system. A fourth institutional change—the coming into effect of the administrative reform that was intended to bolster the party leadership after the LDP came back into power in 1996—provided another complementary institution, enabling greater prime ministerial policymaking leadership. Among the most important of Koizumi's leadership initiatives, as we have seen, was his use of the new CEFP to gain more control over the budget process and also to implement a postal privatization policy. A fifth change in complementary institutions was in the selection process for picking the party leader. As we have seen, implementation of a wider selection process helped undermine the power of the factions in Koizumi's selection, giving him more autonomy to change his cabinet selection process without worrying about the factional balance.

A simple mental experiment about sequencing further illustrates this point. Imagine that television and its political coverage had been more influential in the 1960s and 1970s, and even the early to mid-1980s. This is not inconceivable given that the effects of televised political coverage were being felt significantly in the United States during this period. Would this change in timing have fundamentally altered the influence of the party leadership? Perhaps a bit, as Nakasone showed, but certainly not to the extent that subsequently developed in the 2000s. The competing power centers of the kōenkai, factions, and zoku giin probably would have still remained largely unaffected without the other transformations in the complementary institutions.

Sequencing mattered more in bringing Koizumi to power. One reason the party federations forced the leadership to adopt the wider selection process in 2001 was because of the great fear that the DPJ would win the forthcoming House of Councilors elections. But what if the competitiveness of the DPJ had emerged more slowly and Mori had been prime minister? Would they have dumped Mori so quickly, or changed the selection process so rapidly? And would the federation vote have gone as overwhelmingly for Koizumi rather than the safer and known choice of Hashimoto again? Unlikely. The rapidly rising competitiveness of the DPJ in the new and changed party system were preconditions for the changes that brought Koizumi to power.

Now let us switch the mental experiment. Imagine that electoral reform was imposed in the 1970s, that is, that Kakuei Tanaka's 1972 attempt at reform had succeeded. Would all the same changes we have seen have occurred, but earlier? Probably not. As we have seen, the kōenkai would have adapted to the continued need for a personal vote in the SMDs; the factions would have continued their electoral role (without campaign finance reform) in addition to their control over offices, including the cabinet (without Koizumi), and thus been weakened only a bit. Although the role of the zoku giin might have been diminished because of the successful candidates' need for less policy specialization and the diminution of the role of political pork, they would have continued as they did even with later electoral reform. The constitutional contradiction between cabinet government and parliamentary supremacy in the Japanese system, giving the Diet more influence on policy, would have also continued in place. Without the change in the role and nature of television and without the administrative reform, the party leader's role would have been enhanced, although not as much as it was by the 2000s.

Another confirmation of the importance of this package of exogenous changes all occurring in the 1990s, and their sequencing, is shown by a comparison of the introduction of a party primary to select the leader. Recall that when this was introduced, just as the '55 system factions were at the height of their institutionalized power, it led only to the factions being extended into the electoral districts and a greater linking up with the kōenkai than previously. But when it was reintroduced in the early 2000s with a greater mass of floating voters and the much greater role of a diversified television institution, it led to the Koizumi phenomenon.

All these mental experiments illustrate Paul Pierson's point that "it is *particular aspects* of social relations that become deeply embedded. It therefore matters a great deal when in a broader sequence of development consolidation or institutionalization occurs, and how these embedded aspects interact with more fluid elements of a broader social context" (2004, 77). It was the combination of a range of complementary, exogenous, and "broader social context" changes from the early 1990s to the early 2000s that induced the changes in party leadership that we have seen. Had any one of them occurred previously, its impact on the party leadership and centralization would not have been as great. In many ways, the impact of these exogenous LDP changes was greater downstream from the critical experience (Pierson Ibid., 67–71) of the LDP merger in 1955 than it would have been earlier.

Finally, the increase in the number of floating voters, the new television style of covering politics, and the enhanced role of the party leader in determining many voters' choices, all provided great competitive advantages for a party leader who could manage the video media. Managing an effective media image became an essential component for staying in power. It became increasingly unlikely that any party leader could succeed without having a good media image and personal popular appeal with the public.

Koizumi: The 2005 Election

Generally speaking, many of the changes described so far increased the backbenchers' dependence on the party leader, his image, the party's image, and, as Asano found, the influence of the party leadership on endorsements; however, they did so without eliminating the backbenchers' continued partial dependence on the personal vote and the representatives' own district-mobilization organization and without any change in the attempts of the factions and specialized zoku giin to control the policymaking process in PARC. Despite Koizumi's desire to exercise a strong leadership style, and the new capabilities for doing so, in his first few years in office he had to compromise many of his reform proposals, especially the reform of the way national roads were built, in the face of fierce resistance from the zoku giin. In many ways, therefore, the 2005 election proved to be the culmination of these contrary trends of enhanced party presidential and prime ministerial leadership but continued decentralized party power.

Prime Minister Koizumi's pet project, ever since he had served as minister of posts twenty years before, was postal reform. The postal savings system (the largest financial institution in the world) and the postal insurance parts of the postal system were huge and deeply intertwined with LDP pork-barrel and election politics. The postal zoku giin were one of the most powerful groups within PARC, helping to appoint part-time local postmasters in rural towns and villages in their districts who, in turn, helped mobilize votes for their patrons in elections (Maclachlan 2004, 303–13). Furthermore, these same zoku giin could potentially manipulate the allocations made from the Fiscal Investment and Loan Program (FILP), into which much of postal savings deposits were put and which funded many infrastructural projects ripe for pork-barrel manipulation by politicians. In addition, there were more such postal zoku giin in the main factional rival (296–99) to the Mori faction, in which Koizumi had risen to power within the LDP, and in another zoku giin–rich faction resisting his reforms. The reasons for Koizumi's dedication to postal reform may have been not only to improve its economic efficiency but also to bring about political reform. Postal reform would strike a blow at both the still powerful zoku giin and the weakened, but still existing, rival factions in the party.

The LDP was split on the issue. On July 5, 2005, the postal privatization bill barely passed the House of Representatives by only five votes (233 to 228). The opposition DPJ voted against the bill because of its details rather than the concept itself, but 37 LDP Diet members joined the DPJ members, the reason that the vote was so close (Izumi 2005, 42–46). The postal zoku giin and some in the anti-Koizumi factions led the resistance in the LDP.[6] To get the bills through the House of Councilors, Koizumi and the LDP leadership threatened to dissolve the House of Representatives[7] and call a general election if the bill did not pass. Despite this pressure, twenty-two LDP members still voted against the measure and another eight either abstained or did not show up for the vote; this was enough, combined with the nay votes of the other parties to cause the bill to fail by the rather large margin of 125 to 108 (Foreign Press Center Japan 2005a, 2005b). Against

6. Within these groups, the junior, electorally secure LDP representatives and more senior, anti-Koizumi LDP representatives were the most like to join the rebellion; those in between in seniority were the least likely to. The careers of these in-between politicians were more dependent on their access to the key PARC posts in the party, and thus they were reluctant to jeopardize these consequent advantages to their constituencies and their future careers by defying the party leadership (Nemoto, Krauss, and Pekkanen 2008).

7. The House of Councilors cannot be dissolved by the prime minister because its members serve fixed six-year terms, like U.S. senators.

the advice of other LDP party leaders, Koizumi gambled and called the election immediately.

He also lived up to his threat to punish the rebels in the House of Representatives who had voted against the postal reform bill, even though it had passed in that house—the party refused to nominate them to run as party candidates in the election, effectively kicking them out of the party. Thirty-two of them ran as independents or from newly formed parties, a few even with the support of their local LDP branches, which also joined the rebellion against the central party. Koizumi, Isao Iijima (his main and long-time political assistant and advisor), and Secretary-General Tsutomu Takebe nonetheless took the unprecedented step of personally selecting the LDP candidates to run against the rebels in their districts; the media promptly dubbed these chosen candidates "assassins" (*shikaku*) (source close to Koizumi, pers. comm., September 10, 2005). Several of these were women who were well known in their fields, for example, in media or broadcasting; the media dubbed them "madonnas."

During the short campaign, the DPJ, the main opposition party, concentrated on issues such as pension reform that polls showed the urban voters, who were the core DPJ support base, cared about more than postal privatization. Koizumi, however, hammered away at one theme—postal privatization.[8] In the sponsored advertising competition between the LDP and DPJ, the LDP television ads were slick and skillfully constructed, emphasizing that Koizumi, the party, and their individual local candidates were reformers; these contrasted with the rather scattered and listless DPJ ads.[9] But perhaps the most original media dimension was the manipulation of the wide shows. Koizumi's media advisors knew that these would focus on the celebrity match-ups of famous "assassins" against the key rebels, while almost ignoring many other interesting races, particularly of the DPJ versus LDP, for part of the campaign. And, indeed, although the newspapers focused on many different dimensions of the race, television, and especially the wide shows, concentrated on the celebrity "assassins" versus incumbent races and aspects of the campaign (Hoshi and Osaka 2006, 10–12).

Even the most optimistic LDP supporters must have been shocked by the election results—the party won 296 seats with almost 48 percent of the popular vote, its greatest electoral victory in a quarter century spanning both the pre-and postelectoral reform periods. It gained an additional eighty-four seats, even though it lost the rebel representatives; this was more even than its fifty-seat gain in the previous election (that included them) which had been considered a major victory. The DPJ, on the other hand,

8. An analysis of the content of his speeches (from newspapers) and sponsored debates shows that he devoted over 80 percent of them to that one issue (*Asahi Shimbun*, August 28, 2005, 3; August 30, 2005, 1–5; August 31, 2005, 2; *Nihon Keizai Shimbun*, August 30, 2005, 1–4).

9. Based on observations of the ads appearing on television in Japan during the election.

a party that had made significant gains in the election two years before, won only 113 seats with 36 percent of the popular vote, a loss of 64 seats or approximately one-third of its total seats (see figure 9.7). Also approximately 50 percent of the rebels lost and 80 percent of the "assassins" won in the election through either the SMD or PR portions (*Mainichi Shimbun*, September 12, 2005). The LDP overwhelmingly won in the SMDs, gaining about three-quarters of its seats in that part of the electoral system and, unusually, also outdistanced the DPJ in the PR portion. Many of the losing DPJ SMD candidates remained representatives only by virtue of their having been dual-listed in PR.

Underlying these numbers was the huge swing to the LDP among urban voters, traditionally the weakest LDP constituency. One of the major reasons the LDP did so well in the 2005 election is that it held on fairly well to its perennial base in rural areas, winning seventy-two seats in the one-third of the districts representing the most rural SMD constituencies, a drop of only five from the previous election (whereas the DPJ just maintained its mere eleven seats in this group of districts). Simultaneously, it greatly increased its seats in the one-third of districts that were the most urban SMDs, from thirty-three to seventy-eight (the number of DPJ seats dropped from fifty-nine to eighteen), and the one-third that were mixed urban-rural SMDs, from fifty-eight to seventy-five (the number of DPJ seats dropped from thirty-six to twenty-three).[10] Koizumi's message of postal reform had struck a responsive chord among the urban floating voters. Figure 9.5 illustrates this large change using the votes for the two parties in Tokyo in 2005 and the two previous elections. The overwhelming 2005 LDP victory was magnified, of course, by the large swings that an electoral system with a SMD portion can bring. Recall that the LDP won this huge majority (61 percent of the seats) with less than a majority of the vote (48 percent).[11]

Koizumi's gamble had paid off, and the LDP, with its coalition partner, the New Kōmeitō, now controlled 327 seats out of the 480-seat House of Representatives, a bit over a two-thirds majority. Soon after the election, Koizumi once again presented his postal privatization bill to the Diet. Intimidated by the crushing LDP victory, many recalcitrant LDP members of the House of Councilors who had voted against the bill the first time, now switched their vote, so it passed the House of Councilors as well and became law.

This election dramatically illustrates the pre- and postelectoral reform transitions we have analyzed: the new power of television and the new use of wide shows, especially to influence urban floating voters; the increasing importance of, and dependence of the party electoral fortunes on, the image

---

10. Data are from Ethan Scheiner and are gratefully acknowledged.

11. Indeed, it had picked up a "dividend" of 17 percent more SMD seats than the last election, with only a 3–4 percent increase in the vote, whereas the DPJ had lost approximately half of its SMD strength but had not lost practically any votes in those districts!

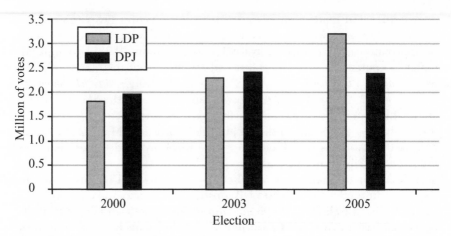

Figure 9.5 Changes in the LDP and DPJ SMD-obtained vote in Tokyo for the 2000, 2003, and 2005 elections (%). DPJ, Democratic Party of Japan; SMD, single-member district.
Source: Constructed from data from newspaper reports after the elections.

of the party leader; the separation of image of the party leader from the image of the party and how a party leader who understood the new system and the resources it could provide took an unpopular party to an electoral victory using his image; the weakening of factional power in the postreform era; and the vagaries of the new majoritarian SMD portion of the election system. Koizumi's successful use of these techniques illustrates the potential capabilities of an astute party leader.

The Limits of Change: Post-Koizumi and the Fall of a Dominant Party

Three prime ministers in the little over three years after Koizumi retired failed miserably to even come close to Koizumi's successes with the party or the government. Shinzō Abe, picked in part because he was young and a Koizumi protégé, had a good media image and was popular with the public, according to polls. He lasted a year and left office amid confusion after his support numbers dropped precipitously when he let former postal rebels back into the party, concentrated on national security reforms instead of domestic concerns, failed to manage well a massive pension records loss by the bureaucracy, and had several of his cabinet members resign facing scandals. Very much because of his unpopularity, the DPJ won the House of Councilors election in July 2007 and gained control of the upper house. His successor, Yasuo Fukuda, picked in part because he was the anti-Abe, was very unmediagenic but was avuncular, conscientious, and reassuring; yet he only weakly handled a Diet where the opposition controlled the upper house. Fukuda watched his popularity plummet within a year as well and was finally urged to resign.

Tarō Asō, Fukuda's successor, was originally somewhat popular with a good and energetic media personality. His support in the polls was approaching that of the infamous former Prime Minister Mori when he was forced to call a general election by September 2009. In that August 30, 2009, election the LDP suffered the first defeat in its history, losing power resoundingly to the DPJ. As figure 9.6 shows, the DPJ recaptured the votes it lost in 2005, and then some. What is particularly surprising was that the DPJ devastated the LDP in the SMD tier, in which the LDP is usually strong because of the personal vote, rather than in the PR tier (the vote by party). In 2009, it completely reversed the votes it had received in this tier in 2005 (47.4 percent versus 36.4 percent in 2005) compared to the LDP (38.6 percent versus 47.7 percent in 2005). The seat results were even worse (see figure 9.7). The DPJ captured 308 seats by itself (221 in the SMD tier and 87 in the PR tier), whereas the LDP won only 119 (64 in the SMD tier and 55 in the PR tier), an even greater victory for the DPJ than Koizumi had won in 2005 for the LDP.

The majoritarian system of the SMD tier gave the DPJ an even greater seat "bonus"—over 55 percent—for its swing of about 13 percent of the vote compared to 2005, than the LDP had received for its smaller swing in 2005. With its coalition partners, the SDPJ and the Kokumintō (People's Party; formed by the former LDP postal rebels after they were expelled from the LDP), the DPJ has a majority of 318 out of the 480 seats in the House of Representatives, essentially the two-thirds majority the DPJ needed to override the House of Councilors if necessary.

What went wrong? Some argue that the LDP 2009 loss was merely a time lagged result, that is, that the effects of the 1994 electoral system reform took a while to gradually take effect. There is some truth to this; the failure

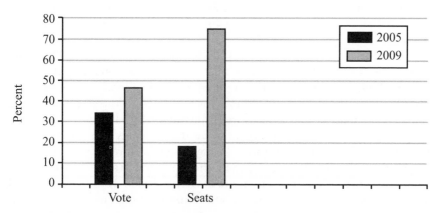

Figure 9.6 Democratic Party of Japan vote and seat results for the 2005 and 2009 elections (%).

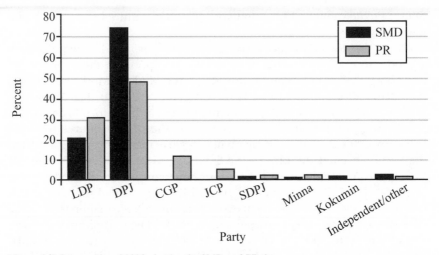

Figure 9.7 Seat results of 2009 election by SMD and PR tiers.
Note: CGP, Clean Government Party; DPJ, Democratic Party of Japan; JCP, Japanese Communist Party; Kokumin, Kokumin Shintō; Minna, Minna no To; PR, proportional representation tier; SDPJ, Social Democratic Party of Japan; SMD, single-member district tier.

of the LDP members to learn the lessons that the 2005 election should have taught them about the changed electoral environment contributed to their defeat. Nevertheless, this argument has two weaknesses. First, as Steven Reed and Michael Thies point out, as "important as where the system is headed is when and how it will get there" (2001b, 381).

Second, up until this election there was no great evidence that the electoral system change was going to bring about the demise of the LDP as the ruling party; indeed, looking at the last election in 2005, we would have predicted exactly the reverse. Beyond just the last election, the LDP had actually been *increasing* its vote share in the SMD tier in every election from the first after the 1996 reform until this one, whatever the variation in seats gained. The electoral system change itself cannot satisfactorily explain this pattern.

Explanations at this point can only be speculative, but we believe the answer lies exactly in our previous analyses of the combination of change and the persistent '55 system institutions that remained. As we have seen, the kōenkai, especially in nonurban areas (although, as the case of Hirasawa shows, in certain urban areas as well), provided the LDP with a strong, if declining, vote-mobilization organization that in many respects kept it in power even after electoral reform. We have seen, however, how in this more competitive electoral environment, in which leadership and the party image count for more, the rural advantage in malapportioned districts was reduced after reform, and rural resentment over diminished benefits was rising, this organization might not have been entirely sufficient to win elections, although it was necessary to elect several of the individual LDP candidates.

The major challenge for the DPJ was to somehow capture more of the rural vote, as it had in the 2007 House of Councilors election, by incorporating rural voters' needs and demands into the DPJ policy platform or by incorporating the remaining anti-Koizumi rebels into their party or coalition but without losing the support of urban voters who were disgusted by exactly these practices by the LDP in the past. The dilemma for the LDP was the reverse—how could it hold on to or gain the support of the floating urban voters as it had in the 2005 general election when it appeared to be backing off from the reforms of the last decade and trying to reinforce its rural base, which was dependent on the kōenkai and pork-barrel clientelistic benefits (Reed, Scheiner, and Thies 2009)?

In the end, the LDP was able to do neither of its challenges, and the DPJ accomplished both of its and was also vastly more successful in coordinating its candidacies with the opposition in 2009 than in any previous postreform election (Smith 2009). Several changes undermined the LDP rural vote. We have discussed the gradual attrition of the kōenkai in chapter 3. More important for the significant change from the 2005 election, this time the powerful support groups traditionally mobilized for the LDP through the kōenkai either supported the DPJ or were passive. The postmasters are an obvious example, but also Nōkyō, the Japan Medical Association, and construction groups either shifted support to the DPJ (at least in some prefectures) or were demobilized due to the slim chances of fat LDP budgets benefiting them. These changes hit at the heart of the kōenkai as the LDP electoral machine and left the LDP even more at the mercy of the floating voters. Another development undermining the LDP was the Heisei merger of municipal units, which was designed to result in more efficient local administration. Many of these municipalities were in rural LDP strongholds (Rosenbluth, Saito, and Yamada 2009, 15 and figure 7), and a reduced number of municipalities also reduced the number of local LDP politicians supporting the Diet candidates who were so important in their clientelistic networks (Scheiner 2006). Also contributing to the precipitous decline in the LDP rural support was an agricultural reform policy that was designed to move Japan from quotas and tariffs to an income subsidy program; but the LDP subsidies were less beneficial to small farmers, who became very discontented with the LDP. The DPJ took advantage of this by coming up with its own income subsidy plan in its manifesto that treated the smaller farmers better. In the new electoral environment in which policy mattered more to even rural voters, both of these changes helped to substantially chip away at the previously solid LDP rural support.

In addition to these causes of the LDP defeat, there were longer-term structural causes related to party leadership and the themes in this book. The kōenkai, factions (even though now weakened), and PARC zoku giin within the party and the national bureaucracy in the government constrained the party leadership from instituting a complete top-down policy-making system. Perhaps the best evidence that the changes in leadership were only partial comes from Koizumi's own track record on getting his reform proposals through. Despite a clear increase in the prime minister's resources and Koizumi's personal public popularity, his record was mixed: a major victory on postal reform; more of a compromise on highway privatization and reform; and generally only little or no progress on rice market reform, health system reform, and other issues. Much of the successful resistance to and the undermining of his plans came from a combination of the national bureaucracy and the party (Mishima 2007, 741–48; Kaihara 2007). The fact that the new electoral system did not completely transform the power of the top leadership of the LDP should not surprise us. After all, even with the SNTV electoral system as a constant, the influence and power of the party leader and prime minister varied greatly over time and was diminished with the entrenchment of the factions, the kōenkai, and PARC and the development of the zoku giin.

The factions perhaps were undermined most by the changes that reform brought, although, as we have seen, they still had some influence due to their continuing influence on the distribution of party posts. Their decline allowed the party leader much more potential for influence in the party, a new capability that Koizumi was able to take advantage of. And that was the problem. Greater influence in the party for the party leader also meant greater potential for a weak or politically unskillful party leader to drag the whole party down with him, as seems to have happened under Abe, Fukuda, and Asō.

In the post-Koizumi climate of public desire for even more reform and no retreat back to the days of the '55 system, the dilemma for the factions was that the LDP collectively could not be seen as going back to old days and influence; thus, even nonfaction members were increasingly able to gain government posts. Yet if this was extended also to the party posts, the last remaining raison d'etre for the factions would be gone. The LDP could not further modernize its personnel practices without sparking further resistance from the leaders of its factions who were threatened by these moves. Not trying to go further to damp down on factional influence gave the media and public the impression the LDP was going backward; trying to do so, however, provoked resistance and reaction from those who benefited from the factions. This seems to be what occurred in the post-Koizumi period within the party, hurting the image that it had gained under Koizumi as a party of reform and giving that mantle back to the now competitive DPJ.

PARC remained and continued to provide the LDP with the training of policy experts within the party and a forum for them to influence policymaking. Its weakening under Koizumi and its integration with the increasing influence of the cabinet on policymaking after the electoral and administrative reforms, however, also allowed the party and governmental leadership to have more influence in the shaping of policy. To the extent that policymaking became more centralized, on the other hand, this also meant that poor leadership and bad policy judgments or responses to crises could make the LDP increasingly unpopular. If the old PARC had one advantage, it was that its bottom-up policymaking ensured more directly that constituency concerns were looked after in the organ that controlled policymaking. That link, given a more influential prime minister who had more influence on the agenda, became more tenuous. Less independence from party leadership also meant PARC could not function as a brake on unpopular policies. This is, in part, what seems to have happened with Abe when his pet foreign policy concerns took precedence over the continuing domestic issues that really mattered to the public and also with Asō when the feedback of growing unhappiness in the rural areas was not translated into policy changes to mitigate that discontent.

Ultimately, the very path-dependent and complete resistance to reform of the kōenkai, the factions, and PARC and the zoku giin helped to doom the LDP. The party made very substantial efforts to respond to and adapt its institutions to the new electoral environment. The problem was that these institutions, and what they represented to new, less rural, less pork-barrel-motivated, and more public-goods-oriented voters were at the heart of the unpopularity of the 2009 LDP. Koizumi was so successful in 2005 because he ran not against the opposition DPJ but against these very persistent institutions of his own party that came to be, for better or worse, associated in the public mind with the problems at the heart of the '55 system.

The guiding research question behind this book was never the success or failure of the LDP at the polls. Nevertheless, we believe our study of party organization does allow us to offer some insights into the causes of the LDP defeat after its long postreform Indian summer of power.[12] We feel that a major cause of the LDP defeat, and interim success, lies ultimately in its incomplete adaptation to the new electoral environment because of its institutionalized party organization.

Liberal Democratic Party Dilemmas of Party Leadership

Applying historical institutional concepts from Pierson, we can see how the particular combination of self-reinforcing path dependence interacted with exogenous changes in the environment to produce the particular mixed outcome it did in party leadership. We can attribute both some of the impetus for and the limits on change to institutional complementarity. Most obviously, the developing institutions of the kōenkai, the factions, and PARC with its zoku giin clearly constrained the power and influence of the party leader prior to electoral reform. Indeed, it was exactly the institutionalization of

12. Of course, some fine works do take the success or failure of the LDP at the polls as their research question; we direct the reader especially to Curtis (1971, 1988, 1999); Scheiner (2006). Note also that Reed (2010) analyzes the various strategies that the LDP adopted to keep itself in power despite its inability to win majorities in elections or in public support in the polls after the 1960s, some of which involve practices we discuss in this book.

these within the LDP that gradually took a more powerful leader, as under Yoshida, and made him the "missing leader" by the 1980s. The institutions were in, and continue to be in, an inverse relationship with the party leadership, even though some of their functions were now partially merged with that of the leadership, as in the case of PARC. That the parliamentary agenda constitutionally was not under the direct control of the prime minister but rather the parliament and that the LDP had a majority on the Diet Management Committee, which sets that agenda, continued to constrain the prime minister's ability to lead and gave the party greater agenda-setting influence, exercised as we have seen in part by PARC.

The influence of television occurred late and then changed, breaking the NHK strong and unchallenged control of political coverage. This change occurred, however, only after the kōenkai, the factions, and PARC had reached the height of their institutionalization within the party, limiting the effects of the media, floating voters, and electoral and administrative reforms and giving an important role to sequencing as well. This meant that all these changes that occurred from the late 1980s to the 2000s did not eliminate these prior institutions but only somewhat diminished and transformed their influence. The negative externalities to candidates who did not have a kōenkai, belong to a faction, or did not developing his or her career as a zoku giin all weakened but continued to exist, providing a counterpoint to the changes in leadership that occurred. Even changes such as the new electoral system, as we have seen, have provided incentives for the continuation of some of these institutions. Thus, the MMM system has reinforced the negative externalities of not having a kōenkai to gather the personal vote due to the "best loser" provisions for PR seat allocation and the party practice of dual listing.

Beyond their mere persistence, however, it appears that the very combination of increased party leader influence and the persistence of these institutions may have introduced a self-reinforcing dynamic to the continuity of the institutions and presented the LDP with some cruel dilemmas. Exactly because the party policy and image of the party leader counted more for voters at a time when the former was unpopular and the latter was bad, the competitive disadvantages of not having a popular leader increased even further. As a mid-level urban LDP politician told us recently while discussing the possibility of the LDP losing the upcoming (2009) election:

> This time the LDP won't win. There also are stupid Diet members who are relying only on the LDP but that group is all going to lose because the LDP isn't popular, no matter what the LDP does. There are those who hate the LDP but who will help me. If it wasn't for that, I wouldn't win the election. Up until now the LDP was strong because of that. Because there were a lot of people who hated the LDP but would help me because I was their representative, the LDP was strong. Up until now because of that I had an individual *kōenkai* and went to funerals too. Simply, the people who will win will win even in the LDP's adverse-wind. (Interview L, October 16, 2008).

Under an unpopular prime minister, the Koizumi reforms and the diminution of pork-barrel spending, along with the rising competitiveness of the DPJ, actually increased the LDP candidate's dependence on the kōenkai for the personal vote. The more flexibility the prime minister had to choose his own cabinet and high party posts without regard to the factions (as changed under Koizumi), the more the remaining party, parliamentary, and cabinet posts increased in value to the individual representatives, enhancing their incentives to belong to one of the factions that continued to control such appointments. The negative externalities of not belonging to a faction also increased, especially because such posts now became even more strictly reserved according to factional seniority to introduce balance into the party.

The more that the prime minister and party leadership gained influence in policymaking because of the Cabinet Office councils and coalition bargaining, the more incentive there was for being active on PARC and the greater the value of that institution to the individual Diet member—the divisions and committees of this institution become the only way that backbenchers could exercise any influence on the process.

Thus, there was a fundamental collective action dilemma that helps explain the problems of the LDP after Koizumi. All the changes that could collectively have improved the chances of the success of the party at the polls (strong centralized leadership, a popular and media-savvy prime minister, and weaker factions and zoku giin) also increased the incentives of individual LDP Diet members to preserve those institutions and to resist further changes.

These changes after electoral reform brought with them, in combination with the continuation of these other institutions, new problems and enhanced risks for the LDP that help to explain the great puzzle of why, after all these changes and Koizumi's success, the LDP could not reform itself enough and finally lost power.

Party Leadership and Historical Institutionalism

Our historical institutional concepts have helped us explain the changes that the LDP underwent in the 2000s in terms of the apparent increasing centralization of the party under its leaders and also the limits of that movement and the constraints and new problems that the path-dependent continuation of the kōenkai, the factions, and PARC brought to the LDP.

Various changes partially transformed the resources and capabilities available to the LDP political leadership, especially those of the party leader (prime minister) and the cabinet. The LDP was no longer at the core of an un-Westminster system (George Mulgan 2003, 73–91) and the almost complete antithesis of the centralized party and government decision making found in the United Kingdom or New Zealand; but neither was it a Westminster system, despite the new electoral system. The party leaders had new resources and capabilities to use if they chose and were able to use them skillfully, but because of the way the party developed historically, they also continued to face the consequences of the institutionalization of the '55 system and the way it combined with these new transformations.

Various LDP prime ministers were able to use those capabilities more or less skillfully; Abe, Fukuda, and Asō clearly were not able to duplicate Koizumi's partial accomplishments. Even most skillfully used, the newly more influential LDP leadership still could not institute as much of a top-down system as in a Westminster-style system. History and the prior development of a party mattered.

The critical experience of the merger of the LDP in 1955, leading to the almost immediate consolidation and institutionalization of the factions, their later extension into the electoral districts and linkage with the kōenkai, and the imposition of their seniority norms on the PARC office-holding processes contained enough elements of path dependence through negative externalities and adaptation to the new electoral system to endure and continue to limit, even if less so, the now greater influence of party leadership. The greater the influence of the party leaders in elections, in appointing personnel to top government and party offices, and in policy-making, however, the more incentives backbenchers had to cling to those three institutions. And thus Japan under the LDP was stuck in a partially centralized but partially decentralized, non-Westminster but not un-Westminster system. Further, as Koizumi's successors demonstrated, neither the advantages the LDP enjoyed nor the disadvantages the DPJ suffered given the new media, increase in floating voters, and MMM electoral system during Koizumi's tenure could be locked in to guarantee a continued process of LDP success.

The DPJ seemed determined both before and after its 2009 victory to be a much more Westminster governing party. Its manifesto clearly laid out this intention, contrasting its goals to what it perceived the LDP dominance through the central bureaucracy, lack of unity and accountability in the cabinet and party, factional politics in cahoots with bureaucratic interests, the "iron triangle" of government-bureaucracy-business collusion, and ministries run as independent fiefdoms. In place of this, the DPJ promised to establish a politician- and cabinet-led government, a unified and accountable cabinet and ruling party, prime ministerial leadership, and ministers working together for the national interests and lives of the people. It even laid out a step-by-step time line for instituting its new measures to achieve these aims once it took power (Democratic Party of Japan 2010).

Clearly determined to decrease the influence of the bureaucracy in policymaking and to have policy decisions made by a centralized cabinet and party political leadership, it began to implement its plans soon after taking office. Among its first acts, it announced that the cabinet would make the important decisions and that the DJP would abolish its own version of PARC and coordinate policy within a centralized State Strategy Office (*Yomiuri Shimbun* Online, September 16, 2009). It abolished the meeting of administrative vice ministers advising the cabinet, an institution it saw as enabling the bureaucrats to persuade the politicians to do their bidding, and it also forbade them from having press conferences, thus concentrating media attention on policy in the cabinet (Nishikawa 2009). Ichirō Ozawa, the new secretary-general of the DPJ, initially banned in principle any DPJ representatives from introducing their own member-sponsored bills, a move, if enforced, that would give a monopoly on legislation to the cabinet (although he later backtracked on this rule; Kawakami 2009, 3). In chapter 10, we discuss the significance of the organization of the DPJ for theories of institutional change.

Although there are thought to be leadership factions as well as ideological divisions in the DJP based on the former progressive or conservative backgrounds of its founding Diet members, these have not congealed into formal, organized, and institutionalized factions of the LDP variety; they are much more fluid and have not prevented the DJP from making decisions by consensus under its four major leaders. Although many of its members have kōenkai, its success as a party electorally has been based much more on its party image, its party policies, and its more centralized mobilization of votes. In short, it may be the DPJ that carries Japanese politics much closer to the Westminster parliamentary model but whether fully so is another question.

In his classic work explaining how Britain developed its "efficient secret" of centralized cabinet government and the fusion of executive and legislative authority (Cox 1987 and 2005), Gary Cox focuses on the outcome of a thirty-year process (1830s to 1860s) of change, explicitly assigning party organization secondary status as a causal variable (Cox 1987 and 2005, 4). Instead, Cox focuses on cabinet-electorate and parliament-electorate relations. In this book on Japan's LDP we adopted a different approach: we are suggesting that party organization, party leadership, and intra-party conflict should be put back into the equation because they and not the electoral system produced Japan's "inefficient secret" of an "unWestminster" (George Mulgan 2003), decentralized yet successful party and government, and then to a large extent maintained it for fifteen years beyond an electoral reform explicitly designed to eliminate it.

We do not know whether Japan's party and government organization will wind up as the Westminster system that the DPJ seems to be striving toward; but if our analysis is correct, it may yet produce a somewhat different outcome to that of nineteenth-century Britain even thirty years after Japan's electoral reform.

The main questions now for the LDP are whether it can refashion itself along similar lines or can find a way to use the three entrenched institutions it developed in ways that function better in the new electoral and party environment and regain power.

Chapter 10

The Liberal Democratic Party out of Time?

Imagine that your friend invites you to the trendiest new restaurant in town, charmingly named "The Modern Social Scientist."...When you arrive, the chef explains that the kitchen is divided into two parts. On the left, she has all the ingredients (which to your puzzlement she refers to as "variables"). On the right is an extraordinary profusion of measuring devices. You express astonishment at their complexity and detailed ornamentation, and the chef explains that each requires years to learn how to operate properly.

The chef proceeds to elaborate her culinary approach: good cooking, she says, amounts to having the perfect ingredients, perfectly measured....As long as you have the correct ingredients and they are properly measured, she insists, how, in what order, and for how long they are combined *makes no difference.*

Few would want to patronize a restaurant with such a philosophy of cooking, but most social scientists are working in that kind of a kitchen.
Paul Pierson (2004, 1)

We are like passengers on the Titanic. The only difference is that the LDP knows it is going to sink. There is nothing more to do now except to wait for it to happen, and then see who can swim.
Personal communication, senior LDP politician to a U.S. academic, July 2008

How did the LDP do it? Seldom particularly popular, the party held power in Japan from 1955 until its disastrous defeat at the polls in 2009 (except during a few months in the early 1990s). Along the way, it weathered storms of protest, endured painful scandals, and surmounted a fundamental electoral reform designed, in part, to get the LDP out of power. Then, four short years after arguably its greatest electoral victory ever, it lost an election for the first time in party history. Despite its defeat, its virtually unbroken record of success in the first five and a half decades of its existence makes the LDP arguably the most successful political party operating in a democracy in the post–World War II era. Surely part of the reason for this success, and a key to the puzzle of how it fell so suddenly, may lie in the way the party organized itself, the central topic explored in this book.

Studying the LDP affords an opportunity to learn more than the secrets of its success and the reasons for its ultimate failure. Political science is now governed by an interest in institutions. In the past, it might have been possible to title a book *Do Institutions Matter?* and have it appear to be an honest interrogative. Today, the chorus of "yea" voices would be deafening.

This book, in contrast, asks questions about institutions on issues still debated among social scientists. The crucial questions of this book are: What determines how institutions change or not? And what determines how much and when they change? We address these questions by examining four political institutions in postwar Japan: the LDP factions, PARC, the kōenkai, and the LDP leadership.

Strong deductive theories predicted there would be dramatic changes in these Japanese party institutions as a result of the 1994 electoral reform. The Japanese postwar electoral system of SNTV (or SNTV MMD) changed with the 1996 election to a MMM system of 300 SMD and 180 (initially 200) PR seats. The reasoning behind the expectations of change seemed sound in each case—the SNTV electoral system provided incentives that sustained the institutions, but the new MMM system did not. Accordingly, change and the likely disappearance of the factions, PARC, and the kōenkai were expected. As it turned out, however, these predictions were not fulfilled or, at least, not completely fulfilled.

It is vitally important to avoid misunderstandings here. We do not fault the predictors for being wrong. In fact, they were smart people, making very good guesses with good deductive logic based, however, on (as it turned out) faulty assumptions about the origins of these institutions. We ourselves have learned much from these predictors, and we respect their scholarship. We simply want to take advantage of the scientific surprise of the predictions' being wrong to refine our theories and understanding of institutional change. We hope readers will not see this book as an attack on the failed predictions or their predictors and, instead, understand that it represents an attempt to refine—as science and scholarship must—theories and understanding.

In refining our understanding of why these political institutions did not vanish, we learn a lot. Of course, we learn a great deal about the LDP and Japanese politics. We also learn about what causes institutions to change or not change. In addition, because of our methodology, we learn about institutional origins. Indeed, although we had anticipated learning primarily about institutional change, our study has inevitably led us to offer important insights on the origins of institutions. We believe this research may shed new light not only on the nature of Japanese politics and broader questions of institutional change but also on still broader questions of methodology and ontology.

In our earlier chapters, we tell the story of how Japanese political institutions arose and developed over time. Here, we lay out the main outlines of our findings. In chapter 1, we set the stage for our study by introducing our central questions of institutional origin and change and party organization, as well providing the context of the '55 system. The chapter painted a picture of the broad importance of the LDP, the most successful party in the history of competitive democracies, as an object of study. In chapter 1, we also make the argument, reprised here, that within-case evidence and an emphasis on process tracing are the appropriate tools to investigate causal arguments about political institutions. In chapters 2–7, we examine the origin, development, and transformation of three political institutions: the kōenkai, the factions, and PARC. In chapters 8–9, we pursue the question of party leadership within the LDP.

Our investigation has produced new findings on three levels: empirical, methodological, and theoretical. At an empirical level, we have analyzed the origin and development of the first three crucial party institutions for the LDP: the kōenkai, the factions, and PARC. We have also closely examined these institutions after the electoral reform to test predictions about how they would transform under the pressure of the new electoral system. Also, we have pursued an analysis of the development and state of the LDP leadership, an institution that (obviously) was not predicted to disappear and did indeed change after the electoral reform, although only partially because of it. In an effort to situate our study for students of Japanese politics, we have also discussed on how these party institutions fit into the larger pattern of Japanese politics both before and after the electoral reform.

At a methodological level, our decision to rely on within-case evidence seems fully validated by the results. Furthermore, this study demonstrates how important process tracing is to establishing causality and reveals some of the limitations of actor-centered functionalist analyses for understanding causation. Although we have relied primarily on qualitative evidence, plenty of quantitative evidence is deployed throughout the book to support our arguments. We prefer to frame the question of methods more clearly as within-case and cross-case evidence, rather than more simplistically as qualitative versus quantitative evidence.

At a theoretical level, we have several major points. For starters, our study makes plain the value of the historical institutionalist orientation. Attention to sequencing, negative externalities, and complementary institutions greatly aids our understanding here of institutional origins, development, and transformation. Any attempt at understanding the origins of and changes over time in these four party institutions would be incomplete or erroneous without attention to these dimensions. Finally, the results of our study have led us to pay special heed to the role of negative externalities and, even more so, of complementary institutions. Much more than has been recognized in the political science literature, complementary institutions hold the key for understanding institutional transformation or persistence.

The issue of delegation, or the tension between the backbenchers and party leaders, perennially intrigues political scientists. And this theme is woven throughout our empirical cases, especially in the chapter on party leadership. Here, we revisit the issue to articulate what this study has to say about the broader issue of delegation within political parties.

We review these three sets of findings in turn, beginning with a brief recap of our empirical findings, moving on to the methodological results, and then turning to the theoretical findings. In the last section, we discuss the import of the transformation or nontransformation of these institutions for understanding the bases of the electoral fortunes of the LDP.

Empirical Findings

We have four main sets of empirical findings to discuss. The three institutions—kōenkai, the factions, and PARC—are each discussed in turn; they constitute the core cases for our questions about institutional origin and change. Our findings on the relationship between the backbenchers and party leaders (delegation) constitute the fourth short summary in this section. Although delegation itself is not an institution (and so these findings are distinct in character from the other three), the issues of delegation infuse the story of the three institutions so powerfully that they are essential to a full understanding. Examining these issues within a separate section not only reflects the attention we pay to delegation in chapters 8–9 but also significantly adds to the generalizable lessons of this book.

Kōenkai

In chapter 2, we scrutinize the birth of the kōenkai in the early postwar years; in chapter 3, we examine the kōenkai after the electoral reform of 1994. As defined in chapter 2, the kōenkai are permanent organizations, or overlapping sets of organizations, with formal memberships devoted to supporting an individual politician and heavily involved in electoral mobilization. Most kōenkai are sets of overlapping organizations built around geography, occupation, interests, or some personal bond to the politician (such as a kōenkai of senior high school classmates). The kōenkai are distinctly *not* LDP organizations (although we elide that distinction for purposes of linguistic convenience when we refer to kōenkai, along with the factions and PARC, as "party institutions"). Instead, they support an individual politician. Earlier analysts posit the creation of the kōenkai as stemming from the nature of social networks in Japanese society or from the transformation of these networks during the rapid economic growth and urbanization in Japan in the early postwar period. Another set of analysts argue that the kōenkai were the necessary result of the need by the LDP to divide the vote among multiple candidates within the same district under the rules of the Japanese SNTV electoral system. That is, to win a legislative majority, the LDP had to win multiple candidates from a single district. And the kōenkai neatly avoided the danger of votes clumping on to the most popular politician, which would cost the LDP seats. This electoral explanation was put to the test when the SNTV system gave way to the current MMM system of 300 SMD and 180 PR seats. Instead of being replaced by party branches, as predicted, the kōenkai have continued as vital, if weakening, organizations for more than fifteen years after electoral reform (see chapter 3).

Contrary to the notion that LDP leaders were rationally supporting or even pushing the creation of kōenkai to divide the vote, the early history of the LDP can be written as a struggle to eliminate the kōenkai and replace them with party branches. In December 1955, with the ink still wet on the merger agreement, the LDP decided to set up local branches (*Asahi Shimbun*, December 4, 1955, 1). It failed in this goal, as it did again in 1956, very seriously in 1960, and again in 1963; after this, the party bowed to the inevitable and de facto accepted the kōenkai. Far from eagerly embracing kōenkai as an efficient vote-division mechanism, the party leadership struggled fiercely to eliminate them and build up the local party organizations.

Although the electoral system plays a role, we see the origin of the kōenkai as being more complex. Kōenkai emerged as a successful institution due in part to the historical sequencing and in part because of negative externalities and complementary institutions. The sequence of events mattered. The LDP formed as a party after several elections in which conservative candidates had built up rival kōenkai that later could not be subsumed into a single local party organization. The kōenkai did not spring up immediately across Japan after SNTV was introduced in 1947; rather, they spread slowly. By the time of the 1955 merger, however, the rival groups of Liberal and Democratic Party politicians still held on to their kōenkai. The electoral system was important as a cause; nevertheless, the electoral system is not sufficient to explain why the kōenkai actually came about.

Negative externalities also mattered. LDP candidates who relied on party branch support lost elections, whereas the candidates who trusted in the kōenkai were victorious. As more and more politicians turned to the kōenkai, the value of the strategy of relying on the party branch diminished. In a way, the weakness of the party label compared to the advantages of the kōenkai contributed to the inability of the party to strengthen its party label with a more vigorous local party organization. The pattern of increase in kōenkai membership from 1967 to 1993 (see figure 2.5) is consonant with this explanation. If the cause had been purely due to the electoral system, there would have shown an immediate jump in membership in 1947 when SNTV was introduced and then an immediate drop in 1994 when the electoral system changed, and party leaders would have been intentionally encouraging the development of the kōenkai instead of resisting it. As the quotation from an LDP politician at the beginning of chapter 9 indicates, those who relied on strong kōenkai in the 2009 election were in a better position to win reelection than those who relied on the party and the image of the party leadership, a fact that bodes well for the continuation of kōenkai even with further centralization of the LDP in the future.

Complementary institutions played a big role as well. The kōenkai grew to mesh quite well with the LDP factions, particularly after the 1978 party presidential primary. The factions were themselves not an inevitable result of the SNTV system, adding another layer of contingency to our understanding of the kōenkai. Perhaps even more important as a complementary institution, however, was the POEL, which heavily restricted campaigning (see chapter 2). These severe regulations made the kōenkai relatively much more attractive as a means to connect to voters—or, to put it as politicians often felt, the POEL left politicians with no recourse except the expensive alternative of the kōenkai to connect to voters.

Kōenkai membership diminished in the decade and a half after the electoral reform, and this is usually interpreted as validating the electoral system explanation of the kōenkai. Such a view, however, ignores the timing and pattern of the kōenkai membership change. Politicians were as keen as ever to establish kōenkai, but over time the voters gradually showed themselves less willing to join. A supply-side explanation might focus on the increase in independent voters (floating voters) perhaps occasioned by the gradually increasing role of the mass media in influencing public opinion, including the new importance of image of the party leader (see chapter 9). In any event, the slow pace of the decline of LDP kōenkai membership (which was still higher in 2003 than it had been in 1972) argues against a purely electoral explanation.

The value of attention to sequencing, negative externalities, and complementary institutions is demonstrated in the origin and development of kōenkai as well as in their persistence after the 1994 electoral reform changed the playing field. Sequencing is obvious. Had Japan adopted the MMM system in 1947 and then switched to SNTV MMD in 1994, we would probably see a very different situation. The logic of negative externalities continued to hold after electoral reform, although with diminishing force. Perhaps most significant, the POEL continued almost completely intact despite the electoral reform of 1994. This is an important reason for why kōenkai were not whisked into the dustbin of history to be replaced by party branches, as some had predicted.

Factions

The story of the LDP factions is similarly rife with misinterpretation, so close attention to the historical record can improve our theories. As shown in chapter 4, before the 1955 merger, the factions in the two smaller conservative parties, the Liberal and the Democratic parties, were different creatures from what they became afterward. The archetypal LDP factions developed later, after the merger and first party presidential election; they bargained with other factions to decide who would become prime minister and controlled the distribution of posts, electoral nominations, and major funding sources. Yet this type of faction came about only in the late 1970s and early 1980s, not immediately after the merger.

Cultural determinist explanations for the factions have often been made, but they are not sustainable in the face of the transformation of the factions over the first postwar decades. Another explanation is rooted in the SNTV electoral system. Here the logic is that the need to run multiple candidates from the same party also drove factionalization within the LDP because each rival faction supported one different contender within any district to prevent candidates within the same faction from competing with one another. But there was, in fact, much more overlap and intrafactional competition than has been claimed, undermining the electoral system argument (see chap. 4). Further, the electoral determinist explanation, like the culturalist claims, is trying to explain change with a constant—from 1947 to 1993, the electoral system did not change but the factions developed and changed greatly. Moreover, the electoral system did change in 1994, but the factions did not disappear. Indeed, the story of the factions is one of almost perpetual change from decade to decade, not of a change from one state before 1994 to another afterward.

We turn again to the insights provided by historical institutionalism and examine how sequencing, negative externalities, and complementary institutions shaped the origin, development, and transformation of the factions. Sequencing was important. If the factions had developed before the kōenkai existed, the faction leaders might well have tried to attract followers by establishing distinctive ideological postures or policy positions. But the kōenkai had already begun to take root before 1956, and the kōenkai and factions both blossomed greatly in the 1956–1958 period, linking them as purely vote mobilization and office-seeking devices with barely any policy or ideological content. Had the faction leaders tried to recruit members based on ideology or policy, they often would have had to exclude those with strong kōenkai (and thus the best chances of reelection) who did not fit the litmus test of ideology.

Negative externalities played a crucial role in the development of the factions. This is most obvious in the distribution of posts. As the factions tightened their grips on the distribution of posts in PARC and the party, the cost to an individual member of not belonging to a faction increased. If only a few members had belonged to factions, the disadvantage of not being in a faction would have been minor. But, with each individual Diet member who added his or her name to a faction membership list, the chance that all posts would be given to faction members increased; thus, the relative disadvantages to nonmembers also increased. This is the path-dependent logic that swept politicians into the factions regardless of their own opinions of the system. And this is the same dynamic we have seen after the electoral reform, as in the example of the Diet member who proclaimed his independence to us in one interview but, when we met him a few years later, had reluctantly joined a faction. Factions continued only because of their role in the distribution of posts, in which negative externalities still made it difficult (even if less so) for politicians to avoid joining a faction. With the LDP now out of power, and thus with no important posts to distribute that have real influence on government policy, it remains to be seen whether the negative externalities of not joining a faction will be strong enough to continue this pattern.

Although the kōenkai were also significantly linked to the factions, the main complementary institution for the factions was the LDP presidential selection mechanism. First adopted in 1956, the selection process changed over time but, almost without exception (save 1978), provided an incentive for ambitious politicians to assemble teams that would vote for them in patron-client exchanges lubricated with money. The drastic revision of the party presidential selection process, especially after Koizumi's selection in 2001, crippled the link between the factions and this complementary institution. The factions changed the most of the three institutions after the electoral reform, in large part because, in addition to the reform's undermining two of its major functions for candidates (nomination and funding) more than it affected the kōenkai and PARC, their most closely associated complementary institution also underwent significant change.

The Policy Affairs Research Council

The third major party institution, was PARC was an extra-legislative party organ devoted to discussion and policymaking (see chaps. 6–7). In addition its policymaking function and the contribution PARC made to developing the politicians' policy expertise, PARC also served an electoral function. Membership in individual PARC divisions ostensibly signaled to voters, particularly voters with a strong economic interest in particular policy issues, that they should vote for LDP candidates in a district, and their representative serving on particular PARC divisions could claim credit for any benefits that PARC provided the district. Organized principally along functional lines (divisions generally paralleled the bureaucratic ministries), PARC was the major policymaking body within the LDP since the party was founded in 1955. LDP Diet members also join Diet committees, but these were always seen as relatively inconsequential compared to PARC. No piece of legislation could be introduced into the Diet without first going through the PARC divisions, even if the legislation had been first drafted by the bureaucracy. The PARC divisions were the front lines of interest coordination (Inoguchi and Iwai 1987, 103). PARC also played an important socialization role for Diet members, as well as structuring their careers through the systematic allocation of positions (primarily the chairs and vice chairs) and even membership in the divisions.

Cultural determinist explanations of PARC emphasize its conformity with traditional Japanese bottom-up decision-making processes. These explanations are typically tautological, at least when applied to PARC processes. The electoral explanation of PARC is more convincing. The PARC system of restricting membership in divisions was argued to be a result of the need to divide the vote; specialization, the story goes, permitted voters to distinguish among candidates. But, to the contrary, the early history of PARC is fraught with discord and also demonstrates the relative irrelevance of PARC in the late 1950s. PARC was the locus of a power struggle between the backbenchers and party leaders over who would influence legislation. In 1960, the LDP Executive Council laid down the requirement that any member's bill must be approved by, among others, the PARC chair. The LDP party leaders, far from encouraging the development and use of PARC for electoral purposes, were constantly trying to keep the policymaking process free of individual member's bills, which, typically, were designed to bring home political pork. This then set the stage for the 1962 Akagi memo, which included government bills as well and marked the beginning of the PARC-based policymaking system that dominated the government in later years.

Nevertheless, there was actually far less specialization among Diet members from the same district as has been claimed, and so PARC division membership never exactly nor completely signaled to voters which LDP candidate to vote, as the dividing the vote hypothesis posits. Instead, PARC division memberships allowed LDP candidates to claim credit with constituents (much as in congressional committee membership in the U.S. SMD system). There is no empirical basis for the assumption that, just because candidates were elected via SNTV, candidates from the same district specialized on different PARC divisions. Indeed, given the likelihood that many in the same district would choose to become members of the same major divisions (Agriculture and Forestry, Commerce and Industry, and Construction—the Big Three), that there were costs associated with *not* specializing in these popular committees makes much more sense than the specialization hypothesis overall. Rather than PARC, the geographical concentration of the vote (abetted by the kōenkai) seems more important in understanding dividing the vote. As such, although PARC was also seen as headed for a rapid demise, or at least a total makeover, once the need for candidates to differentiate themselves from their rivals in the same party under a SNTV system was gone, after the electoral reform in 1994 PARC still flourished because it could still perform its credit-claiming and vote mobilization functions, as well as the functions of policy-training and -making.

As it turned out, PARC did indeed change after the electoral reform. Before 1994, membership on PARC divisions was strictly controlled; after 1994, membership in the divisions was opened to any and all interested legislators. Membership lists were no longer kept. Nevertheless, PARC did not disappear; instead, it continued to serve other important functions for the governing party. And, although membership was open, the leadership posts within PARC were still contested as scarce resources and still controlled by the factions as paths for career advancement.

The origin of PARC can be attributed more to policymaking concerns and intraparty factional rivalries between mainstream and antimainstream forces than to concerns about dividing the vote. In terms of Strøm's (1990) tripartite division of the vote-seeking, office-seeking, and policy-seeking functions of parties, the importance of PARC for the first was overemphasized, perhaps at the expense of understanding its significance for the latter.

In terms of understanding how PARC came about, developed, and transformed after the electoral reform, we find again that attention to sequencing, positive externalities, and complementary institutions is valuable. PARC began as a vehicle to bring about the preliminary integration of the Liberal and Democratic parties before they merged. In the early years, the backbenchers (and antimainstream faction members) were the main participants in PARC, and it was not closely connected to policymaking influence. The running struggle between the backbenchers and leaders continued for several years until the 1962 Akagi memo struck a compromise that allowed the backbenchers some influence on bills but let party leaders channel backbenchers' demands through the hierarchical system of PARC executives. This is what we mean when we say that PARC served in place of a party whip for the LDP (Krauss and Pekkanen 2004, 21). Recall that the LDP was very unusual among major democratic parties in not having such a position. The sequence of rapid economic growth and then PARC systematization was critical for the functioning of PARC. Had rapid economic growth delivered sufficient resources to the mainstream factions by the late 1950s, they might have been able to consolidate their hold on the policymaking process without acceding to the compromise on PARC that invested it with policymaking influence.

The system gained acceptance as individual Diet members bought into the notion that seniority within PARC was the means to become a zoku giin and to develop influence over policy. Members invested in specialization because, as more Diet members did so, it became a losing strategy not to. Specialization because of a long-term career incentive was far more important than any incentive to divide the vote.

The main complementary institution for PARC was the factions because the factions controlled access to the important executive posts (and, before 1994, membership) in the divisions. This is why PARC is a middle case in terms of change after 1994. PARC no longer restricted membership in the divisions, so it cannot be said to have had any important role in dividing the vote; moreover, the importance of PARC for dividing the vote has probably been overestimated. In any event, the significant role of PARC in policymaking and office allocation (and specialization) continued until the LDP loss in August 2009. Because the LDP is now not making government policy, PARC offers slimmer benefits to Diet members, and this loss of power will affect the dynamics of institutional change.

Relations between the Backbenchers and Party Leaders

In the creation of the '55 system party, as we have seen, the conflicts among party leaders (factional rivalry) played a major role in creating a competing and unconcentrated party leadership. Conflicts between the backbenchers and party leaders, for example, over party branches versus kōenkai and over control over budget bills and private member bills (leading to the Akagi memo), were instrumental in the development of a political party in which the central leadership did not control vote mobilization, the distribution of offices, or policymaking. Factional rivalry for the prime ministership in 1978 led to the greater linking up of the factions and kōenkai at the grassroots level and to the changes in the allocation of party, parliamentary, and government posts due to the faction seniority rules and proportional distribution. Indeed, overall, we can conclude that the role of conflict among party leaders and between the leaders and backbenchers for control of the party played a more significant role than did the SNTV electoral system in the origins and development of the LDP as a decentralized non-Westminster system.

Even after the electoral reform, in the movement of the LDP away from its being a '55 system party (but not to a Westminster party), the conflict between prime ministers (especially Koizumi) and the faction leaders and zoku giin also was instrumental, along with the role of television, administrative reform, and electoral reform. Electoral systems matter; but so do intraparty conflict and rivalry. A summary of the development of the institutions appears in table 10.1.

Methodological Matters

Methodology matters greatly in determining the quality of the answers we receive to our research questions. Earlier attempts to understand why the kōenkai, the factions, or PARC existed frequently relied on actor-centered functionalism. In other words, analysts looked at who benefited from the existing institutional arrangements, in a snapshot of time, and then implied or argued that the beneficiaries were the ones who had brought about the system to capture those benefits. In our view, such analyses are ill-suited to genuine investigations of causation. For example, although we could argue that the kōenkai was an effective or necessary means to divide the vote for the LDP under SNTV, it is a fallacy to then argue that the kōenkai must have come about as a solution to a need to divide the vote for the party.

TABLE 10.1
Development of key Liberal Democratic Party institutions

	Kōenkai	Factions	PARC	Party Leadership
Antecedents	*Origin:* Before 1955; exist in small numbers	Exists prewar and early postwar but loose and nonexclusive	Exists prewar and earlier postwar but not important	
1950s	Growth spurred by LDP merger; 1956 party branch strategy fails	*Origin:* Leadership conflict after first LDP presidential election in 1956 drives exclusive and organized actional formation	Not important and haven for antimainstream factions	*Origin:* Hatoyama-early 1950s-Yoshida rivalry spurs Yoshida's changing party organization, elevating Sec-Gen and PARC chairs and increasing party leader's power
1960s	*Early development:* Major party pushes to replace kōenkai with party branches fail in 1960 and 1963; kōenkai develop in number and size	*Early development:* Factional conflict induces institutionalization of first faction, then party rules about seniority and proportionality	*Origin:* Mainstream/anti-mainstream and government-backbencher conflicts lead to Akagi Memo, which is pivotal in giving PARC influence on government bills	*Early development:* Conflict leads to pattern of collective leadership, strong norms in executive post allocation, and Akagi Memo; these, and kōenkai, undermine central leadership
1970s	Kōenkai continue to grow; 1978 party presidential race enmeshes factions and kōenkai more	Factional conflict leads to 1978 party presidential primary and stronger links between factions and kōenkai	*Early development:* Management of factional conflict through norms of seniority and proportionality leads to factional bargaining over posts and also to accumulation of experience in PARC divisions over time	Weak leadership continues
1980s	Kōenkai continue to grow	Factions well systematized in governance of LDP	Specialization and influence of *zoku giin* increases	Rise of TV strengthens potential power of PM
1990s	*Transformation:* Electoral reform, the rise of TV, and the rise of the "floating voter" diminish kōenkai	*Transformation:* Electoral reform and change in party presidential selection rules weaken factions	*Transformation:* Electoral reform dramatically changes PARC crediting-claiming function; new PARC division membership rules	*Transformation:* Administrative reform gives Cabinet and PM new powers; TV and "floating voters" make party more reliant on PM; new party presidential selection rules strengthen PM
2000s	Kōenkai persist in somewhat weakened state	Factions persist and play a role in executive post allocations below cabinet level	Struggle for policy influence through PARC and executive posts within PARC continues	Cabinet and especially PM more powerful in policymaking and more important for electoral success of party

Note: PARC, Policy Affairs Research Council; PM, prime minister; Sec-Gen, secretary-general.

Instead, we argue that the proper way to investigate causality is using within-case evidence. Within-case evidence comes in two forms: process tracing and congruence testing. In chapters 2–7, we apply rigorous process-tracing methodology to find out how the kōenkai, the factions, and PARC came about and developed. We find that the electoral system was important, but the evidence placed more emphasis on sequencing, negative externalities (and path dependence), and complementary institutions.

Getting Methodology Right

In recent years, there has been a broad but quiet revolution in the theory of qualitative methods.[1] Although this research extends to areas as disparate as Boolean algebra, necessary and sufficient causation, negative cases, concept formation, measurement validity, and unit homogeneity, a few areas are especially relevant for this book.

One of the central claims of the new literature on qualitative methods, and one that is often conceded even by the staunchest quantitative methods advocates, is that, although statistical analysis can reveal correlation, *causation* is better or can only be established by process tracing (sometimes called colligation; Roberts 1996). For us, this means that to examine the causality behind the political institutions in Japan we have to do two things. First, we have to examine the causality behind the transition or nontransition in 1994, and second, we have to go back to the origin of these political institutions to examine exactly what caused them to come into being in the first place. Powerful deductive theories have sought to account for the existence of the factions, PARC, and the kōenkai, with compelling explanations in each case. Nevertheless, without establishing the actual causality through process tracing, these theories are vulnerable to charges of actor-centered functionalism (Pierson 2004). That is, scholars analyzing the situation as it existed ask the question of who benefits. Once they have determined this, they assume that the institutions must have come about, or at least been maintained, to secure those benefits for the actors. This may be a wonderful way to generate hypotheses to test, but it does not constitute proof about actual causality or causal mechanisms. That can only be done with process tracing.

Process tracing is not the same thing as within-case evidence. In fact, the close examination of cases can produce two kind of evidence. First, process tracing produces evidence about causal linkages. The second kind of evidence from within-case studies is not directly related to the causal

1. See, for example, Bennett and Elman (2006a, 2007); Brady and Collier (2004); Clemens (2007); George and Bennett (2006); Gerring (2001, 2004, 2007, 2009); Hall (2003); Lieberman (2005); Mahoney (2004, 2007, 2010); Mahoney and Goertz (2004, 2006); Mahoney and Rueschemeyer (2003); Pierson (2004); Ragin (2000); Thelen (1999); and numerous articles in special issues of *Journal of Politics* 70(1) in 2008, *Comparative Political Studies* 40 in 2007, and *Political Analysis* 14 in 2006.

linkages but, rather, comes from additional opportunities to examine the observable implications of theories. Searching for this type of evidence is sometimes called congruence testing. In our study, for example, in addition to the direct evidence about the kōenkai in the LDP (in which they are said to have divided the vote), we can examine the role of kōenkai in other political parties. We can then examine whether the observable implications of our theories are congruent with the facts in those cases or not. Process tracing and congruence testing are tremendous contributions to our methodological tool kit, whose value has been clarified and strengthened by the development of qualitative methodology in recent years.

Detailed case studies employing these methodologies are the appropriate approach to use in exploring why and how our political institutions did or did not change. Of course, we value highly the contributions made by scholars employing quantitative methods (and we use them ourselves both in this book and elsewhere). Our argument is not about which set of tools is better; rather, it is that the choice of tools must fit the problem to be investigated.[2] This is not a question of the trade-off between parsimony and explanation. Causal analysis requires process tracing (and that means qualitative and detailed case study) methodologies. Because we are concerned with the questions of the origin and development of institutions and because of the mistaken theoretical predictions concerning the impact of electoral reform, this study demands causal analysis.[3]

Another virtue of detailed case studies is that they can nicely pick up the interconnectedness of variables that is often obscured by the current method of quantitative analysis. In our study, we can see the interconnectedness of the factions, PARC, and the kōenkai as causal elements in each of the other case studies.

Time in Politics

Neither path dependence nor the notion of sequencing is a method (like process tracing) or an approach (like historical institutionalism); each is a concept. Because many historical institutionalists employ path dependence,

2. Detailed case studies also are superior to regression analyses in avoiding problems such as omitted variable bias, uncovering Galton's problem, and maintaining measurement validity (Mahoney 2004). Although case studies are superior for determining whether a variable matters causally (causal mechanism), quantitative methods are usually superior for assessing how much that variable matters compared to others (causal effects) (George and Bennett 2006).

3. Process tracing is probably especially appropriate in before and after comparisons because it allows special attention to be paid to the most threatening of the confounding variables: maturation and exogenous shocks (Campbell and Stanley 1973, 467). For more discussions of process tracing, which according to Gerring "might also be labeled 'causal-process' observations...or alternatively, colligation, narrative explanation, pattern-matching, sequential explanation, genetic explanation, and causal chain explanation" (2009, 116, n. 55), see Gerring (2001, 2004, 2007, and esp. 2009); George and Bennett (2005, chap. 8); Little (1991, 1995, 43–44); Scriven (1975 and 1976); Seawright and Collier (2004); Tarrow (1995, 472).

this concept is often misidentified as being coterminous with historical institutionalism. But historical institutionalism simply emphasizes the importance of studying time as a variable; this does not mean that every such study must invoke path dependence. Path dependence is just one element of several in the attention to time that constitutes historical institutionalism. Moreover, path dependence applies to a somewhat narrow selection of circumstances. As in so much of social science, different authors use the concept differently (Bennett and Elman 2006b; Page 2006; Pierson 2004). Our use here is closest to Pierson (2004), although we emphasize negative externalities more than the rarer positive returns (Page 2006).

In our analysis, we take time seriously, not just through our examination of path dependence but also through the attention we pay to sequencing. The sequence in which events occur is another important element identified by an emphasis on time. Sequencing can matter to how events play out. On a commonsense level, it can hardly evoke any dissension to say that the sequence of events can powerfully affect outcomes. (Try walking through a door before opening it if you disagree.) For political analysis, too, sequencing can be very important. For example, Thomas Ertman (1997) argues that different patterns of state building in early modern Europe stemmed from the timing of the onset of military competition. Different states experienced this military competition at different stages of the development of their bureaucracies. The choices available to the state to respond to the threats similarly varied, and this had long-term influence: "differences in the timing of the onset of sustained geopolitical completion go a long way towards explaining the character of state infrastructures found across the continent at the end of the 18th century" (Ertman 1997, 26). In the twelfth century, literacy was not widespread and the best response was to rely on proprietary office holding and tax farming. Countries that faced intense military competition later, however, were able to draw on more literate populations to construct superior bureaucratic structures. Thus, sequencing in politics matters profoundly. We pay attention to sequencing in our study and also find that it is remarkably important.

Methods Employed

We use detailed case studies, which we consider the appropriate methodology to examine causal questions. Our case studies include detailed archival research, interviews with scores of politicians, and statistical analysis. We present a variety of within-case evidence of process tracing to establish causality, as well as congruence testing of other observable implications that we can examine within our cases. We have found that some institutions can complement others. We are hardly unique in this approach, but our case study focus has also allowed us to analyze the interactions of important variables and to isolate exactly how institutions can be mutually reinforcing.

Armed with this more accurate understanding of the causes of these institutions, we are better prepared to understand what happened to them after the electoral reform of 1994. It is far less puzzling that these institutions did not disappear after 1994 once we grasp that their electoral causes had been overestimated. In explaining the persistence and adaptation of these institutions, we have turned, again, to historical institutionalist insights. To understand the variation in the degree to which the institutions were or were not affected by electoral reform, however, we need to refine our understanding of the role of complementary institutions.

Theoretical Take-Homes

We believe our intensive examination of the LDP and its party institutions during the postwar period reveals several valuable lessons. In the previous two sections, we detail our empirical findings and spell out how we see our study contributing to the current methodological debates in political science and sociology; here, we turn our focus to other theoretical contributions of the book. First, we discuss how our study pushes forward the historical institutionalist approach to political analysis. Then, we suggest a reframing of our understanding of how political parties confront or solve delegation problems. In particular, much of the relationship of the party leadership and backbenchers, as well as the role of party institutions, are best understood as the incomplete delegation by the LDP of key functions to the party center. We also consider why this particular pattern of delegation occurred.

Historical Institutionalism

Process tracing and congruence analysis are methods. Historical institutionalism, on the other hand, is a theoretical orientation or approach. Some historical institutionalists engage in large comparisons (across cases or across time), whereas others are more modest in scope and examine slices of time or space. Kathleen Thelen distinguishes rational choice institutionalism and historical institutionalism "in terms of the relative centrality of 'equilibrium order' versus 'historical process' in the analysis of political phenomena (Thelen 1999, 381; see also Orren and Skowronek 1994). Thelen continues, "Whereas rational choice theorists tend to view institutions in terms of their coordinating functions, historical institutionalists see institutions as the legacy of concrete historical processes" (Thelen 1999, 382) and this brings to the fore questions of temporality rather than questions of equilibrium order (Orren and Skowronek 1994, 312). Thelen points out that "this does not mean that historical institutionalists are uninterested in regularities and continuities in politics; it just means that the emphasis tends to be on political development as a (structured) process and on the way institutions emerge from particular historical conflicts and constellations" (Thelen 1999, 382). We give credit where it is due, acknowledging the importance of electoral systems in structuring the political process. However, we place this book within the historical institutionalist tradition.

Our study both has been informed by historical institutionalist insights and attention to time as a variable and seeks to advance that research agenda. In our examination of institutional origin, development, and transformation or persistence, we have repeatedly found evidence for the importance of sequencing, negative externalities (path dependence), and complementary institutions. The sequence of key events, such as the introduction of a new electoral system, the merger of political parties, and degree of implementation of divergent individual legislators' strategies, have profound consequences for institutions.

For example, the merger of the LDP in 1955, binding together the Liberal Party and the Democratic Party and their constituent legislators, came nearly a decade after the introduction of the SNTV electoral system under the restored Japanese democracy. Different strategies for voter mobilization could have been pursued by the party if it had been unified at the outset, but the weakness of the LDP party branches and the reliance of party members on the kōenkai to mobilize voters were heavily influenced by this sequence in two ways. First, the merger meant that politicians in 1955 running under the LDP banner had had, until a few months before, totally separate organizations. They were loathe to merge their operations, despite repeated party offensives to strengthen local party branches at the expense of the kōenkai. Second, the successful candidates were those who had adopted kōenkai strategies, whereas those who relied on the party label were severely disadvantaged in electoral competition. This created a disincentive for politicians to commit to building party branches and negative externalities for those who tried. Upon a moment's reflection, the importance of the sequence of events is blindingly obvious in the impact of electoral reform and electoral systems. Had Japan adopted MMM before adopting SNTV, it is unclear whether the kōenkai would have ever developed to the extent that they did. Electoral systems certainly matter, but to understand how they matter, we need to study their effects in time as well as in the abstract.

Examining how negative externalities create a path-dependent process that drives a system toward a certain equilibrium presents another example of the importance of paying attention to time. The factions within the LDP make a good example. As more and more politicians joined factions, the cost of not being in a faction (the negative externality toward nonmembers) increased. When there were only a few legislators in a faction, the cost of not being in a faction was not great, despite factional control over the legislative and party office allocation system. But, as more and more members joined, the risk to legislators of being completely shut out of offices or being given very undesirable offices increased. This pushed more members to join factions regardless of their personal proclivities. This accounts for the LDP legislator who reluctantly joined a faction to end his being shut out of important positions in the party and legislature. Conversely, once negative externalities decrease, as happened when factional loyalty and faction leadership control decreased after the electoral reform, the number of those who do not join factions increases.

Note that the distinction between negative externalities and positive returns is important. Positive returns (also called increasing returns) are ever-larger payoffs, a situation that contrasts with the typical decline in returns for every marginal input. Scholars have argued that both negative externalities and positive returns can create path dependence. In our study, we have found that both positive returns and negative externalities spurred the process, although negative externalities were more common.

Many historical institutionalist and organizational sociology scholars identify complementary institutions as important in affecting the processes of institutional evolution (e.g., Baum and Oliver 1992, 1996; Baum and Singh 1994). Our study highlights how critical complementary institutions are in explaining the persistence or transformation of institutions on both the systemic and individual institutional levels.

On the macro level, multiple interlocking institutions that are complements to one another can be self-reinforcing. In our study, we have seen how the weakness of the party branches and strength of the kōenkai supported factionalism, whereas factional control of PARC appointments strengthened the role of PARC as a policymaking body and, in addition, seniority in the factions determined the allocation of posts in PARC. These three party institutions grew to mesh quite well together but only gradually and across an extended period (from 1955 until the late 1970s). In fact, the role that complementary institutions play in institutional persistence or transformation is surprisingly large. In his *After Victory*, John Ikenberry (2000) argues that interlocking institutions were the reason the international system experienced surprisingly little change after the end of the Cold War dramatically changed the balance of power. We see a similar result in our research in that the interlocking institutions of the kōenkai, the factions, and PARC allowed surprisingly little change in the LDP organization after the transformation of the electoral system.

When we separate out each of these institutions for individual study, we can isolate the role that complementary institutions play. Taking advantage of our distinct cases, we can push forward this type of reasoning. Specifically, we find in our study that a key variable in explaining institutional change after the Japanese electoral reform was whether key complementary institutions also changed (see table 10.2).

To avoid misinterpretation, we want to make a few things clear. Although we do not see the electoral system as the sole cause for these three party institutions, we do acknowledge the significance of the electoral system for these institutions. When the electoral system changed in 1994, these three

TABLE 10.2
Complementary institutions and institutional change

Institution	Complementary Institution	Change in Complementary Institution	Change in Institution
Kōenkai	Public offices election law	Low	Low
Factions	Party presidential election system	High	High
PARC	Factions	High	Medium

Note: PARC, Policy Affairs Research Council.

party institutions did not disappear; nevertheless, they did undergo varying degrees of transformation. In part, we explain this variation as a misspecification of the original causal arguments. For example, electoral systems mattered less as a cause for the origin of the kōenkai than has been thought, and even after 1994 change in other variables—such as the media—mattered more. In part, we point to time as a crucial variable in why the institutions continue. For example, the factions were sustained by negative externalities, such as in the allocation of party posts, that continue to this day, and, of course, sequencing matters for all three institutions.

Another piece of the puzzle in explaining the variation in transformation is the extent to which complementary institutions were restructured at the time of the electoral reform. Perhaps particularly because these three institutions were interwoven to a degree, but we suspect more generally, change in the complementary institutions had an unusually large effect on how much party institutions transformed after 1994. For example, the POEL remained virtually untouched. As a result, the transformation of the kōenkai has been slow. The way that the kōenkai mobilize voters remains virtually the same as it was in the 1950s; politicians continue to expend effort and resources to build up the kōenkai, and the weak party branches do not show convincing evidence of becoming more muscular. In contrast, the system for choosing the LDP president changed dramatically. Correspondingly, we see a substantial change in the factions (although this stopped far short of the evaporation of the factions). The factions lost their long-standing influence over nominations and funding, but they remained a force in the allocation of offices below the cabinet level. We can attribute this to the fact that the logic that sustained the factions in office allocation remained unbroken, as our attention to sequencing and path dependence reveals. Still, there is no question that the factions changed. PARC also changed. The complementary institution for PARC is the factions, and the factions controlled the appointments to PARC offices. After the electoral reform, however, PARC changed its spots and began to admit any willing LDP legislator to the PARC divisions. This was an important change, although the use of PARC for legislative specialization to divide the vote was probably not as great as previously thought (see chap. 6). In addition to the leadership positions within PARC continuing to be controlled by the factions, PARC also continued its substantial role as a policymaking body and as a party whip.

The implications of this for understanding institutional transformation are significant. Scholars, politicians, and policymakers alike have long seen that institutional reforms do not always accomplish the intended aims or accomplish them quickly. We point here toward the unheralded importance of getting complementary institutions right too in order to accelerate change.

Delegation: Why the Liberal Democratic Party Is a Non-Westminster Party

The story of political parties is the story of delegation. Voters delegate their sovereignty over the government to representatives universally chosen, in the modern democratic world, on the basis of political party competition. Even this fundamental observation is not the end of the story, however, because political parties themselves embody a series of delegations. Scholars have argued that political parties exist to solve certain collective action dilemmas (Aldrich 1995; Cox and McCubbins 1993; Longley and Hazan 2000; Nyblade 2004). These dilemmas continue within the hearts of the political parties in the form of the tension between the interests of the individual legislators and the party leaders. To varying extents, backbenchers delegate control over these core functions to the party leadership while holding the leaders accountable for the outcomes or results. The ideal typical expression of this principle at its logical conclusion is in the Westminster system. The party leaders hold control over the three major functions of the party. They control vote-seeking behavior through their scripting of election campaigns and through their control over nominations as well as (if in power) the timing of the election itself. Party leaders also control office-seeking behavior, doling out offices and positions to the rank-and-file legislators, and policy-seeking behavior through a top-down process of policymaking.

As we have mentioned, however, there is a large variation in the extent to which backbenchers delegate these functions to their leaders and how. This, in turn, accounts for the differences among political parties in the democratic world, even those with somewhat similar parliamentary institutional contexts. How do we explain these variations? Specifically, how do we explain the unusual organizational and delegation structure of the LDP? With vote-seeking maintained in the hands of backbenchers through the kōenkai, office-seeking largely in the hands of rival leadership factions, and policy-seeking mostly controlled by PARC in which backbenchers broadly controlled the process, the LDP was one of the most decentralized major parties in the world. Yet, at the same time, with PARC and the formalized membership factions, the party was elaborately structured to a very unusual degree. With this combination, under the '55 system the LDP party leader and the prime minister of Japan (and these offices, almost without exception after 1955, were held by the same person) were among the weakest democratic leaders in the world.

Our findings can be read as an explanation of exactly how this limited delegation came about and why. There is no one simple explanation; but if we were looking for one primary cause, the origin of the party in the merger of two smaller rival conservative parties in 1955 would be a prime candidate. The decision of the fledgling party to select its leader by party convention led, as we have seen, to the development of exclusive and highly competing leadership factions. Right off the bat, party leadership was shared among several party leaders, especially the coalition that formed around the winning candidate (the mainstream coalition), rather than being centralized in the party leader. When the factions linked up with the kōenkai and the backbenchers resisted the attempts by some party leaders to use party branches for vote-seeking instead, the fate of a more centralized electoral mobilization style was sealed. With the Akagi memo and the compromise between the party leaders and backbenchers that it entailed, policy-seeking became more decentralized, and as faction seniority rules penetrated also into the system for assigning party and government posts, the rigid hierarchical but decentralized policymaking of the '55 system was institutionalized. By the early 1980s, the limited-delegation system had been established fully; the party refused to fully delegate its most important functions to the party leader in party affairs and to the prime minister and cabinet in governmental affairs. Thus, despite some superficial institutional resemblances to the Westminster systems of the United Kingdom and New Zealand, Japan never developed a cabinet government with a full set of delegations.

The changes wrought by the electoral reform, television, and administrative reform partially changed this (see chap. 9). More functions were delegated to the prime minister, including his choice of cabinet and more policymaking decisions. With the fusion of PARC and the prime minister's policymaking role after Koizumi, the weakening (but not the elimination) of the factions, and the greater importance of the party and party leader's image, and the continued maintenance of the kōenkai, the LDP had more delegation than under the '55 system, although still more limited than under a Westminster system. As a result, the LDP by 2009 was neither the fish of the '55 system nor the fowl of the Westminster system.

Lessons from Defeat: The LDP out of Time

The historic victory of the DPJ in the August 30, 2009, election offers an unusually rich opportunity for learning. We mean this not in the sense that the LDP can learn from its defeat, institute reform, and then return to power; every election produces losers who can reflect on the need for reform. Rather, the loss of power by the LDP after such a long period of rule provides a rare opportunity for us to study how defeat transforms the party organization of a party singularly unused to losing—a valuable new window on historical processes of transformation. Here we first examine how defeat could affect the kōenkai, the factions, PARC, and the party leadership. In particular, we are interested in how defeat disrupts the path-dependent processes that have sustained these institutions. We discuss the lessons we can draw from the study of defeat and party organization. Next, we discuss the theoretical implications of the DPJ party organization. Finally, we offer some analysis of what we call the halfway adaptation of the LDP as the cause of its prolonged success and ultimate defeat.

A Historic Defeat and Historical Institutionalist Processes

After its holding power for decades, the LDP defeat presents a rare and valuable research opportunity. How does defeat affect the time-dependent processes we have examined? Specifically, how do we expect defeat to affect these processes and thus the kōenkai, the factions, and PARC?[4] For a century political scientists have argued that defeat provides a greater stimulus to change (Lippmann 1914), but this has not been specified theoretically.[5] We contribute to that discussion here, addressing why defeat matters for institutional change.

The scale of the LDP defeat offers two contrasting lessons about the kōenkai for Diet members. First, the rise in the number of floating voters, the influence of mass media, and the increased importance of the party label all lessened the centrality of the kōenkai for elections. The DPJ wave that swamped the LDP could not be stopped by kōenkai sandbags. But, in addition, those LDP politicians who won were disproportionately those who had strong kōenkai and who stemmed the tide locally because of their unusually strong sandbag levies. We expect this to influence the development of the LDP party organization in the following way. The current LDP parliamentary delegation may feel that they do not need to build up a strong party branch network at the district level to win the next election. After all, they have won reelection in 2009, when things are at their worst, through reliance on their kōenkai. Therefore, the mobilization of the vote probably will continue through the decentralized efforts of the individual Diet members beyond what is optimally efficient. They may, however, respond to the changed electoral environment and increased importance of the party label in other ways—perhaps with more aggressive media campaigns, more telegenic leaders, and stronger manifestos. If, contrary to our expectations, a strong party

4. Party leadership will undoubtedly be affected greatly, but because it is less closely tied to the time-dependent processes we examine in this book, we feel our thoughts on the transformation of the party leadership are too speculative to include at this point.

5. The argument dates back at least to 1914, although we suspect it is much older (Lowi 1963, 571; Lippmann 1914).

branch network is built, then it will have become possible only because so few LDP members won the election in 2009 and so the party has a fresh opportunity to build an organizational infrastructure in most districts in the country. Either way, the influence of sequencing and positive returns will remain as the LDP charts the future of the kōenkai and party branches.

We believe the development of the factions as an institution will be strongly influenced by the defeat of 2009. After the loss of its nomination, party presidential selection, and funding functions, the factions have been sustained by a path-dependent process. Their influence over the distribution of posts in the party and legislature created negative externalities for Diet members who did not belong to a faction. In a sense, factions became the QWERTY keyboards of the LDP—inefficient or illogical, but entrenched and difficult to change. But the 2009 defeat changes all this because the costs of not being in a faction have suddenly dropped. Being disadvantaged in the allocation of posts costs much less when the posts are worth much less. For this reason, we would not be surprised to see the atrophy of factions. This is especially likely if the LDP does not win power in the next two or three elections but new individual LDP Diet members are elected. Such individuals will have very little reason to join a faction. Should factions not diminish greatly, it will be because so few new members have won elections, starting in 2009.

PARC has been and will be similarly affected by the LDP loss of power. A policymaking body has much less to do when it cannot make policy. Of course, it could formulate manifesto planks, but such a level of abstraction was never the focus of PARC. With its real policymaking powers lost, PARC will be eclipsed by the party leadership, which will spearhead the development of manifestos. LDP President Sadakazu Tanigaki's moves after the 2009 defeat to form something like a shadow cabinet and to combine the functions of PARC and the Diet Strategy Committee may be only the first step in this direction. The decline of the factions as a complementary institution delivers a further spur to the transformation and decline of PARC. How far this goes may depend in part on how long the LDP is out of power.

In all three cases, it is not just defeat per se, or defeat providing a stimulus to change, that will lead to institutional change but, rather, the way that defeat disrupts time-dependent processes. We suspect that this is not specific to Japan but is a general result.

Two examples are found in Ireland and New Zealand, although some of the changes were made as much in campaign tactics or methods as in party organization. In Ireland, after a stunning defeat in 1973 at the hands of Fine Gael and Labour, the Fianna Fail party was expected to lose again in 1977. Instead, Fianna Fail transformed its tactics:

> In facing for the first time the prospect of two defeats in a row, the party therefore invested considerably in building up its organizational resources.... They

were to initiate a new style of campaigning in Irish politics, and were at least partly responsible for the publication of the party's first—and very glossy and voter-friendly—election manifesto in 1977. Rapidly, and quite abruptly, Fianna Fail had therefore moved from being close to the other extreme, where the key motor was provided by party central office, the national leadership and the national election programme. (Mair and Marsh 2004, 246)[6]

And while researching political parties in New Zealand, David Denemark (2003) discovers much less change in campaign tactics between 1987 and 1996 (the first mixed member proportional, MMP, system campaign) than he expected. After all, SMD and MMP systems provide startlingly different incentives for parties to campaign; in the former, parties should spend their resources only in hotly contested seats and ignore uncompetitive districts, but in the latter, the party is rewarded for earning votes anywhere in the country. Nevertheless, parties in New Zealand did not transform their campaign strategies or tactics before the 1996 election. Instead, there was a slow and uneven shift. In 1996, the parties illogically continued to concentrate their campaign spending in competitive districts. Denemark remarks that "especially at the constituency level, these imperatives were unevenly realized...thus pointing to the ability of inertia—by political elites and candidates, as well as by voters—to stymie the willful transition from one framework of electoral campaign logic to the next" (2003, 602). Denemark cautions that this incomplete transition should remind us that parties are not unitary actors "responding as one to the imperatives of adaptation. Rather, their differential responses to uncertainty point to the difficulties of political learning and adjustment, as political actors gauge the relative benefits and costs of change" (2003, 615). Similarly, Fiona Barker and Elizabeth McLeay argue that electoral reform in New Zealand had a clear impact, although it was not as decisive as might have been anticipated:

> despite the increase in the number of significant parties and its potentially radical implications for the relationship between party and government, the New Zealand parliamentary party system demonstrated several significant continuities under the new electoral rules....An electoral system is merely one variable, albeit a highly influential one....Other exogenous forces, especially societal forces, and other systemic and endogenous ones, explain why change has been limited in certain other aspects. (2000, 132)

Denemark reflects that, "while electoral systems theoretically provide imperatives for pursuing the sort of campaign best-suited for maximizing votes, defeat—or the threat of it—may represent a necessary, but not sufficient, impetus for the transformation of the election campaign" (2003, 608).

---

6. We thank Steve Reed for pointing out this parallel and citation to us.

We believe that the insights of Peter Mair and Michael Marsh, Denemark, and Barker and McLeay about inertia, other endogenous factors, and the spur of defeat can be profitably analyzed further in terms of time-dependent processes. Reliance on electoral uncertainty as an explanation for organizational change (Agranoff 1978) misses the point. The logic of such analyses implies that defeat and near defeat (or the prospect of either) are not distinguished greatly in the minds of calculating actors; a narrow victory should have almost as much impact on pushing forward changes as a narrow loss because both reveal electoral uncertainty. In contrast, our argument is that even a narrow defeat can produce very distinct outcomes from a paper-thin victory and that the results of actual defeat will differ greatly from an avoided expected defeat. Moreover, a purely electoral system approach may assume that, with a change in the overall institutional environment (i.e., the electoral system), party institutions will be compelled to adapt because the incentives to parties and politicians have changed. This confuses the reason for adaptation with the causal mechanism of adaptation. As a simple stimulus-response adaptation to the environment model, this approach shares several similarities with early theories of evolution. Like early pre-Darwinian evolutionary theories, such as those of Lamarck (Howard 1982, 22–23), it assumes that the environment itself acts as the causal mechanism stimulating adaptation; in contrast, one of Charles Darwin's major contributions was to show that the natural selection process is the causal mechanism. Similarly, for political parties, although the stimulus of defeat certainly is important, how the party adapts depends also on the "political natural selection" mechanisms of time-dependent processes.

Lessons from the Victors: The Organization of the Democratic Party of Japan

Unlike the LDP, the DPJ is a child of the MMM system. Although the DPJ absorbed individual Diet members from a bewildering variety of parties, its organization in 1996 offered a fresh opportunity to mold a party organization to fit the times. Most observers view the DPJ as having greater top-down leadership than the LDP and as being organizationally better suited to the current electoral environment. This is often taken as evidence that the electoral system provides strong incentives to shape party organization. We agree. But we also believe that the contrast between the party organizations of the LDP and DPJ is instructive. After all, if the DPJ has created a structure better suited to MMM, why has the LDP not followed suit? Both parties face a very similar electoral environment, after all. Of course, we find the answer in the time-dependent processes this book investigates. Still, it is worth remarking that the divergence in party organization between a relatively well-adapted new party and a less well-adapted old party should not be simply taken for granted but, rather, analyzed and explained. In explaining why the LDP did not adopt a more efficient and better-suited organizational structure immediately, we need to turn to the tools of historical institutionalism—path dependence, sequencing, and complementary institutions.

The Halfway Adaptation of the Liberal Democratic Party

We began our study by asking why three party institutions that had been expected to disappear in the wake of electoral reform were still tenaciously clinging to existence a decade and a half later. Their persistence *prima facie* calls into question causal arguments based on the electoral system. We have demonstrated that the correct methodology to assess causation in these cases is within-case evidence featuring process tracing. Our own investigation along those lines has revealed the importance of conceiving of causation in temporal terms. Thinking in terms of time, we have highlighted the importance of sequencing and negative externalities (path dependence). Our study also displays the importance of complementary institutions in understanding the persistence or transformation of institutions over time.

Here we consider implications of the LDP electoral success. In our view, ironically, the very institutions that drove the LDP electoral success—the kōenkai, the factions, and PARC—were its undoing. After the electoral reform, these institutions did not disappear. Instead, for reasons we have discussed at length, they remained in place. These institutions had a powerful influence on the vote-seeking, office-seeking, and policy-seeking behaviors and the success of the party. Unfortunately, they eventually proved to be drags on the party. Instead of building new institutions to compete in the changed electoral and policy landscape, the LDP adapted and transformed its old standby trio to a degree. In the short term, this proved adequate; however, transformation did not go far enough, and the institutions eventually began to weigh down the electoral prospects of the LDP in an age of not only a new electoral system but also a more competitive party system, a changed role for the media, and transformed voter appetites. Politicians continued to turn to the kōenkai while party branches were nascent, but voters wanted to turn the TV on instead. The factions had never earned the LDP good press, and in the age of the new hypermedia environment and more floating voters interested in the image of the party leader and in policy outcomes, the costs of voter antipathy and media sneers were too high for the office-distribution function they played. The power of the prime minister and party leadership grew due to the increased relevance of TV, administrative reform, and the restructuring of the Prime Minister's Office. Yet the continued power of PARC in the policymaking process and of the factions in their control over party appointments provided a breeding ground for internal strife, from the forces of resistance to the postal rebels.

But what about Koizumi's great successes in using the new capabilities in his position as party leader and prime minister? How did the LDP go from its greatest majority since its formation in the 2005 election to being on the verge of losing power? There is no one simple answer to this question; the answer lies in a convergence of several of the changes we have discussed. First, the LDP was operating in a new environment, perhaps the most important component of which was the emergence of a second major centrist political party that offered voters a real choice, if not so much in policies, at least in expressing discontent. As Scheiner (2004) has argued, it was not the popularity of the LDP as a party that kept it in power but the lack of "quality candidates" of the opposition parties and the personal vote that its individual candidates mobilized through their kōenkai. Now, when the LDP continued to be unpopular, those not tied into such personal networks could easily decide to vote for the DPJ, a respectable conservative party itself.

This brings us to the second factor—the increase in the number of floating voters combined with (and abetted by) the increase in the importance of television has made volatility and "swings" from election to election far more likely. The third factor is that, exactly because of the new role of party leader and party image in the decisions of voters since the electoral reform, the question of leadership (agency, if you will) has combined with structure to make much more of a difference. We see that with Koizumi; but we see it even more strongly in the contrast with the *post*-Koizumi era. None of the three prime ministers who followed him understood or knew how to skillfully use the new capabilities now inherent in the prime minister's office. By not knowing how to use the television medium skillfully (Fukuda), making poor appointment choices to the cabinet that now also mattered more to voters (Abe), seeming to revert back to the old politics of the factions and undermining the previous party message of reform under Koizumi (Aso), or a combination of all of these, the LDP quickly lost the momentum it had gained from Koizumi and his 2005 victory.

The precipitous loss of advantage by the LDP after 2005 also raises a more fundamental question: How did the intraparty institutions that had served the LDP so well in the past suddenly become so ineffective? Of course, neither we nor other analysts claim that party organization alone explains electoral success, and we consider the party organizational institutions to be dependent, not independent, variables. Still, we offer some thoughts on the question. In the new, more competitive environment today (brought about by electoral reform, party realignment, television, and more floating voters), these LDP institutions grew increasingly ineffective for the its goal of staying in power. At the same time, they still provided many individual representatives advantages for their reelection. The LDP was thus caught in a vicious circle. The more the party did not supply popular leadership with a good media image and public-goods policy that many voters now expected, the more some of its individual representatives had to rely on their personal vote, use factional affiliation to attain good positions on PARC to provide political pork, and claim credit in their constituencies to get reelected. And the more representatives who did that, the less the party provided the effective popular leadership and public-goods policy many other voters now wanted and that was needed for the collective success of the party. And the cycle started again. The negative externalities for the individual LDP representatives that sustained these intraparty institutions become a major disadvantage for the party as a whole for its attaining the level of popular support in the new environment that it needed to stay in power.

The LDP organizational structure that had served it so well for so long seemed to be able to maintain it as a major party but was unable to ensure its dominance in the new environment. Its fusion of prereform continuity and postreform adaptations had sufficed to keep it in power for a decade and a half in the new environment. Now that the LDP has tasted defeat, we expect the party to find a new appetite for organizational change.

Given what political scientists have argued for a century, we are hardly innovators to suggest that we'll see the LDP tinkering with the electoral machine while stalled in the wilderness. If it succeeds in that enterprise, it will surely return to power even should that require several elections; the electoral landscape has transformed so that no party can attain the perpetual dominance of the LDP's initial decades (Krauss and Pekkanen 2010). If it fails, however, the party could be supplanted by another party or parties better suited to the contemporary competitive environment.

Coded Interviews

Diet Members

Code	Party	House	Interview Date	Notes
A	LDP	HOR	November 30, 2001 June 27, 2002 June 22, 2004	
B	LDP	HOR	October 12–17, 2003 September 15, 2005 October 5, 2007 Mar 13, 2008 October 4 2008	
C	LDP	HOR	December 7, 2001	Relatively young former cabinet minister
D	LDP	HOC	December 2001	
E	LDP	HOR	December 2001	
F	LDP	HOC	October 10, 2003 June 22, 2004	
G	LDP	HOR	December 11, 2001	
H	LDP	HOR	December 12, 2001	
I	LDP	HOR	July 10, 2002	
J	LDP	HOR	July 1, 2002	LDP party executive involved in post allocations
K	LDP	HOC	July 1, 2002	
L	LDP	HOC	October 7, 2003	Veteran Diet member
M	LDP	HOR	July 4, 2002	LDP Diet member who was elected under both systems,; member of one of the largest LDP factions
N	LDP	HOR	July 9, 2002 June 29, 2004 September 7, 2005	At this time, a junior Diet member

Diet Members—cont.

Code	Party	House	Interview Date	Notes
			October 5, 2007	
			October 16, 2008	At this time, a senior LDP Diet member
O	LDP	HOR	July 11, 2002	
P	CGP	HOR	December 11, 2001	
			June 26, 2002	
Q	DPJ	HOR	June 27, 2002	
			October 9, 2003	
R	DPJ	HOR	July 2, 2002	
S	CGP	HOR	October 15, 2003	
T	NCP	HOR	December 6, 2001	Former prime minister
U	LDP	HOR	September 24, 2003	
V	DPJ	HOR	2001 December	
W	LDP	HOR	December 15, 2003	
X	DPJ	HOR	December 15, 2003	
Y	LDP	HOR	December 16, 2003	
Z	LDP	HOR	December 17, 2003	
			June 19, 2004	
AA	LDP	HOC	December 17, 2003	
BB1	LDP	HOR	December 17, 2003	
			October 28, 2008	
BB2	LDP	HOC	June 22, 2004	
CC1	DPJ	HOC	December 17, 2003	
CC2	LDP	HOR	June 27, 2004	
			August 26, 2004	
			September 10, 2005	
			October 4, 2007	
DD	DPJ	HOR	August 5, 2004	
EE	LDP	HOR	August 6, 2004	
FF	DPJ	HOR	August 6, 2004	
GG	DPJ	HOR	August 6, 2004	
HH	LDP	HOR	August 6, 2004	
II	DPJ	HOR	August 6, 2004	
JJ	LDP	HOR	August 26, 2004	
KK	DPJ	HOR	August 26, 2004	
LL	LDP	HOR	August 29, 2006	
			October 5, 2007	
MM	LDP	HOR	November 8, 2005	
NN	LDP	HOR	November 8, 2005	
OO	LDP	HOR	October 3, 2007	Former cabinet minister
			October 20, 2008	
PP	DPJ	HOR	October 4, 2007	
QQ	LDP	HOC	July 17, 2008	
SS	LDP	HOR	October 29, 2008	

Notes: HOC, House of Councilors; HOR, House of Representatives.

Party and Diet Members' Staff

Code	Party	Staff	Interview Date	Notes
PA	LDP	Party staff	June 27, 2002	
			August 5, 2004	
			October 3, 2007	
PB	LDP	Party staff	June 27, 2002	
			January 1, 2004	
			August 5, 2004	
PC	LDP	Party staff	June 27, 2002	
PD	LDP	Party staff	October 16, 2003	
PE	LDP	Party staff	October 13, 2003	
PF	LDP	Party staff	January 1, 2004	
			August 5, 2004	
PG	LDP	Party staff	January 1, 2004	
			August 5, 2004	
			October 3, 2007	
PH	LDP	Party staff	June 20, 2004	
PI	LDP	Diet member's staff	June 22, 2004	
PJ	LDP	Diet member's staff	June 24, 2004	
PK	LDP	Diet member's staff	June 29, 2004	
PL	LDP	Party staff	September 7, 2005	
PM	LDP	Party staff	September 7, 2005	
PN	LDP	Party staff	September 10, 2005	
PO	LDP	Party staff	October 3, 2007	
PP	LDP	Party staff	October 3, 2007	

Note: Almost all interviews were conducted in Tokyo. For interviews conducted elsewhere, locations are given in text when cited. For interviews conducted in Tokyo, no location is noted in text.

References

Abe, Hitoshi, Muneyuki Shindō and Sadafumi Kawato. 1994. *The Government and Politics of Japan*. Tokyo: University of Tokyo Press.

Adachi, Koichi. 1960. "Warera wa jimintō no chihō orugu" [We Are Local LDP Activists]. *Chuo Koron* 75 (4): 88–102.

Agranoff, Robert. 1978. "The New Style of Campaigning: The Decline of Party and the Rise of Candidate-Centered Technology." In *Parties and Elections in an Anti-Party Age*, ed. Jeff Fishel. Bloomington: Indiana University Press.

Aldrich, Howard E., and Jeffrey Pfeffer. 1976. "Environments of Organizations." *Annual Review of Sociology* 2: 79–105.

Aldrich, John H. 1995. *Why Parties?: The Origin and Transformation of Political Parties in America*. Chicago: University of Chicago Press.

Altman, Kristin Kyoko. 1996. "Television and Political Turmoil: Japan's Summer of 1993." In *Media and Politics in Japan*, ed. Susan J. Pharr and Ellis S. Krauss. Honolulu: University of Hawaii Press.

Akagawa, Roy K. 2003. "Like the Dodo, LDP Factions a Thing of the Past." *Asahi Shimbun*, September 12, 2003.

Amburgey, Terry L., and Hayagreeva Rao. 1996. "Organizational Ecology: Past, Present, and Future Directions." *Academy of Management Journal* 39 (5): 1265–86.

Asahi Journal. 1967. "Sō senkyo no Naka no Habatsu Koso" [Factions in the Election]. 9 (6). February 5. 19–24.

——. 1969. "Jiban Rire no Hisaku to Kono." 11 (52). December 28. 97–101.

——. 1972a. "Habatsu Senkyo, Yatō Kō sei Irimidareru." 14 (45). November 3. 107–9.

——. 1972b. "Susamajii Jimin no Habatsu Senkyo." 14 (50). December 1. 109–10.

Asahi Shinbun Seijibu, ed. 1968. *Seitō to Habatsu* [Political Parties and Factions]. Tokyo: Asahi Newspapers.

Asahi Shinbun Niigata Shikyoku. 1982. *Tanaka Kakuei to Etsuzankai*. Tokyo: Yamate Shobou.

Asano, Masahiko. 2006. *Shimin Shakai Ni Okeru Seido Kaikaku: Senkyō Kōhōsha Riku-ruto* [System Reform in Civil Society: Recruiting Election Candidates]. Tokyo: Keio Daigaku Shuppankai.

Bardi, Luciano. 2004. "Party Responses to Electoral Dealignment in Italy." In *Political Parties and Electoral Change,* ed. Peter Mair, Wolfgang C. Muller, and Fritz Plasser. London: Sage.

Barker, Fiona, and Elizabeth McLeay. 2000. "How Much Change?: An Analysis of the Initial Impact of Proportional Representation on the New Zealand Parliamentary Party System." *Party Politics* 6(2): 131–54.

Baum, Joel A. C., and Christine Oliver. 1992. "Institutional Embeddedness and the Dynamics of Organizational Populations." *American Sociological Review* 57(4): 540–59.

———. 1996. "Toward an Institutional Ecology of Organizational Founding." *Academy of Management Journal* 39(5): 1378–427.

Baum, Joel A. C., and Jitendra Singh. 1994. "Organizational Niches and the Dynamics of Organizational Founding." *Organizational Science* 5(4): 483–501.

Bennett, Andrew, and Colin Elman. 2006a. "Complex Causal Relations and Case Study Methods: The Example of Path Dependence." *Political Analysis* 14: 250–67.

———. 2006b. "Qualitative Research: Recent Developments in Case Study Methods." *Annual Review of Political Science* 9: 455–76.

———. 2007. "Case Study Methods in the International Relations Subfield." *Comparative Political Studies* 40: 170–95.

Bettcher, Kim Eric. 2005. "Factions of Interest in Japan and Italy: The Organizational and Motivational Dimensions of Factionalism." *Party Politics* 11(3): 344.

Bouissou, Jean-Marie. 1999. "Organizing One's Support Base under the SNTV: The Case of Japanese Koenkai." In *Elections in Japan, Korea, and Taiwan under the Single Non-Transferable Vote: The Comparative Study of an Embedded Institution,* ed. Bernard Grofman, Sung-Chull Lee, Edwin A. Winckler, and Brian Woodall. Ann Arbor: University of Michigan Press.

———. 2001. "Party Factions and the Politics of Coalition: Japanese Politics under the 'System of 1955.'" *Electoral Studies* 20(4): 581–602.

Brady, Henry, and David Collier, eds. 2004. *Rethinking Social Inquiry: Diverse Tools, Shared Standards.* Lanham, Md.: Rowman & Littlefield.

Cain, Bruce, John Ferejohn, and Morris Fiorina. 1987. *The Personal Vote: Constituency Service and Electoral Independence.* Cambridge, Mass.: Harvard University Press.

Calder, Kent. 1991. *Crisis and Compensation.* Princeton: Princeton University Press.

Campbell, Donald T., and Julian C. Stanley. 1973. *Experimental and Quasi-Experimental Designs for Research.* Chicago: Rand McNally College Publishing.

Campbell, John Creighton. 1977. *Contemporary Japanese Budget Politics.* Berkeley: University of California Press.

Campbell, John Creighton, and Ethan Scheiner. 2008. "Review Essay: Fragmentation and Power: Reconceptualizing Policy Making under Japan's 1955 System." *Japanese Journal of Political Science* 9(1): 89–113.

Carey, John M., and Matthew Soberg Shugart. 1995. "Incentives to Cultivate a Personal Vote: A Rank Ordering of Electoral Formulas." *Electoral Studies* 14: 417–39.

Carlson, Matthew. 2007. *Money Politics in Japan: New Rules, Old Practices.* Boulder, CO: Lynne Rienner.

Cason, Jeffrey. 2002. "Electoral Reform, Institutional Change, and Party Adaptation in Uruguay." *Latin American Politics and Society* 44(3): 89–109.

Cheng, Tun-Jen. 1989. "Democratizing the Quasi-Leninist Regime in Taiwan." *World Politics* 41(4): 495–96.

Christensen, Raymond V. 1994. "Electoral Reform in Japan: How It Was Enacted and Changes It May Bring." *Asian Survey* 34(7): 589–605.

———. 1996. "The New Japanese Electoral System." *Pacific Affairs* 69(1): 50–70.

———. 1998. "Putting New Wine into Old Bottles: The Effects of Electoral Reform on Campaign Practices in Japan." *Asian Survey* 38: 986–1004.

Clemens, Elisabeth. 2007. "Toward a Historical Sociology: Theorizing Events, Processes, and Emergence." *Annual Review of Sociology* 33: 527–49.

Cowhey, Peter, and Mathew McCubbins. 1995. "Introduction." In *Structure and Policy in Japan and the United States,* ed. Peter Cowhey and Mathew McCubbins. Cambridge, UK: Cambridge University Press.

Cox, Gary. 2005. *The Efficient Secret: The Cabinet and the Development of Political Parties in Victorian England.* Cambridge: Cambridge University Press.

———. 2005. "The Organization of Democratic Legislatures." In *The Oxford Handbook of Political Economy,* ed. Barry Weingast and Donald Wittman. Oxford: Oxford University Press.

Cox, Gary, and Mathew McCubbins. 1993. *Legislative Leviathan.* Berkeley: University of California Press.

Cox, Gary, and Emerson Niou. 1994. "Seat Bonus under the Single Nontransferable Vote System: Evidence from Japan and Taiwan." *Comparative Politics* 26: 221–36.

Cox, Gary, and Frances M. Rosenbluth. 1994. "Reducing Nomination Errors: Factional Competition and Party Strategy in Japan." *Electoral Studies* 13(1): 4–16.

———. 1996. "Factional Competition for the Party Endorsement: The Case of Japan's Liberal Democratic Party." *British Journal of Political Science* 26(2): 259–97.

Cox, Gary, Frances Rosenbluth, and Michael F. Thies. 1999. "Electoral Reform and the Fate of Factions: The Case of Japan's Liberal Democratic Party." *British Journal of Political Science* 29(1): 33–56.

Curtis, Gerald L. 1970. "The 1969 General Election in Japan." *Asian Survey* 10(10): 860–62.

———. 1971. *Electoral Campaigning, Japanese Style.* New York: Columbia University Press.

———. 1988. *The Japanese Way of Politics.* New York: Columbia University Press.

———. 1999. *The Logic of Japanese Politics: Leaders, Institutions, and the Limits of Change.* New York: Columbia University Press.

Democratic Party of Japan. 2009. "Standing Officers Council Formerly [sic] Approves Limitations on Hereditary Politicians." June 9, 2009. Available at: http://www.dpj.or.jp/news?num=16242 (accessed September 18 2009).

———. 2010. "Manifesto: Acting Hand in Hand with the People toward the Establishment of a New Government." Available at: http://www.dpj.or.jp/english/manifesto_eng/04.html (accessed November 25, 2009).

Denemark, David. 2003. "Electoral Change, Inertia and Campaigns in New Zealand: The First Modern FPP Campaign in 1987 and the First MMP Campaign in 1996." *Party Politics* 9(5): 601–18.

Desposato, Scott, and Ethan Scheiner. 2009. "Governmental Centralization and Party Affiliation: Legislator Strategies in Brazil and Japan." *American Political Science Review* 102(4): 509–24.

Dore, Ronald. 1958. *City Life in Japan.* Berkeley: University of California Press.

Dore, Ronald. 2004. "Speech at Chatham House." February 25. Available at: http://www.rieti.go.jp/en/papers/contribution/dore/03.html (accessed April 9, 2009).

Dower, John W. 1993. *Japan in War and Peace: Selected Essays.* New York: New Press.

Druckman, James N. 2003. "The Power of Television Images: The First Kennedy-Nixon Debate Revisited." *Journal of Politics* 65(2): 559–71.

Duverger, Maurice. 1954. *Political Parties.* New York: John Wiley.

Ehrhardt, George. 2004. "Crashing the Party: Prefectural Federations and the April 2001 Liberal Democratic Party Presidential Primary." Workshop in Political Theory and Policy Analysis, Indiana University, Bloomington.

Epstein, David, David Brady, Sadafumi Kawato, and Sharyn O'Halloran. 1997. "A Comparative Approach to Legislative Organization: Careerism and Seniority in the United States and Japan." *American Journal of Political Science* 41(3): 965–98.

Ertman, Thomas. 1997. *Birth of the Leviathan: Building States and Regimes in Medieval and Early Modern Europe.* Cambridge: Cambridge University Press.

Estévez-Abe, Margarita. 2006. "Japan's Shift toward a Westminster System: A Structural Analysis of the 2005 Lower House Election and Its Aftermath." *Asian Survey* 46(4): 643–44.

Falconieri, G. Ralph. 1990. "The Impact of Rapid Urban Change on Neighborhood Solidarity." In *Social Change and Community Politics in Urban Japan,* ed., J. W. White and F. Munber. Chapel Hill: Chapel Hill Institute for Research in Social Science, University of North Carolina.

Fenno, Richard F. 1978. *Home Style: House Members in Their Districts.* New York: Little, Brown.

Finkelstein, Sydney, and Craig Urch. 2001. "The Boston Red Sox and the Integration of African-American Players." Case no. 1-0088. Tuck School of Business, Dartmouth University.

Fiorina, Morris. 1974. *Representatives, Roll Calls, and Constituencies.* Lexington, Mass.: Lexington Books.

Foreign Press Center Japan. 2005a. "Postal Reform Bills Narrowly Passed by the Lower House, but the Political Situation Might Get Unstable." Japan Brief 549. Tokyo, Japan.

———. 2005b. "Prime Minister Koizumi Calls General Election After Upper House Rejects Postal Privatization Bills." Japan Brief 562. Tokyo, Japan.

Foster, James J. 1982. "Ghost-Hunting: Local Party Organization in Japan." *Asian Survey* 22(9): 843–57.

French, Howard W. 2000. "Premier, It Seems, Isn't Alone in Seeing Japan as Divine." *New York Times Online,* May 31, 2000. Available at: http://www.nytimes.com/2000/05/31/world/premier-it-seems-isn-t-alone-in-seeing-japan-as-divine.html.

Fukui, Harahiro. 1970. *Party in Power: The Japanese Liberal-Democrats and Policy-Making.* Berkeley: University of California Press.

Fukui, Haruhiro, and Shigeko N. Fukai. 1996. "Pork Barrel Politics, Networks, and Local Economic Development in Contemporary Japan." *Asian Survey* 36: 268–86.

Fukuoka, Masayuki. 1983a. "Naze tsuyoi Kakuei seiji?" (Why Are Kakuei Politics so Powerful?). *Chuo Kouron:* 112–22.

———. 1983b. "Tanaka Kakuei's Grass Roots." *Japan Echo* 10(1): 33–39.

Fuwa, Tetsuzou. 1991. "Presidium Report." Tokyo: *Akahata.*

Gaunder, Alisa. 2007. *Political Reform in Japan: Leadership Looming Large*. New York: Routlege.

George, Alexander L., and Andrew Bennett. 2005. *Case Studies and Theory Development in the Social Sciences*. Cambridge, MA: MIT Press.

George Mulgan, Aurelia 2000. "Japan's Political Leadership Deficit." *Australian Journal of Political Science* 35(2): 183–202.

———. 2002. *Japan's Failed Revolution: Koizumi and the Politics of Economic Reform*. Canberra: Asia Pacific Press.

———. 2003. "Japan's 'Un-Westminster' System: Impediments to Reform in a Crisis Economy." *Government and Opposition* 38(1): 73–91.

———. 2006. *Power and Pork: A Japanese Political Life*. Canberra: Asia Pacific Press.

Gerring, John. 2001. *Social Science Methodology: A Critical Framework*. Cambridge and New York: Cambridge University Press.

———. 2004. "What Is a Case Study and What Is It Good For?" *American Political Science Review* 98 (2): 341–54.

———. 2007. *Case Study Research: Principles and Practices*. Cambridge and New York: Cambridge University Press.

———. 2009. "What Standards Are (or Might Be) Shared?" In *Workshop on Interdisciplinary Standards for Systemic Qualitative Research: Cultural Anthropology, Law and Social Science, Political Science, and Sociology Programs*, ed. Michele Lamont and Patricia White, pp. 107–23. http://www.nsf.gov/sbe/ses/soc/ISSQR_workshop_rpt.pdf.

Gotoda, Masaharu. 1998. *Jo to Ri* [Emotion and Rationality]. Tokyo: Kodansha.

Gray, Virginia, and David Lowery. 1996. "A Niche Theory of Interest Representation." *Journal of Politics* 58(1): 91–111.

Grofman, Bernard. 1999. "SNTV: An Inventory of Theoretically Derived Propositions and a Brief Review of the Evidence from Japan, Korea, Taiwan, and Alabama." In *Elections in Japan, Korea, and Taiwan under the Single Non-Transferable Vote: The Comparative Study of an Embedded Institution*, ed. Bernard Grofman, Sung-Chull Lee, Edwin A. Winckler, and Brian Woodall. Ann Arbor: University of Michigan Press.

Grofman, Bernard, and Arend Lijphart, eds. 1986. *Electoral Laws and Their Political Consequences*. New York: Agathon Press.

Gunther, Richard, and Jose Ramon Montero. 2002. "Introduction: Reviewing and Reassessing Parties." In *Political Parties: Old Concepts and New Challenges*, ed. Richard Gunther, Jose Ramon Montero and Juan L. Linz. Oxford: Oxford University Press.

Hall, Peter. 2003. "Aligning Ontology and Methodology in Comparative Politics." In *Comparative Historical Analysis in the Social Sciences*, ed. James Mahoney and Dietrich Rueschemeyer. Cambridge, UK: Cambridge University Press.

Hall, Peter A., and Daniel W. Gingerich. 2009. "Varieties of Capitalism and Institutional Complementarities in the Political Economy: An Empirical Analysis." *British Journal of Political Science* 39: 449–82.

Hall, Peter A., and Rosemary C. R. Taylor. 1996. "Political Science and the Three New Institutionalisms." *Political Studies* 44(5): 936–58.

Hamamoto, Shinsuke. 2007. "Senkyo Seido Kaikaku to Jimintō Giin No Seisaku Senko: Seisaku Kettei Katei Hen'yō No Haikei" [Electoral System Reform and LDP Diet Members' Policy Activities]. *Revaiasan* 41: 13–27.

Hastings, Sally Ann. 1995. *Neighborhood and Nation in Tokyo, 1905–1937*. Pittsburgh, PA: University of Pittsburgh Press.

Hayao, Kenji. 1993. *The Japanese Prime Minister and Public Policy.* Pittsburgh: University of Pittsburgh Press.

"Heisei 12-nenban yoron chōsa nenkan: Zenkoku yoron chōsa no genkyō" [Opinion Survey Yearbook 2000: The Condition of National Opinion Surveys]. 2001. Cabinet Ministers' Secretariat Public Relations Office, Tokyo.

Hennesy, Peter. 2000. *The Prime Minister: The Office and Its Holders since 1945.* New York: Penguin Books.

Herron, Erik S., and Misa Nishikawa. 2001. "Contamination Effects and the Number of Parties in Mixed-Superposition Electoral Systems." *Electoral Studies* 20(1): 63–86.

Hibbing, John R. 1999. "Legislative Careers: Why and How We Should Study Them." *Legislative Studies Quarterly* 24(2): 159.

Hirano, Shigeo. 2006. "Electoral Institutions, Hometowns and Favored Minorities: Evidence from Japanese Electoral Reforms." *World Politics* 59 (1).

Hirasawa, Katsuei. 2007. *Seijika Wa Rakuna Shobai Janai* [It Ain't Easy Being a Politician]. Tokyo: Sobisha.

Hoffmann, Steven A. 1981. "Faction Behavior and Cultural Codes: India and Japan." *Journal of Asian Studies* 40(2): 231–54.

Horiuchi, Yusaku, and Jun Saito. 2003. "Reapportionment and Redistribution: Consequences of Electoral Reform in Japan." *American Journal of Political Science* 47(4): 671–73.

Hoshi, Hiroshi. 2004. "Jimintō Seichōkai-to Seisaku Kettei Katei [The LDP's PARC and the Policy-Making Process]." In *Gendai Nihon Seitō Shiroku, vol. 5: 55-Nen Taisei—Ikō-no Seitō Seiji* [Japanese Political Party Records, vol. 5, the '55 System and Party Politics], ed. Koichi. Kitamura. Tokyo: Daiichi Hōki.

———. 2005. *Jimintō to Sengo—Seiken Tō Gojyū-Nen* [The LDP and the Postwar-Fifty Years Ruling Party]. Tokyo: Kodansha.

Hoshi, Hiroshi, and Iwao Osaka. 2006. *Terebi Seiji—kokkai hōdō kara TV "Takkuru" made.* Tokyo: Asahi Shimbunsha.

Howard, Jonathan. 2001. *Darwin: A Very Short Introduction.* Oxford: Oxford University Press.

Hrebenar, Ronald J. 2000. *Japan's New Party System.* Boulder: Westview Press.

Ida, Masamichi. 2007. *Nihonseiji No Chōyū Daitōryō Seika, Nidaiseitō Ka, Datsuseitōka* [The Current Trends of Japanese Politics: Presidentialization, Two-Partization, and Non-Partisanization]. Tokyo: Hokujyushuppan.

Igarashi, Akio. 1989. "Daigishi Kōenkai no seishinteki soshiteki Kōzō [The Organizational Structure of Representatives Kōenkai]." *Shiso* 779 (May): 79–99.

Iijima, Isao. 2006. *Koizumi kantei hiroku* [The Secret Record of the Koizumi Prime Minister's Office]. Tokyo: Nihon Keizai Shimbunsha.

Ike, Nobutaka. 1978. *A Theory of Japanese Democracy.* Boulder: Westview Press.

Ikenberry, G. John. 2000. *After Victory: Institutions, Strategic Restraint, and the Rebuilding of Order After Major Wars.* Princeton: Princeton University Press.

Inoguchi, Takashi, and Tomoaki Iwai. 1987. *Zoku Giin no Kenkyu* [Research on Tribe Diet Members]. Tokyo: Nihon Keizai Shimbunsha.

Inou, Takashi. 1984. *Giinsan wo tetteiteki ni riyou suru hō* [A Comprehensive Guide to Using Your Representative]. Tokyo: Kigensha.

Iokibe, Makoto, Motoshige Itoh, and Katsuyuki Yakushiji. 2007. *Mori Yoshirō: Jimintō to Seiken Kotai* [Mori Yoshirō: The LDP and Alternation in Power]. Tokyo: Asahi Shimbunsha.

Iseri, Hirofumi. 1988. *Habatsu Saihensei*. Tokyo: Chūō Kōronsha.

Ishibashi, Michihiro, and Steven R. Reed. 1992. "Second-Generation Diet Members and Democracy in Japan." *Asian Survey* 32 (4): 366–79.

Ishikawa, Masumi. 1979. "Jimintō: tairyō tōin seitōka no jisshitsu" [The LDP: The Truth behind a Large Number of Party Members]. *Sekai* 398: 200–204.

Ishikawa, Masumi, and Machisada Hirose. 1989. *Jimintō: chōki shihai no kōzō* [LDP: The Structure of Long-Term Rule]. Tokyo: Iwanami Shoten.

Itoh, Mayumi. 2003. *The Hatoyama Dynasty: Japanese Political Leadership through the Generations*. New York: PalgraveMacmillan.

Iwai, Tomoaki. 1990. *Seiji Shikin no Kenkyū*. [Research on Political Funds]. Tokyo: Nihon Keizai Shimbunsha.

Iwami, Takao. 1978. "Jimintō 150-man Tōin no 'Atsui Natsu'" [The "Hot Summer" of the LDP's 1.5 Million Members]. *Chūō Kōron*. 93(8): 158–65.

Izumi, Hiroshi. 2005. "Koizumi States All on Snap 'Postal Election.'" *Japan Echo* 10: 42–46.

Jain, Purnendra C. 1995. "Electoral Reform in Japan: Its Process and Implications for Party Politics." *Journal of East Asian Affairs* 9(2): 402–27.

Japanese Communist Party Central Committee. 1984. *Sixty Year History of Japanese Communist Party 1922–1982*. Tokyo: Japan Press Service.

Japan Times. 2002. "Urban-Rural Vote Disparity Narrows but Still Skewed." September 3, 2002.

Jimintō Kishadan. 1963. "Jimintō-no habatsu" [LDP Factions]. *Chūō Kōron* 78(9): 130–51.

Jiyūminshutō. 1987. *Jiyū Minshutō Tōshi Shiryōhen* [LDP Materials]. Tokyo: Jiyū Minshutō.

Johnson, Chalmers. 1995. "Tanaka Kakuei, Structural Corruption, and the Advent of Machine Politics in Japan." In *Japan: Who Governs?* New York: W. W. Norton.

Kabashima, Ikuo, and Ryosuke Imai. 2002. "Evaluation of Party Leaders and Voting Behaviour—an Analysis of the 2000 General Election." *Social Science Japan Journal* 5: 94.

Kabashima, Ikuo, and Gill Steel. 2007. "How Junichiro Koizumi Seized the Leadership of Japan's Liberal Democratic Party." *Japanese Journal of Political Science* 8(1): 96.

Kaihara, Hiroshi. 2007. "The Advent of a New Japanese Politics: Effects of the 1994 Revision of the Electoral Law." *Asian Survey* 47(5): 757–59.

Kaneko, Yuko. 1999. "Government Reform in Japan." Paper presented at the annual IIAS conference, Asia-Pacific Panel on Public Administration, London.

Katz, Richard. 2001. "Reforming the Italian Electoral Law, 1993." In *Mixed-Member Electoral Systems: The Best of Both Worlds?* ed. Matthew S. Shugart and Martin P. Wattenberg. Oxford: Oxford University Press.

Katz Richard, and Peter Mair, eds. 1994. *How Parties Organize: Change and Adaptation in Party Organizations in Western Democracies*. London: Sage.

Kavanagh, Dennis. 2000. *British Politics: Continuities and Change*. 4th ed. Oxford: Oxford University Press.

Kawakami, Osamu. 2009. "DPJ's Diet Management under Fire/Ozawa's Approach to Party Affairs Seen as Inconsistent, Sowing Confusion in Diet." *Daily Yomiuri Online*, November 22, 2009. Available at: http://www.yomiuri.co.jp/dy/national/20091122TDY02309.htm (accessed November 24, 2009).

Kawato, Sadafumi. 1988. "Shū-san dōjitsu senkyo to Nakasone ninki" [The House of Representatives-House of Councilors Same Day Election and Nakasone's Popularity]. *Hokudai Hōgaku Ronshū* 39(2): 238–80.

———. 1996a. "Jimintō ni okeru yakushoku jinji no seidōka" [LDP Personnel Management System]. *Hōgaku* 59: 34–46.

———. 1996b. "Shinioritei ruru to habatsu-jimintō ni okeru jinji hibun no henka" [Change in Personnel Distribution through the LDP Factions' Seniority Rule]. *Rebuaiasan* [Leviathan] special supp. issue: 111–45.

———. 1999. "1950-Nendai Giin Rippō-to Kokkaihō Kaisei" [The 1955 Revision of the Diet Law and the Decline of Member Bills]. *Hōgaku* 63(4): 481.

———. 2005. *Nihon No Kokkai Seido to Seitō Seiji* [The Japanese Diet and Party Politics: Creation, Transformation, and Political Outcomes of Legislative Institutions]. Tokyo: University of Tokyo Press.

———. 2006. "Parliamentary Supremacy and Parliamentary Cabinet System in Japan." Lecture, International Institute Lecture Series: Citizenship at Risk, February 1, University of Michigan.

Key, V. O., Jr. 1964. *Politics, Parties and Pressure Groups.* 5th ed. New York: Crowell.

Kikuchi, Miyoshi. 1990. "Chōnaikai no kinō [Functions of Neighborhood Associations]." In *Chōnaikai to chiiki shūdan* [Local Groups and Neighborhood Associations], ed. Susumu Kurasawa and Ritsuo Akimoto. Tokyo: Minerva Shobou.

Kingdon, John W. 1981. *Congressmen's Voting Decisions.* New York: Harper and Row.

Kitaoka, Shinichi. 1985. "Jiyū Minshutō" [The Liberal Democratic Party]. In *Gendai Nihon-No Seiji Kōzō*, ed. Kamishima Jirō. Kyoto: Hōritsu Bunka Sha.

Kitaoka, Shinichi. 1995. *Jimintō* [The LDP]. Tokyo: Yomiuri Shinbunsha.

Kobayashi, Kichiya. 1982. *Jitsuroku Etsuzankai* [The Etsuzankai]. Tokyo: Tokuma Shoten.

Kohno, Masaru. 1992. "Rational Foundations for the Organization of the Liberal Democratic Party in Japan." *World Politics* 44(3): 369–97.

———. 1997. *Japan's Postwar Party Politics.* Princeton: Princeton University Press.

Köllner, Patrick. 2004. "Factionalism in Japanese Political Parties Revisited or How Do Factions in the LDP and DPJ Differ?" *Japan Forum* 16(1): 93.

Köllner, Patrick. 2009. "Japanese Lower House Campaigns in Transition: Manifest Changes or Fleeting Fads?" *Journal of East Asian Studies* 9 (1): 121–49.

Komiya, Hitoshi. 2005. "Yoshida Shigeru no seiji shidō to sōshiki" [The Political Leadership of Yoshida Shigeru and Party Organization]. *Nihon Seiji Kenkyū* 2(1): 1–13.

Kosugi, Kei. 1967. "Soshiki naki jiminto no soshiki" [The Organization of the LDP that Is Not Organized]. *Chūō Kōron* 82(9): 152–59.

Krauss, Ellis S. 1996. "Media Coverage of U.S.-Japan Relations." In *Media and Politics in Japan*, ed. Susan. J. Pharr and Ellis. S. Krauss. Honolulu: University of Hawaii Press.

———. 2000. *Broadcasting Politics in Japan: NHK and Television News.* Ithaca: Cornell University Press.

———. 2006. *NHK vs. Nihon seiji.* Trans. J. Gotō. Tokyo: Tōyō Keizai Shimpōsha.

———. 2007. "The Prime Minister, Cabinet, and Policymaking: The Changing 'Core Executive' and 'Presidentialization' in Japan." In *Core Executive and the Civil Service System in Comparative Perspective*, ed. Michio Muramatsu. Kizu, Japan: International Institute for the Advancement of Science.

Krauss, Ellis S., and Elizabeth Coles. 1990. "Built-in Impediments: The Political Economy of the U.S.-Japan Construction Dispute." In *Japan's Economic Structure: Should It Change?* ed. Kozo Yamamura. Seattle: Society for Japanese Studies.

Krauss, Ellis S., Kuniaki Nemoto, and Robert Pekkanen. Forthcoming. "Reverse Contamination: Burning and Building Bridges in Mixed Member Systems." *Comparative Political Studies.*

Krauss, Ellis S., and Benjamin Nyblade. 2005. "'Presidentialization' in Japan?: The Prime Minister, Media and Elections in Japan." *British Journal of Political Science* 35(2): 362.

Krauss, Ellis S., and Robert Pekkanen. 2004. "Explaining Party Adaptation to Electoral Reform: The Discreet Charm of the LDP?" *Journal of Japanese Studies* 30(1): 1–34.

———. 2010. "The Rise and Fall of Japan's Liberal Democratic Party." *Journal of Asian Studies* 69(1): 5–15.

Kreuzer, Marcus. 2009. "How Party Systems Form: Path Dependency and the Institutionalization of the Post-War German Party System." *British Journal of Political Science.* 39(4): 669–97.

Lam, Peng Er. 1996. "The Japanese Communist Party: Organization and Resilience in the Midst of Adversity." *Pacific Affairs* 69(3): 361–79.

———. 1999. *Green Politics in Japan.* London: Routledge.

Leiserson, Michael. 1968. "Factions and Coalitions in One-Party Japan: An Interpretation Based on the Theory of Games." *American Political Science Review* 62(3): 770.

Liberal Democratic Party. 1987. *Jiyuu Minsutou Toushi: Sihryou hen* [History of the LDP: Materials]. Tokyo: Jiyuu Minshutou.

Lieberman, Evan. 2005. "Nested Analysis as a Mixed-Method Strategy for Comparative Research." *American Political Science Review* 99: 435–52.

Lippmann, Walter. 1914. *A Preface to Politics.* New York: Mitchel Kinnerly.

Little, Daniel. 1991. *Varieties of Social Science Explanation: An Introduction to the Philosophy of Social Sciences.* Boulder, CO: Westview.

———. 1995. "Causal Explanation in the Social Sciences." *Southern Journal of Philosophy* 34: 31–56.

Longley, Lawrence D., and Reuven Y. Hazan, eds. 2000. *The Uneasy Relationships between Parliamentary Members and Leaders.* London: Taylor & Francis.

Lowi, Theodore. 1963. "Toward Functionalism in Political Science: The Case of Innovation in Party Systems." *American Political Science Review* 57 (3): 570–83.

Mabuchi, Etsuo. 2001. *Jimintō no kinkyū.* Hamamatsu: Shizuoka Shimbunsha.

Maclachlan, Patricia L. 2004. "Post Office Politics in Modern Japan: The Postmasters, Iron Triangles, and the Limits of Reform." *Journal of Japanese Studies* 30(2): 303–13.

Mahoney, James. 2004. "Comparative-Historical Methodology." *Annual Review of Sociology,* vol. 30, ed. Karen S. Cook and John Hagan, pp. 81–101.

Mahoney, James. 2007. "Qualitative Methods and Comparative Politics." *Comparative Political Studies* 40: 122–44.

Mahoney, James, and Dietrich Rueschemeyer, eds. 2003. *Comparative Historical Analysis in the Social Sciences.* Cambridge: Cambridge University Press.

Mahoney, James. 2010. "After KKV: The New Methodology of Qualitative Research." *World Politics* 62 (1): 120–47.

Mahoney, James, and Gary Goertz. 2004. "The Possibility Principle: Choosing Negative Cases in Comparative Research." *American Political Science Review* 98: 653–69.

———. 2006. "A Tale of Two Cultures: Contrasting Quantitative and Qualitative Research." *Political Analysis* 14: 227–49.

Mahoney, James, and Dietrich Rueschemeyer, eds. 2002. *Comparative Historical Analysis in the Social Sciences*. Cambridge, UK: Cambridge University Press.

Mair, Peter, and Michael Marsh. 2004. "Political Parties and Electoral Markets in Postwar Ireland." In *Political Parties and Electoral Change*, ed. Peter Mair, Wolfgang C. Müller, and Fritz Plasser. London: Sage.

Mair, Peter, Wolfgang C. Müller, and Fritz Plasser, eds. 2004. *Political Parties and Electoral Change*. London: Sage.

Martin, Alex. 2009. "DPJ Submits Bill to Cut Back on Culture of Hereditary Politicians." *Japan Times Online*, June 2. Available at: http://search.japantimes.co.jp/cgi-bin/nn20090602b1.html (accessed September 18, 2009).

Martin, Curtis H., and Bruce Stronach. 1992. *Politics East and West: A Comparison of Japanese and British Political Culture*. Armonk, N.Y.: M. E. Sharpe.

Massey, Joseph A. 1976. *Youth and Politics in Japan*. Lexington, Mass.: Lexington Books.

Masumi, Junnosuke. 1964. "Sen-kyūhyaku-gojūgo-nen no seiji taisei." *Shisou* (June): 55–72.

———. 1965. *Nihon Seitōshiron* [History of Japanese Political Parties]. Tokyo: Tokyo University Press.

———. 1967. *Jiyuu Minshutō no Soshiki to Kinō* [The Organization of the LDP]. Nenpou Seijigaku: 34–77.

———. 1995. *Contemporary Politics in Japan*. Trans. L. E. Carlisle. Berkeley: University of California Press.

Masters, Coco. 2008. "Fukuda's Last Stand." *Time,* May 1, 2008. Available at: http://www.time.com/time/magazine/article/0,9171,1736513,00.html.

Mayhew, David. 1974. *Congress: The Electoral Connection*. New Haven: Yale University Press.

McCubbins, Mathew, and Frances Rosenbluth. 1995. "Party Provision for Personal Politics: Dividing the Vote in Japan." In *Structure and Policy in Japan and the United States*, ed. Peter F. Cowhey and Mathew D. McCubbins. Cambridge, UK: Cambridge University Press.

McElwain, Kenneth. 2008. "Manipulating Electoral Rules to Manufacture Single-Party Dominance." *American Journal of Political Science* 52(1): 32–47.

McKean, Margaret A. 1989. "Equality." In *Democracy in Japan*, ed. Takeshi Ishida and Ellis S. Krauss. Pittsburgh: Pittsburgh University Press.

McKean, Margaret A., and Ethan Scheiner. 2000. "Japan's New Electoral System: La plus ça change...." *Electoral Studies* 19: 447–77.

Mishima, Ko. 2007. "Grading Japanese Prime Minister Koizumi's Revolution: How Far Has the LDP's Policymaking Changed?" *Asian Survey* 47(5): 727–48.

Miyake, Ichirō. 1977. "Yūkensha Kōzō" [The Structure of Voters]. In *Nihon Seiji Gakkai ed. Nenpō Seijigaku*. Tokyo: Iwanami Shoten.

Mochizuki, Mike Masato. 1982. "Managing and Influencing the Japanese Legislative Process: The Role of Parties and the National Diet." PhD diss., Harvard University.

Moriwaki, Toshimasa. 1984. "Election and Daily Activities of Local Assemblymen in Japan." *Kwansei Gakuin Law Review*: 7–31.

Morgenstern, Scott J. 1996. "The Electoral Connection and the Legislative Process in Latin America: Factions, Parties, and Alliances in Theory and Practice." PhD diss., University of California, San Diego.

Mughan, Anthony. 2000. *Media and the Presidentialization of Parliamentary Elections*. New York: Palgrave.

Müller, Wolfgang C., and Kaare Strøm, eds. 1999. *Policy, Office or Votes?* Cambridge, UK: Cambridge University Press.

Murakawa, Ichirō. 1984. "Jiyū Minshutō Seimu Chōsakai No Yakuwari" [The Role of PARC in the LDP]. *Juristo* 805: 46.

——. 1989. *Jimintō no seisaku kette Sisutemu* [The LDP's Policy-Making Process]. Tokyo: Kyōikusha.

Muramatsu, Michio. 1987. "In Search of National Identity: The Politics and Policies of the Nakasone Administration." In *The Trade Crisis: How Will Japan Respond?* ed. K. B. Pyle. Seattle: Society for Japanese Studies.

——. 2005. "Seikan kankei wa dō kawatta no ka-1976–2002 kanryō mensetsu chōs kara yomitoku" [How Have Political Relationships Changed—Understanding from Bureaucrats' Interview Surveys]. *Ronza* (July): 159.

Muramatsu, Michio, and Ellis S. Krauss. 1984. "Bureaucrats and Politicians in Policymaking: The Case of Japan." *American Political Science Review* 78(1): 126–48.

——. 1987. "The Conservative Policy Line and the Development of Patterned Pluralism." In *The Political Economy of Japan: The Domestic Transformation*, ed. Kozo Yamamura and Yasukichi Yasuba. Stanford: Stanford University Press.

Nagel, Jack H. 1994. "What Political Scientists Can Learn from the 1993 Electoral Reform in New Zealand." *Political Science and Politics* 27(3): 527.

Nakane, Chie. 1967. *Tate-Shakai no ningen kankei: Tan'itsu-shakai no riron* [Human Relations of a Vertical Society: A Theory of a Homogeneous Society]. Tokyo: Kodansha.

——. 1970. *Japanese Society*. Berkeley: University of California Press.

Naoi, Megumi, and Ellis S. Krauss. 2007. "Who Lobbies Whom?: Electoral Systems and Organized Interests' Choice of Bureaucrats vs. Politicians in Japan." Paper presented at the conference on Modeling Power Relationships in Japanese Democracy, Centre for the Study of Democratic Institutions and the Japan Society for the Promotion of Science, University of British Columbia.

Nemoto, Kuniaki, Ellis S. Krauss, and Robert Pekkanen. 2008. "Policy Dissension and Party Discipline: The July 2005 Vote on Postal Privatization in Japan." *British Journal of Political Science* 38: 499–525.

Nemoto, Kuniaki, Ellis S. Krauss, Robert Pekkanen, and Nigel Roberts. Forthcoming. "Legislative Organization in MMP: The Case of New Zealand." *Party Politics*.

Nihon Keizai Shimbunsha, ed. 1985. *Jimintō Seichōkai* [LDP Policy Affairs Research Council]. Tokyo: Nihon Keizai Shimbunsha.

Niigata Nippō Sha. 2004. *Za Etsuzankai* [The Etsuzankai]. Niigata: Niigata Nippō Jigyō sha.

Nishikawa, Yukio. 2009. "Unknown Territory for Bureaucrats and Media." Reuters Blogs. September 4. Available at: http://blogs.reuters.com/japan/tag/democratic-party-of-japan/ (accessed November 25, 2009).

Nonaka, Naoto. 1995. *Jimintō Seiken Ka no Seiji Erito* [The Political Elite under LDP Rule]. Tokyo: Tokyo University Press.

Nonaka, Naoto. 2008. *Jimintō no seiji no owari* [The End of LDP Politics]. Tokyo: Chikuma Shinsho.

North, Christopher Titus. 2005. "From Technocracy to Aristocracy: The Changing Career Paths of Japanese Politicians." *Journal of East Asian Studies* 5 (2): 239–72.

Nyblade, Benjamin, and Steven Reed. 2008. "Who Cheats? Who Loots? Competition and Corruption in Japan, 1947–1993." *American Journal of Political Science* 52: 926–41.

Nyblade, Benjamin. 2004. "The Dynamics of Dominance: Party Government Duration and Change in Parliamentary Democracies." Ph.D. Dissertation, Department of Political Science, University of California, San Diego.

Okushima, Sadao. 2006. *Jimintō Sōsaisen* [LDP Party Presidential Selection]. Tokyo: Chūō Kōron Shinsha.

Orren, Karen, and Stephen Skowronek. 1994. "Beyond the Iconography of Order: Notes for a 'New' Institutionalism." In *The Dynamics of American Politics*, ed. L. C. Dodd, and C. Jillison. Boulder, CO: Westview.

Otake, Hideo. 1998. "How a Diet Member's Koenkai Adapts to Social and Political Changes." In *How Electoral Reform Boomeranged: Continuity in Japanese Campaigning Style*, ed. Hideo Otake. Tokyo: Japan Center for International Exchange.

Packard, George R., III. 1966. *Protest in Tokyo: The Security Treaty Crisis of 1960*. Princeton: Princeton University Press.

Page, Scott E. 2006. "Path Dependence." *Quarterly Journal of Political Science* 1: 87–115.

Palmer, Geoffrey, and Matthew Palmer. 2004. *Bridled Power: New Zealand's Constitution and Government*. 4th ed. South Melbourne, Australia: Oxford University Press.

Park, Cheol Hee. 1998. "The Enduring Campaign Networks of Tokyo's Shitamachi District." In *How Electoral Reform Boomeranged: Continuity in Japanese Campaigning Style*, ed. Hideo Otake. Tokyo: Japan Center for International Exchange.

——. 2000. *Daigishi no tsukurare kata—Shousenkyoku no senkyo senryaku* [The Birth of a Representative]. Tokyo: Bunshun Shinsho.

——. 2001. "Factional Dynamics in Japan's LDP since Political Reform: Continuity and Change." *Asian Survey* 41(3): 433–34.

Park, Gene, and Ezra Vogel. 2007. "Japan in 2006: A Political Transition." *Asian Survey* 47(1): 30.

Pekkanen, Robert. 2000. "Japan's New Politics: The Case of the NPO Law." *Journal of Japanese Studies* 26 (1): 111–48.

——. 2003. "Molding Japanese Civil Society." In *The State of Civil Society in Japan*, ed. Frank J. Schwartz and Susan J. Pharr. Cambridge, UK and New York: Cambridge University Press.

——. 2004. "Japan Social Capital without Advocacy." In *Civil Society and Political Change in Asia: Expanding and Contracting Democratic Space*, ed. Muthiah Alagappa. Stanford, CA: Stanford University Press.

——. 2006. *Japan's Dual Civil Society: Members without Advocates*. Stanford: Stanford University Press.

Pekkanen, Robert, Benjamin Nyblade, and Ellis S. Krauss. 2006. "Electoral Incentives in Mixed Member Systems: Party, Posts, and Zombie Politicians in Japan." *American Political Science Review* 100(2): 183–93.

——. 2007. "Where Have All the Zoku Gone?: Electoral Reform and MP Policy Specialization in Japan." Paper presented at the 65th Annual Midwest Political Science Association National Conference, Chicago.

———. Unpublished paper. "The Logic of Ministerial Selection: Electoral Reform and Party Goals in Japan." La Jolla, Seattle, and Vancouver.

Pekkanen, Robert, Kuniaki Nemoto, and Ellis S. Krauss, "The Collective Action Problem under SNTV: The Case of Factional Overnominations in Japan." Unpublished paper in process.

Pekkanen, Saadia, and Paul Kallendar-Umezu. 2010. *In Defense of Japan: From the Market to the Military in Space Policy.* Stanford, CA: Stanford University Press.

Pempel, T. J. 1982. *Policy and Politics in Japan: Creative Conservatism.* Philadelphia: Temple University Press.

———. 1990. *Uncommon Democracies: The One Party Dominant Regimes.* Ithaca: Cornell University Press.

Pierson, Paul. 2000. "Increasing Returns, Path Dependence, and the Study of Politics." *American Political Science Review* 94: 251–68.

———. 2004. *Politics in Time: History, Institutions, and Social Analysis.* Princeton: Princeton University Press.

Pierson, Paul, and Theda Skocpol. 2002. "Historical Institutionalism in Contemporary Political Science." In *Political Science: The State of the Discipline,* ed. Ira Katznelson and Helen Milner. New York: W. W. Norton.

Polsby, Nelson W., Miriam Gallaher, and Barry Spencer Rundquist. 1969. "The Growth of the Seniority System in the U.S. House of Representatives." *American Political Science Review* 63(3): 787–807.

Ragin, Charles. 2000. *Fuzzy-Set Social Science.* Chicago: University of Chicago Press.

Ramseyer, Mark J., and Frances McCall Rosenbluth. 1993. *Japan's Political Marketplace.* Cambridge, Mass.: Harvard University Press.

Reed, Steven R. 1992. "Factions in Japanese Conservative Politics." Unpublished paper, Tokyo.

———. 2003. "Conclusions." In *Japanese Electoral Politics: Creating a New Party System,* ed. Steven R. Reed. New York: RoutledgeCurzon.

———. 2009. "Party Strategy or Candidate Strategy: How Does the LDP Run the Right Number of Candidates in Japan's Multi-Member Districts?" *Party Politics* 15:295–314.

———. 2010. "The Liberal Democratic Party: An Explanation of Its Successes and Failures." In *The Routledge Handbook of Japanese Politics,* ed. Alissa Gaunder. New York: Routledge.

Reed, Steven R., and John M. Bolland. 1999. "The Fragmentation Effect of SNTV in Japan." In *Elections in Japan, Korea, and Taiwan under the Single Non-Transferable Vote,* ed. Bernard Grofman, Sung-Chull Lee, Edwin A. Winckler, and Brian Woodall. Ann Arbor: University of Michigan Press.

Reed, Steven R., and Ethan Scheiner. 2003. "Electoral Incentives and Policy Preferences: Mixed Motives behind Party Defections in Japan." *British Journal of Political Science* 33: 469–90.

Reed, Steven R., Ethan Scheiner, and Michael F. Thies. 2009. "Party-Centered, More Volatile: New Ballgame in Politics." *Oriental Economist* (October): 8–9. Available at: http://faculty.psdomain.ucdavis.edu/escheiner/research/published-work/Reed,%20Scheiner%20-%20Thies%202009,%20TOE.pdf.

Reed, Steven R., and Michael F. Thies. 2001a. "The Causes of Electoral Reform in Japan." In *Mixed-Member Electoral Systems: The Best of Both Worlds?* ed. Matthew S. Shugart and Martin P. Wattenberg. Oxford: Oxford University Press.

———. 2001b. "The Consequences of Electoral Reform in Japan." In *Mixed-Member Electoral Systems: The Best of Both Worlds?* ed. Matthew S. Shugart and Martin P. Wattenberg. Oxford: Oxford University Press.

Reischauer, Edwin O. 1988. *The Japanese Today.* Cambridge, Mass.: Belknap Press, Harvard University Press.

Reitman, Valerie. 2001. "Japan Vents Its Ire at Premier over Sub Crash." *Los Angeles Times* online, February 16, 2001. Available at: http://articles.latimes.com/2001/feb/16/news/mn-26172.

Richardson, Bradley. 1967. "Japanese Local Politics: Support Mobilization and Leadership Styles." *Asian Survey* 7(12): 860–75.

———. 1974. *The Political Culture of Japan.* Berkeley: University of California Press.

———. 1977. "Stability and Change in Japanese Voting Behavior, 1958–72." *Journal of Asian Studies* 36(4): 675–93.

———. 1988. "Constituency Candidates versus Parties in Japanese Voting Behavior." *American Political Science Review* 82(3): 695–718.

———. 1998. *Japanese Democracy: Power, Coordination, and Performance.* New York: Yale University Press.

Richardson, Bradley, and Dennis Patterson. 2001. "Political Traditions and Political Change: The Significance of Postwar Japanese Politics for Political Science." *Annual Review of Political Science* 4: 93–115.

Roberts, Clayton. 1996. *The Logic of Historical Explanation.* University Park: Penn State University Press.

Rochon, Thomas R. 1981. "Electoral Systems and the Basis for the Vote: The Case of Japan." In *Parties, Candidates and Votes in Japan: Six Quantitative Studies,* ed. John C. Campbell. Ann Arbor: Center for Japan Studies.

Rose, Richard. 2001. *The Prime Minister in a Shrinking World.* Oxford: Polity Press.

Samuels, Richard J. 2003a. "Leadership and Political Change in Japan: The Case of the Second Rinchō." *Journal of Japanese Studies* 29(1): 1–31.

———. 2003b. *Machiavelli's Children: Leaders and Their Legacies in Italy and Japan.* Ithaca: Cornell University Press.

———. 2007. "Securing Japan: The Current Discourse." *Journal of Japanese Studies* 33(1): 125–52.

Satō, Seizaburō, and Tetsuhisa Matsuzaki. 1986. *Jimintō seiken* [LDP Regime]. Tokyo: Chūō Koronsha.

Seawright, Jason, and David Collier. 2004. "Glossary." In *Rethinking Social Inquiry: Diverse Tools, Shared Standards,* ed. Henry E. Brady and David Collier. Lanham: Rowman & Littlefield.

Scheiner, Ethan. 2004. "Analysis of the 2004 Japanese House of Councilors Election." *Foresight Magazine,* August 21—September 17, 2004, 70–71.

———. 2006. *Democracy without Competition in Japan: Opposition Failure in a One-Party Dominant State.* New York: Cambridge University Press.

Schickler, Eric. 2001. *Disjointed Pluralism: Institutional Innovation and the Development of the U.S. Congress.* Princeton: Princeton University Press.

Schlesinger, Jacob. 1999. *Shadow Shoguns: The Rise and Fall of Postwar Japan's Political Machine.* Palo Alto: Stanford University Press.

Schoppa, Leonard James. 1991. *Education Reform in Japan: A Case of Immobilist Politics.* New York: Routledge.

Scriven, Michael. 1975. "Causation as Explanation." *Methods and Research* 20 (4): 428–55.

Scriven, Michael. 1976. "Maximizing the Power of Causal Investigations: The Modus Operandi Method." In *Evaluation Studies Review Annual*, ed. G. V. Glass. Beverly Hills: Sage.

Seisaku Geppō. 1964. "Seichōkai Jūnen no Ayumi wo Kataru" [Talking about the Path of the Policy Affairs Research Council's Ten Years]. *Seisaku Geppō* 100: 142.

Shinoda, Tomohito. 2000. *Leading Japan: The Role of the Prime Minister.* Westport, Conn.: Praeger.

———. 2003. "Koizumi's Top-Down Leadership in the Anti-Terrorism Legislation: The Impact of Political Institutional Changes." *SAIS Review* 23(1): 23–24.

Shiota, Ushio. 2007. *Minshutō No Kenkyū* [Democratic Party Research]. Tokyo: Heibonsha Shinsho.

Shugart, Matthew Soberg, and Martin P. Wattenberg. 2001a. "Electoral 'Efficiency' and the Move to Mixed-Member Systems." *Electoral Studies* 20: 173–93.

———, eds. 2001b. *Mixed-Member Electoral Systems: The Best of Both Worlds?* Oxford: Oxford University Press.

Sinclair, Barbara. 1995. *Legislators, Leaders, and Lawmaking: The U.S. House of Representatives in the Postreform Era.* Baltimore: Johns Hopkins University Press.

Skocpol, Theda, ed. 2006. *Protecting Soldiers and Mothers: The Political Origins of Social Policy in United States.* Cambridge, Mass.: Belknap Press.

Smith, Daniel Markham. 2009. "Coalition and Cabinet Formation." Presentation at IR/PS, UCSD Roundtable on Japan's 2009 Lower House Election, September 30, 2009, La Jolla.

———. 2009. "Political Inheritance under the Single Non-transferable Vote Electoral System in Japan." Unpublished paper, University of California, San Diego.

———. 2010. "Political Dynasties in Democracies: The Causes and Consequences of Hereditary Politics." Ph.D. dissertation prospectus. Political Science Department, University of California, San Diego.

Smith, Henry D. 1978. "Tokyo as an Idea: An Exploration of Japanese Urban Thought until 1945." *Journal of Japanese Studies* 4 (1): 45–80.

Soma, Masao. 1963. *Nihon-no Senkyo Seiji.* [Japanese Electoral Politics]. Tokyo: Aoki Shoten.

Steinmo, Sven, Kathleen Thelen, and Frank Longstreth, eds. 1992. *Structuring Politics: Historical Institutionalism in Comparative Analysis.* New York: Cambridge University Press.

Strøm, Kaare. 1990. "A Behavioral Theory of Competitive Political Parties." *American Journal of Political Science* 34: 569–98.

Strøm, Kaare, Wolfgang C. Müller, and Torbjörn Bergman, eds. 2006. *Delegation and Accountability in Parliamentary Democracies.* New York: Oxford University Press.

Sveinsdóttir, Hulda Thóra. 2004. "For Disharmony and Strength: Factionalism within the Conservative Parties in Japan, 1945–64." PhD diss., University of Newcastle upon Tyne.

Takahara, Masao. 1959. "Hoshu Seitou no Soshiki Katsudou." *Shisou* 420 (June): 91–99.

Takayasu, Kensuke. 2005. "Prime-Ministerial Power in Japan: A Re-Examination." *Japan Forum* 17(1): 163–84.

Taniguchi, Masaki (2004) *Gendai Nihon no Senkyo Seiji: Senkyo Seido Kaikaku wo Kensho Suru* [Contemporary Japanese Electoral Politics: Investigating Electoral Reform]. Tokyo: University of Tokyo Press.

Taniguchi, Masaki. 2007. "Changing Media, Changing Politics in Japan," *Japanese Journal of Political Science* 8(1): 147–66.

Taniguchi, Naoko. 2008. "Diet Members and Seat Inheritance: Keeping it in the Family." In *Democratic Reform in Japan: Assessing the Impact*, ed. Sherry L. Martin and Gill Steel. Boulder, CO: Lynne Rienner Press.

Tarrow, Sidney G. 1995. "Bridging the Quantitative-Qualitative Divide in Political Science." *American Political Science Review* 89 (2): 475–81.

Tatebayashi, Masahiko. 2004. *Giin Kōdō no seiji keizaigaku-Jimintō shihai no seido bunseki* [A Political Economy of Diet Members: A System Analysis of Rule]. Tokyo: Yuhikakusha.

Tatebayashi, Masahiko, and Margaret McKean. 2002. "Vote Division and Policy Differentiation Strategies of LDP members under SNTV/MMD in Japan." Unpublished paper Presented to Association of Asian Studies, Washington D.C.

Thayer, Nathaniel B. 1969. *How the Conservatives Rule Japan.* Princeton: Princeton University Press.

Thelen, Kathleen. 1999. "Historical Institutionalism in Comparative Politics." *Annual Review of Political Science* 2: 369–404.

Thies, Michael F. 2002. "Changing How the Japanese Vote: The Promise and Pitfalls of the 1994 Electoral Reform." In *How Asia Votes*, ed. John F.-S. Hsieh and David Newman. New York: Chatham House.

Tiberghien, Yves. 2007. *Entrepreneurial States: Reforming Corporate Governance in France, Japan, and Korea.* Ithaca: Cornell University Press.

Tkach-Kawasaki, Leslie M. 2003. "Politics@Japan: Party Competition on the Internet in Japan." *Party Politics* 9(1): 109.

Tsujinaka, Yutaka, Robert Pekkanen, and Hidehiro Yamamoto. 2009. *Gendai Nihon no jichikai chōnaikai* [Contemporary Japanese Neighborhood Associations]. Tokyo: Bokutakusha.

Tsurutani, Taketsugu. 1980. "The LDP in Transition?: Mass Membership Participation in Party Leadership Selection." *Asian Survey* 20(8): 844–59.

Turnbull, John. 2007. "'It Wesnae a Goal, Geoff': Worldwide, Scots Lend 'Fitba' Their Distinctive Style." Global Game: Soccer as a Second Language. Available at: http://www.theglobalgame.com/blog/2007/05/it-wesnae-a-goal-geoff-worldwide-scots-lend-fitba-their-distinctive-style/ (accessed October 5, 2009).

Uchida, Kenzō. 1983. *Habatsu* (Factions). Tokyo: Kodansha.

Usui, Chikako, and Richard A. Colignon. 2004. "Continuity and Change in Paths to High Political Office: Ex-Bureaucrats and Hereditary Politicians in Japan." *Asian Business and Management* 3: 395–416.

Wahara, Nobuo. 1990. "Kōenkai katsudō no kihon mondai" [The Basic Problems of Koenkai Activities]. *Zenei* 599: 30–56.

Ward, Robert E. 1951. "The Socio-Political Role of the *Buraku.*" *American Political Science Review* 45 (4): 1025–40.

Ward, Robert E. 1978. *Japan's Political System.* 2nd ed. Englewood Cliffs, N.J.: Prentice-Hall.

Watanabe, Kōzō. 1981. *Mizubasho Nikki* [Mizubasho Diary]. Tokyo: Nagata Shobo.

Watanabe, Tsuneo. 1958. *Habatsu: Hoshutō-No Kaibō* [Factions: A Dissection of the Conservative Party]. Tokyo: Kōbundo.

———. 1977. *Seiji no Jōshiki* [Common Knowledge of Politics]. Tokyo: Kōdansha.

Watanuki, Joji. 1991. "Social Structure and Voting Behavior." In *The Japanese Voter*, ed. Scott Flanagan, Shinsaku Kohei, Ichiro Miyake, Bradley M. Richardson, and Joji Watanuki. New Haven: Yale University Press.

Weingast, Barry R. 2002. "Rational-Choice Institutionalism." In *Political Science: The State of the Discipline,* ed. Ira Katznelson and Helen Milner. New York: W. W. Norton.

Winckler, Edwin A. 1999b. "Electoral Equilibria on Taiwan." In *Elections in Japan, Korea, and Taiwan under the Single Non-Transferable Vote: The Comparative Study of an Embedded Institution,* ed. Bernard Grofman, Sung-Chull Lee, Edwin A. Winckler, and Brian Woodall. Ann Arbor: University of Michigan Press.

Yamada, Masahiro. 1993. "Jimintō daigishi no shūyō shistemu" [The Vote-gathering System of Representatives]. Ph.D. Dissertation. University of Tsukuba, Japan.

Yamada, Masahiro. 1996. "Seitō soshiki no douno rikigaku." *Leviasan* (special issue): 184–90.

Yamada, Masahiro. 1997. "Kōenkaiseiji no bunsekiwakugumi" [An Analytic Framework of Kōenkai Politics]. *Hō to Seiji* 48 (1): 387–408.

Yomiuri Shimbun Tokyo-Honsha Yoron-Chosabu. 2004. *Nidaiseitosei no akebono* [The Dawn of the Two-Party System]. Tokyo: Bokutakusha.

Yoshioka, Masatsugu. 2007. "Is Japanese Politics 'Un-Westminster'?: Examining the Role of the PARC." *Electronic Journal of Contemporary Japanese Studies,* discussion paper 3. Available at: http://www.japanesestudies.org.uk/discussionpapers/2007/Yoshioka.html.

Yuasa, Hiroshi. 1986. *Kokkai 'Giinzoku'—Jimintō 'Seichō' to Kasumigaseki* [Kasumigaseki's "Diet Member Tribe"]. Tokyo: Kyōikusha.

Zuckerman, Alan. 1979. *The Politics of Faction: Christian Democratic Rule in Italy.* New Haven: Yale University Press.

Index

Page locators with an "f" indicate figures; page locators with a "t" indicate tables.

labor unions, 15, 18, 50
Lam, Peng Er, 60, 61
Lamarck, 284
Leiserson, Michael, 109, 110
Liberal Party, 51, 54, 62, 106, 123, 152,
161–62, 206–7, 233, 264, 276
Lockheed Scandal, 116, 117, 168, 220

Machimura, Nobutaka, 139
Mair, Peter, 284
Manabe, Kenji, 79
Manabe, Takeshi, 78t, 79, 81
Mannoo Town, 71t
Marsh, Michael, 284
Martin, Curtis, 155–56
Marugame City, 68–71, 74, 76
Masumi, Junnosuke, 31, 52, 55, 63–64
Matsuoka, Toshikatsu, 38–39
Matsuoka Toshikatsu New Century Politics
and Economic Discussion Association,
39
Matsuoka Toshikatsu Policy Research
Association, 39
Matsutomokai, 38–39
Matsuzaki, Tetsuhisa, 1, 113–14, 169, 170
McArthur, Douglas, 206–7
McCubbins, Mathew, 172–75, 196
McKean, Margaret, 171, 175
McLeay, Elizabeth, 283–84
media coverage, 24, 48, 90, 94, 97, 103, 115,
215f, 218–24, 227–31, 237–38, 240, 243f,
244–46, 256, 281, 285
meibō, 133
Meiji, 49
Meisuikyō data, 32–33, 92f, 136f, 137f
members of parliament (MPs), 66, 156
Miki, Bukichi, 107
Miki, Takeo, 57–58, 117, 121–22, 124, 136f,
137f, 138, 213, 230f
Mikoda, Junichi, 84t
military operations, 15, 49, 110, 217, 274
Ministry of Agriculture, Forestry, and
Fisheries, 156
Ministry of Finance, 68, 162, 217, 222, 240
Ministry of International Trade and Industry,
156
Ministry of Posts and Telecommunications,
156
Minseitō, 111
Minshutō, 106, 107
Mito City, 39
Mitsubishi, 111
Mitsui, 111

mixed-member majoritarian (MMM) system,
3, 62, 78, 89, 97–98, 189, 190, 201, 256,
261, 264, 276, 284
mixed-member proportional (MMP) system,
283
Miyamoto, Shigeru, 61
Miyazawa, Kiichi, 22, 143f, 222, 228, 230f
Mori, Yoshirō, 119–20, 139, 141, 143f, 145f,
168, 233, 237–38, 241f, 245
Morita, Hajime, 76, 77t, 78–79, 83
Mughan, Anthony, 203
Mulgan, Aurelia George, 38
multi-member district (MMD), 22–23, 46, 49,
62–64, 88, 97, 171, 182, 236, 261, 265
Muramatsu, Michio, 169, 214, 242
Murayama, Tomiichi, 3, 237

Nagasaki, 54
Nagata-cho, 72
Nakanan Town, 71t
Nakasone, Yasuhiro, 62, 114, 121–22, 136f,
137f, 143f, 220–24, 229–30, 234, 240,
243–44
National Organization Committee, 57
National Police Agency, 81
National Railways, 234
negative externalities, 12, 14, 27–28, 63, 118,
127, 147–48, 151, 152, 185, 201, 256–58,
264–67, 276–78, 287
neighborhood associations, 45, 69, 85–86
Nemoto, Kuniaki, 123
New Frontier Party (NFP), 77t, 84t, 91, 232,
233
New Kōmeitō, 249
New Liberal Club (NLC), 34f
New Renaissance Party (NRP), 77t
New Year's celebrations, 35, 36, 61, 83, 86
New York Yankees, 12, 13
New Zealand, 5, 7, 15, 23, 155–56, 206, 257,
280, 282–83
News Station, 227–28, 230, 234, 244
Newsweek, 237
NHK network, 219, 223, 227–28, 230, 244, 256
Niigata, 33, 49
Niigata Prefecture Etsuzankai, 38
Nioo Town, 71t
nisei giin, 43, 44f, 78, 144, 145f, 146, 195,
211
Nishikouri, Atsushi, 84t
Nixon, Richard, 218
Nōkyō, 80, 253
Nonaka, Naoto, 58, 154
Nukaga, Fukushiro, 39, 42, 242